Running
a Perfect BBS

Mark L. Chambers with
Dave Gibbons
John R. Harris
George Peace
Markus W. Pope

QUE

Running a Perfect BBS

Library of Congress Catalog No.: 94-67941

ISBN: 1-56529-919-1

97 96 95 94 6 5 4 3 2 1

Interpretation of the printing code: the rightmost double-digit number is the year of the book's printing; the rightmost single-digit number, the number of the book's printing. For example, a printing code of 94-1 shows that the first printing of the book occurred in 1994.

Publisher: David P. Ewing

Associate Publisher: Corinne Walls

Publishing Director: Brad R. Koch

Managing Editor: Anne Owen

Product Marketing Manager: Greg Wiegand

Dedication

This book is dedicated to my mother Adelle and my father Troy, who've been there for me since "Line Number One."

Mark L. Chambers

Credits

Publishing Manager
Steve Schafer

Acquisitions Editor
Steve Schafer

Product Director
Jim Minatel

Production Editor
Mitzi Foster Gianakos

Copy Editors
Kelli M. Brooks
Theresa Mathias

Technical Editor
Paul McIntire

Figure Specialist
Cari Ohm

Book Designer
Amy Peppler-Adams

Cover Designer
Dan Armstrong

Editorial Assistant
Theresa Mathias

Acquisitions Assistant
Ruth Slates

Production Team
Angela Bannan
Amy Cornwell
Terri Edwards
Theresa Forrester
Joelynn Gifford
Dennis Clay Hager
Beth Lewis
Malinda Lowder
Erika Millen
Steph Mineart
Nanci Sears Perry
Beth Rago
Kaylene Riemen
Clair Schweinler
Dennis Sheehan
Kris Simmons
Michael Thomas
Johnna VanHoose
Mary Beth Wakefield

Indexer
Michael Hughes

Composed in *Stone Serif* and *MCPdigital* by Que Corporation

About the Authors

Mark L. Chambers has been a PC software technical writer and bulletin board system operator for over ten years. He and his wife Anne live in Columbia, Missouri, with their daughters Erin and Chelsea. He has contributed work for the Que books *Introduction to PC Communications* and *Using PC Tools 8*, as well as numerous technical editing projects. Mark is also the author of several successful TBBS online door programs, including "Lord of the Boards" and "CD Review."

Mark established The Batboard in 1984 as a single-line BBS running on an 8-bit Atari computer running custom software; the BBS is dedicated to the character Batman in film, TV, and comics. Since then, The Batboard has run on a TRS-80 Model 4 and several PC systems, with software ranging from RBBS, QuickBBS, and its current multiline system, TBBS. The Batboard offers FidoNet and Internet connections, as well as two CD-ROMs, .QWK mail, RIP and NAPLPS graphics, online games, and much more. The Batboard was also voted one of *Boardwatch Magazine's* Top 100 bulletin boards in 1993.

Dave Gibbons is a former technical trainer and writer for DATASTORM TECHNOLOGIES in Columbia, Missouri, and LaserMaster Technologies in Eden Prairie, Minnesota. He began his professional writing career in chilly Cando, North Dakota, at age 16. Now a freelance writer and consultant, Dave spends much of his free time rock climbing on the Internet (`dgibbons@bigcat.missouri.edu`).

John R. Harris is a partner in the Atlanta, Georgia, intellectual property law firm of Jones & Askew. He practices patent, trademark, and copyright law, with special emphasis in the computer and electrical arts. He received a J.D. and M.B.A. from Emory University in 1979, and a bachelor's degree in electrical engineering from the Georgia Institute of Technology in 1973. During the mid-1970s, John was a computer system design engineer at Harris Corporation, in Melbourne, Florida. He is a contributing author to the book, *Using the Internet*, Chapter 5, "Legal Considerations of Internet Usage," Que Corporation (1994), and can be reached on the Internet (`jharris@jonesaskew.com`).

George Peace, sysop, software author, consultant, and Internet provider based in Harrisburg, Pennsylvania, has been active in BBSing since '81. George is cofounder of an early L.A.-area computer user group and served two terms as board member of First Osborne Group. Since discovering FidoNet in '86, he has served as Mid-Atlantic and North American Coordinator and currently serves as its International Coordinator and a central mail and file distribution hub. His recent software credits include popular FidoNet utilities such as Areafix QM, FLAME, and Raid.

Markus W. Pope is a quality assurance technician for DATASTORM TECHNOLOGIES, INC. He received a position in the Information Systems department at Springfield Remanufacturing at age 19. Markus has attained several computer-related positions in various companies since 1988 including computer operator for Springfield Remanufacturing, Inc., programmer/analyst for Midwest Equipment Rental, Inc., technical support specialist for DATASTORM, and quality assurance technician also for DATASTORM.

Acknowledgments

I would like to express my thanks to a few people without whom this book simply wouldn't have happened:

- Dave Gibbons, John Harris, George Peace, and Markus Pope, whose excellent contributions gave this book great strength.
- Jim Minatel and Mitzi Foster Gianakos, whose guidance and editorial comments brought this book to a new level.
- And Anne, Erin, and Chelsea, who always encouraged and supported me. During the writing of this book, they put up with a great deal of neglect but never once complained.

Special thanks and acknowledgment to Les Bessenger, who assisted John Harris in his research and drafting for Chapter 7, "Legal Aspects of Operating a BBS."

Les Bessenger was a law clerk for Jones & Askew in 1994. He received a bachelor's degree in electrical engineering from the University of Florida in the 1980s, and expects to receive his J.D. from the University of Florida Law School in 1994. His professional experience includes working as an engineer with E-Systems, St. Petersburg, Florida, and Hewlett-Packard, Ft. Lauderdale, Florida.

Trademarks

Contents at a Glance

Contents

Foreword

by Jim Harrer
President/CEO
Mustang Software, Inc.

Usually a BBS is started by a single person who accepts the responsibility of running the system. Somewhere along the way, we started calling this person the system operator. It is probably a throwback from the mainframe days, and you must admit, it sounds important. It didn't take long before we shortened it to sysop (sis'op).

I take it, the reason you're holding this book in your hands is because you want to join the ranks and become a sysop. I've been one since 1984, and am still one today. Over the course of the past ten years, I have had the pleasure of meeting thousands of sysops. Running a BBS is a really neat experience. I'll never forget the first time I spent a weekend installing my BBS, getting the welcome screens just right, logging in from the console, leaving my first "welcome" message and getting the BBS "Ready for Calls."

I left a few messages on other local BBSs, giving out my new BBS phone number. I was ready; it was time for my BBS to take over, unattended. I stared at the "Waiting for Call Screen," waiting for someone—anyone—to call. Minutes seemed like hours, until my modem lights flashed! The screen changed to "Ring Detect" and I knew something was happening! A chill went down my back as I watched my computer—without me doing a single thing—take over to answer the phone, establish a connection, and send my "prelog file" to callers, welcoming them to my BBS and prompting them for their name.

I was hooked; this was really, really cool. I stayed up all night watching that computer screen. I couldn't believe it—people actually called at 3:00 a.m.! I knew, because I was up watching them! As time went on, I experienced my first long-distance call, my first international call, and my first upload (where the caller actually contributed to my BBS by sending me a file).

Today, some of my best friends are people I've met online. I met my business partner at Mustang, Rick Heming, and our V.P. of Engineering, Scott Hunter, through my BBS. It's safe to say, running a bulletin board has made a major change in my life. Most sysops have similar war stories to tell. Like most things, running a BBS is a people business and as the sysop, you're the one who controls the interaction. The BBS's ultimate success rests solely in your hands.

So that brings us to this book. Mark Chambers, the contributing authors, and and the Que staff have done a GREAT job of covering all essential areas of running a BBS. They seem to cover a great deal of ground from creating an image to legal issues, doors, CD-ROMs, FidoNet, and the Internet. I wish I had this book when I started out; it would have saved me a lot of time and mistakes. Reading this book reminded me of sitting around the table visiting with sysops, there is a lot of knowledge, experience, and depth in these pages. Whether you're new to BBSing or a veteran of cyberspace, this book will teach you the critical areas of setting up and managing your BBS. As time goes by, it will become your reference guide as you expand into new areas like off-line mail and Internet gateways.

As the developers of the Wildcat! Bulletin Board System (BBS), we wanted to help you apply the ideas and concepts of this book by including a "Lite" version of our BBS product. Make no mistake, this is a fully-functional BBS package that is currently being used by tens of thousands of sysops worldwide! You'll be among some of the finest sysops in the world—the Wildcat! Sysop Family, which is a helpful and resourceful group. Plus you'll also have access to the hundreds of third-party utilities that have been written for Wildcat! v3.

So, with this book and our Wildcat! v3 "Lite" software, you're ready to become a sysop. I hope the experience will change your life, as it did mine. I hope it becomes as great as you want it to be. But more importantly, I hope you experience that same "chill" when your BBS takes its first call; it will make all the work leading up to getting your BBS online worth it.

See you online!

Introduction

In 1983, when I first became interested in the online world, every connection was an adventure! I'd call one of the two bulletin boards available in my local area at the time, strap the receiver of my telephone onto the rubber cups of my 300-baud acoustic modem, and sit in awe as the stream of characters flowed slowly across the screen. The action was definitely no-frills: there were no graphics or games, no online chat, no message networks, and only a handful of files to transfer with Xmodem. But the excitement and the magic was there; my friends and I were communicating, and the simplest message usually received dozens of replies. I don't remember getting much sleep—there were less busy signals after midnight!

Soon, I decided that it would be fun to provide others with a BBS of my own, and my "communications center" took shape around an Atari 400 and a single floppy disk drive. I wrote the BBS software myself, and spent almost as much time tinkering with it as I did reading my mail and calling long distance. To be a sysop, it was necessary to know your BBS hardware and software inside-out, and whatever you needed you usually had to build or write yourself.

It's fun to look back just a decade ago now that everything has changed. Today, the exchange of electronic information is one of the primary uses for the PC; according to one estimate, there are over 20 million BBS users worldwide! The advances in the field of PC communications reflect this: modems that transfer data at 14,400 bps are plentiful for under $200, networking packages for an entire office can be installed in a day, and thousands of public and private bulletin boards have appeared worldwide (with nearly 60,000 bulletin boards in the United States alone). Huge information services like CompuServe and global information networks like the Internet provide electronic mail and file transfer services anywhere you can reach a telephone jack.

Today, a sysop's job is different in many ways as well. A sysop is no longer primarily concerned with simply keeping everything working for the next call. Modern bulletin board programs are much more reliable, easier to set up, and less trouble to maintain than they were a decade ago, even for the novice computer owner. Although it always helps to know as much about your equipment as possible, you no longer need to be a computer expert to run your own system.

However, to run a successful BBS today, you'll have to perform tasks that "old timer" sysops never considered: you'll have to market and advertise your BBS, connect it to external services like FidoNet and the Internet, maintain CD-ROM file libraries, and check your download files for viruses. The focus of a sysop's attention has subtly moved away from the basic hardware and software—it now faces outward, toward national and international users, as well as toward advanced services like CD-ROMs and fax transmissions.

Whether you're an experienced BBS user or a casual caller, this book and the accompanying Wildcat! Lite software have been designed to provide you with everything you need to build a complete single-line BBS, with no restrictions or "crippled" functions. Once you've installed and customized your system, we'll introduce methods of improving it, adding lines and services, and making a profit. I've focused primarily on starting a hobby bulletin board (although sysops starting bulletin board systems for profit or support will benefit from this book as well). Hobby boards make up the vast majority of systems, and they're the most common type of board run by beginning sysops.

In Chapter 1, "Understanding Bulletin Boards," you'll be introduced to the three types of bulletin boards—the hobby system, the profit system, and the business/support system—as well as the hardware and software you'll use to run your BBS. We'll discuss important files used by every bulletin board, and common terms used by sysops everywhere.

Chapter 2, "Understanding PC Communications," helps you make sense out of the confusing technology and terminology surrounding data communications. You'll learn how PCs transfer data through a serial connection, as well as how your modem and serial port work together. We'll also cover the tremendous recent advances in modem technology, including data compression and error correction.

Chapter 3, "Hardware Requirements," discusses much more than the basic requirements for Wildcat! Lite; in addition, you'll find information on BBS-related hardware and software used by most sysops. We'll present all the details on the telephone line you'll need, including extra services you might need—and those you definitely won't! Finally, Chapter 3 explains the critical differences between *integrated* BBS programs that run on a single machine and *networked* programs that run on a local area network.

In Chapter 4, "Creating an Image," you'll build the foundation of your BBS step-by-step. You'll select an overall theme, a name for your system, and a set of services you'd like to provide for your users. You'll also design your menu system, consider security issues, and outline your message and file areas. In addition, you'll be introduced to the possible profit (and headaches) involved with charging your users for access.

Chapter 5, "Installing the Software," leads you step-by-step through the installation and basic configuration of your Wildcat! Lite software. You'll also find hints and tips that will come in handy for any BBS program. Once you've completed this chapter, your BBS will be ready for your first local logon.

We'll customize your system to a much higher degree in Chapter 6, "Getting Up and Running." You'll learn how to create your own ASCII and ANSI menus and welcome screens. We'll examine important files that every sysop should offer, such as disclaimers and rules bulletins. Finally, you'll see how you can perform usability tests before your BBS goes online, and how you can recruit a co-sysop if you'll need help running your system.

In Chapter 7, "Legal Aspects of Operating a BBS," we'll cover your legal responsibilities (and rights) as the system operator of a BBS. This important chapter may hold a few surprises for even experienced sysops, as the legal issues surrounding bulletin boards have multiplied dramatically in the last few years.

Chapter 8, "Protecting Your BBS," provides you with valuable techniques in handling problem users and protecting your BBS data from viruses and Trojan horses. You'll also learn about copyrighted material, including how to protect your own creative work and how to handle copyrighted work from other sources.

Chapter 9, "Sysop Maintenance and Administration," discusses internal and external automatic system events, and how you can use them to help maintain your Wildcat! BBS. We'll also cover the important commands available from your Wildcat! sysop menu, and how you can run DOS programs and use DOS commands from a remote location.

How—and, equally important, when—should you expand your BBS with extra services and additional lines? You'll learn all the details on adding more to your bulletin board in Chapter 10, "Expanding Your BBS." We'll also cover methods of adding a subscription system to your BBS, as well as credit card and 1-900 support.

Chapter 11, "Marketing Your BBS," is a complete guide to publicizing and advertising your bulletin board as inexpensively as possible! We'll outline methods of attracting new users and generating renewed interest in your system among your current callers.

In Chapter 12, "BBS Success Stories," you'll see firsthand how some of the most successful sysops have built their bulletin boards, and how they've applied techniques introduced earlier in this book.

Chapter 13, "Shareware," details everything you'll need to know on one of the most popular services available on most bulletin boards: downloading shareware files. This chapter describes the differences between shareware and commercial software, and it provides you with possible sources for shareware that you can offer on your system.

Chapter 14, "Using Offline Mail," explains how you can provide your users with the capability to read and reply to messages offline, and then upload their responses to your BBS! This is another popular service, especially among your long-distance users.

Chapter 15, "Adding Doors," introduces you to the external programs you can offer on your BBS. Whether you decide to feature games, databases, periodicals, or DOS applications, this chapter will help you add them to your system. We'll also give tips on using and maintaining your doors.

Chapter 16, "Adding CD-ROM Support," will introduce you to the CD-ROM drive, which has proven to be one of the most exciting advances in online technology in the last several years. With your Wildcat! Lite BBS, you can offer your callers a huge, "ready-to-run" library of download files on CD-ROM with just an hour of work! We'll cover what you should look for when buying both your drive and BBS-ready CD-ROMs.

In Chapter 17, "RIP Graphics, External Protocols, and Viewers," we'll cover additional ways you can add functionality to your Wildcat! Lite bulletin board, including a full examination of RIP graphics, external protocols, and an external file viewer.

Chapter 18, "Understanding External Connections," introduces you to the idea of external connections that can link your BBS to the outside world through FidoNet, the Internet, local area networks, and chat networks.

In Chapter 19, "Connecting to FidoNet," we'll concentrate on how you can link your Wildcat! Lite BBS to the international FidoNet message and file network, and what that connection will mean to you and your users.

Chapter 20, "Connecting to the Internet," focuses on how you can offer Internet electronic mail and public message forums to your callers. Whether you have international business connections or you'd like to communicate with friends overseas, Internet electronic mail is probably the most important external connection you can make!

In Chapter 21, "Advanced External Connections," you'll learn more about advanced external connections such as satellite antennas, long-distance chat links, and X.25 packet connections. Although they're expensive, these techniques can make your BBS extremely attractive to your callers.

Finally, the appendixes at the back of this book include a comparison of popular bulletin board software packages—which can help you if you're planning to purchase another program—and an ANSI reference guide.

Welcome, then, to the myriad challenges that await you as the manager of your own online service! I believe you'll find this book a valuable guide in setting up your BBS, and I sincerely hope you'll enjoy inviting your users into your "corner of cyberspace" as I have these last ten years! I welcome any comments or questions you may have about this book. I can be contacted via Internet e-mail at `sysop@batboard.org`.

Mark L. Chambers

Part I

Bulletin Board Basics

Chapter 1

Understanding Bulletin Boards

by Mark L. Chambers

At first glance, the BBS community appears to be a vast number of individual islands, each completely different and separate from the others. Every system you call reflects the personality and goals of its sysop, with different services, rules and regulations, and a different theme; in effect, the caller enters a unique electronic "world" with each connection to a new board! Exploring a new BBS is a big part of the fun.

However, this first impression is actually misleading. Although your system will be different than any other, it will still fit into one of the three types of bulletin board systems we briefly mentioned in the introduction to this book: the hobby BBS, the profit BBS, and the business/support BBS. If your users are going to enjoy themselves while visiting your BBS, you'll have to plan how it looks, how callers will navigate it, and what features it will offer—just as other successful sysops have planned their systems "from the ground up."

In this chapter, you'll learn the common elements shared by every bulletin board system—no matter what software a BBS uses, how many lines it features or what services it provides. Your bulletin board will be a singular extension of yourself (or your business), but it will be based on the same concepts, planning, and technology as any other well-run BBS.

Three Types of Bulletin Boards

Nothing can doom a new bulletin board system to failure faster than lack of a clear goal. A hobby system is not designed to turn a profit, just as a profit BBS will do more damage than good as a support tool for your business. Many of your callers are not interested in paying for online time, while others will be dissatisfied if you don't offer the more expensive features that profit systems can afford. Users calling for support are even more focused; they want the latest Windows video driver, or the chance to leave a message for your support staff, and they want it **quickly**! Thus, the image your system portrays will even affect which users will frequent your BBS on a regular basis.

Of course, there is certainly no reason why one type of system can't offer some of the features from another type. For example, a hobby board can accept subscriptions and donations of hardware from its users, as long as it continues to provide some sort of free membership to the public. A profit BBS can provide specific support for certain games or application software. In the same spirit, it's common for a hobby board to become a profit bulletin board over time—if the sysop takes the right steps to expand and advertise the BBS. However, such a metamorphosis usually takes a few years, a cash reserve, and a dedicated sysop who's not afraid to take risks.

Therefore, it's imperative that beginning sysops decide which type of board they will run. Before you turn on your modem, install a single program, or design your first ANSI screen, let's review each type of system in detail.

The Hobby System

As you might have already guessed, the first bulletin boards (founded in the late '70s) were hobby systems running custom hardware; the software was usually written by the sysop. Such boards offered free public access to everyone, sometimes with no online time limit (after all, most of these pioneer bulletin boards were limited to storing simple messages and displaying text files, and only other technical experts had the knowledge to call them). Sysops of today's hobby systems should be proud that they can trace their roots back to those early bulletin boards! Figure 1.1 shows a typical main menu screen from a hobby system.

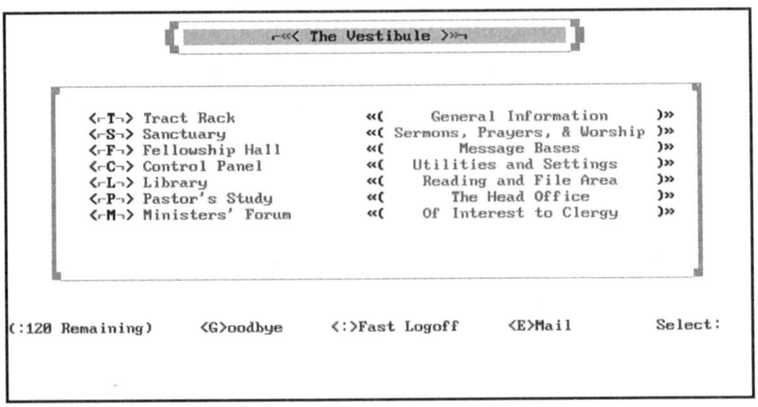

Fig. 1.1
The main menu from a hobby system, showing the strong theme and services you might find on a hobby BBS.

What are the typical features of a hobby system?

- **Some form of free public access.** Today's hobby bulletin boards haven't changed in this regard; to be counted as a hobby board at all, your BBS will have to allow every caller a certain set of standard features free of charge. These features typically include the message bases and a set limit on the number or size of download files (perhaps also imposing a download *ratio*, where the user must upload a certain number of files or bytes for every file or byte downloaded). Subscribers receive extra privileges, more online time per day and a larger download ratio (or no download restrictions at all). Other hobby boards still allow unlimited free downloading and free access to every feature, but they're becoming harder and harder to find. Technical support boards usually offer most or all of their features free of charge as well.

> **Tip**
>
> When you consider the image you want to project to your callers, even a profit bulletin board should offer some type of free access! Nothing can be more frustrating to your callers than to connect to your system and discover there's nothing for them to do unless they become a paying member (especially those calling long distance). Neglect to create a good first impression, and you're likely to be rewarded immediately with a quick disconnect from a visitor who'll never return!

- **Single-line operation.** Again, this is not an ironclad indicator of a hobby board, but it certainly describes the vast majority. Most hobby bulletin boards are run on a tight budget, and therefore cannot afford the additional expense of multiple lines. Business/support boards and profit systems, on the other hand, must have multiple lines to be successful.

- **A dedicated theme.** Hobby sysops often start their bulletin boards to share a particular passion with other enthusiasts, and this is reflected in the theme of almost every hobby BBS. These boards try their best to tailor every prompt, menu, and command to match their theme. The online world attracts a large number of science fiction and fantasy fans, and many boards are dedicated to popular cult classics of these genres like *Star Trek* and *The Lord of the Rings* series. If you run one of these systems, you might cast yourself as a starship captain and your BBS as your "vessel," or perhaps you might be a wizard and your BBS would be your "castle." Other favorite themes include space travel in general, music, animation and comic heroes, TV and film classics, and role-playing games. You'll even find cyberspace equivalents of a "local tavern" environment, where you can pull up a virtual bar stool and chat with your fellow patrons!

Profit boards usually don't work hard at such a close identification with a particular topic because they must appeal to a broad range of callers to attract as many subscribers as possible; their themes usually center around how many services they provide. For example, popular themes for profit systems include acting as an "international message center" (because profit boards usually feature several networks) or a "public file library" (because of a large number of files).

Also, a business-oriented bulletin board or support system builds its theme around the company's product; after all, because a business BBS is a functional extension of the business itself, it's not a wise choice to link your product support bulletin board closely with *Lost in Space* or the *Green Hornet*!

Now let's look at the hobby board from another angle: what advantages and disadvantages does a hobby system bring to you as a sysop? What can you expect if you decide to run one?

On the plus side, a hobby system is the easiest of the three types to start and maintain. Your callers expect you to maintain your system, but they certainly don't require the same attention and hard work required by either a profit system or a business/support BBS. In this regard, it really is a hobby—and, like any other hobby, you get as much out of it as you choose to put into it. Hobby systems provide the sysop with an immediate connection with others who share common interests, so it makes a great meeting place if you're looking to share information and files of a certain type (for instance, a BBS devoted to cycling attracts callers who can recommend a particular bicycle or track, and you're likely to find news files detailing cycling events).

On the negative side, a hobby BBS can be a financial drain; even if you charge subscribers, it's not likely you'll break even. For a single-line system, your costs will remain low, but there's always the additional phone bill. Unexpected repair bills for hard drives and modems can result from operating your PC around the clock. Finally, your computer will be constantly running the BBS, so you'll either have to go without or purchase another PC for yourself. If your machine is powerful enough to run your BBS software with multitasking software, you can operate the BBS and continue to use your computer, but—unless it's a fast PC like a 486 or Pentium and your line count is fairly low—its performance is likely to be sluggish.

The Profit System

The profit BBS is often considered the pinnacle for a sysop: your hobby has become your full-time employment, and you can devote your entire day to maintaining and improving your system. For many sysops who run hobby boards, it sounds like the perfect career.

Don't be fooled by this common misconception! Any sysop earning a living from a bulletin board will tell you that running a profit system involves constant work, perhaps even more than a regular business. Your service doesn't stop at 5:00 or 6:00 p.m. like a more traditional business; it must work flawlessly at 4 a.m. as well. If you're not adding hundreds of files or answering countless messages from your users, you're probably worrying about the forthcoming increase in the rate the telephone company charges for those 32 lines! Figures 1.2 and 1.3 show two implementations of a profit system—one with a plain text, straightforward appearance, and the other with extensive ANSI graphics. You'll notice, however, that both systems offer an impressive set of services.

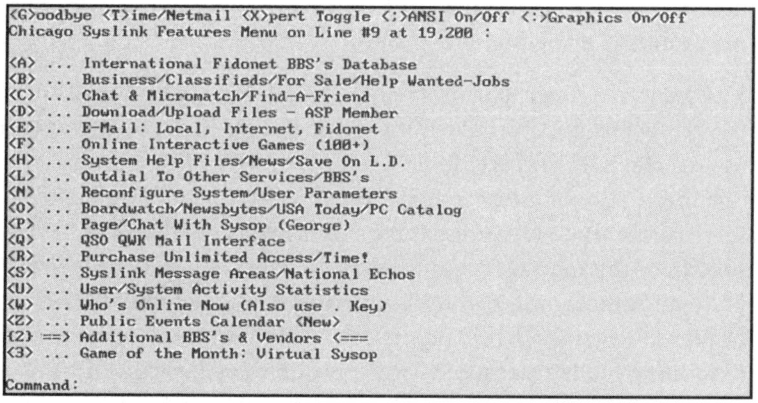

Fig. 1.2 The main menu from a profit system showing a straightforward approach.

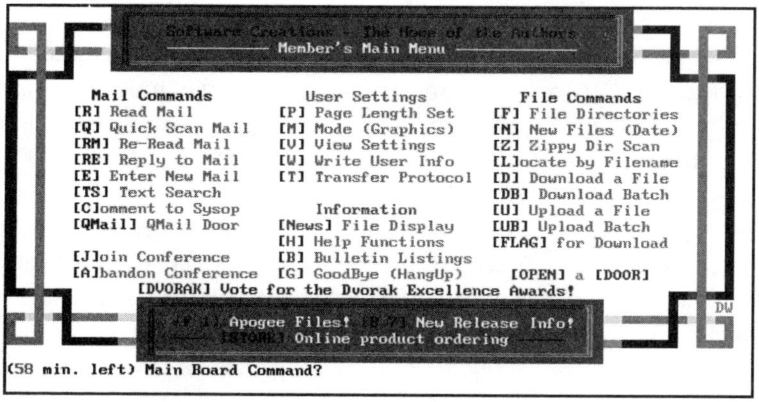

Fig. 1.3 The main menu from a profit system displaying extensive ANSI graphics.

What are the typical features of a profit system?

- **Financial risk.** Building even a 4-, 6-, or 8-line bulletin board involves an investment in hardware, software, and time, and today's computers are well known for their high depreciation rate. The profit sysop must be ready to advertise nationally to attract users because most cities are not large enough to support more than a handful of profit boards. Long-distance subscribers are all-important to a large system. If the BBS is a success, the sysop will probably have to hire additional help in the form of office and technical support employees.

- **Multiline operation.** Nothing irritates a subscribing user of your profit BBS more than calling your system and hearing a busy signal. Unless your BBS will have a very large number of lines, it's important that you reserve one or more "private" numbers that only your subscribers can call (most of the large bulletin board programs available today allow you to disconnect a caller from a specified line if the caller's access is not high enough). Your lines should also provide a *rollover* function so that a call made to your first telephone line will roll to the next number if the first line is busy.

- **The best services.** To attract enough callers to become self-sufficient, the profit BBS must provide more features and make them easy for the user to reach. It's no accident that most profit bulletin boards carry not one international message network, but several. FidoNet, RIME, and the Internet are three favorites, and a profit BBS is likely to carry most, if not all, of the message areas for each network. Profit boards that are known for their online entertainment often have hundreds of challenging games, while others offer online want-ad services or online "shopping malls." Because a large portion of callers concentrate on downloading programs, profit bulletin boards can feature dozens of CD-ROM drives and many, many gigabytes of hard drive space. Several large boards act as official distributors for shareware authors, while other profit boards specialize in custom graphics by creating their own pictures in .GIF format (short for CompuServe's Graphic Interchange Format). A considerable number of profit systems center around multiline chat—a function very much like the CompuServe CB Chat simulator—by allowing users to talk and play games with each other in both public and private virtual "rooms." Finally, many successful profit boards appeal specifically to adults, offering sexually-oriented messages, programs, pictures, and chat areas for individuals of every sexual preference.

- **A high legal risk.** As you can imagine, the more users you accept, the higher your chances of involvement in a civil suit (or even allegations of criminal activity). Recently, the media has focused attention on adult boards, and several have been shut down or confiscated. Surprisingly enough, however, other profit boards with little in the way of adult material have also been the targets of legal attack. Some of these systems were found to offer "pirated" commercial software mixed in with their shareware and freeware titles, while at least one BBS was seized because it was suspected of harboring "hackers" exchanging confidential information and phone card numbers. Your profit BBS **must** be well protected legally. Display a professionally-written disclaimer to every new user, and make sure you require tangible proof of age before granting adult access. Each upload you receive should be checked individually, if possible, to prevent someone from uploading commercial software. Discourage the discussion of pirated software or illegal activities within your message bases. These simple precautions help keep your system clean in the eyes of the law! You'll learn more about these legal measures in Chapter 7.

The Business/Support System

Finally, we come to the bulletin board that is run by a company or government agency for support of the company or agency. These systems are usually an extension of more traditional voice technical support for a product—the more high-tech the product, the more likely the company is to invest in a support board. Government agencies, on the other hand, use bulletin boards to disseminate public information quickly and inexpensively.

If the BBS supports a particular product, the sysop may have one or more technical support personnel devoted to answering technical questions posted in the system's message base. If the BBS does not offer direct technical support, it could have a large file library of the latest in software and instructional text files, and experienced customers could offer a form of support through their messages.

Businesses also make use of bulletin boards as remote e-mail (short for electronic mail) servers—for instance, each member of a sales force could logon to the company BBS and answer mail, upload and download sales information, and stay on top of late-breaking events within the company. Because many bulletin board packages also feature automated fax services, a caller can even upload a message that the BBS computer will automatically send with its faxmodem. Figure 1.4 shows a typical main menu screen from a business/support system.

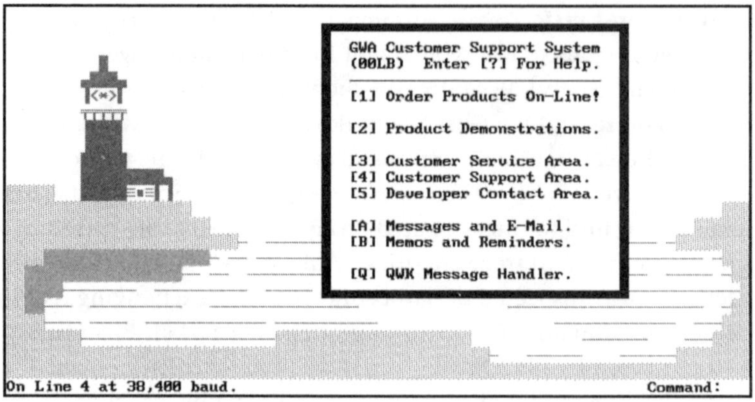

Fig. 1.4
The main menu from a business/support system, showing the basic menu structure and product-oriented services typical of the type.

What are the typical features of a business/support system?

- **Secure funding.** Unlike the sysops of hobby and profit boards, a business/support BBS sysop has funding from the parent organization—in other words, no sleepless nights wondering where to find the money to afford a replacement monitor!
- **Multiline operation.** Again, a support system must offer enough lines to avoid busy signals.
- **Company advertising and sales.** Most business/support boards understand the potential of their system as an "online billboard," and you're likely to find bulletins concerning new products and menu screens advertising the company logo; some of these bulletin boards also provide online methods of ordering replacement parts, third-party software, or books concerning their products.
- **Fewer features.** Of course, this is not to say that a call to a business bulletin board results in a single spartan menu and a handful of commands; however, a business system usually includes only those functions required by callers, so you won't find any online games or ANSI art galleries on most support boards. Menus are usually structured to make it as easy as possible to download support files or jump directly to the product support message base.

Now that you're familiar with the purpose of each system, you should select one of the three BBS types to use for your own system. Because the purpose of each system is well defined and addresses a different set of goals on your part, this should be an easy decision to make. Throughout most of this book, we'll concentrate on building a hobby system—they're the most popular and they make up the vast majority of bulletin boards around the world. However, we'll mention the other two types of bulletin boards whenever they differ a great deal from a hobby system.

What Makes Up a BBS?

As you learned earlier, most sysops work hard to make their system unique in the caller's view, and usually the BBS becomes a reflection of the sysop's opinions and goals as well. To illustrate this, think of a typical evening spent calling other bulletin boards: your first call during an online evening might be to a local gun enthusiast's hobby system, where you might join in a discussion for or against gun owners' rights. The next call might connect you to a long-distance profit system; if you subscribe, you'll probably spend the duration of the call listing the new files made available during the last week and downloading the files that catch your eye. Finally, you might logon to another local board patterned after a coffee house that specializes in online chat and FidoNet messages. You'd probably find five or six users conversing with the sysop in the Chat Lounge, and you might join in before you download your FidoNet mail using the system's .QWK door.

If all this sounds like complicated work for the sysops running those boards, it's actually more complex from the caller's standpoint! If you've already spent time online with your modem, you know that switching from one BBS to another can sometimes bring with it a miniature version of culture shock. For the sysops of each of our imaginary systems, however, the view behind the scenes is much the same.

In the early days of bulletin boards, the hardware that made up a bulletin board had to be built from the ground up, and the sysop usually wrote the bulletin board software. Today, virtually every sysop uses similar, standard equipment and one of several commercial or shareware bulletin board programs; once you're familiar with the basic setup, you'll see that your BBS will actually be quite simple in daily operation.

Note, however, that this does not mean that your BBS will automatically be easy to set up! Most bulletin board programs include a basic system already configured with menus, files, and message areas. If you're going to personalize your system at all, however, you'll have to create your own menu design, message bases, and file sections—and the more customized your system becomes, the more work is involved.

Let's examine the two components that make up any bulletin board system: hardware (like the computer and modem) and software (such as your BBS software and user management utilities). You'll also learn about four specific files required by practically every bulletin board, and how your BBS will use them.

The Hardware

At a minimum, every bulletin board system includes the following pieces of hardware:

- **A computer.** In this book, we'll assume you have an IBM AT, 80386 or 80486 computer (or compatible). Older PC and XT-class machines also perform quite well in a single-line environment. If you have a Macintosh computer, there are several shareware and commercial bulletin board systems written for Macs. Some larger bulletin boards operate with UNIX computers, but they require a much higher level of technical knowledge than bulletin boards based on personal computers.

- **At least one "Hayes-compatible" modem.** In Chapter 2, you'll learn more about the Hayes standard AT command set and modems in general.

- **At least one RS-232 serial port (external modems only) and cable connection to the modem.** In Chapter 2, you'll learn more about the inner workings of your PC serial port.

Those are the minimum hardware requirements of any bulletin board—we'll outline the specific hardware required by your Wildcat! bulletin board system in Chapter 3.

The Software

At a minimum, every bulletin board system includes the following software programs:

- **The bulletin board program itself.** This is the main executable you run to put your BBS online, and your system will probably run this particular program nearly 24 hours a day. The BBS software is designed to be as self-maintaining as possible, exiting back to DOS only when you bring the system down for some reason or during an *external event.* An external event is a scheduled time every night when the sysop has set the BBS to automatically bring itself down for maintenance purposes.

- **A user management program.** This program allows you to add, delete, and modify the data stored by the system for each caller. This may be built into the BBS program itself, or it may be a separate executable.
- **A configuration program.** You'll run this program when you first install your BBS software to specify all of the options and settings available that control your BBS—for example, the brand and model of modem you're using, the maximum number of lines that can be stored in each message, and whether or not your users are allowed to delete their own messages. The configuration program is also used whenever you change or upgrade your hardware, or if you need to make a global change to the way your system operates.

Putting Hardware and Software Together

To illustrate how your BBS hardware and software will work together, let's outline the progress of a hypothetical call to your bulletin board:

1. You run your BBS program, which sends the proper commands to initialize the modem and prepare it for answering incoming calls.
2. The modem detects an incoming call on the telephone line and automatically answers it. The two modems "negotiate" and then connect, establishing a communications link between your BBS and the caller's computer on the other end of the telephone line. The modem then sends a result code to your PC indicating that a user is now online.
3. Your BBS software sends the logon prompts to the modem, which in turn sends them over the line to the other computer. The prompts request the caller's name and password, which are returned by the remote modem.
4. Your BBS software compares the answers to the prompts. Is the name recognized by the BBS software as that of an existing user? If not, the caller enters the BBS as a new user. If the name is recognized, the password is compared against the password provided by the caller—if they match, the user has been identified and is allowed access to the BBS menu. If the password is not right, the caller is given one or two more tries to type it correctly—if the caller fails to get the password right after repeated attempts, the BBS sends a command to the modem to hang up the connection.

5. Once the caller has been identified, the BBS loads certain information into memory from the userlog records it has stored on disk. The data includes a personal access level that determines what you will allow the caller to do while online.

6. The caller selects commands from your menu system to navigate through your BBS, run games, compose and read messages, upload and download files—whatever your board offers. Each feature or service has its own minimum access level, and the caller can only use that feature with a personal access level greater than or equal to the minimum required level.

7. Your caller selects the "Goodbye" or "Exit" command at the end of the call, indicating that the BBS should disconnect and reset itself for the next caller. The BBS program sends the required command to the modem, which breaks the connection, and the modem begins waiting for the next call.

Of course, this is only the basic procedure your BBS follows to answer incoming calls and interact with users; there are many circumstances that can alter the flow of our hypothetical call. For example, the connection might be broken due to a power failure while your user is in the middle of reading a message—in such a case, the modem would indicate to the BBS that it's no longer connected, and the BBS program must "clean up" the aborted message and reset for the next caller. In another example, the user might be interrupted by a knock at the door, leaving the PC and the connection to your BBS idle for several minutes. To prevent a caller from wasting too much time during a call by standing idle, your BBS can automatically force the modem to disconnect if a preset amount of time passes by and the user has not pressed a key. A well-written BBS program is hard to "break," no matter what the circumstances—in fact, most sysops encourage their new users to try any feature they like while online, knowing that the callers can't hurt the system!

Your Userlog, Message Base, File Directories, and Logfile

We'll finish this section of this chapter by discussing the following four types of files universally used by bulletin boards:

- **The Userlog File.** Your userlog file is probably the single most important system file created by your BBS. It contains the logon names and passwords for all of your users, as well as extra data such as address information, home telephone numbers, and each user's preferences for graphics and system settings. As we discussed earlier, the userlog also contains a privilege level that you've assigned manually (or the default value that's automatically assigned to new users after they fill out your registration questionnaire).

Each time an existing user logs onto your BBS, the bulletin board program loads part of the corresponding userlog entry into memory and keeps a record of how many files the caller receives from the system, how long the user remains online, and the number of messages the caller writes. This statistical data is often used by the bulletin board program or external utility programs to create reports, flag those who are not participating (by sending files to your system and entering messages), and award extra time and services to those members of your system who do more than their share.

Tip

Any experienced sysop can tell you the value of maintaining regular backups of your BBS files—it's foolish not to protect your valuable data from hardware failure or a misplaced DOS delete command in the wrong directory! Because the userlog file is so valuable, however, many sysops take an extra step and back it up separately every night during their maintenance event. To do this, simply add the DOS Copy command to your maintenance batchfile and create a copy of the userlog file in a special subdirectory under your BBS directory. By using this technique, you ensure that you never lose more than a single day's worth of userlog changes and new user additions.

- **The Message Base.** One of the most popular services provided by any good bulletin board is its message base, where users can read and write messages and reply to messages left by others. Many bulletin boards also provide connections to message networks such as FidoNet and the Internet, and messages from these connections are added to the base, where your callers can reply to them as well.

  The text from these messages and their accompanying address data (who the message is from, who it's to, the message subject, and the date it was posted) is stored in one (or perhaps two) large message base files. As you might imagine, this file can grow to dozens of megabytes, depending on the amount of message traffic your BBS produces and how long you allow the messages to remain before the system deletes them. When a caller reads messages, your bulletin board software searches through your message base and displays those messages that match the caller's specifications—for instance, all new messages received since the last time the caller logged on to your system.

- **The File Directories.** Downloading files is another popular online pastime for your callers; in fact, many profit systems are wholly supported by their huge file libraries, which feature megabytes of new files added every day. To decide which files to download, your users will refer to a database of file descriptions, which usually includes one or two sentences describing what each file contains, when it was uploaded, how long it is, how many times it has been downloaded, and what requirements your PC needs to run the program.

  This descriptive data is stored in individual files called *directories*, and each section of your file library usually has its own directory. When a caller lists your file descriptions, your bulletin board software searches through each of these directories and displays those filenames and descriptions that match the caller's specifications—for example, all files containing the string "VGA" in their name or description.

- **The Logfile.** Although the name sounds similar to your userlog file, the logfile serves a completely different purpose: it simply records **every** activity taken by both your bulletin board software and your callers. This is valuable information for determining what features your callers are using the most. There are many external logfile processing utilities that create reports on a daily and weekly basis.

  You'll also find your logfile to be helpful when you're tracking exactly what happened at a particular time—if the BBS returned an error, the logfile can help pinpoint the circumstances leading up to it. You can follow the activity of a problem user as well, and many sysops include excerpts from the logfile in warning messages. We'll discuss how to handle problem users—including warning messages—in Chapter 8.

Common BBS Terms—A Short List

If you're already experienced in calling bulletin boards, you'll already be familiar with most of the terms used in this book; however, if you're new to the world of PC communications, a conversation with a BBS sysop might seem like a foreign language exam! In this short glossary, we'll list a few of the most common BBS terms.

- **ANSI or ANSI-BBS.** The most common terminal emulation in use on PC bulletin boards today. A terminal emulation is a set of codes transmitted between your bulletin board and the caller's communications software that control the colors, graphic characters, and cursor positioning for the caller's screen. ANSI allows your callers to display colors, simple animation, and even music.

- **Chat.** Chat refers to an online conversation between two or more people. There are three forms of chat: public chat (rather like the CompuServe CB simulator, where everyone can read what everyone else types), private chat (where two or more people can converse without anyone else reading their words), and sysop chat (where a caller chats directly with the sysop).

- **Disclaimer.** A disclaimer is a legal notice seen by all of your new users during their first logon that indicates your system follows all applicable laws regarding bulletin board services.

- **Downloading.** The process of a user retrieving files from the bulletin board with a transfer protocol to the user's computer. In effect, the user receives a copy of the file—exactly as it exists on your BBS—once the transfer has completed.

- **External event.** Bulletin board programs allow the sysop to set up a periodic event (usually at midnight or in the early morning) where the BBS program automatically exits to DOS and runs a DOS batch file with the name you specify. This batch file usually includes deletion of older messages from the message base, online game maintenance, and so forth. Once the event has completed, the DOS batch file reloads the BBS, and your system is again ready to accept calls.

- **Logon or logging on.** The process by which a caller identifies himself or herself to the bulletin board by typing in a name (or alias) and a password. This process occurs after the modems connect but before the BBS allows the caller into your menu system.

- **Networks.** Over the years, many bulletin boards have joined together to form message and file networks. If your board is a member of a network, a message posted by one of your users in a network area is echoed (or copied) to every other network BBS. The most popular and largest PC network is called FidoNet.

- **Piracy.** Software piracy involves the distribution of commercial software without renumeration to the author(s); usually, the software protection scheme, if any, has been removed by the pirate. Pirate bulletin boards do exist, but they are blatantly illegal and software manufacturers actively investigate them whenever possible.

- **Shareware.** Shareware refers to software that you can try out before you buy—if you like the program, you send money directly to the author. Shareware can be legally distributed from your BBS, while the commercial software you buy in a store **cannot** be distributed from your system.
- **Uploading.** The process of a caller sending a copy of an existing file on the caller's drive to your bulletin board with a transfer protocol. Once you approve these files and move them to the appropriate sectors, other callers can access them.

Summary

This chapter provided you with a basic understanding of what components make up your BBS, how it works, some of the more important files you'll be maintaining, and an introduction to some of the common terms used by sysops. In the next chapter, "Understanding PC Communications," you'll learn the details of PC serial communications and the hardware your BBS will use.

Chapter 2

Understanding PC Communications

by Mark L. Chambers

For most of us, the telephone is a familiar, ordinary part of life. Picking up the receiver and dialing a number is so automatic, we hardly think about the steps involved—and we naturally assume that the person on the other end of the connection speaks the same language with the same dialect, so there will be no problem communicating.

Although the steps involved are actually quite similar to the process used during a voice call, newcomers to PC communications are often overwhelmed by the hardware and software required to connect with a bulletin board. The telephone is even replaced by a device called a modem, which seemingly complicates the entire idea of calling another computer!

The online world also comes complete with its own cryptic language, which unfortunately includes many confusing terms like data bits, serial port, and the AT command set. As a sysop, you may find yourself frustrated as you try to help a caller who is not yet familiar with this new language.

In this section, we'll discuss the basics of PC communications: the hardware and the underlying technology that everyone uses to send information between computers over telephone lines, beginning with the data itself. You'll learn about the serial port your PC requires to use a modem. We'll explore how a modem works and how your PC will control it to answer incoming calls. Finally, you'll learn more about the techniques used by today's advanced high-speed modems, which are rapidly becoming standard equipment for today's bulletin boards.

The Basics of Serial Communications

The Bit

Computers store and share information in many formats, but they all use a single common foundation called the bit. Think of a bit as the simplest of storage methods; it's like a container that's either completely full or completely empty. The electronic equivalents of these two states are "on" and "off," exactly like a light switch (in fact, the earliest "thinking machines" were simply banks of switches). Computers assign a value of 1 to the on state, and a value of 0 to the off state. As you might have already guessed, those two values can also be represented as positive and negative electrical signals, allowing computers to communicate directly through cable connections.

The Byte

Of course, the storage represented by a single bit is severely limited—it's hard to transmit anything of substance with only two possible values! How does the PC use bits to represent a character from the alphabet, for example? And how does it send that character to another computer?

The answer is quite simple: computers group eight bits together into a single unit called a *byte*. A byte can store values from 0 to 255, and it's the standard building block for storing and transmitting numbers and text. To send (or store) a single character, your computer represents it with a byte value from 0 to 255; when a program needs to display the contents of a byte, the computer substitutes the corresponding character instead.

This implies the need for a set of standard character values, because two computers assigning different values to the same character would never be able to communicate. For many years, computer manufacturers have recognized the American Standard Code for Information Interchange (or ASCII) character set as the standard for 128 of the most common characters you'll find on a typewriter or computer keyboard—for example, the number and letter keys, punctuation keys, and dedicated keys like Enter. The 128 characters are the most common subset of the 256 available byte values. This allows your PC to communicate text information with most other computer brands available today; for example, both an IBM PC and an Apple Macintosh recognize the same ASCII code for a lowercase b.

Other character sets apply only to a certain brand. This is the case with the IBM extended character set, which contains a number of special graphics characters like line drawing and international symbols. These symbols take up the additional 128 characters, so the extended set uses all 256 byte values.

Most PC-based bulletin boards use this enhanced graphic character set; in order for your callers to display these symbols, their terminal program must recognize the same set.

Serial or Parallel?

As we mentioned earlier, computer communications over a cable simply consists of positive and negative voltages, each of which indicates the setting of an individual bit. To understand how your PC exchanges data with your modem, we must explore the idea of serial communications—beginning with how it differs from parallel communications. If you're using a printer connected directly to your PC, it's probably attached to one of the LPT parallel ports.

In a *parallel* connection, each bit in a byte is assigned its own unique wire within the cable, as in figure 2.1. An extra wire, called a *circuit strobe*, indicates that a new byte has been sent, making it easy for the receiving hardware to tell each incoming byte from the preceding one. Remember, all eight lines of our parallel connection are changed at once, so the entire byte is received as a single unit.

As you might guess, this is one of the fastest methods of transmitting data, with very little time spent waiting between data bytes. In fact, this is the method used by your computer to read and write data to memory. Older computers are referred to as 8-bit or 16-bit, meaning that they access data with a circuit much like our example. Newer computers are 32-bit, meaning that they can read and write 4 bytes (each containing 8 bits) of memory storage at a time, allowing much faster access.

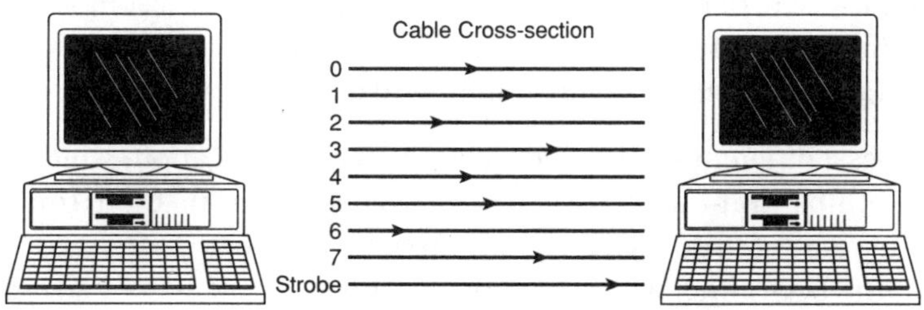

Fig. 2.1
A schematic of a parallel circuit.

Serial communications, on the other hand, only requires a single wire, making it far more desirable for communications over long distances. For this reason, serial communications became the standard among computers. In a serial circuit, the individual bits that make up a byte travel at a predetermined rate down the same wire, as shown in figure 2.2.

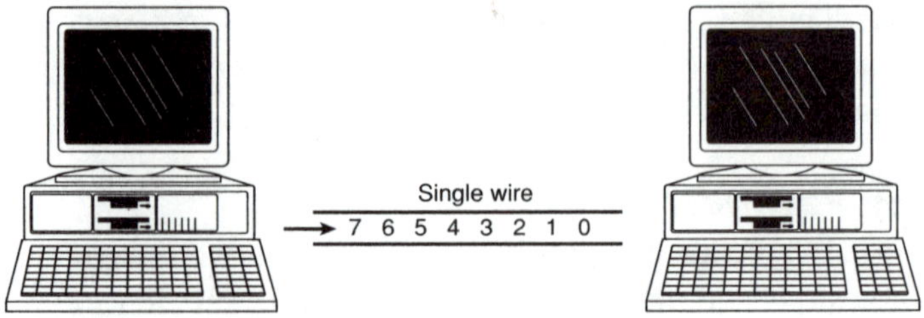

Fig. 2.2
A schematic of a serial circuit.

As long as the receiving hardware delays the same amount of time between bits as the sending machine, the two of them can communicate. This common transmission rate can be expressed in two ways:

- Bits-per-second. Usually written as bps. This is the actual throughput of the connection, written as the number of bits sent each second.
- Baud rate. A term coined by the French inventor Baudot. The baud rate of a connection indicates the number of data packets sent each second. Note that each data packet may contain more than one bit, depending on the hardware involved.

For a simple direct connection like the one we're discussing here, the baud rate and bps rates are always the same, because each packet is actually a single bit; when we discuss modem speed later in this chapter, however, you'll see that the two speeds are usually different because the modem can transfer several bits per packet.

Of course, this method of serial communications requires that both machines remain perfectly synchronized for the receiving computer to correctly receive and store each byte of data; this is why it's called *synchronous* communication. Synchronous links require high-grade telephone lines, and are usually only used for mainframe and minicomputer data communications.

Your PC uses a different method, *asynchronous* communication, which is slower by comparison—however, with the asynchronous method, timing is far less important. In the asynchronous method, each byte is "framed" by a *start bit* at the beginning, which is always 0, and a *stop bit* at the end, which is always 1 (see fig. 2.3). With these bits indicating the beginning and ending of each byte, the connection between the two computers need not remain perfectly consistent because the receiving computer can recognize each data byte.

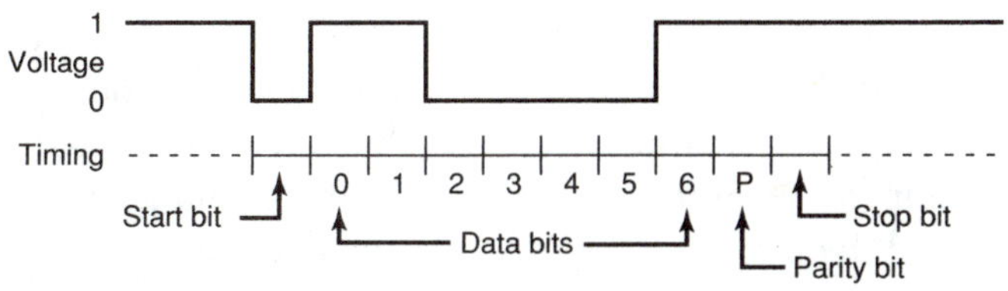

Fig. 2.3
Start and stop bits framing a byte.

Note

It is possible to add 2 stop bits at the end of each byte, but this slows the transfer because extra data has to be sent. For this reason, 1 stop bit has become a universal standard for all PC data communications, and you'll probably never encounter a transfer where 2 stop bits are necessary. If your callers ask how many stop bits they should set within their terminal program, **always** recommend they use a single stop bit.

Data Bits

As you learned earlier, it takes 256 character set positions to send the entire IBM extended character set, so all 8 data bits are necessary. Other computers (particularly mainframe and minicomputers) have no use for IBM graphics, so they use only the first 128 character set positions and 7 data bits per byte. Online services like CompuServe are often run on these large computers, and therefore require 7 data bits instead of 8. Of course, this is due to the basic premise you've already learned about serial communications: both machines must use the same number of bits in each byte and the same number of start bits and stop bits in order to successfully transfer data.

It's important that your callers understand that your BBS will use 8 data bits, and that their terminal software must be set to 8 data bits as well. The bad news is that many terminal programs call this number by different names, such as "word length" or "byte length." However, as we've already discussed, 8 bit serial communications is the standard on PCs, as well as the Macintosh; therefore, most programs use 8 data bits as their default.

Using Parity

You've probably heard telephone static (sometimes called line noise) during a voice call. As you might imagine, such interference plays havoc with a serial connection, corrupting data so that it arrives at its destination with a completely different value. The final component of PC serial communications is a form of error detection that's applied to each byte called *parity*.

When parity is used, the sending PC totals each of the first 7 bits within each incoming byte and changes the eighth bit so the sum comes out odd or even (depending on the parity setting you select). The receiving computer totals all 8 bytes and compares them to the parity setting; for example, if the parity is set to "even" and the sum of all 8 bits is odd, the receiving computer knows that the byte has been incorrectly received, and requests that it be sent again (see fig. 2.4). Similarly, "odd" parity sets the eighth bit so that the sum is an odd number.

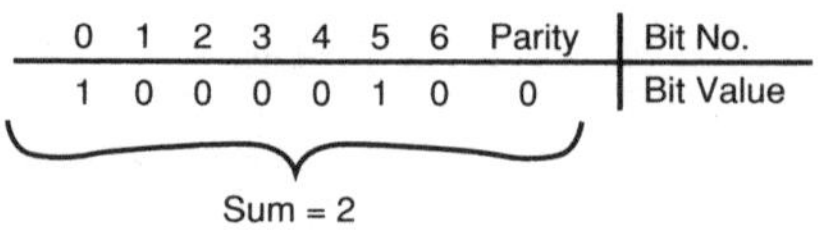

Fig. 2.4
Counting the bits in an even parity connection.

As you might imagine, this is a rather simplistic form of error detection. In fact, data can still be corrupted and pass the parity check, as long as the sum of the bits is still odd or even as required. Other parity values are even less precise: mark parity merely sets the eighth bit to 1, while space parity sets the parity bit to 0, and these bits are the only data checked by the receiving computer. Parity checking also slows down the transfer slightly, just like using 2 stop bits. PCs also have an additional problem using parity, because the IBM graphics character set requires all 8 bits to send all 256 possible characters, and a setting of even parity forces your PC to depend on only those first 128 characters for display.

For these reasons, PC serial links are almost always set to no parity, meaning that all 8 data bits are used within a byte and parity is never calculated.

This is yet another area where the mainframe/minicomputer world differs from the PC world. Mainframe computers almost always use even parity for communications (as we said before, there's no need for extended graphics, so the eighth bit in each byte is unused anyway). Again, this is why CompuServe requires a setting of even parity for a successful connection. This is a major cause of confusion in the online world, because callers with their PCs set to 8 bits and no parity will connect with a 7 bit service using even parity only to find that all they receive are strange characters or a blank screen with no response.

Because no parity is the common default for PC communications software, your users may never encounter this frustrating problem, but it never hurts to ask them what communications settings they're using. Many sysops make sure their communications settings of 8 data bits, no parity, and 1 stop bit appear on their welcome screen to remind every caller.

The PC Serial Port

So far in this chapter, we've discussed the basics of serial communication, but you haven't been introduced to any specific hardware that you'll use in setting up your bulletin board system. In this section, you'll move to the PC serial port, which is the basic hardware unit that makes serial communications among PCs possible.

As we mentioned earlier, your PC uses the parallel method of moving data to and from memory, so the computer must rely on its serial port to convert bytes in parallel format to serial format before they can be transferred. In addition, the port must also receive incoming signals from the other side of the link and organize them back into bytes that the computer can use.

The RS-232 Standard

Your serial port sends to and receives data from your modem through a standard configuration of circuits arranged according to the RS-232 standard, which was officially adopted by the Electronic Industries Association in 1969. The standard defines the voltages allowed along each of 25 wires and the additional control signals that can be sent along with the data. The standard signals are presented in table 2.1.

Table 2.1 RS-232 Signal Definitions

ISO Pin #	RS-232 Name	DTE/ DCE	RS-232 Function
1	FG		Frame (protective) ground
2	TD	DCE	Transmitted data
3	RD	DTE	Received data
4	RTS	DCE	Request to send
5	CTS	DTE	Clear to send
6	DSR	DTE	Data set ready
7	SG		Signal ground
8	CD	DTE	Received line signaldetec
9		DTE	Reserved for testing (+ voltage)
10		DTE	Reserved for testing(- voltage)

(continues)

Table 2.1 Continued

ISO Pin #	RS-232 Name	DTE/ DCE	RS-232 Function
11		DTE	Supervisory transmit data
12	SCD	DTE	Secondary received line signal detect
13	SCTS	DTE	Secondary clear to send
14	STD	DCE	Secondary transmitted data
15	TC	DTE	Transmitter clock
16	SRD	DTE	Secondary received data
17	RC	DTE	Receiver clock
18			Unassigned
19	SRTS	DCE	Secondary request to send
20	DTR	DCE	Data terminal ready
21	SQ	DTE	Signal quality detect
22	RI	DTE	Ring indicator
23		DCE	Data rate selector (direction optional)
		DTE	EIA/CCITT code changes with direction
24	ETC	DCE	External transmit clock
25		DCE	Unassigned

If you look at your serial cable leading to your modem, you might find that the cable only has 9 pins on the connector that attaches to your serial port. Where did the extra wires go? The answer is that most PC manufacturers have dropped the specialized signals that aren't used by modems or serial printers in the intervening years because the adoption of the RS-232 standard. Many serial cards offer both a full 25 pin port (called a DB-25) and a 9 pin port (called a DB-9); because either one provides all the signals necessary to operate your modem, you can use either one for your BBS.

Several signals are of particular interest to sysops, because they can be used by the BBS software to control your modem:

Pins 4 (Request to Send) and 5 (Clear to Send). These signals are used for hardware flow control (also commonly referred to as RTS/CTS Pacing). Practically all high-speed modems use this form of flow control to temporarily halt the flow of data while your serial port is busy or your PC is writing to disk.

Pin 8 (Carrier Detect). The CD signal indicates that your modem has made a successful connection, and it remains on as long as the connection continues. Your BBS software will probably monitor this signal constantly to make sure that the caller has not been disconnected.

Pin 20 (Data Terminal Ready). Most modems can be set to hang up whenever they sense that the DTR signal has dropped; this is an easy and fast method for your BBS to disconnect a call.

Addresses and Interrupts

Naturally, your PC must be able to control your serial port and read the data it's collecting, even while the port is processing data. The RS-232 port provides the pathway for both data and control signals between your modem and your serial port, but how do your serial port and your PC communicate?

The answer is through reserved locations in your PC's memory called *port addresses*. A port address is accessed by your PC in much the same manner as it accesses its memory storage. The computer reads data received by the serial port from the modem, writes data to be sent to the modem, and controls the operation of the port through these addresses. Your PC can support up to four ports at once, each with its own standard address. These addresses are usually referred to as COM1 through COM4, and their port addresses are expressed in hexadecimal numbers as 0x3f8, 0x2f8, 0x3e8, and 0x2e8 respectively.

Note

If your PC uses the Microchannel bus, your first two port addresses are the same as those listed in the previous paragraph; however, your COM3 address is 0x3220 and your COM4 address is 0x3228. Unfortunately, IBM did not follow the ISA standard for the last two port addresses, and many an IBM PS/2 owner has experienced problems with using COM3 and COM4.

In return, the serial port is provided with a method of alerting your PC that it has received data, allowing the PC to continue with other processing in the meantime. The port sends a signal called an *interrupt* (or IRQ) to the PC, which then processes the data from the corresponding port address.

If you're going to connect more than one serial device to your PC—including a serial mouse—it's important to make sure that your serial ports are kept separate, and that no two devices attempt to share the same port address or interrupt line. It's always safe to use COM1 and COM2 together, but an IRQ conflict may result if you connect a serial mouse to COM1 and a modem to COM3.

Note

With the use of special "intelligent" serial cards, your PC can access additional ports, allowing you to run more lines on one machine.

The 16550 Series UART

The heart of your serial port is a Universal Asynchronous Receiver-Transmitter (or UART) chip, which handles the parallel-serial conversions you learned about earlier in this section. IBM PCs have been fitted with a number of UART revisions over the years; the first was the 8250, while the most common UART chip version in use today is the 16450.

While the 16450 is vastly improved, it was never designed to cope with two of today's hottest advances in serial communications: the rapid increase in high-speed modems that run at 9600 bps or faster, and the rise in popularity of multitasking environments like Windows, DESQview, and OS/2. Under these circumstances, the use of a 16450 UART will almost always result in repeated errors whenever your callers are transferring files to and from your system (no matter what file transfer protocol they use). If your BBS will use a high-speed modem or you're planning on running in a multitasking environment, it's absolutely essential that your serial ports be equipped with the latest UART chips—the 16550 series.

Where the 16450 UART could hold only a single incoming character before requiring processing time from the computer, the 16550 UART can hold a total of 16 incoming characters. Under Windows or DESQview, this extra buffer provides your PC with the extra time it needs to process multiple tasks; with high-speed modems, the serial port is not overrun by incoming bytes faster than it can process them. Earlier versions of the 16550 chip did not handle the buffering of incoming characters correctly, so make sure your chip carries the designation "AF" or "AFN."

If you're upgrading your PC or purchasing a new PC to handle your bulletin board system, make sure that the serial ports it comes with are equipped with

16550 UARTS. If you're experienced with electrical hardware, you can also purchase these chips separately and install them yourself; however, make sure the UART you'll be replacing is mounted in a socket so that you can remove it, rather than soldered directly to the card!

Note

If you're unsure whether your serial port or internal modem has the older 16450 or a newer 16550 UART, open your PC and unplug the card. The UART is usually one of the largest chips on the card, and the top of the chip should be labeled with some derivative of "16450" or "16550AF" (for example, your chip might have "16C450N" written on it, but the number 16450 can still be recognized within the label). As mentioned previously, serious problems with file transfers using a high-speed modem or multitasking software can also be symptoms of an older 16450 UART chip.

If you've installed Windows 3.1 or MS-DOS version 6, you can also determine your UART type by running the Microsoft Diagnostics utility MSD. From the MSD main menu, press **C** for COM Ports to display both the UART chip and the port address for each of your COM ports.

Tip

If you're upgrading from an internal 2400 baud modem to a new high-speed modem, you can easily upgrade both your modem and your UART chip at the same time! Because internal modems are equipped with their own UART, simply make sure the high-speed modem you buy has a 16550-series UART (or equivalent chip) onboard; check with the salesperson before you decide on a particular modem.

What Is a Modem?

If the serial port is the key to PC serial communications, your modem is an extension of the same idea: it acts as the key to serial connections over telephone lines. More than any other piece of PC hardware, the modem is probably surrounded with the densest magical aura; most experienced callers rank their modems as the "eighth wonder of the world," and know less about how they work than any other PC peripheral! For your callers, this impression of the modem as a black box is harmless. As long as the box works and they can connect to the online world, the modem can remain a mystery.

As a sysop, however, your BBS will often depend upon your knowledge of your modem and how it operates. If your modem is not properly set, your BBS may be unable to answer an incoming call, disconnect a user, or take advantage of advanced modem features like high-speed connections, error correction, and data compression. Many a new sysop has left a message on another BBS across town asking for instructions on how to disable that irritating modem speaker or how to "busy" the BBS telephone line while the bulletin board is down.

In this section, we'll shed some light on the mystery surrounding your modem, as well as provide you with an introduction to the standard Hayes AT command set used by most modems. We'll end this chapter with a discussion of the data compression and error correction offered by today's high-speed modems.

Tip

The very attractive discount programs offered by modem manufacturers to sysops are an unexpected bonus of running a bulletin board. Naturally, the manufacturer does this to promote the product among your users. Before you purchase a modem from a catalog or a local store, call the modem's manufacturer and see if you can purchase the modem under a sysop discount plan!

Digital vs. Analog Signals

Up to this point, we've tracked data from the basic methods your PC uses to store information to the point where it passes through your serial port and reaches your modem. How is that same data transferred across a telephone line to a modem on the other side?

First, take a moment to consider the fundamental difference between human speech and the digital signals computers use to communicate. When you speak over the telephone, the sounds of your words are converted into an electromagnetic signal that varies in frequency; at the other end of the connection, this acoustic signal is converted back into the corresponding sound wave. These electromagnetic waves are called an *analog* signal, and they have formed the basis for not only the telephone but most methods of recording sound as well.

As you've already learned, however, your PC uses *digital* signals that vary from 0 to 1, each signal representing an individual bit. Computers cannot create analog signals by themselves, so they cannot use a voice telephone line to transfer data without help of some sort.

This, then, is the job performed by your modem. It *modulates* the digital signals produced by your PC into an acoustic sound wave called a *carrier* and sends that analog signal across the telephone line. On the receiving end, the modem *demodulates* the acoustic signal, converting it back into digital form (see fig. 2.5). In fact, these two terms formed the basis for the word modem, which stands for *mo*dulator-*dem*odulator!

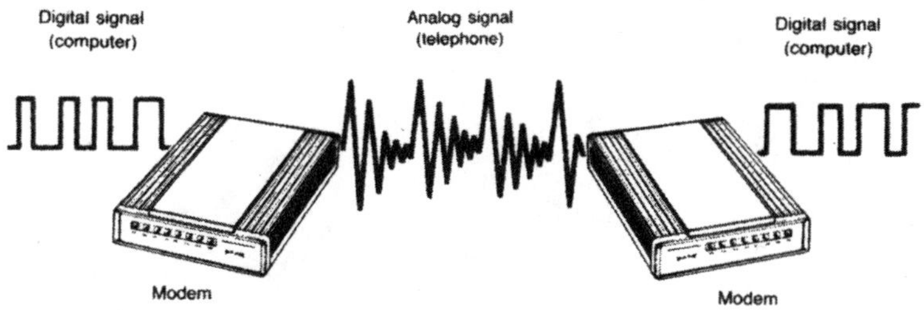

Fig 2.5
Two modems on either end of a connection, showing how data is converted.

Early modems used acoustic couplers, which held a phone receiver tightly against two cups (see fig. 2.6). The cups allowed sound to pass from the modem and through the receiver's mouthpiece, while incoming signals were picked up from the receiver's earpiece. Today's direct connect modems are far faster and less prone to error because the acoustic signal need never actually pass through the air before it's converted by the modem; instead, the telephone line runs directly from the wall plug to the modem. Most modems have a second phone jack built in, allowing you to plug in a telephone and use the line for voice calls when the modem is turned off.

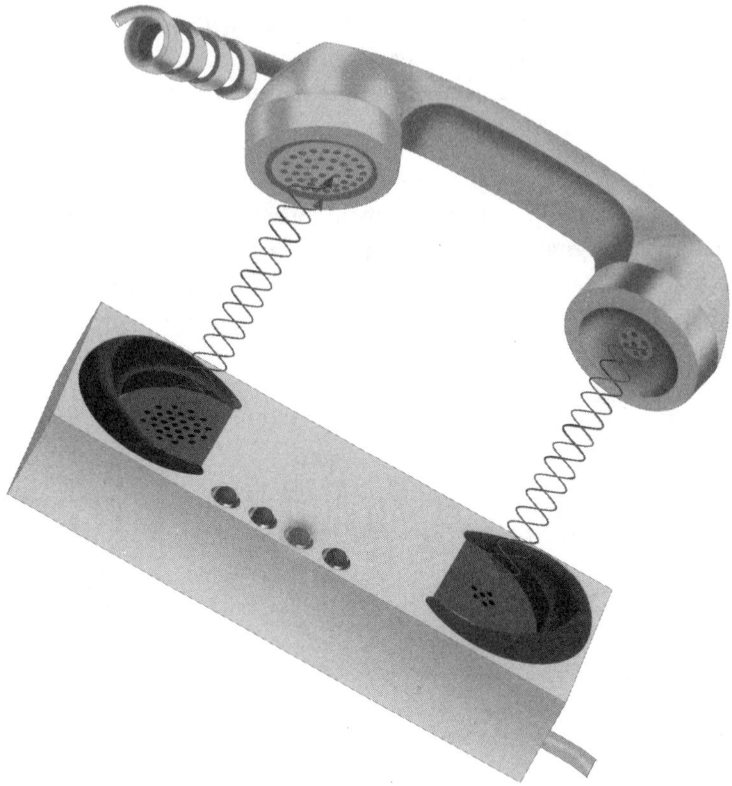

Fig. 2.6
An acoustic coupler modem.

Internal vs. External Modems

Although internal and external modems have their own advantages and disadvantages, they operate exactly the same. If you're making a decision on which type to buy for your bulletin board, this section will help by describing the differences between them.

An external modem is housed in a separate box with its own power supply, making it easy to connect to a variety of computers (see fig. 2.7). For example, you can disconnect an external modem from a Macintosh computer and use it with an IBM PC—the two computers use two different serial connections, but all that's required is the corresponding cable. The modem will work equally well with either computer. Because of the case and power supply, external modems are usually a bit more expensive than their internal counterparts, and they require a separate serial port, serial cable, and power outlet.

Most external modems also feature a number of status lights on the front panel, which many sysops find invaluable in monitoring and debugging the operation of a BBS. These lights indicate when the modem is online and a connection has been made, when data is being sent and received, and (for advanced high-speed modems) when a high-speed connection has been made.

On the other hand, an internal modem is a standard plug-in expansion card that you install inside your PC, so it cannot be used with non-IBM computers (see fig. 2.8). An internal modem is entirely self-contained and requires no separate power supply, serial port, or serial cable.

Fig. 2.7
An external modem.

Fig. 2.8
An internal modem card.

Understanding Modem Speeds

Earlier in this chapter, you learned that the terms bps and baud refer to the number of bits and the number of data packets sent per second (respectively) through a serial link. When you discuss the speed of a modem, you're talking about its speed in bits per second; however, somewhere in the past the two terms became practically synonymous, so you'll often see references to a 2400 baud modem when the correct modem speed is actually 2400 bps. The modem transfers 2400 bits per second, but does it at 600 baud; the faster throughput is due to the fact that a 2400 bps modem actually sends 4 bits per data packet, and 4 bits per packet at 600 baud yields 2400 bits per second.

This confusion of terms is so common that you'll find baud and bps used interchangeably by users and programmers alike; for example, the popular PROCOMM PLUS terminal package refers to modem baud rate instead of bps throughout. The only problem you're likely to encounter if you substitute baud for bps is an occasional online scolding by one of your technically proficient users!

Today's modems are categorized by a handful of standard speeds ranging from 300 bps to 28800 bps; speeds of 14400, 16800, 19200, and 28800 are usually abbreviated with a decimal point, as in 28.8 for 28800. Of course, your users will appreciate the fastest speed you can provide, and the recent drop in high-speed modem prices over the last two or three years has made the 14.4 modem the most popular speed. Although you'll still receive a large number of 2400 bps calls (which was the standard speed during the late '80s and early '90s), their number will continue to decrease rapidly, especially because these modems usually offer no data compression or error correction.

Talking to Your Modem—The Hayes AT Command Set

Until now, our discussion of modems has focused on the hardware itself and how it accomplishes the task of connecting your PC to the online world through a telephone line. Your modem is the link that exchanges data between your bulletin board system and the users that will call it.

However, the modem's job is essentially done once the connection has been established; from that point on, it simply continues sending and receiving data and monitoring the connection to make sure it hasn't been broken. The modem depends upon your BBS software to identify your callers, display the menus and information they request, send and receive files, and even indicate when to break the connection and hang up.

This brings up another question: how does the bulletin board operate your modem? For example, how can your BBS detect an incoming call? Or, how can it disconnect a user once the daily online time limit is reached? For reasons like these, your bulletin board software must be constantly aware of your modem's current condition, and it must be able to control your modem at all times.

Almost all modern modems make use of a set of alphanumeric commands originally developed by Hayes Microcomputer for their Hayes Smartmodem 300. The popularity of the Hayes Smartmodem series established this command set—commonly referred to as AT commands, because each command recognized by the modem is prefaced with the attention characters AT—as the de facto standard. Modems that adhere to this standard are labeled Hayes-compatible. The original AT command set contained less than 40 commands, which are included in table 2.2. This number has grown significantly to support the advanced modem features available today (we'll discuss these in detail in the next section).

Table 2.2 The Original Hayes AT Commands

Command	Function
AT	Prefixes all other commands
A/	Reissues the last command given
A	Manually answers an incoming call
C0	Disables transmit carrier
C1	Enables transmit carrier
DP	Dials, using pulse method
DT	Dials, using DTMF tone method (number follows)
E0	Disables echo of command input
E1	Enables echo of command input
F0	Sets half-duplex mode
F1	Sets full-duplex mode
H0	Places phone on hook (hangs up)
H1	Takes phone off hook (goes busy)
I	Returns modem product code (manufacturer code)

(continues)

Table 2.2 Continued

Command	Function
I1	Returns internal ROM checksum (manufacturer code)
I2	Performs modem internal memory test
L1	Sets speaker to low volume
L2	Sets speaker to medium volume
L3	Sets speaker to high volume
M0	Turns speaker off
M1	Turns speaker on when dialing and off when carrier detected
M2	Turns speaker off always
O	Returns on-line if connected
Q0	Returns modem command result codes
Q1	Does not return modem command result codes (acknowledgement of command operation or failure)
Sn=x	Sets S register to value (controls several internal timing and modem features)
Sn?	Displays current value of an S register
V0	Returns numeric result codes
V1	Returns text result codes
X*n*	Sets result code completeness level to *n* (higher values enable call progress monitoring, baud rate detection, and other extended result codes)
Z	Resets the modem internally and restores last stored values for all parameters
+++	Enters command mode if currently in data mode

You'll note that one of these modem commands looks a little strange; unlike those AT commands beginning with a letter of the alphabet, the +++ command can be used without the AT prefix. This special pattern of three plus signs is called the escape sequence, and it's used only when your modem is connected to another computer. The escape sequence tells the modem that the characters to follow are not part of the data it's sending to the other computer; instead, they are AT commands sent by the BBS to control your modem.

Once you understand the concept of your BBS sending commands to the modem, the interaction between them is simple to understand. The BBS sends a command to your modem instructing it to answer incoming calls. The modem replies with some sort of message, usually "OK." When a connection is made, the modem sends another message to your BBS telling it that a caller is now online and the speed of the connection. The BBS sends its logon prompt, and the interaction begins between your BBS software and the caller. When the caller hangs up or your BBS disconnects, another command is sent to the modem telling it to hang up the telephone and reset itself for the next call, and the entire process begins again.

Let's illustrate the use of some common AT commands sent to a BBS modem:

- **ATS0=1.** When you first turn on your modem, it may not be programmed to automatically answer incoming calls. The BBS usually sends ATS0=1 to turn over this important function to the modem. The command S0=1 sets Hayes-compatible modems to answer an incoming call on the first ring. If you wanted your BBS to answer calls on the third ring, you'd use the command ATS0=3 instead. To disable this auto-answer feature, you'd send the modem the command ATS0=0.

- **ATM0.** This command disables the modem speaker, which is usually on by default during the connection process. For a while, you may enjoy hearing the tones your modem generates during the connection process—somewhere down the line, however, most sysops eventually turn the speaker off.

- **ATH0 and ATH1.** These commands place the modem "on hook" and "off hook," respectively. If you're exiting your BBS and taking it offline for a few minutes, it's best to send the modem an ATH1 command, so that callers attempting to reach your system get a busy signal instead of ringing without answering. Once you're finished and the BBS is back online, it will send the modem the command ATH1 to put the modem on hook, ready to receive calls again.

Note

Many bulletin board programs send an escape sequence (+++) and ATH0 to force the modem to disconnect a caller at the end of an online session.

- **ATDT5551212.** If you're familiar with calling bulletin boards, you'll probably recognize this as a command instructing the modem to dial the telephone number 555-1212. Your bulletin board or a special "front-end" program for FidoNet/Internet communications may use this command to call another system to exchange messages and files.

Another common command combination is E1 V1, which forces your modem to respond with text result messages like "OK."

> **Note**
>
> As mentioned before, almost all bulletin board programs automatically configure your modem during installation. As long as your modem is directly supported by your BBS software, you'll probably never have to send a single AT command manually, and any changes you make to the modem commands will be made from the BBS configuration menu. We cover them here so you'll understand how your BBS program and your modem work together.

Advanced Modem Topics

In addition to an increase in raw speed, today's advanced modems offer two important advantages over older 300, 1200, and 2400 baud modems: they offer higher throughput with data compression, and they correct errors that occur during transmission. Keep in mind, however, that compatible modems must be used on each side of the connection in order to use these features.

Error Correction Protocols

Earlier in this chapter, we discussed the simple error detection principle of parity checking, and we also noted that your PC typically uses all 8 bits in a byte for graphics, which makes it impossible to use parity anyway. File transfer protocols can assure that you accurately send or receive data, but they're only effective while transferring a file.

Error-correcting modems can both detect and correct errors caused by static and line noise immediately, without requiring any intervention from your PC or your terminal software. If corrupted data is detected by the receiving modem, the data is automatically transmitted again. The international standard for error correction is called v.42, and it forms the basis for most of the error-correcting modems available on the market today. If your modem does not support the v.42 standard, the modems will connect without error correction.

Data Compression Standards

Data compression is an easy method of reducing the amount of time required to transfer data between modems—the effective speed of the transfer (sometimes called the *throughput* of the transfer) rises, even though the modems are not actually sending data any faster.

A modem compresses data by reducing a series of characters to one or two "symbols," which are then sent to the other modem instead of the actual character string. The process is rather like the idea of a character set (which we introduced at the beginning of this chapter), but taken in reverse. With a character set, your PC performs a substitution when it displays a single character represented by the 8 bits in a byte; in effect, a modem with data compression would send the single character, which would then be expanded back into the 8 original bits at its destination. Most modems can practically double their throughput with data compression.

Like many other areas of PC communications technology, several manufacturers have created their own proprietary compression schemes in the past, including Hayes and Microcom. Today, however, these have been largely replaced by the international v.42bis compression standard, which includes the older MNP compression method if a v.42bis connection cannot be made. v.42bis is an "intelligent" compression method, meaning that it is only applied to data that will benefit from compression—such as a text file—rather than data that has already been compressed—such as a .ZIP archive.

Summary

In this chapter, you've been introduced to the basics of serial communications: how your PC stores information, how that data is sent to your serial port and then to your modem, and finally how your modem converts the data into signals that can be sent over a telephone line. In the next chapter, "Hardware Requirements," we'll examine the hardware you'll need to install and operate your Wildcat! BBS.

Chapter 3

Hardware Requirements

by Mark L. Chambers

In the previous chapter, you learned a wealth of fundamental knowledge concerning how your PC stores and uses data, how it sends data across a serial connection, and how your serial port and modem work. In this chapter, we'll apply what you've learned by turning our attention specifically to bulletin board hardware and software questions—what type of PC will you need for your BBS? How many lines should you operate? Should you use the latest technology in telephone services? Will you need a computer network, or an integrated system that runs on a single PC? We'll answer all of these questions.

First, we'll cover what hardware and software are required for you to run the Wildcat! Lite BBS included with this book. You'll learn more about the two methods of operating larger multiline systems. Finally, we'll discuss advanced serial multiport hardware like the Digiboard and Galactibox.

Single-line Bulletin Boards

Single-line bulletin board systems make up a large majority of the BBS community around the world. One of the reasons for their popularity is the relatively inexpensive hardware they require to operate. If you're running a BBS on a "dedicated" PC, for example—without attempting to run multitasking software like Windows or DESQview—you could run a single-line BBS with:

- A 80286 or 80386SX-based computer with 1 meg of RAM.
- A serial port with a 16550-series UART.
- A 9600 bps high-speed modem.

At today's hardware prices, a new system with those specifications would cost well below $1000, and a similar system bought used would probably bring the price under $500. For a hobby that provides as much enjoyment as running a bulletin board, that's a small price to pay!

Your BBS will also require a certain amount of hard drive space. The following are the determining factors here:

- **The number and size of download files you'll offer.** If your file library will feature only a few sections, or if you'll be carrying only the latest files and deleting older files, you'll probably require anywhere between 20 and 40 megabytes of hard drive space. Larger libraries can occupy an entire 300-meg hard drive! If your system will offer general shareware files like applications and games, consider adding one or more CD-ROM drives to your system; they can actually reduce the amount of hard drive space you need at the same time they expand your selection of files! We'll discuss adding a CD-ROM later in the book.

> **Tip**
>
> As your file library grows, you can either dedicate additional hard drive space to it or mark older files as offline and keep them on floppy disk or a tape cartridge. The latter method is a popular alternative because it allows you to maintain a larger "virtual" file library than you can actually offer online, and some BBS software packages provide specific support for offline files. Of course, the disadvantage is that you must manually add the requested files to your file library and then delete them once they've been downloaded.

- **The size of your message base.** A busy system with a popular message base may require 5 megabytes of hard drive space just to store your message files! Even if your local message bases aren't that active, you can easily expect to double that to 10 megabytes or more if you offer FidoNet echoes or Internet newsgroups, which always contain new messages every day.

Tip

Just as with your file library, there's a simple way to provide additional messages online while still conserving hard drive space. Most bulletin board programs allow you to automatically delete messages based on their age—if you need to save space, set this figure so that messages only remain on your system for anywhere from two weeks to a month after they're added to your message base. Because your system will store messages for a shorter period of time, you can add a message area or two without significantly increasing the amount of space your message base files will require.

- **The number of external doors you provide.** Most online game doors occupy less than 500K of drive space, but some of the larger and more popular multiline games (and games with immense universes like Trade Wars) can eat up 2 or 3 megabytes of space each. If you offer online matchmaking databases or an online shopping mall, you're likely to find that these also take several megs to hold your data files.

With these criteria in mind, an average single-line hobby system with a file library of around 50 megabytes should be able to fit comfortably in 120 to 150 megabytes of hard drive space, while 200 to 250 megabytes should provide you with plenty of elbow room for starting a BBS.

Wildcat! Requirements

Now that you have an idea of the requirements for a typical single-line hobby BBS, let's check the specific minimum requirements you need to run the Wildcat! Lite BBS packaged with this book:

- **An IBM PC or compatible.** Although your BBS will run on an XT, it's recommended that you provide at least the 80286-based AT computer mentioned earlier in this chapter; this will allow you to run a high-speed modem of 9600 bps (or faster) without errors.

- **A minimum of 512K RAM, of which at least 350K must be available for use by Wildcat!** As before, it's recommended that your PC have at least 1 meg RAM, and the more memory the better (any extra memory can be used for a hard drive cache and a RAM disk).

- **MS-DOS or PC-DOS, version 3.3 or higher.** With the proper configuration, Wildcat! Lite can also be run under DESQview or OS/2.

- A minimum of 6 megabytes of hard drive space.

- **A Hayes-compatible modem.** As you learned in Chapter 2, this simply means that your modem should recognize the standard Hayes AT command set. Many sysops prefer an external modem so that they can monitor the connection by watching the modem's status lights, but an internal modem will operate exactly the same.
- **A serial port (required only if you'll be using an external modem).** If you're going to use a high-speed modem, make sure your serial card has a 16550-series UART (as explained in Chapter 2).
- **A standard RS-232 PC-to-modem cable (required only if you'll be using an external modem).** These cables are typically available just about anywhere that computers or computer peripherals are sold.

Although this listing covers all the required hardware and software you need to operate your Wildcat! BBS, it doesn't include many of the niceties that most bulletin board sysops find to be invaluable when operating a BBS. Some of these items are included to protect your system and its components, while others are added for your convenience. We'll use the rest of this section to discuss these common extra requirements.

Using an Uninterruptible Power Supply

Some sort of electrical protection is a good idea for any computer system, but it makes especially good sense for a BBS system; your PC will be running 24 hours a day, 7 days a week, and a single voltage surge through your home wiring during a lightning storm could cripple both your PC and your modem.

> **Tip**
>
> Some sysops take the extra precaution of bringing down their BBS and unplugging the equipment during a lightning storm because even the more expensive surge surpressors cannot protect your system from a strike on an electrical line—this is usually true even for those units that offer an equipment replacement guarantee.

Although a voltage surge is a very rare occurrence, electrical brownouts and temporary power failures are commonplace, and they can also cause damage over time. As you have already learned, bulletin board software is designed to be as rugged and stable as possible, but even the best of programs can inadvertently corrupt your data and your hard drive's FAT table if power is lost for a split second. For this reason, a standard electrical surge protector is really not a complete solution for a BBS.

Bulletin board sysops need the protection of a full uninterruptible power supply (usually called a UPS), which provides an immediate backup source of battery power for several minutes during a brownout or blackout. Most UPS units also sound an alarm to alert you that power has been lost, so in many cases you can simply bring down your BBS safely and turn off your PC until commercial power is restored. UPS systems are usually rated for higher surge voltages, and they also filter voltage spikes, so they eliminate the need for a surge protector as well. Several manufacturers offer UPS models under or around $100 that are perfect for a single-line BBS.

Tip

Many sysops don't consider the possibility of a surge through their telephone lines, however you should make sure your modems are protected from telephone line voltage surges as well. Inexpensive telephone line surge supressors are often advertised in *Boardwatch Magazine*, and they can make the difference between a working modem and a costly doorstop!

Using a Hard Drive Optimizer

A bulletin board's hard drive undergoes much tougher treatment than the same drive installed in a typical family PC; it runs constantly, and it rarely has an idle moment (especially drives used in multiline systems). If you're familiar with hard drive maintenance, you know that the more a drive is used, the more often it should be *defragmented*. Data used and modified by your PC is usually not written back to the same location, resulting in the fragmentation of large files like your message base and your userlog. The more fragmented these files become, the longer it takes for your PC to read them, eventually resulting in an appreciable slowdown of your system.

If possible, optimize your BBS hard drive(s) at least once a week with a program like Norton's Speedisk or PC Tools' Compress, either manually or automatically as part of your maintenance event.

Using a Hard Drive Cache

For the same reasons that you need to defragment your drives, you also need to boost the performance of your board's hard drive with a software *cache* program (such as Microsoft's SMARTDrive). These programs reserve a part of your PC's RAM as a buffer, holding data that your BBS software accesses often in memory, where it can be read and written without having to retrieve it from the hard drive. A good example is your userlog, which your BBS will refer to constantly.

If you're not already using a hard drive cache, add one today! You'll find that it will speed up the operation of every program you run, not just your bulletin board software.

Using a RAM Disk

As a sysop, you'll often find yourself performing disk operations that require quite a bit of temporary space—for instance, unarchiving .ZIP files to check them for viruses, unpacking FidoNet mail packets, or trying out a new online door before you actually decide to add it to your system. Usually, this involves writing the files to a temporary directory on your hard disk, using them, and then deleting the directory or erasing the files. This is a perfect opportunity to use a RAM disk instead of your hard drive, which you'll find will save you quite a bit of clutter and several extra steps, as well as reduce the fragmentation on your drive.

If you've never used a RAM drive, it's a simple concept: you load a special driver that reserves some of your RAM and fools your PC into thinking that the RAM space is another hard drive. Your PC assigns the new "drive" a unique letter, and you can use it exactly as if it was a physical hard drive. Depending on the amount of total RAM you've installed in your system, your RAM disk can range from half a megabyte to 10 megabytes or more! Consult your DOS manual to find the exact syntax necessary to create a RAM disk for your specific DOS version; usually the driver is called RAMDRIVE.SYS or VDISK.SYS, and it's loaded within your CONFIG.SYS file. There are also several shareware RAM disk programs that create a drive and then let you shrink or increase its size.

There are three distinct advantages and two important disadvantages when using a RAM disk. On the positive side, because a RAM disk uses your PC's RAM as its media, any program that uses a RAM disk for storage or execution runs much faster than it would from a hard drive. A RAM disk need never be defragmented. Finally, a RAM disk need never be replaced, because there are no moving parts to wear out. On the down side, because your PC's RAM loses its contents each time you turn the computer off, your RAM disk will only hold its contents as long as your PC is turned on. If you have any important data you want to keep permanently, copy it from your RAM disk back to your hard drive as soon as you're finished with it. Also, larger RAM disks can be quite expensive compared to hard drive space, especially with the rapid drop in hard drive prices.

Using a Tape Drive

Every PC owner should back up system data to disk or tape at least once a week, but this common sense protection is especially important to the sysop. Losing your userlog or message base can not only interrupt your service to your callers, but it can actively discourage them from calling again; after all, who wants to re-register all over again for a second or even third time? Additionally, you can imagine the chaos that will occur if you lose your file library descriptions, or some of your library download files themselves.

Although it's perfectly acceptable to backup to floppy disk, as your BBS message base and file library grows you'll find your backup to be an increasingly tedious job, and it will take more and more time that your BBS could be online. If you can afford a QIC-compatible tape drive, it's highly recommended that you add one to your system; it can handle the task largely unattended, and it's usually faster than a floppy backup of the same data. Tape backups are quite inexpensive; for example, a good model that can store up to 250 megabytes of compressed data on a single tape will probably cost under $200.

Basic Multitasking

Finally, it's time to introduce the basics of *multitasking* software. A multitasker is an operating environment (such as DESQview) or a full-fledged operating system (such as OS/2) that allows your PC to run your BBS software as a hidden background task, while you continue to use it for other applications. The multitasker does this by forcing your PC to alternate its processing time between each task; for example, the multitasker gives your BBS three clock ticks of processing time, then gives your word processor three ticks, then returns to your BBS, and so on. That's a simple explanation of preemptive multitasking, but it illustrates that your PC can never give its full attention to your bulletin board unless the BBS is the only program running.

At first glance, multitasking sounds like the ideal way of running a bulletin board system (especially a single-line BBS), because you can still use your PC for word processing, database, or spreadsheet work while your callers are completely unaware that you're sharing your PC with them. However, it's not as simple to run a system under this scenario as it first appears. You need to consider the following possible disadvantages before deciding to use a multitasker for your single-line system.

- **Multitasking requires extra horsepower.** To avoid sluggish operation for both your BBS and your local applications, you're going to need a considerably faster PC. At a minimum, if you're running a high-speed modem under DESQview, you should have a 80386 33mhz PC. If you decide to use the greatly enhanced features of OS/2, a 80486DX 33mhz PC with 8 megabytes of memory is your minimum requirement for a single-line BBS running in the background.

> **Tip**
>
> It's not recommended to attempt running a DOS-based BBS under Microsoft Windows because DESQview and OS/2 offer more efficient multitasking of DOS programs. However, if you have a sufficiently-fast PC, the PowerBBS Windows-based bulletin board package will allow you to run other Windows applications while your BBS operates in the background.

- **Multitasking requires extra RAM.** Your PC will need extra RAM to run and use multiple applications.

- **Multitasking requires careful configuration.** Unlike the simple and straightforward changes necessary to AUTOEXEC.BAT and CONFIG.SYS under a pure DOS environment, a multitasker will usually require experimentation and careful configuration before you have your system running to your satisfaction.

- **Multitasking may affect stability.** A misbehaving DOS application may cause your multitasker to freeze, which also locks up your BBS. Although this possibility is less of a problem with OS/2, no multitasker is as safe and stable as DOS alone.

Of course, multitasking can indeed be the perfect environment for you as a sysop if you can work your way around these disadvantages! The decision is up to you: if you can devote an entire PC to running your BBS, it's recommended that you use a pure DOS environment. If, however, you only have a single PC and you'll have to use it from time to time, there's no reason not to try multitasking. After all, in this section we've only considered multitasking as it relates to a single-line hobby system; in the rest of this chapter, you'll learn that multiline packages from PCBoard and Wildcat! rely on DESQview or OS/2 for their multitasking abilities, while other multiline packages like TBBS and the Major BBS rely on their own internal multitaskers.

Your Telephone Service

So far in this chapter, we've considered single-line systems and their requirements. In the last decade, most hobby boards began as single-line systems—but recently, more and more new sysops envision their boards as online services capable of turning an immediate profit, and thus begin their systems with multiple lines from the start. This recent surge in multiline systems is also due to the rapid drop in PC hardware and modem prices, making it economically feasible to provide multiline service as a hobby (instead of an investment on the scale of a small fortune, as it once was).

But how do you determine how many lines you'll need? Isn't it always better to operate as many lines as you can afford? And will you need any of the special functions offered by your telephone company? In the next section, you'll learn more about how you can predict the number of lines you'll need, and what types of telephone services sysops want and don't want.

How Many Lines Will I Need?

The idea that you should always offer as many lines as you can afford is one of the most common misconceptions held by new sysops. As any sysop of a profit board can tell you, there's no mistake more costly than spending your money fruitlessly on 32 telephone lines when you could have served your callers just as well with eight lines! Most bulletin board vendors price their programs by line count as well, so it's more expensive to buy software that will operate 16 lines rather than four lines.

There are three factors that make it easier to determine how many lines you'll need for your BBS:

- Are you within local calling distance of a major city? If so, it's probably a safe bet that a higher line count would attract more callers. The same is true for a college or university.
- How long will you allow a single caller to remain online? Remember, a single-line BBS can only accept 24 callers if each remains online for an entire hour! Of course, the average call time will be much lower than that for most callers, even for boards that focus on file transfers. If you allow your standard-level users 30 minutes of online time per day, you should expect about 50 calls per day, per line.
- Will your BBS have strong competition? Are there already existing multiline bulletin boards in your local calling area that will offer the services you plan to have on your BBS? If the answer is yes (and you'll be running a profit board), then consider whether you can offer at least half of the line count offered by your competition.

> **Tip**
>
> Remember, you need not necessarily exceed (or even equal) the number of lines offered by your competition. However, you must generate interest and perceived value on the part of your callers, and it's harder to do that without a competitive number of telephone lines.

Before all else, keep this basic rule in mind: it's **much** easier to add lines in the future (when you're sure you need them) than it is to pay for lines now and then take them down in the future. Naturally, the addition of extra lines makes a great press release, and enhances the stature of your BBS in your calling area—the subtraction of lines, however, has the reverse effect.

Will your BBS focus on multiline chat? If so, then the number of incoming lines to your system becomes much more important, and the rules change completely: you **should** consider adding as many lines as possible, as long as your BBS is within local calling distance of a large city. Pure chat boards are generally considered to be much harder to establish, and your system must provide enough incoming lines to allow for lively, interesting conversation.

> **Tip**
>
> One of the benefits of running a board devoted solely to multiline chat is that you can offer 2400 bps as your standard modem speed, because 2400 bps is considered a comfortable rate for reading and typing. Also, the advanced features of error correction and data compression often result in a choppy display, so they're usually not supported. It's not uncommon for a major chat board to offer 32 lines to the public, each of which offers a generic 2400 bps modem!

Once you've established your system, you'll find it easier to monitor your line usage (the amount of time that each telephone line is busy), and this value will determine whether you need to add additional lines. Some BBS programs offer line usage tracking as a part of the program; if your software doesn't provide this important figure as a built-in function, use a utility that reads your logfile or userlog and creates a report, and run it as part of your maintenance event.

Caller ID and Call Waiting

Among the extra services offered by your telephone company, caller ID, distinctive ring, and call waiting are of special interest to sysops; the first service is a possible advantage, while the last is a decided disadvantage.

Caller ID allows a modem to display the telephone number where an incoming call originated, making it an ideal security feature for bulletin boards. Unfortunately, only the latest modem technology supports this feature, so it's not supported on most modems made as recently as two years ago. Also, only a few bulletin board programs directly support caller ID, so you must be running one of these packages to use the service. If you have the right modem and software, though, you'll find that this feature will greatly reduce the number of prank calls and problem users you must deal with on your system. BBS programs supporting caller ID typically log the originating number to a separate file or the system logfile.

On the other hand, call waiting generates a signal (usually a series of tones or a clicking noise) indicating that someone else is attempting to call you. Of course, this makes no sense on a BBS telephone line, but many of your callers will probably have this service, and that signal usually results in a disconnection! It usually takes several unexpected disconnects before a new caller who's unfamiliar with this problem leaves an angry message to you demanding to know why your BBS (or you personally) keeps hanging up. Handle these calls politely, for the user has no way of knowing the real reason; you can also indicate that the caller can usually add a "disable" string to the modem's dialing command that turns off call waiting for the duration of the current call. This string of characters varies across the country, so check with your local telephone company for the string that works in your area.

What Are Hunt Groups?

If you've decided to run a multiline BBS with more than two or three lines, you'll probably want to arrange for your telephone company to handle your lines in a *hunt group* (also referred to as forward on busy). Using this system, only the first of your numbers should be made available to the public. If a caller is currently online, line 1 is busy and the next call to your system is automatically routed to line 2. If line 2 is also busy, the caller is routed to line 3, and so on. Finally, if all lines are busy, the caller receives a busy signal and tries again later.

This is an ideal setup for a multiline system because many of your users will only try one number when they call your system (even if they know all 15 other numbers, your system is busy as long as line 1 is busy). Arranging your lines in a hunt group ensures that your system is always used to its full potential. Some sysops differentiate their hunt groups based on modem speed as well. Note, however, that if you decide to reserve certain numbers as subscriber-only lines, those numbers cannot be added to the hunt group (unless you set them up in a separate group).

Multiline Bulletin Boards

Now that you've learned more about determining whether you need multiple lines—and why you should arrange those lines in a hunt group—it's time for us to turn our attention to multiline systems. In this section, we'll introduce you to the two methods of providing multiline service (integrated and networked) and provide examples of each, discuss the hardware needs of a multiline system, and discuss the multiport serial cards that make it possible to offer as many as 256 lines on a single PC. Note that the term "network" in this section refers to a group of PCs in the same room or building, all connected together by cables.

Integrated vs. Networked Multiline BBS Software

By definition, a multiline bulletin board program allows more than one caller to simultaneously access all of the services provided by your BBS. Multiple users can read and post messages, interact with each other through multiline chat and multiline games, and even download the same file at the same time. For this to be possible, the BBS program must prevent situations from occurring that would lead to DOS file and program errors, including locking files to prevent two lines from simultaneously writing to the same file and allowing multiple users to run the same BBS program at the same time.

Over the years, BBS software developers have settled on two methods of providing multiline access from the DOS platform: the *integrated* system and the *networked* system. Both of these solutions have their advantages and disadvantages, and it's important that every sysop planning to operate a multiline BBS understand the pros and cons of each method before deciding on one or the other.

Integrated Multiline Software

The integrated bulletin board system allows multiline access on a single PC, allowing up to 64 and even 256 simultaneous users! Integrated systems use a built-in custom multitasker, so there's no need for a separate multitasking environment like DESQview or OS/2. Integrated programs allow you to run all 16 lines of your budding online service from a single monitor and a single PC without the headaches of additional computers or file servers. Figure 3.1 shows an illustration of a typical multiline BBS running integrated software.

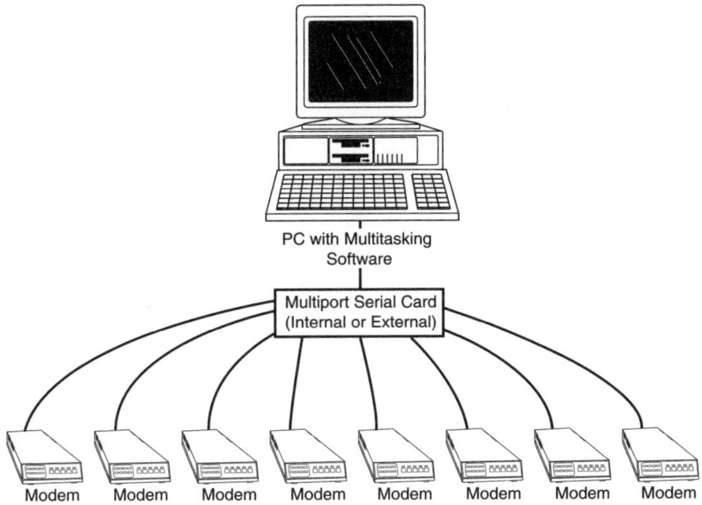

Fig. 3.1
An illustration of the system architecture of a multiline BBS running integrated software.

But wait—how can a single PC operate that many serial ports? As you'll remember from Chapter 2, the IBM PC standard architecture allows only two serial ports, and the de facto standard adds another two ports; that's a total of four, using port addresses COM1 through COM4. The answer is simple: integrated bulletin board programs use advanced multiport serial cards that sidestep the PC's limit, with as many as 16 complete ports on each card. The ports use a special cable with a single connector on the PC end that branches out into the corresponding number of RS-232 cables on the modem side; these complex cables are often called octo-cables because of their unique design.

The two most popular integrated BBS programs are The Bread Board System (commonly called TBBS) from eSoft, and The Major BBS (commonly called MBBS) from Galacticomm. These two programs are quite similar in many respects, as they share both the advantages and the disadvantages common to integrated BBS software. Both programs have been in existence for several years now, and both of them are popular choices for profit and business/support systems because of their reputation for rock-solid stability and dependability. Both systems come with a base package containing all the standard services featured on most boards, and both TBBS and MBBS offer add-on modules that you buy separately to expand the capabilities of your system. Of course, you can run either system as part of a PC network, but this is usually done to provide an additional level of connectivity through the network (for example, so that employees of a company can logon to the system without needing a modem). Figure 3.2 shows the main Sysop console screen from a TBBS system. Figure 3.3 shows the main Sysop console screen from a MBBS system.

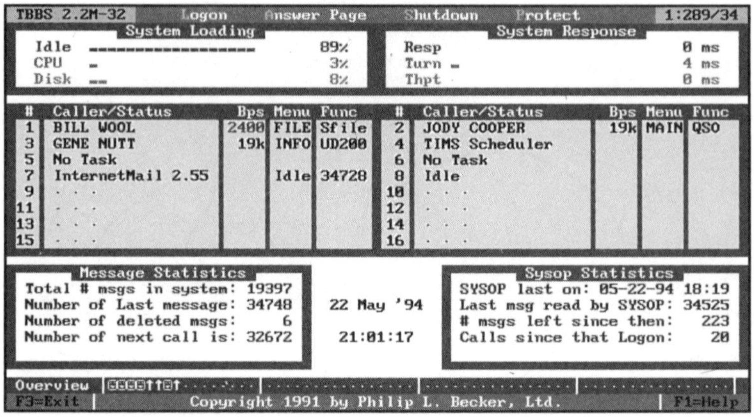

Fig. 3.2 The sysop console screen from the author's TBBS 2.2 system.

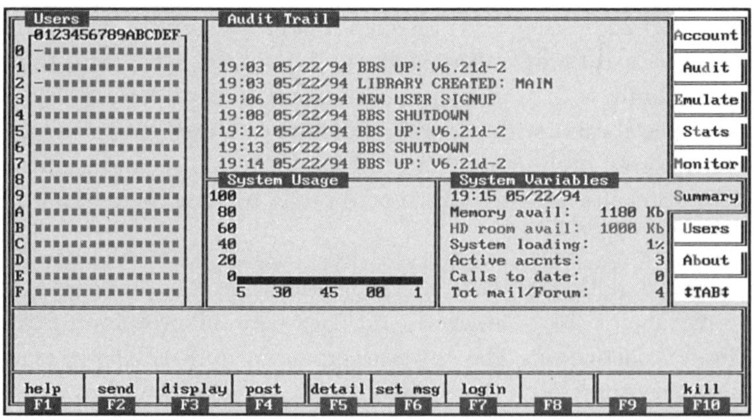

Fig. 3.3 The sysop console screen from a Major BBS 6.2 system.

What are the advantages of running one of these integrated BBS programs?

- **Low cost per line.** Because only a single PC is required to operate an integrated BBS, the relatively high cost of the BBS software is more than offset by the savings in hardware over a networked system.

- **Ease of installation and maintenance.** An integrated system takes less space and requires far less maintenance time than a room full of networked PCs, and all you need to install is the BBS itself, instead of the BBS software and the network software. You also save the time you'd spend fine tuning your network for operation with your BBS.

- **Stability and reliability.** As mentioned earlier, integrated bulletin boards are inherently far more stable than networked systems, which often encounter problems with network-specific software and hardware cards. The multitasker built into an integrated BBS program takes complete control of your PC at the lowest level, providing the various functions your users expect without requiring interaction with any other software or another PC. Sysops of integrated systems are fond of pointing out that they can leave their bulletin boards for an entire vacation without worrying about a system crash due to the BBS software!

On the other hand, what are the disadvantages of using integrated BBS software?

- **No direct access to DOS.** Because your BBS program is constantly running, an integrated system can never "drop to DOS" like a networked system. Instead, both TBBS and MBBS offer sysops DOS emulator modules, which look and act like DOS. However, this inability to shell directly to DOS also prevents integrated systems from running the standard external door programs used by networked boards; instead, TBBS and MBBS doors must be specially written and compiled so that the BBS program can run them internally.

- **Loss of processing speed.** No matter how good the multitasker, an integrated BBS program cannot deliver the same processing power to each node as a networked solution because the integrated BBS program must share resources between lines and the networked system uses one PC per line. For this reason, integrated systems with a large number of lines are usually run on the fastest 80486 and Pentium platforms available.

- **Poor performance under DESQview and OS/2.** Because integrated BBS software includes its own multitasker, TBBS and MBBS have traditionally run rather poorly under DESQview and OS/2. It can be done, but the intent of these programs is that you dedicate an entire PC to your bulletin board.

Networked Multiline Software

Networked bulletin board systems provide multiple lines with a group of PCs, all connected together on a standard DOS network (for example, a Novell or Lantastic network). Each PC in the network usually runs a single line (or *node*, as lines on a networked BBS are often called); this provides the best possible response time for the user. However, each PC can run more than one node (usually a maximum of around eight per PC), if it runs a copy of an external multitasker such as DESQview. Figure 3.4 shows an illustration of a typical multiline BBS running networked software.

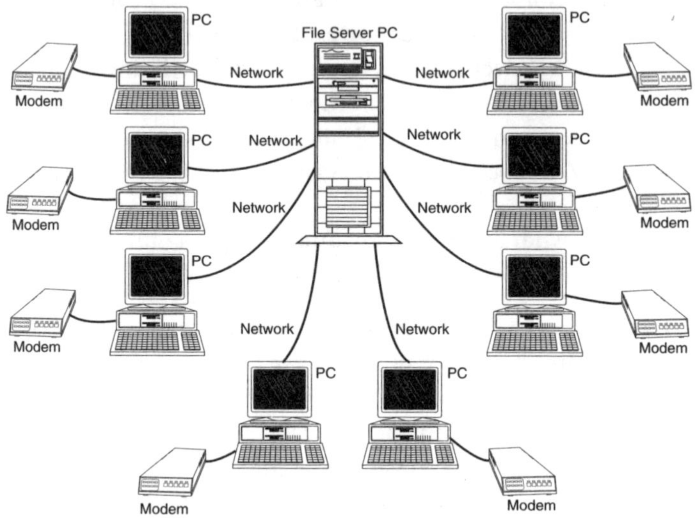

Fig. 3.4
An illustration of the system architecture of a multiline BBS running integrated software.

Sysops of networked bulletin boards also usually assign their fastest 80486 or Pentium PC as a dedicated file server, which means it holds most of the hard drive files and CD-ROM storage used by the other PCs in the network. This is a convenient method of providing a very fast PC for disk-intensive functions, while the rest of the PCs that actually handle incoming calls can be slower 80386 machines.

The two most popular network BBS programs are Wildcat! from Mustang Software, and PCBoard from Clark Development Company. Both of these programs have recently added support for multiport serial cards to their products, which blurs the distinction slightly between them and the integrated programs we covered earlier—however, both of these network programs still require you to provide your own multitasking environment if you're going to run multiple lines on one PC, and they support a maximum of eight lines on a single computer (far less than either TBBS or MBBS). It's important to note that network BBS programs like Wildcat! don't require a network connection if you plan to operate only eight lines—the network is only required if you need to run a higher number of lines. Figure 3.5 shows the main Sysop console screen from a Wildcat! multiline system.

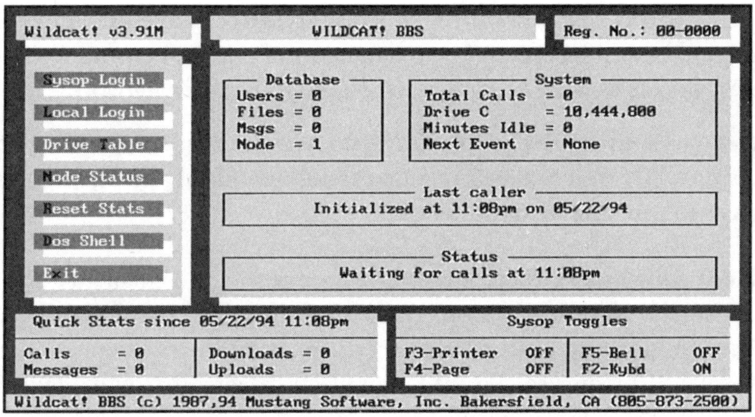

Fig. 3.5
The sysop console screen from a Wildcat! multiline BBS.

What are the advantages of operating a network multiline system?

- **Direct access to DOS.** A network bulletin board program can shell to DOS without dropping carrier, so you can access a true DOS prompt remotely and run programs that you wouldn't be able to run on an integrated system. You can also choose from a huge number of external DOS doors, so your selection of games, database programs, and other online programs is much larger with a network system.

- **Network connectivity.** In addition to the advantage of a central file server, your PCs will be able to access peripherals like printers and CD-ROMs from anywhere on the network—a decided improvement over trying to cram all those drives and expansion cards inside a single PC chassis.

- **Faster processing speed.** If your network system dedicates one PC to each node, your users will enjoy faster throughput and response time than any integrated system.

- **Excellent performance under DESQview and OS/2.** These systems are built with multitasking software like DESQview and OS/2 in mind.

Unfortunately, though, networked bulletin board systems do have their disadvantages:

- **Considerable hardware investment.** If you've bought and sold computer equipment in the past, you know how PC hardware depreciates rapidly in value. If you decide to devote 16 complete PCs to your networked bulletin board, make sure you're prepared to keep them running!

- **Additional installation and maintenance worries.** Unlike an integrated system, you'll have to maintain multiple PCs and a computer network, as well as the software required to run that network.
- **Network instability.** By nature, no network is as solid and reliable as a single PC. Your BBS will require careful fine tuning on an ongoing basis to run reliably day after day.
- **Heat and Electricity.** A large network of PCs in a small area will generate a great deal of heat. To avoid equipment breakdowns, you may need to look into air-conditioning the room(s) where the network is. Several PCs may also overload your electrical circuit. You may need to hire an electrician to install additional circuits.

Digiboards and Intelligent Serial Cards

It's obvious that multiport serial cards have played an important role in the evolution of the PC-based bulletin board. Without one or more of these cards, your PC is limited to a maximum of four lines; with four Digiboards installed, a system running TBBS can jump to 64 lines and truly call itself an online service. How do these boards work?

Probably the best-known manufacturer of multiport serial cards is Digiboard Incorporated, which offers 16-bit IBM PC expansion cards with 4, 8, and 16 fully-functional serial ports onboard, each of which has a configurable port address. These serial ports can be accessed by your communications software with a special device driver, but integrated and networked multiline BBS programs that use Digiboard hardware normally talk directly to the card, and don't require the device driver. As mentioned earlier, cards like the Digiboard are connected to external modems via a special cable, with one connector on the PC end and up to 16 connections on the modem end.

Galacticomm, maker of the Major BBS package, also offers a unique expansion interface for internal modems called the GalactiBox. This external case holds and powers up to 16 internal modems (which, as you recall, are usually somewhat cheaper than the external versions of the same modem). The box is in turn connected to an expansion card within your PC. Up to 16 GalactiBoxes can be strung together, for a maximum of 256 internal modems connected to a single PC!

Summary

In this chapter, you learned more about the specific hardware you'll need to run a single-line board like your Wildcat! Lite BBS, as well as the hardware required to run multiline integrated and networked bulletin board systems. We also discussed peripherals and extras that help make life easier for any sysop. Finally, we presented the factors that can influence how many lines you offer to your callers, the telephone services you want, and those that you don't want.

In the next chapter, "Creating an Image," you'll learn how to create your system's overall structure by developing a combination of a theme, a set of services, and your menu system.

Chapter 4

Creating an Image

by Mark L. Chambers

In this chapter, we'll explore how you can design your BBS around a theme of your choice, as well as the services you should offer, and the structure your menu system should take. All three of these—theme, services, and menus—must work together to create the online image you want to present to your callers. It's this image that makes your BBS memorable and, most importantly, causes new callers to add your BBS to their directory of bulletin board numbers!

You'll also learn more about charging your users. Should you charge a fee for all callers, or just accept donations? How will your users pay you for a subscription? We'll cover those questions and more.

Beginning with this chapter, from time to time we'll refer specifically to the Wildcat! Lite software included with this book. However, the procedures we'll cover in this chapter apply equally to the design of any bulletin board running any software package.

Matching Theme to Function

As mentioned in Chapter 1, your bulletin board's theme must fit the function it will serve in order to attract callers. Hobby boards perform well with a theme based on your personal interests. A profit board theme emphasizes the services it can offer to subscribers. Business/support boards stress the company's product line whenever possible.

In this section, we'll build a theme for an example hobby system, and then provide ideas for all three types of bulletin boards. Make sure you have a pad of paper and a pencil handy for your own design!

An Example Hobby Theme

The first step in building your board's theme is to select which one of your interests you'd like to see online. If you need ideas, write down your top five hobbies and interests—don't worry whether they're general (like cars and driving or animals) or specific (like Greek mythology or World War II airplanes). A theme can be as specific or as general as you wish, and you can express it in one or two words or an entire paragraph.

Now select an interest from your list that you feel will match these criteria:

- **Interesting to others.** To attract users and keep them calling your system, your theme should be interesting to a segment of the general public. Remember, your theme can be as simple as "inviting the user into my house," and you can call your board "My Place BBS"—but will that image for your board attract callers? If a caller does logon, will your BBS theme be memorable, or will it tend to be mixed in with the dozen other boards the caller tried that evening? You'll likely gain a regular group of local callers, but such an image isn't likely to draw long-distance users into making that important first call.

- **Unique or singular.** As mentioned in Chapter 1, sysops have used certain images so many times while creating their systems that the themes can practically be considered classics—for example, themes based on *Star Trek*. Certainly, you can follow suit, but your BBS will make more of an impression if you select something less common for your theme.

- **Lends itself to the BBS structure.** Do you have a large number of text files, programs or graphics related to this interest? It's always an advantage to offer text and files from your own collection, whether they be programs, text files, digitized sounds, or graphics. Of course, these files must be within the public domain, or you cannot distribute them from your system. For example, if your board will center around photography, you probably already have shareware and freeware programs you've collected to aid you in preparing your darkroom or cataloging your negatives. If you don't mind scanning photographs you've taken into .GIF or .JPG format pictures and releasing them to the public, you can provide exclusive files available nowhere else—and you can even add your logo to the pictures as a form of advertising, which we'll cover in Chapter 11.

- **Brings you into contact with your peers.** If you've decided to run a hobby system, you're interested in making your PC into an automated communications center, not a business—and therefore your theme should attract people with whom you share a common interest, rather than anyone who happens to own a modem. If you pick a popular theme, you're likely to receive calls from around the country (and perhaps from around the world) once you advertise your system!

Of course, these are suggestions to keep in mind, not rules—in fact, one of the attractions of running a bulletin board is the complete freedom you have in creating your own world within cyberspace! If you select an adult theme, however, take the opportunity to check your local laws concerning the distribution of adult material, particularly the minimum age and what types of materials are considered illegal.

Profit and Business/Support Themes

If you've decided to run a profit system, your theme should be much more general to accommodate any potential subscriber; you need not pick a theme as unique as a hobby board to help cement the relationship between BBS and caller. For a board that will concentrate on files, for example, you might consider a library analogy, where the user checks out software, or a bank analogy, where the user can deposit and withdraw files. Message boards can be transformed into newsrooms or radio stations. If your board will specialize in online games, the theme of an online arcade (complete with a change machine that represents your credit card payment system) is a natural. Other profit boards represent themselves as a distribution center for certain shareware publishers or custom picture files scanned by the sysop. If your profit board will center around online shopping, by all means paint your system as a shopping mall—and the more stores, the better!

The business functions of a support system need not render it completely without a theme; your board might use the analogy of a suggestion box (for employee messages) or a telephone switchboard (as an extension of telephone technical support). Other business bulletin boards tie their appearance to company newsletters, which can be quite effective in sending a corporate message to the caller. Whether your business/support board uses a theme or a strict businesslike e-mail appearance, however, it should always reflect your company logo, and additional information on your company's products and services should always be available from the main menu. A caller to a support system is already an owner of the product, or is at least interested in purchasing it, so offer detailed descriptions of your company's products or free demo software for downloading.

For our example system, let's say we've decided upon classical music as a theme. In order to make our hobby BBS unique, we'll further narrow the theme to a favorite composer—in this case, let's say you pick Mozart because you have a wide variety of recordings and literature detailing his life—and you decide to devote the system to reviewing classical music on compact disc. Now you've developed a theme, and you can add as much or as little detail to it as you like! Some sysops choose to immerse the caller completely in another world, while other sysops use their theme as a common thread, without adding extensive detail.

Selecting a Name

Typically, the next step in the process of creating your system's image is the selection of a name, because you'll need it as you create your welcome screen, menus, and other system files. If you'd rather determine the name for your bulletin board at a later time, skip to the next section and return here when you're ready.

As you might expect, your system name should reflect part of your theme, but it must also catch the eye and provide some clue as to the nature of your BBS. Often, the only information carried in a BBS listing is the name of your system, the telephone number, and your modem's maximum speed. Also, the name should be fairly short, as a longer name will be harder for your callers to remember and harder to fit into the cramped space usually provided by a terminal program's telephone directory. If you need help in deciding on a name—and it can be harder than you think—enlist the help of your friends and family, or check a national BBS list and see what other sysops have named their systems.

For our example, we want to tie Mozart, our representative classical composer, to the compact discs our callers will review. Because compact discs are in digital format, how about the name "The Digital Mozart BBS?" Luckily, this also has a double meaning because it can just as easily refer to your computer (as you learned in Chapter 2, your PC uses digital signals).

Whatever you select as a name, be prepared to advertise it heavily! In Chapter 11, we'll explore how you can promote your system nationally for the price of a phone call or a stamp.

Providing the Right Services

At this point, if you've been working along with the development of our example BBS, you've

- decided on a general theme for your BBS.
- chosen a name for your BBS.

Now it's time for the next step in designing your system: building a list of the services you'll provide to your users. In this section, you'll learn more about the basic services provided by virtually every bulletin board—and then we'll select the additional services that best fit the type of BBS you plan to run.

It's important to note here that the term *services* does **not** include the number of lines you'll offer to the public. Instead, services are features of either your bulletin board software or external programs you add to your system, which your users access through menu commands.

You may be asking, "Why map out my services now—why not simply add them as my users demand them?" The answer is twofold: first, you'll attract and keep more users from the very beginning if you offer a fair number of the services they're looking for. Second, it's harder to expand your system to add singular features piece-by-piece without repeated periods of downtime and irritated users.

Tip

It always pays to plan ahead, especially as a sysop. Your BBS can grow and succeed only as long as it remains online—therefore, you should perform as much maintenance and upgrade work as possible in the shortest amount of time. Rather than bringing your system down for two hours every Sunday just to back up your hard drive, plan ahead to take care of other jobs at the same time. For instance, if you must take down your system for 24 hours to add network software, why not add one or more of those online game doors you've been collecting? Many sysops find that their users are pleasantly surprised by the arrival of several new services at once, which gives the impression that your system is rapidly expanding to meet public demand.

What Do Your Users Expect?

Although there's no set package of services that's standard across all bulletin boards, we can accurately estimate what services your users will expect in a baseline system for all three types of bulletin boards. Our method is simple: take a cross-section of the successful systems in each type and mark the services that most of them have in common.

> **Tip**
>
> Where does a new sysop find information specifically concerning running a bulletin board? If you're experienced in the online world, you're probably already familiar with the monthly magazine *Boardwatch*. If you've never seen a copy, then run, don't walk, to your neighborhood newsstand and pick one up! Even though Boardwatch focuses on all aspects of the BBS world, including the Internet and all of the major online services, you'll find that it's an invaluable reference tool for any sysop, with columns on hardware, legal issues, and the latest information on upgrades to all of the major bulletin board software packages. As an added bonus, Boardwatch carries advertising that's aimed directly at BBS sysops, so you can keep tabs on the street prices for just about any purchase you need to make for your BBS. Another prime source of information is the CompuServe IBMBBS Forum, where you can find an answer (or at least several pointed opinions) on just about any BBS topic by leaving a public message. The IBMBBS Forum also includes a well-stocked library of freeware, shareware and demo BBS programs, utilities, and doors.

Common Services for Hobby Boards

Each of our three types of bulletin boards share the following basic services.

- A local electronic mail center, including some method of sending messages to the sysop. In this case, *local* refers to messages that originate on your BBS for other users of your BBS; they're not part of a network like FidoNet.
- A general public message base, where users usually post messages to "ALL." This base acts as a suggestion box for the sysop, as well as a good spot for posting messages of system-wide interest.
- A bulletin menu or database. The sysop typically posts the system rules here, as well as the latest news, help text for new features and such.

- A chat function between the sysop and the caller.

That's it! Notice that this core list doesn't include some features you may have considered standard, like a file library; that's due to the fact that some successful multiline chat bulletin boards have operated in recent years with few or no files available to download. Of course, you'll probably want to include more for your callers, so here are the other common hobby services:

- One or more special interest message bases, at least one of which usually concerns the board's theme.
- A selection of online game and database doors. When we refer to a *database* door, we're talking about a program that displays and manipulates data of some type (your users may or may not be able to add records). For example, matchmaker programs are database doors; each user fills out a personal questionnaire that can then be compared with the existing records to find the closest match.
- A FidoNet network connection, which provides both public message echoes and private FidoNet *netmail*. You'll learn more about setting up FidoNet on your system later in the book.
- An offline mail facility. This allows your callers to download their messages, read and reply to them offline, and then upload their replies. As you might imagine, offline mail is very popular with long-distance callers because it allows them to participate without the expense of composing messages online.
- A download file library. At least one file section usually concerns the board's theme. This service also includes the ability for your callers to upload files to share them with others.

Together with the standard four core services, this list makes up the common services most often found on hobby boards.

> **Tip**
>
> Unless you'd like to supply your users with a large number of download files, your hobby system can probably maintain a reasonable file library with user uploads alone (plus the occasional long-distance download session on your part). Hobby boards are not generally expected to compete with profit boards when it comes to the number of files available for download, especially since most profit boards offer multiple CD-ROMs online. However, if you do want to attract users to your hobby system with a larger file library, try assigning a download ratio—perhaps 1 byte uploaded for every 10 bytes downloaded. Many bulletin boards provide automatic ratio calculation using the upload/download statistics stored for each user in the userlog file; if your BBS software doesn't support ratio control, it's very likely that there's a shareware utility you can use to accomplish the same task. Users who don't maintain the ratio are locked out from downloading until they upload the necessary bytes.

Common Services for Profit Boards

Common services for profit boards run the gamut of technology, depending on the most important service, whether it be downloading, messages, games, or online chat. Together with the standard four core services, you might find any of these services:

- One or more complete message networks! The latest technology enables larger profit boards to purchase a satellite antenna and download all Fido echoes, Internet newsgroups, RIME message areas, and even obtain current weather radar images and national TV listings—all without placing a single telephone call. Other boards use the standard method of calling a network hub and downloading their messages over the phone. You'll learn more about both of these methods later in the book.

- Multiple CD-ROM file libraries. Some of the largest profit systems offer 20 or even 30 CD-ROMs online, offering an incredible selection of files. CD-ROM storage has proven to be one of the most successful technological advances for profit boards, as a single 6 disc CD-ROM jukebox offers more download opportunities than were ever available when bulletin boards depended solely on hard drive storage. Again, we'll cover how to add a CD-ROM to your system later in the book.

- Electronic newspapers like *USA Today* and electronic magazines like the online version of *Boardwatch*. It's hard to find a profit board that doesn't have an extensive reading room of these digital periodicals.

- Multiline, multiplayer games of every imaginable type, from casino card games to fantasy role-playing adventures. Callers can chat together while they compete, and profit boards usually award monthly prizes on some games for the highest scores.

- Huge online chat areas. A line count of 32 or 64 lines is common for these mega-chat systems! Several bulletin board programs even allow these mega-chat systems to connect with each other transparently, so that callers can converse with users on other boards.

As you can see, profit bulletin boards can pick from an impressive number of features to entice the caller into spending money on a subscription, and they try to make that online purchase as easy as possible for their users by accepting credit cards or using a 1-900 system to assign charges to the caller's telephone bill. We'll explore both of those systems later in the book.

Common Services for Business/Support Boards

Finally, we come to the services commonly offered by business and support boards. Along with the four core services, these systems usually offer:

- An extensive download library containing support programs, utilities, help files, and user feature requests for the company's products. This file library is almost invariably free of any download ratio or cost.

- Hidden menu selections which can be seen and used only by employees. These features usually connect employees to the company e-mail system. Sysops of these boards also offer public message bases for employees only or allow them to transfer files to and from a private file area if they work at home.

- An online catalog and ordering system for callers who would like to purchase company products during a call.

- A public message area devoted to each of the company's products, where customers can answer each others' questions (and, optionally, exchange messages with company technical support representatives).

As we learned earlier, these services are focused directly at two groups of callers: customers calling for support and company employees. Therefore, most bulletin boards of this type actually have fewer services than a hobby system.

Balancing Your Services

Now that you have an idea of what base services your users will expect, it's time to adjust the importance of each service for your specific BBS—after all, your bulletin board will be your online home, and therefore you should balance the services it provides to match your personal preferences. You may want to drop one of the services while greatly expanding the importance of another.

Remember our example system, "The Digital Mozart BBS?" Let's apply this process to the services it will provide:

1. Because our callers will use all four of the core services, we'll decide to keep them: e-mail, a general public message base, a bulletin menu, and a sysop chat function.
2. We'll add a special interest message area for Mozart, an area for classical music in general, a compact disc message area, and a MIDI computer music message area.
3. Games are of no interest to us, so we'll drop them. However, there are database doors that can hold the music reviews our callers will write, so such a door becomes one of the most important functions on our system.
4. FidoNet has both a MUSIC echo and a HISTORY echo to add to message areas, and callers to Digital Mozart can use netmail to communicate far outside our local calling distance, so we'll decide to connect our system to FidoNet before we ever accept our first caller.

> **Tip**
>
> It's very hard to turn down a FidoNet connection for other reasons, as well. Although Internet e-mail is much faster and covers more locations, FidoNet netmail is still a very popular method of private communication between users on systems far distant from each other. FidoNet public echoes exist for hundreds of topics, and each of them is moderated in some fashion (meaning that improper language and conversations are stopped as soon as possible, and off-topic message threads are roped in by the moderator). An Internet newsgroup, on the other hand, can contain just about anything, including insulting flame messages. For these reasons, most bulletin boards pick up FidoNet as their first network, and it's recommended that you do, too!

5. Because a large portion of our callers will be long-distance, we'll decide to add an offline mail program.

6. Finally, we'll decide to keep a basic file library, but it will feature only programs and files related to Mozart, classical music, MIDI music, and system utilities (such as archive programs, virus scanners, and .QWK mail reader programs). We'll also decide to stock the library with our public-domain collection of MIDI classical melodies, making sure that new users will have something to download.

If you're following along with pencil and paper, apply this same process to your list of services to determine which of them you want to offer your callers. Along with your personal preferences, keep these guidelines in mind:

- **File maintenance time.** Among the list of hobby services, the feature that will take the highest toll of your resources is undoubtedly your file system. Uploads should be individually screened whenever possible before you post them, old downloads and duplicates will have to be eliminated and all of the files you offer will have to be backed up to disk or tape in case of a drive failure. A common mistake of novice sysops is the assignment of far too many file areas (most of which remain empty, or hold only a few files)—try to remain conservative as you plan your file library.

- **System stability.** Each time your BBS software releases control of a call to another program—usually either a game door, database door, or offline mail generator—there is a slight risk that an error could occur that could lock your system or render it incapable of taking calls. This doesn't happen often at all, but if your company relies on the system you're going to build, consider using as few external programs as possible. Note that this reliability issue typically doesn't affect the sysop of an integrated system because an integrated BBS never actually drops to DOS to run doors.

- **Sysop availability.** If you're going to be running your system remotely from another location, or if you'll be away from the keyboard for long periods of time, you may wish to disable your system's sysop chat function, which requires you to be physically present at the BBS console. This prevents callers from spending their online time in a vain attempt to page you for a sysop chat. Instead, include a bulletin to your users informing them that they should leave you mail if they need to contact you. If your BBS allows users to page you, will the page bell disturb you while you sleep? We'll describe later how you can set up timed internal events for your Wildcat! BBS that disable the sysop chat command automatically during the hours you determine.

Selecting a BBS Program

This book includes a fully-featured, single-line Wildcat! BBS program that you can use to create an excellent entry-level bulletin board system. If you're a new sysop or you feel that Wildcat! Lite meets your requirements for a BBS package, you can run your system indefinitely with this software; it offers considerable power and the chance to expand your services through external doors through the foreseeable future.

However, you may have decided to start a multiline BBS, or you may wish to investigate other BBS packages before making a decision. Perhaps you're looking for a particular feature that isn't offered in Wildcat! Lite. In this section, we'll outline the points you should consider while selecting a BBS program.

As a first step, read Appendix A at the back of this book. This appendix contains information on several of the most popular commercial, shareware, and freeware BBS programs currently available, with general comments covering their strengths, weaknesses, and suitability for certain applications. If you're uncertain exactly what you'd like to offer on your BBS, this is also an ideal source of possible services.

Once you're familiar with what's available, select those that fit your requirements, contact each of the manufacturers, and ask for information and specifications for their programs. Manufacturers of commercial BBS software can provide you with brochures and demonstration copies of their program, while shareware manufacturers offer a manual on disk and the program itself.

You can use these brochures and data to create your own chart or spreadsheet for the particular program features that interest you the most. Enter each feature on the left of the chart, and create a column for each program you're considering. Put a Y in the column if the program provides the feature and an N if it doesn't. Table 4.1 illustrates an example BBS feature chart. The top three or four programs with the highest number of features make up your group of "semi-finalists!"

Table 4.1 An Example Feature Chart

Program Name	Multiline?	.QWK Support?	RIP Graphics?	External DOS Doors?	LAN-ready?
A-BBS	Y	N	Y	Y	N
B-BBS	N	N	N	Y	N
C-BBS	Y	Y	N	N	N
D-BBS	Y	Y	Y	Y	N
E-BBS	N	Y	N	N	Y
F-BBS	Y	Y	Y	Y	Y
G-BBS	N	Y	Y	N	N
H-BBS	Y	N	Y	Y	N
I-BBS	N	Y	Y	N	N

Now install the demonstration copies of these top choices. Compare the feel of each program from both the user and the sysop's side. If a demonstration version of a program is not available, contact a local sysop who's running that package and see if you can drop by to view the sysop's side of the BBS.

While you're evaluating each system, consider these general criteria:

- **Complexity.** Is the program simple to install? Is it easy enough for you to design menus? Can you configure it without resorting to calling the manufacturer's technical support? Does the BBS program automatically configure modems? Does the software build or create a sample system you can experiment with right away? You should feel certain that you can master the operation of your BBS software in a fairly short time, especially if you've decided to start a profit or support BBS—users of profit or support boards are much less likely to forgive sysop mistakes than hobby BBS users!

- **User-friendliness.** This term is often overused in the computer industry, but it applies perfectly to BBS software. If your users cannot easily navigate your board or the commands it uses are cryptic, they won't be comfortable and they simply won't call back. Put yourself in the caller's place and try common user commands like switching graphics modes, reading messages, and downloading files; if you're not certain what you're doing, will your callers know?

- **Expansion.** Make sure the program can grow in the direction you envision for your BBS. Total line count is important if you're going to be running a large system, but that's not the only factor—for example, is the program limited to a certain number of messages, or message sections? Is there a maximum number of doors? How many files can you add? Consider the services you selected in the previous section and be sure the program supports them. It's important that you're not "locked in" with a BBS program you're likely to outgrow in two or three years, as switching from one program to another can be extremely difficult.

- **Cost.** This generally isn't a problem for a shareware BBS program, but it can be the determining factor when a commercial program is involved. Remember to check the upgrade policy for multiline board software, because the manufacturer is likely to charge you for a version of the program that can support additional telephone lines.

- **Reliability.** Commercial BBS software is almost certain to be more reliable than a shareware offering. If you're purchasing a program for a profit or business/support BBS, it's recommended that you consider only commercial software, because you'll have professional technical support if you need it; additionally, any downtime caused by a bug in your BBS program is equivalent to lost profit or irritated customers.

To help you in making your choice, Appendix A addresses these questions for each of the programs it includes. Once you've narrowed down the selection to a single program that meets your needs the best, buy your copy and start reading the manual from cover to cover!

Designing Your Menu System

You've now reached another important point in the design of your bulletin board system—a point where you'll build the menu system your callers will use to navigate from point to point within your BBS. In this section, you'll learn several simple rules that will prevent you from creating a menu system that's too simple or too complex for your callers. We'll also continue the development of our example hobby system.

Investigating Other Systems

If you're experienced in using bulletin boards, take a moment to consider one or two of your favorite systems—or, even better, load your communications software and call them. Now, ask yourself these questions about each of those boards:

- Did you ever feel lost while you were online, even after you had called several times?
- Were you ever faced with a menu with so many choices you felt a little overwhelmed?
- Did you ever find yourself wishing you had someone to help?

If you enjoyed your calls to these boards, you probably answered no to most or all of those questions—and those are the same questions you should ask yourself about the menu structure of your own system after we've completed this section. A good BBS menu system is arranged intuitively, so the caller can often predict where features are located even if they don't appear on that particular menu.

If you already have a modem handy, take an evening and visit your local systems to study their menus. Remember, no bulletin board program is infinitely configurable—for example, your Wildcat! system includes hardcoded menus that you can't change in some ways—but you can still tell when a sysop has taken time in preparing a menu system. Is online help available on most of the board's menus? Are the menu command descriptions logical and correctly spelled?

Most of the systems you call will offer a set of global keys that perform the same functions no matter what menu you're using, and these keys will become second nature to your regular callers in a surprisingly short time. For example, some systems use a single key throughout the BBS to return to the main menu, while another key takes you back to the preceding menu. Other display keys show who's online, the amount of time you've been connected, and who else has called today. New callers will make use of a global online help key as well; whatever menu they're using, they know they can display a help file. Finally, your callers will greatly appreciate a quick logoff key that bypasses any intervening menus and disconnects immediately—just make sure that it's not a key that's often pressed by mistake!

During your investigation of other systems, you'll also see how certain keys have an almost universal meaning from system to system. Whenever possible, most sysops would rather use the F key to display the File menu, the M key to display the Message menu and the G key to display the Goodbye (logoff) menu. There's no need to feel like you're plagiarizing another sysop's design if you decide to use these same keystrokes; they've been used for those purposes since the first BBS went online. Remember, however, that you should only use the standard alphanumeric keys available on any computer keyboard, so that your callers using other brands of computers can access your BBS as well.

Tip

As we mentioned in the previous section, many bulletin board programs have one or more "hard-coded" menus—for example, your Wildcat! Lite program—that can restrict you in some ways while designing your menus. Other BBS programs may not impose limitations on menu structure, but they require more work to complete the menus you've designed because you must build them from scratch. It's a good idea to buy the BBS software you've selected and read its documentation before you start charting your menu system, so that you'll be aware of the menu designs that are possible with your program.

Basic Charting

Creating your own menu design is easier than you think, as long as you approach it systematically. The idea is to provide your users with the fastest access possible to the commands they'll use the most; for this reason, we'll use a relatively flat menu design that uses a main menu and a single layer of submenus. Good menu design also entails grouping your commands together logically. Certain commands belong together, and your users will expect them to be on the same menu.

If the idea behind good menu design is to provide the fastest access possible, why not simply put as many commands as will fit on the main menu? This is actually the approach taken by many sysops, and even the default menus on some shareware and commercial BBS packages try to pack all of their commands on a single screen. An example is Figure 4.1, which illustrates a main menu that many new users would find chaotic and confusing.

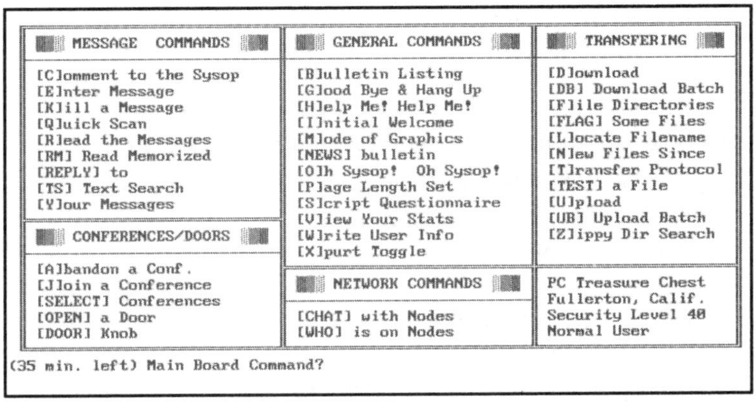

Fig. 4.1
The main menu from a BBS largely based around a single menu screen.

Our goal in designing your menu system is to reassure your new callers that they've reached a user-friendly BBS, and therefore we'll build submenus. Of course, this introduces an additional keystroke between the main menu and all those commands, but it's a sure bet that your users won't mind pressing that one extra key! The best approach to take is to divide your services into major groups—message functions, file functions, and utility commands, for instance—and place each of those groups on a separate menu. Figure 4.2 is an example of this user-friendly design. Compare it with Figure 4.1, and you'll see why users prefer a bulletin board with submenus.

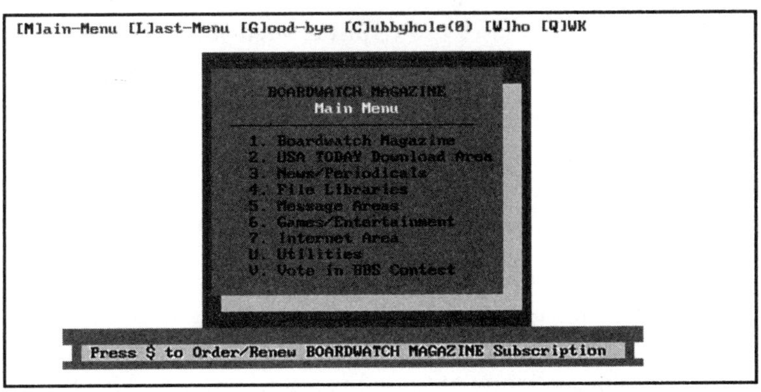

Fig. 4.2
The main menu from a BBS using submenus to separate its services.

With this rule in mind, take the listing of services you created in the last section and follow these steps:

1. Circle each service that you think will require its own menu. For some services, like your message base and file library, a separate menu is a tradition that makes sense. For services like your online games menu, the sheer number of commands usually warrants a separate menu just to hold all the possible choices. However, there's no reason why your bulletins and electronic periodicals can't share a menu (they perform a similar function), and most users would expect your electronic mail commands to be included on the same menu as your public message bases. Group services like these together whenever possible. Also, don't forget a utility menu where your callers can change their passwords, modify their terminal settings, and select their file transfer protocol.

2. Tear off a separate sheet of paper for each service or group that requires a separate screen, and write a descriptive name of one or two words at the top of the page. Under the name, jot down the services that will appear on that screen. Feel free to switch and substitute services among pages if one of your groups doesn't seem to fit together logically (this is the time to make changes, rather than after you've created the screen files). Try to separate each service into component commands whenever possible—for example, your message services will include "Read Messages" and "Write a Message" commands. Describe each of these commands with a phrase. You've just created your *submenus*, which will exist one level below your main menu.

3. Once you've separated your services into individual units, count the number of submenus you've created. If you find you have more than seven submenus, you may wish to reconsider how you've grouped your services together (unless you're designing a profit board with a large number of services).

4. Once you're satisfied with your individual submenus, it's a simple matter to create your main system menu. First, arrange your submenus in alphabetical order. If any of the submenu names start with the same character, think of another name for one of the submenus; because our main menu commands will key on the first letter of each submenu name, we can't use two that are the same. Once each submenu name begins with a unique character, write them down in order on another sheet of paper, and label that sheet "Main Menu."

Congratulations, you've just created a menu chart for your bulletin board! Hold on to your chart until Chapter 6, where you'll use it as a reference while you create the ASCII and ANSI menu screens themselves.

An Example Hobby Menu Structure

Now, to illustrate the process with an example, we'll apply this method to create the menu system for The Digital Mozart BBS.

1. First, we'll select those services that should have their own submenus. After examining our service listing, we'll pick the following as being important enough to warrant a separate submenu: the message bases, the file areas, the bulletins, and the CD review database. Our utility menu will allow callers to change their settings, and it will also have the sysop chat and offline mail commands. We'll also include global key commands for logging off, displaying the system time, returning to the previous menu, and returning to the main menu.
2. We'll count the number of submenus, and come up with five. That's within our acceptable range, so there's no need to shuffle services around.
3. Now we'll build our main menu with the following commands: [B]ulletin menu, [C]D Reviews, [F]ile menu, [M]essage menu, and the [U]tility menu.

Avoiding Menu Pitfalls

Depending on your bulletin board software, the process we just used to create a menu system can be easier or harder. Some structured systems allow very little change to their basic menu structure, so there's very little planning involved at all. Other programs are almost totally free-form, so that with a lot of detailed planning and work, you can design a system from the ground up to do exactly what you wish.

No matter whether your BBS software leans to the simple or the complex when it comes to menu design, make certain you avoid these general problems while you're creating your BBS architecture:

- **Menu dead ends.** Ensure that each of your menus includes a command to return to the main menu and a command to return to the previous menu. Usually, both of these functions are covered by your global commands, and they're activated with the same keys no matter where your callers are within your BBS.

- **Vague command descriptions.** Long-distance and local users alike will be frustrated if they spend extra keystrokes discovering what you mean by "Door 1" or "Set Criteria." Whenever possible, describe menu commands (both on your chart and on your screens) with a phrase instead of just a name. This is also a common problem with boards that are closely tied to a theme—for example, the sysop of a board creates a menu system that parallels a favorite film or book, with commands that mirror items or actions from that source. Unfortunately, not every caller will recognize the sysop's clever symbolism!

- **Overloading your menus.** Just as you can overload your main menu by filling it with too many submenus, you can also overload your submenus with too many individual commands. While you're designing your menu system, try to anticipate how many commands each service will offer, and keep the number somewhere under 15 commands per submenu. Note that this limit should not include global key commands because these keys will become second nature to your callers very quickly; they're available on every menu, and they should appear in the same location on each screen.

- **Lack of jump navigation commands.** If possible, provide your callers with a way to jump directly to the two or three most important menus in your system. These keys can also be global, if you like. This is a great convenience feature for those callers who download and read messages, because they can travel directly between those two menus without returning to the main menu.

Building Your Message and File Areas

As an optional step that will save you a little time in the future, you can map out your message and file areas. This will help as you create the actual screens in Chapter 6.

On your Message submenu page, indicate any specific message areas you know your system will carry—in our example, we had our general message area, e-mail, and special interest areas for Mozart, classical music in general, compact discs and MIDI computer music. We also know our system will carry FidoNet netmail and the MUSIC and HISTORY echoes.

Our Files submenu is considerably smaller, because we have only three file areas: Mozart, classical music, and MIDI music. However, we'll also decide to add another section for "System files," which will include copies of our archive utilities, a virus checking program, and a master list of all of our files.

A final directory, "Uploads," will hold files uploaded by callers; the security level on this section will be higher, so only you can access these files until you've had a chance to check them for viruses and content.

Planning Access Levels

Every BBS should have at least two security access levels, which determine the menus, features, and services available to each caller. At a minimum, your system will require a Sysop access level for yourself and a standard access level for your users; however, it's much more flexible to provide additional levels, and they're a requirement for a profit BBS that allows subscribing members higher access.

As an example, Wildcat! Lite uses a *level* system to allow you to quickly and easily specify which combination of functions, message folders, and file sections is available to each of your users—typically, the higher the level, the more functions are available. To access a service or a function, the user must have a level either equal to or greater than the level you assign the service during your configuration. For example, if you specify that level 10 users can read a certain message folder, then any caller with an access level of 10 or greater can read those messages, but a level 5 user cannot read them.

When planning your security levels, keep in mind whether you'll be charging for access (which we'll discuss in the next section) and whether or not you'll need the help of a co-sysop (which we'll cover later in the book). If you decide to charge subscribers or allow a co-sysop high access, you'll need separate security levels for them as well.

Should I Charge?

To end this chapter, we'll discuss whether or not you should charge your users for access to your system. You'll learn more about methods of billing your callers later in the book—at this stage in the development of your system, all you really need to decide is whether to charge at all.

Because it's assumed you'll be running a hobby system, the question of charging your users separates you from profit systems (for obvious reasons) and business/support boards (which almost universally never charge their callers). If we assume you'll start with a single-line hobby system, your only expenses in running your system will be the additional charge for installing and using another telephone line and the electricity involved in running your PC 24 hours a day (which is so minimal you're likely not to notice it). If these bills are within your budget, then you can operate a very popular free BBS (often called a *no-fee* system), which doesn't charge its members at all for use of any services. As you learned earlier, your no-fee BBS might enforce upload/download ratios, but you almost guarantee the success of your system by offering it as a free public service.

On the other hand, our example system will be connected to the FidoNet message network, and that will entail your PC automatically dialing out late at night to exchange mail with at least one other system (which is usually a long-distance call). This is a very important point: review your services **carefully** before you decide whether or not to charge, because there may be hidden expenses in some of the services you're going to offer.

The question of whether or not to charge your users also depends on your view of your callers. If you feel your callers owe you for the privilege of using your PC and the hard work you've put in building your system, you're more likely to charge them. If, on the other hand, you feel privileged that callers frequent your system, and your BBS will be easy for you to afford, then you'll probably lean more toward opening it as a free BBS.

Keep these points in mind as you consider the question of charging for access:

- If you do decide to charge, you should keep a standard access level free of charge to avoid being classed as a profit system.
- Receiving subscription money from your users also involves a commitment on your part to provide them with the services they've paid for—and that means more work for you.
- If you charge for access, you must also maintain tax records on the amount you collect.
- You can begin charging at any point.
- If you begin to charge, you may need to obtain a local business license, depending on the regulations in your state or locality.
- If you begin to charge, your telephone company may charge you business rates, which are higher than residential rates. Consult your local telephone company for details.

As a general recommendation, most new sysops should run their hobby systems as no-fee boards for at least six months. This time period allows your BBS to build a following, as well as providing time for you to work the kinks out of your bulletin board and get it running smoothly. If you decide to charge at that time, you can introduce your subscription plan simultaneously with the announcement of one or more new services reserved for your paying subscribers.

Summary

In this chapter, you learned how to create your system's image by developing a combination of a theme, a set of services, and your menu system. You explored how to balance the services you selected and learned basic charting skills that you used to build a road map of your new BBS. Finally, you considered the possibility of charging your users for higher access to your system.

In the next chapter, "Installing the Software," we'll cover the process of installing your Wildcat! Lite bulletin board, complete with a basic default menu system.

Chapter 5

Installing the Software

by Mark L. Chambers

Now that your preparations have been made and you have a firm concept of the theme, the services, and the menus you'd like to offer your users on your BBS, this chapter will lead you through the installation and configuration of the Wildcat! Lite single-line system provided with this book.

For many new sysops, the installation and configuration of their BBS software is the most troublesome phase of creating their system—that's why we'll take you through the entire setup process step-by-step. If you'd like to get your bulletin board up and running in the shortest time, the default Wildcat! configuration will require few changes to create the basics of your system, and we'll cover those in this chapter; however, you'll probably want to apply what you learn in the next chapter as well, where we discuss how to customize the look and feel of your bulletin board. To illustrate the default configuration process, we'll use the example system we created in Chapter 4.

If you're installing a different shareware or commercial BBS package, don't automatically skip ahead! Although this chapter provides step-by-step instructions on installing Wildcat! Lite, we'll still cover information and tips that will help you no matter which BBS software you've chosen.

At the end of this chapter, we'll also cover how you can upgrade your Lite version of Wildcat! and receive the latest single-line (Wildcat! 'S') or multiline (Wildcat! 'M') version of the program.

Tip

In addition to the electronic online Help available throughout your Wildcat! system, you can also obtain additional help with the installation of your Wildcat! Lite BBS on CompuServe—type GO PCVENA at any CompuServe prompt and select Section 9 for Mustang Software.

Installation Step-by-Step

In this section, we'll install your Wildcat! Lite system with the INSTALL program; then we'll use the MAKEWILD configuration editor to configure the BBS environment to your specific system.

Installing the Files

To install your BBS files, follow these instructions:

1. Insert the *Running a Perfect BBS* disk into your drive.
2. You're now ready to run the Wildcat! installation program from your disk. Type **<drive letter>: install.exe** and press Enter. The screen in figure 5.1 appears.

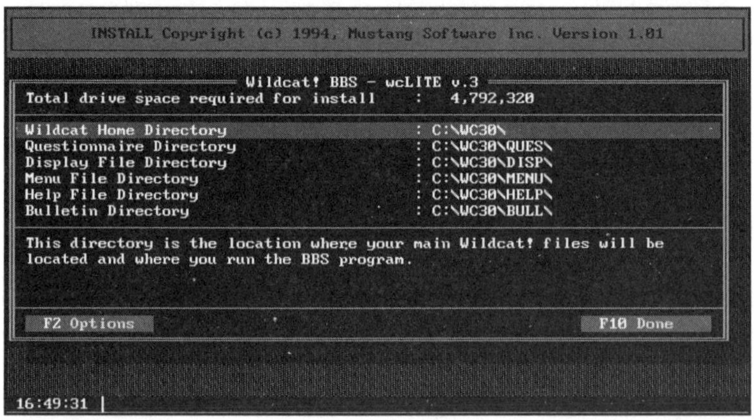

Fig. 5.1
The initial menu screen from the INSTALL installation.

3. Enter the drive letter of the disk source drive. Press Enter to confirm your choice.
4. INSTALL allows you to disable the installation of certain functions of Wildcat! Lite to conserve disk space, and allows you to select different directory paths than the program defaults. If you wanted to install only part of the files, you could press F2 to select which files to omit (see fig. 5.2). Because we'll be using all of the functionality of the BBS program and we want to use the default subdirectories, press F10 to indicate that you want to copy all of the program files.

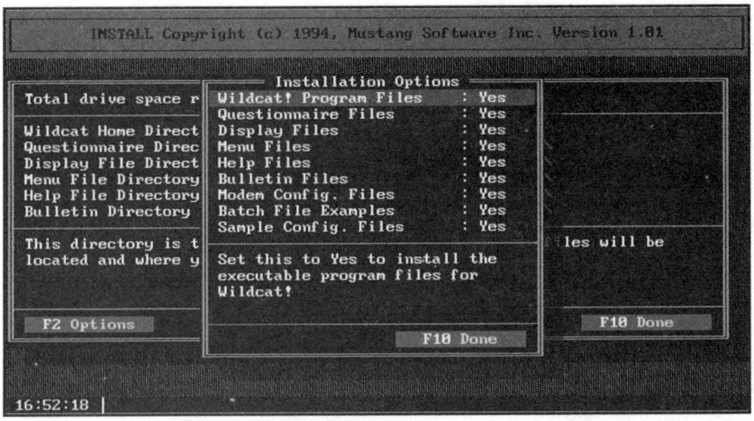

Fig. 5.2
The Options selection screen from the INSTALL installation program.

Tip

No matter what BBS software you're installing, use the default subdirectory names and locations unless you have a strong reason for changing them. Why? Third-party utilities, doors, and add-on modules for your BBS program usually default to these standard directory names and locations as well, saving you time and possible mistakes as you expand your system later. For example, if your BBS software default directory is C:\HOST, most external programs written for your BBS will use that default directory as well. Note that some programs work more efficiently in a RAM disk, but because the contents of a RAM disk are lost when you reboot or turn off your PC, it should be used only for temporary or work directories.

5. The installation program now begins to extract and copy all of the BBS files from the disk to the default directory \WC30 (see fig. 5.3). Once the installation is complete, press Enter to return to the DOS command prompt.

6. Because Wildcat! must open, read, and write several files while your BBS is running, your next step is to ensure that your CONFIG.SYS file includes the two statements

   FILES=40

   BUFFERS=40

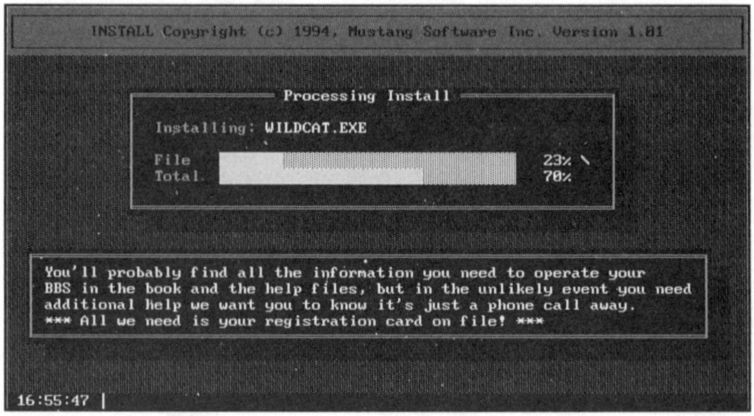

Fig. 5.3
INSTALL shown during the copy process.

The CONFIG.SYS file should be located in the root directory of your C: drive, along with your AUTOEXEC.BAT file. Use your favorite text editor (or the EDIT program supplied with recent versions of DOS) to load the CONFIG.SYS file; if the FILES and BUFFERS statements don't exist, add them to the top of the file. If they do exist, make sure they are set to at least the minimum values specified previously.

> **Tip**
>
> If you've never used a text editor before, you can also load and edit a text file within most DOS and Windows word processors. However, make sure you save the modified file in "pure ASCII" or "DOS text" mode, because your PC will not be able to use the file if it's saved in your word processor's native mode.

Configuring Your BBS

Now that you've installed all of your BBS system files to the \WC30 directory, we'll use MAKEWILD.EXE to configure your software for your specific PC and modem.

Note that we're only going to make the changes necessary for you to put your system online for now; in the next chapter, we'll modify more of these settings to personalize your BBS even further. However, Wildcat! Lite allows you to customize almost every function of your BBS—therefore, to get your system online quickly, we'll leave many of these values set to their defaults. Your BBS will operate well with the changes that we make, but if you want to take advantage of the full power of Wildcat! Lite, it's highly recommended that you use the comprehensive built-in online Help wherever you need it within the configuration program. The online Help contains additional information on every one of the fields in MAKEWILD, including those that we don't change in this book.

Follow these instructions:

1. Change to the WILDCAT directory by typing **cd \wc30** and pressing Enter.

2. You're now ready to run the Wildcat! Lite configuration program. Type **makewild** and press Enter. The screen in figure 5.4 appears.

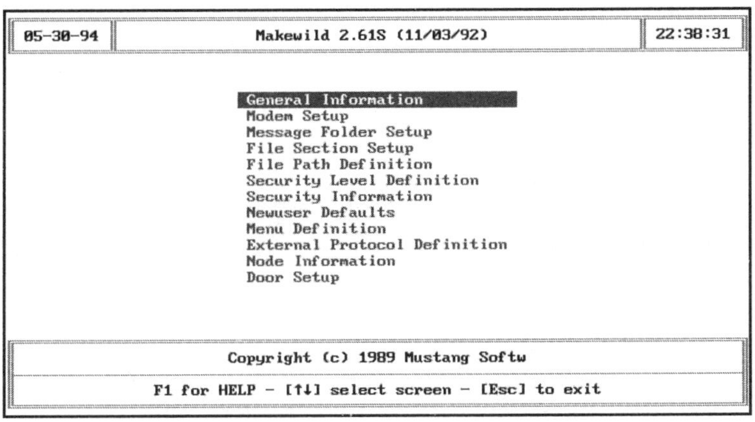

Fig. 5.4
The initial menu screen from the MAKEWILD configuration program.

3. First, we'll make a few changes to your General Definition settings; these values affect your entire system. Because the highlight bar you use to select a screen is already on General Definition, press Enter. The screen in figure 5.5 appears.

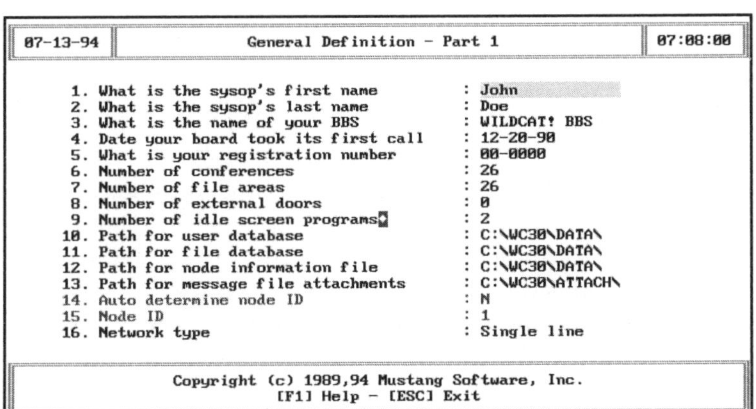

Fig. 5.5
The initial General Definition screen from the MAKEWILD configuration program.

> **Tip**
>
> The MAKEWILD utility sports an extensive context-sensitive online Help system—if you need additional information on any field within MAKEWILD, simply highlight the field by moving the cursor to it and press F1. The PageUp and PageDown keys scroll through the Help text, and the Escape key will return you back to MAKEWILD.

4. You need to enter the values for your name and the name of your BBS. As you can see, the highlight is now in field 1, indicating that MAKEWILD is ready to accept your typing in that field. Press Delete until the field is empty and type your first name. If you need additional help for a field, press F1. To return to the previous screen, press Escape.

5. Now press Enter (or the down arrow key) to move to the next field. Type your last name.

> **Tip**
>
> Remember, it's not necessary for you or your callers to use your real names—if you like, you can allow your callers to use aliases. Many sysops find that aliases add to the participation on their systems, especially bulletin boards that offer adult messages or material. If you do decide to allow aliases, make sure you obtain the real name of each of your callers during the registration sequence; many bulletin boards offer direct support for both aliases and real names.

6. Press Enter to move to field 3 and type the name of your BBS. For our example, we'll enter **The Digital Mozart BBS**.

7. Press the down arrow once to move to field 4, where you should enter today's date in mm/dd/yy format. This date represents the birthday of your Wildcat! Lite system!

8. That completes the changes we need to make to Part 1 of the General Definition screens. Now press Page Down to display Part 2 (see fig. 5.6). Press Enter until the highlight has moved to field 12—we're going to force your BBS to take the modem off-hook whenever you shut down the system. The default setting is N, indicating that Wildcat! Lite will not force the modem off-hook. Change this value to Y, so that the BBS line will not ring and your callers will receive a busy signal.

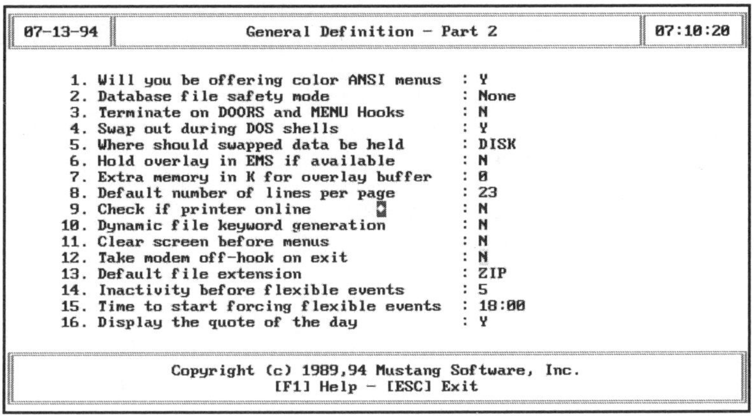

Fig. 5.6
Part 2 of the General Definition screen from the MAKEWILD configuration program.

9. That completes the changes we need to make to the General Definition screens. Now press Escape to return to the MAKEWILD main menu. Use your down arrow key to move the highlight to Modem Definition and press Enter. The screen in figure 5.7 appears.

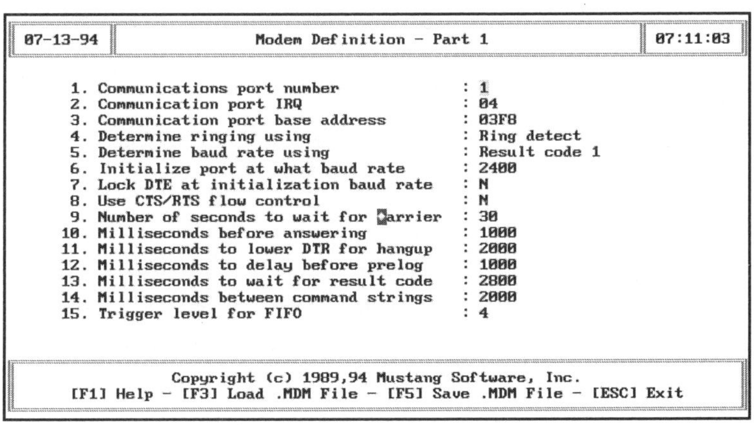

Fig. 5.7
The Modem Definition screen.

10. First, press F3 to pick your modem type from a list of supported brands and models. MAKEWILD displays the selection box shown in figure 5.8. If your modem is listed, move the cursor using the down arrow key and press Enter when your modem is highlighted. MAKEWILD automatically enters the required settings. If your modem is not listed, use one of the generic standard modem setups described in the online Help screen—most unlisted 2400 baud modems that were manufactured in the last two or three years will use the STD_2 setup.

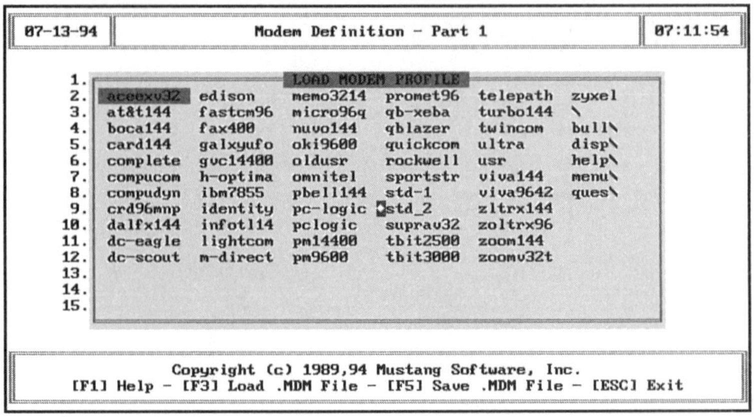

Fig. 5.8
The modem selection box displayed when you press F3 on the Modem Setup screen.

Tip

Nearly all major commercial and shareware bulletin board programs now offer automatic modem installation similar to your Wildcat! Lite system—however, if you select the wrong modem configuration, your BBS will work erratically or not at all. If you're having continual problems with your modem, call the manufacturer's support board and ask other sysops what settings to use, or contact the manufacturer's technical support department.

11. If your modem will not use COM1, type the number of the COM port you'll use for your BBS.

12. Now press Enter repeatedly until you reach field 6. Press the spacebar until the number displayed equals the highest speed offered by your modem.

13. If you're using a high-speed modem with a baud rate of 9600 or faster, press Enter one more time and press Y to indicate that Wildcat! should lock the baud rate between your PC and your modem. If you're unsure of the values for fields 6 and 7 on this screen, check your modem manual and see if it recommends that you use a locked baud rate. If so, use the value it provides for the speed value in field 6, and set this field to Y.

> **Tip**
>
> If you're using a high-speed modem, lock the baud rate whenever possible to provide the fastest possible throughput. With a locked baud rate, your modem may even deliver faster throughput than its rated speed!

14. That completes the changes we need to make to the Modem Definition screen. Now press Escape to return to the MAKEWILD main menu. Use your down arrow key to move the highlight to Conference Definition and press Enter. The screen in figure 5.9 appears.

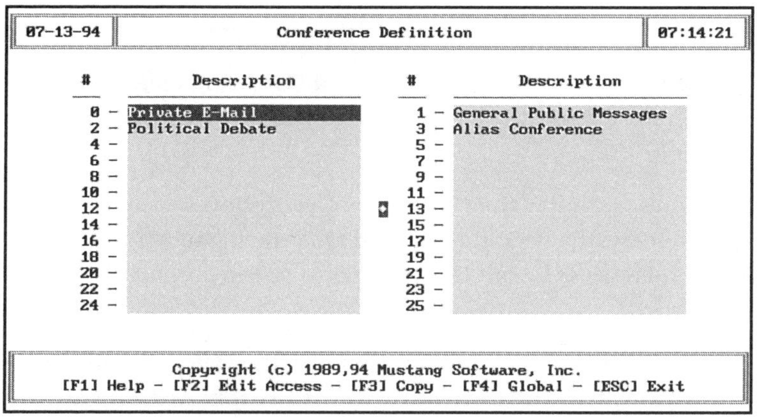

Fig. 5.9
The Conference Definition screen.

Wildcat! Lite refers to its message database areas as *conferences*, an analogy that will help those who have never used a bulletin board before to understand the concept of electronic mail and public messages. If you remember from Chapter 4, we planned for six *local* message areas for our example BBS: the general message area, e-mail, Mozart, classical music in general, compact discs, and MIDI computer music. *Local* indicates that these message areas originate and remain on our example system—in other words, they're not message network echos (like FidoNet) or newsgroups (like Internet). We'll cover FidoNet and the Internet later in the book.

If you have decided to offer more than the default 26 message conferences (Wildcat! allows 1000 areas), make sure you change the value for Field 6, which appears on Part 1 of the General Definition screen. This field—"Number of conferences"—determines how many conference "slots" are provided on this screen. Of course, you'll substitute the topic names you decided upon for your system in Chapter 4, and you may have more or less than six folders; for this example, however, we'll stick with the default and modify the names to reflect our hypothetical BBS.

> **Tip**
>
> Some sysops don't allow new users to access messages until they've been upgraded, while other sysops prefer to allow their new callers to participate immediately—it's an issue of how much you trust your callers! If you're concerned about the security of your system (and the possible damage that a problem user can cause if you allow immediate access to your message areas), allow message access only to standard users that you've upgraded.

15. Because the names "Private E-Mail" and "General Public Messages" are acceptable, press the down arrow key to move the highlight to number 2.

16. Press Enter to display the Conference Description screen. Use the Delete key to remove the default name and type the name **All About Mozart**. Press Esc to exit the description screen and highlight conference 3.

17. Press Enter for the Description screen. Use the Delete key to remove the default folder name and type the name **Classical Music**. Press Esc to exit the description screen and highlight conference 4.

18. Press Enter for the Description screen. Type the conference name **Classical Compact Discs**. Press Esc to exit the description screen and highlight conference 5.

19. Press Enter for the Description screen. Type the name **Let's Talk MIDI!**.

20. You've created your message conferences! Now press Escape to return to the MAKEWILD main menu. Use your down arrow key to move the highlight to File Area Definition and press Enter. The screen in figure 5.10 appears.

In Chapter 4, we planned for five file sections for our example BBS: programs and files related to Mozart, classical music, and MIDI music; a system area with commonly-used shareware like the PKZIP/PKUNZIP archive utilities and virus scanning software; and an uploads area that's available only to you, so that you can examine uploaded files before placing them in the correct section.

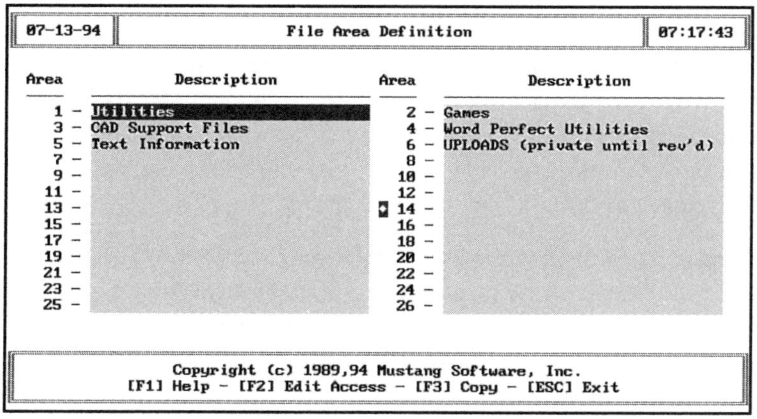

Fig. 5.10
The File Area Definition screen.

If you have decided to offer more or less than the default five file sections (Wildcat! allows a maximum of 1000), make sure you change the value for Field 7, which appears on Part 1 of the General Definition screen. This field—"Number of file areas"—determines how many slots of the alphabet are provided for file areas on the File Area Definition screen. Each slot has a File Area Description screen, where you can specify the path for the file sections.

Tip

Whenever possible, place all directories for your BBS download files, online games, and external programs under your BBS home directory (in this case, \WC30). For example, an online game directory should appear as a subdirectory of your \WC30 directory, such as \WC30\AGAME. In addition to keeping your hard drive as uncluttered as possible, this also makes it easier to remember the locations where you've stored your various system files.

21. Press Enter to display the File Area Description screen. Use the Delete key to remove the default name and type the name **Mozart**. Press Enter and specify the path where the Mozart files would be located (for our example, leave the path as it is). Press Esc to exit the description screen and highlight section 2.

22. Press Enter to display the Description screen. Use the Delete key to remove the default section name and type the name **Classical Music**. Press Enter and specify the path where the Classical Music files would be located (for our example, leave the path as it is). Press Esc to exit the description screen and highlight section 3.

23. Press Enter to display the File Area Description screen. Use the Delete key to remove the default name and type the name **MIDI Music**. Press Enter and specify the path where the MIDI Music files would be located (for our example, leave the path as it is). Press Esc to exit the description screen and highlight section 4.

24. Press Enter to display the Description screen. Use the Delete key to remove the default name and type the name **User Utilities**. Press Enter and specify the path where the User Utilities files would be located (for our example, leave the path as it is). Press Esc to exit the description screen and highlight section 5.

25. Press Enter to display the Description screen. Use the Delete key to remove the default name and type the name **Uploads**. Press Enter and specify the path where the upload files would be located (for our example, leave the path as it is). Press Esc to exit the description screen.

> **Tip**
>
> Most sysops do not allow uploads to be immediately visible to their users, because the files should be checked for viruses and commercial content before being made available for downloading.

26. If you were actually creating our sample BBS, you'd delete the name and path for file section 6, because we wouldn't need it. Now press Escape to return to the MAKEWILD main menu.

27. Press Escape from the MAKEWILD main menu to exit back to DOS. MAKEWILD prompts you for confirmation that you wish to exit the program, which will automatically save the changes you've made to your configuration. Select Yes. MAKEWILD then asks if you'd like to check the current directory paths throughout your configuration to make sure they exist; select Yes, and indicate you'd like for MAKEWILD to create any directories that don't already exist.

That's it—you've just finished the basic configuration needed to get your BBS running! You can actually go online right now, if you wish, but it's highly recommended that you read through the next chapter first (at least the portion describing your first logon to your BBS). With only an hour or two more of extra work, you can personalize your BBS to a much higher degree with a custom welcome screen, additional bulletins and ANSI menus, a newsletter, and much, much more.

Upgrading Your Wildcat! System

The Wildcat! Lite BBS you've just configured uses version 3.95 of the bulletin board software. Mustang Software has provided this older version of their full commercial package to allow you to "try before you buy"; in other words, you can experience what it's like to be a sysop of a Wildcat! system. The Lite version of Wildcat! is actually the previous release of the software; at the time this book was written, the current version of Wildcat! is 4.0, and it includes a wealth of features not available in your Lite system.

Wildcat! Lite will work well as is for single-line hobby applications (as well as a simple single-line business/support board), and you can continue to use it for as long as you like—however, it is limited to a single line, so if you would like to expand your BBS into a multiline system, you'll have to upgrade.

Upgrading your Wildcat! Lite system is as simple as purchasing the latest version, which is available through mail order, directly from Mustang Software and many of the larger retail software stores. Make sure you check the advertisements in *Boardwatch Magazine*, as you'll probably find the mail-order method offers the lowest prices. Once you've purchased your commercial package, you'll be offered the chance to upgrade your current Wildcat! Lite userlog and data files during the installation process; this makes the process easy for both you and your callers!

Let's briefly outline the versions of Wildcat! that are currently available:

- Wildcat! 'S' Single Line. This is the latest commercial version of your single-line program, making it the perfect upgrade path if you wish to continue running a single line, but you would like to take advantage of all the new features of the 4.0 release.

- Wildcat! 'M' Multiline. This version uses the network method of providing multiple lines, but you can still run up to four nodes under

DESQview on a single PC—or, if you like, you can take the more traditional approach and run multiple PC workstations on a network, each of which handles one node (or two under DESQview). The 'M' version supports up to 10 lines.

- Wildcat! 'P' Multiline. This version is the same as the 'M' version, but it supports a whopping 250 lines!
- Wildcat! 'I' Multiline. The flagship of the Wildcat! line, the 'I' version is especially designed to support the Digiboard multiport serial cards you learned about in Chapter 3. Up to eight lines can be run on a single PC, and multiple PCs can be linked together over a network for even more power.

Summary

In this chapter, we installed your Wildcat! Lite bulletin board software and configured it with the basics needed to get you online with your own BBS!

In the next chapter, "Getting Up and Running," we'll continue to customize your BBS with your own ANSI and ASCII screens, text files, and more. You'll logon to your BBS for the first time, and we'll fine-tune its operation. Finally, we'll discuss co-sysops who can help you run your bulletin board!

Chapter 6

Getting Up and Running

by Mark L. Chambers

Now that you've installed your BBS software and made the necessary changes to the system configuration, it's your decision how much additional work you will do to further personalize it. Of course, you can make these changes later, but most sysops customize their systems long before their first caller connects. To give you an idea of what your basic system looks like as is, we'll begin this chapter with your first local logon.

Our primary purpose in this chapter is to illustrate how you can customize your menus and standard text files that no BBS sysop should be without. Because these are guidelines, you can pick and choose the changes you'd like to make. We'll cover the possible pitfalls in building ANSI menus, as well as how to create a good first impression with a custom BBS welcome screen. You'll learn what to include when writing a basic disclaimer to protect you and your callers, as well as a set of rules and regulations that will help you to run your system with a minimum of hassle and the maximum of enjoyment.

We'll also introduce you to the idea of *usability testing,* a process that has become very important for today's software developers. This is one step that every new sysop should perform before the first caller logs on—it's easier to debug your system before a hundred or so users have left you e-mail complaining about problems with your BBS!

Finally, we'll close this chapter with a tribute to the unsung hero of sysops everywhere: the *co-sysop*. Will you need help maintaining and improving your BBS? If so, a mature and reliable co-sysop is as important to your bulletin board as your modem or your BBS software. You'll find out how to choose a co-sysop, how to present that person to your callers, and which duties your co-sysop should (and should *not*) perform.

Your First Logon!

To get an idea of what your default Wildcat! Lite system looks like, it's time for you to "connect" yourself as a user from the BBS PC keyboard. This process is called a *local logon*, and it's an excellent way to:

- **Participate on your own system.** Through a local logon, you can read and post messages, play a game, chat with others in teleconference mode—just about anything you could do if you connected with a modem. Of course, your BBS will recognize you as the sysop, so you'll likely have many more commands and features to choose from than one of your users. Still, the majority of your local logons will be made just to enjoy your bulletin board!
- **Test your system.** Most BBS programs allow you to logon locally in two ways: as the sysop and as a regular user. The first method is convenient when you've added a new feature to your system and you'd like to check it to make sure it works. The latter method is practically a requirement, especially to new sysops, because you should logon at least once as a temporary user at each security level. This allows you to see and do exactly what will be available to a user at that level, so you can make sure that message bases and files that should be private for a security level actually are private. We'll discuss this in detail when we cover usability testing later in this chapter.

Tip

Most bulletin board programs today allow a regular user to logon from the local console, as well—therefore, if one of your users is visiting you, that user can logon and use your BBS normally, just as if he had connected with a modem. However, keep your system's security in mind; depending on which BBS software you're using, your visitor may also be able to use sysop console commands, so it may be necessary to keep an eye on your local caller!

- **Maintain your system.** The Wildcat! sysop menu is available during a local logon, and you can add files locally as well. We'll discuss this menu and file maintenance in detail in Chapter 9.

During this local logon, you'll enter your personal information as a new user, and then upgrade yourself to sysop status with a single keystroke! You'll then take a short tour around your system to familiarize yourself with some of the functions available to your users. Follow these steps:

1. Change directories to your \WC30 directory.

> **Tip**
>
> No matter what BBS software you use, make sure you add the path to your BBS "home" directory to your DOS PATH statement in your AUTOEXEC.BAT file. This will allow you to run your system no matter what drive and directory you're in at the moment—in our case, it will allow us to type the command CAT anywhere, instead of having to change to \WC30 each time. When you're ready to go online, don't forget to add your BBS batch file name as the last line of your AUTOEXEC.BAT file—this will allow your BBS to reload itself after a power outage.

2. Type the command **CAT** and press Enter. This runs the CAT.BAT batch file that loads your Wildcat! BBS program, putting your BBS online for callers (and allowing you to logon locally).

No matter which BBS program you run, it's a good idea to run a DOS *startup* batch file that runs the actual BBS program (instead of running the BBS program executable directly). This allows you to perform associated tasks immediately before your BBS runs. For example, you might copy BBS data files from your hard drive into a RAM disk or unload an anti-virus scanning program. The more complicated your BBS, the more likely you'll need a startup batch file.

> **Tip**
>
> If you decided to install your Wildcat! software in the default directory \WC30 on your C: drive, you should be able to run the CAT.BAT batch file without any modification. However, if you installed on a different drive or in a different directory, edit the batch file and change the commands that change the drive to C: and the directory \WC30 to whatever you specified during installation.

The screen in figure 6.1 appears; this is your Wildcat! BBS *Waiting for Calls* screen, the offline "control center" of your BBS. From here, you can see the status of your system at a glance, as well as upgrade users, enter a chat with one of your users, toggle the printer on and off, shell to DOS, and shut down your system. Depending on your BBS software, you may see more or less status information and commands.

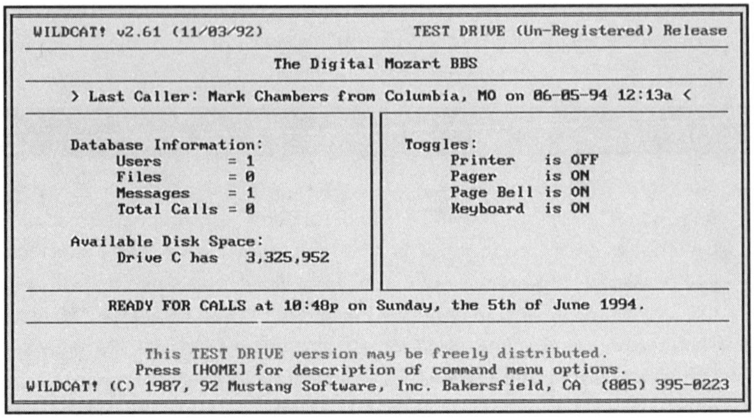

Fig. 6.1
TheWildcat! Waiting for Calls screen.

On the left side of the Calls screen, you'll see a row of console commands that allow you to logon locally, shell to DOS, shut down the BBS, and display different information about your system. You can use these commands by holding down the Alt key and pressing the highlighted character in the command name (for instance, a Sysop Login is available with the Alt-S sequence).

From the default status screen on the upper right, you can see the current total number of callers in your userlog, files in your file section and messages in your message base, and the total number of calls your system has received since you first went online. Wildcat! also displays the amount of space free on the drive where your \WC30 home directory is located, as well as the current status of your system—in the figure, this line indicates that your BBS is ready to take calls. If a caller was online, it would display the caller's name. The status screen can change when you use certain Sysop commands (such as the Drive Table command).

Finally, at the bottom of the Calls screen, Wildcat! displays whether your printer is toggled on or off, whether users can page you outside of the hours you specify in MAKEWILD, whether the sysop page will sound a tone from your PC's speaker, and whether your keyboard is toggled on or off. (You can turn your keyboard off to prevent children or the occasional cat from locking out a user by accidentally pressing a key!) The Quick Stats fields show statistics accumulated during shorter periods of time. To reset them, press Alt-R.

If your screen suddenly goes black, don't panic—most bulletin boards offer a built-in screen saver to protect your monitor. If a caller is currently logged on, Wildcat! Lite displays the name in the screen saver box. To return to the Waiting for Calls screen, simply press the Escape key.

Table 6.1 shows a short description of each command key available to you from the Calls screen. Take the time to learn these commands!

Table 6.1 The Online Help Description Displayed When the Home Key from the Waiting for Calls Screen is Pressed

Idle screen:	
F1 or Alt-S	Sysop logon
F2	Keyboard control of user session on/off
F3	Printer on/off
F4	Page hour override on/off
F5	Page bell on/off
F10 or Alt-X	Terminate Wildcat! Lite
Alt-D	Display DOS menu
Alt-L	Local logon
Alt-T	Drive table display
Alt-R	Reset stats
While a caller is online:	
F6	Start or end local chat or page
F7	Add time in 5 minute increments
F8	Subtract time in 5 minute increments
F9	Upgrade user security
Alt-U	User record window
Alt-V	EGA/VGA video toggle
Alt-W	Screen display on/off

3. As noted in the preceding table, the Sysop local logon key is F1 (or you can use Alt-S). Press it now, and Wildcat! starts a logon with the first and last name you supplied while configuring your BBS with MAKEWILD. In other words, when you press F1 or Alt-S for a Sysop logon, Wildcat! assumes it's you at the keyboard; when you press Alt-L, you can logon as any user (or a visitor can logon locally).

4. Because this is your first logon, Wildcat! cannot find you in its userlog files, so it asks you to verify that you spelled your name correctly. (Because most users type their names quickly, this is a common problem online.) Press **Y** to indicate that your name is correct.

5. Wildcat! now prompts you for your password. This is a **very** important choice. Make sure you use a brand new password that you've never used on any system before, and then make it even more unique by appending a number to it (for example, mustang3). Wildcat! then asks you for the same password a second time to verify it.

> **Tip**
>
> Remember that this password is essentially your access to the system, including the Shell to DOS function—never give it to anyone or use it on another BBS or online service, and change it every month or so to ensure the security of your BBS.

6. Type a company name, if you like, at the next prompt, or leave the field blank to skip it. Press Enter to continue.

7. Now type the first line of your street address and press Enter to continue.

8. If necessary, type the second line of your street address and press Enter to continue.

9. Type your city at the next prompt and press Enter to continue.

10. Next, type your state abbreviation and press Enter.

11. Type your ZIP code and press Enter.

12. Complete your address information by typing your country name (or leave it blank for the default of USA) and pressing Enter.

13. Enter your voice telephone number and verify that it's correct by pressing **Y**. You'll hear sysops refer to someone's "voice" number all the time—it refers to the number where you can be reached for a voice conversation, not a "data" number that may be answered by a modem.

14. Next, enter your BBS telephone number.

15. Enter your birth date in mm/dd/yy format at the next prompt and verify that it's correct by pressing **Y**. Wildcat! uses your birth date as a form of periodically verifying your identity—this form of continuous verification of your caller's identity is growing more and more popular with sysops, and more programs are implementing it.

16. Enter the name of your BBS as the "From" field—this is a plus for your callers, who may want to be identified as being from a company or another location. At this point in the process, your screen should look like figure 6.2.

```
Looking up Mark Chambers... Please wait.

The name "Mark Chambers" was not found in the user database.

Is this name spelled correctly? y

Where are you calling from [City, State or Country] ? Columbia, MO
"Columbia, MO" - Correct [Y/n]? y

Please Select a Password     : mustang3
Re-enter Password to verify  : ********

What is your Computer Type   : IBM 486DX/50
"IBM 486DX/50" - Correct [Y/n]? y

For later verification please enter your Birth Date: MM-DD-YY 06-01-61
06-01-61, Correct [Y/n]? y

Please Enter your VOICE phone number:
XXX-XXX-XXXX
```

Fig. 6.2
The logon prompts seen by your new users.

17. Select your PC type at the next prompt and press Enter to continue.

18. Select your gender and press Enter to continue.

19. The next prompt asks for a default file transfer protocol value (or you can choose Select, where Wildcat! will prompt you for a protocol before each transfer). Most terminal software now supports ZMODEM, so select it by pressing **Z**.

20. Your users can control Wildcat! in two ways: by "stacking" commands as a single string (with each command separated by a space or semicolon), or with "hot keys" (where a single key calls the command without

requiring you to press Enter). Stacking commands allows the fastest navigation, but the Enter key is required. The hot key method is slower, but your users will get an immediate response from your system. For now, press **Y** to indicate you'd like to use hot keys.

21. Next, the BBS asks you which form of default text entry you'd like to use when composing messages. You can elect to use the line editor (which accepts one line of text at a time), a full-screen editor (which resembles a text editor program, but requires you to use ANSI)—or, you can choose which editor you'd like to use each time you compose a message. By far, the most popular of these is the ANSI full screen editor, so select it by pressing **F**.

22. Your answer to the next prompt determines whether or not the BBS will use ANSI, ASCII, or RIP menus and display files, or whether the system should automatically detect which display type you're using at logon. We'll demonstrate all three of them later in this chapter—typically, of course, you'll probably want to use your ANSI menus locally, and the Auto detect setting will take care of this for you. Like virtually all other BBS programs, Wildcat! has no local RIP support for the BBS sysop. Therefore, RIP menus and display files will not be shown correctly on your local console screen, so don't select RIP for your local logons! If your users see a string of odd characters instead of ANSI colors and graphics, they should select No color here and the system will send them your ASCII menus. Your users can also change this setting later.

> **Tip**
>
> At the time of this writing, only a single BBS program—the commercial Searchlight BBS package—offers RIP support for local logons. If you're concentrating on offering RIP to your users, take a close look at Searchlight; it's one of the programs covered in Appendix A.

23. The next prompt asks you whether you'd like to erase the -pause- prompt displayed by Wildcat! Lite whenever it pauses for a full page of text. Although this delays the next screen of text slightly, it "cleans up" your display (and, depending on the terminal software you're using, it may delete those extra characters if you're capturing text to a disk file). Press **Y** for Yes.

24. As a final step, the BBS requests you enter your mother's maiden name! This might seem like a strange (and rather personal) request, but Wildcat! uses it as a security feature in case you've forgotten your password.

That completes the logon process! Now that you've completed registration, Wildcat! displays a local sysop status bar at the bottom of the screen, with the information you entered, the baud rate, the user's security, the user's age, the current menu or display file name, and the amount of time the caller has remaining. Note that the user never sees these two lines; this information is for your eyes only. This is the display you'll use most often as a sysop. At this point in the process, your screen should look like figure 6.3.

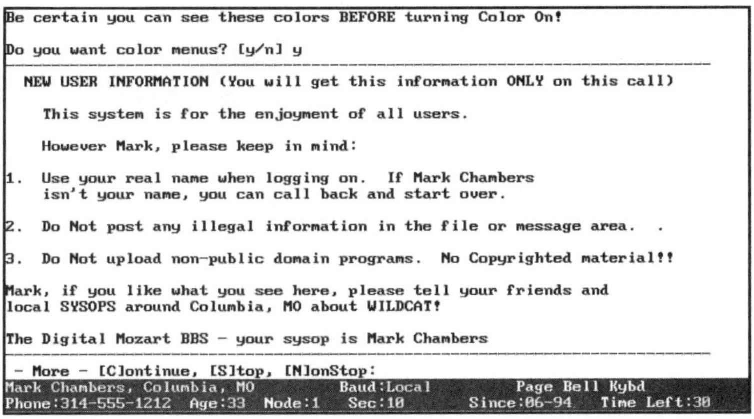

Fig. 6.3
The local status bar, seen only by the sysop on the BBS screen.

The first task performed by most bulletin board programs once a caller is online is a *mailbox check*, which means the BBS displays any electronic mail or public messages addressed to the user. Because this is your first logon, you don't have any.

Upgrading Your Access

Your BBS now displays its main menu (see fig. 6.4), and it's time to award yourself the high honor of the sysop security level! Right now, you have only the NEWUSER security level, so the menu automatically displays only those commands with NEWUSER access (or less): these are the Comments to Sysop and Goodbye commands.

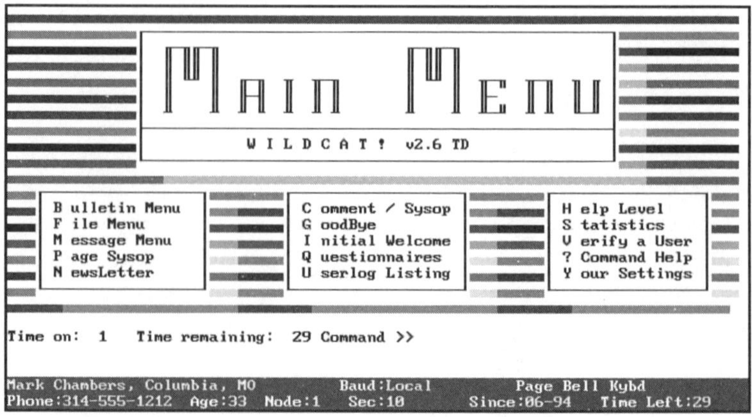

Fig. 6.4
The default main menu for new users on your Wildcat! Lite system.

> **Tip**
>
> Most bulletin board programs now offer insertion parameters (like embedded Wildcat! "@" codes, which we'll cover later), and it's a good idea to use them often. Your users will notice the personal touch when they see their names and locations within your text files, bulletins, newsletters, and menus. You can also use insertion parameters to create a user information bulletin that your callers can check on upload and download bytes, time remaining this call, and much more.

Press F9 to display the Upgrade Security Level window (see fig. 6.5). This is the same method you'll use when a caller is online and you'd like to change his or her security level immediately. You'll notice that Wildcat! displays three default security levels—move the highlight cursor over the word SYSOP with your right arrow key and press Enter. Congratulations, your BBS now recognizes you as the sysop!

You'll also notice that a new command, Sysop Menu, has appeared; this is your sysop menu. You'll do all of your online maintenance from this menu.

Although you've awarded yourself sysop access, you'll notice from the local sysop status bar that you still have less than 30 minutes of time remaining! How can you give yourself (or one of your callers) additional time during a BBS session? As a permanent method, you can assign additional online time within the MAKEWILD security profile screens; for now, though, press F7 several times. Each time you press F7 on your console keyboard, the BBS will add an extra five minutes of online time for the current session (in other words, this time disappears after the caller hangs up, or you exit a local logon).

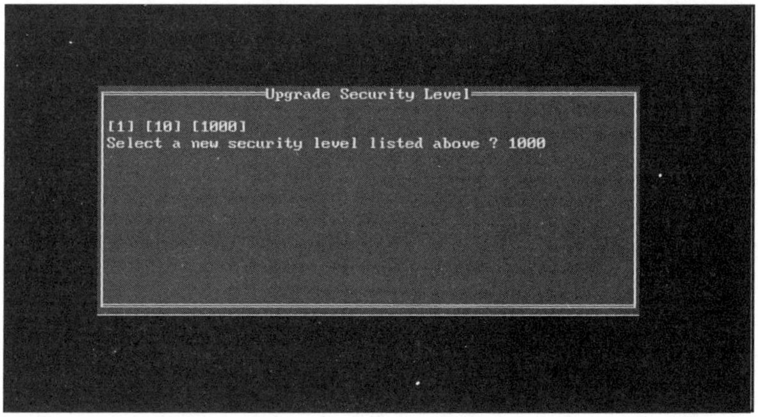

Fig. 6.5
The Upgrade Security Level window, which you can use to immediately upgrade the current caller from your BBS console.

Take a few minutes now and try out the various commands on each default menu. From the main menu of your BBS, make sure you visit each of your submenus as well: press **B** for the Bulletin submenu, **F** for the Files submenu, **Q** for the Questionnaire submenu, **1** for the Sysop submenu, and **M** for the Message submenu. You may notice that the Files and Message submenus each have commands that jump directly to the other; because most users will visit your message submenu and your file submenu each call, this is a real convenience. Of course, you can't upload or download a file locally, but try leaving and reading a message, answering the sample questionnaire, reading a bulletin, and displaying your system settings.

You should also press **H** from the main menu to try both of the other *help levels*: regular level, where you see only the commands available from the current menu, and expert level, where the BBS displays only the name of the current menu. Once you and your users get familiar with the commands, one of these two help levels will probably save you a considerable amount of time as compared to the novice level. Each menu also includes an online help screen, so your users can always display more detailed information on each command if they need it.

Tip

If you're using a different BBS package that doesn't provide some form of online help, consider taking the time and effort to create your own online help screens! Help text should be available on each menu, and you should describe each command with at least a sentence or two; these help screens will be invaluable to your callers, and you'll have taken a big step toward making your system more user-friendly. Even if your BBS software has no method of providing online help, you can still make your help text available as a download file, and your callers can view or print them offline.

First Impressions

As you move around your new BBS, pull out your trusty paper and pencil and jot down your impressions of the default menus. Is the File submenu clear to you, or could the commands be more intuitive if they were grouped differently? Should the BBS display the number of times a user has called on the main menu? What information could you obtain from your callers with a new questionnaire? Do you really need to offer the initial welcome display as a command? Are the menus too colorful, just right, or not elaborate enough?

It's important to record all of your impressions, good or bad, major or minor. This is probably the last time you'll be completely non-biased about your system, and soon the menus and commands will become second-nature to you, so approach your new system just as if you were a caller and not the sysop. Consider this the first phase of your usability testing—if you like or don't like what you see, there's a good chance many of your users will feel the same.

You may decide to leave one or all of the default menus untouched, and (as we said earlier) this is the easiest and fastest method of getting your system online. Later in this chapter, you'll learn about how to create alternate menus in ASCII, ANSI, and RIP—but if you like the default menus, they are yours to use. Many Wildcat! sysops choose this route, and their users never know that they didn't lift a finger to create those beautiful, multicolored 3-D ANSI menus!

Leaving Your System

When you're ready to exit your system, use the Goodbye command from the main menu. Wildcat! returns to the Waiting for Calls screen. To shut down your system and return to DOS, press F10. Wildcat! will take your modem off hook, so incoming callers will receive a busy signal.

Tip

Remember how we mentioned that external modems are usually preferred by sysops? If you have an external modem, you can always check whether your modem has been taken off-hook by glancing at its lights. Most Hayes-compatible modems have a light marked OH, which will be lit if the modem is off-hook.

Creating Your System Files

In this section, we'll build and modify several of your system files to illustrate how you can personalize your system with a minimum of time and trouble. You'll learn more about:

- How your Wildcat! system uses .BBS, .SCR, and .RIP menu files, as opposed to dynamically "building" a basic set of menus automatically.
- A couple of new programs. THEDRAW is the most popular shareware ANSI editor available, and no matter which BBS program you run, you'll likely be using it to create your ANSI menus. MAKEQUES is the questionnaire utility we'll use to create a simple voting booth.
- The graphical possibilities of the RIP and NAPLPS emulations.
- The system files you may wish to modify for your BBS.

Building Custom Menus

By default, Wildcat! uses a sophisticated method of creating the four major menu screens—Main, Message, File, and Sysop—within your BBS on the fly, based on the security level of your caller and the corresponding menu commands. Mustang Software calls these *dynamic* menus. Callers presented with dynamic menus see only those commands that they can actually use; other commands on the same menu with a higher security level are stripped from the menu and are not displayed. If you'd like a simple text-only menu system that's fast, no trouble to create, and easy to use, dynamic menus are a good idea. Most other bulletin board programs also offer some sort of automatic menu creation based upon the caller's security level or access.

However, your Wildcat! software also gives you the power to display menus that you create—both in ASCII text (with the extension .BBS) and ANSI color graphics, which you've already seen earlier in this chapter (with the extension .SCR). You can also use RIP graphics by creating a separate set of menus with the .RIP extension. These menu files must be located in the MENU directory specified on the MAKEWILD Conference Definition screen. If a .SCR menu is found and the user has selected ANSI color, Wildcat! Lite displays it; if no such file exists, the BBS next searches for a .BBS ASCII file. If neither of these files are available, Wildcat! displays a dynamic menu.

> **Tip**
>
> If you're using Wildcat! Lite, you can also use text-based color codes to add ANSI color within your .BBS files. On the positive side, this requires only one set of menus for both ANSI and ASCII callers, as long as the menus are nearly alike—however, most sysops prefer using separate menus for ASCII and ANSI, since the ANSI menus tend to be radically different in format and complexity, and therefore require separate files. The color codes also make the file harder to read and edit by hand, so most Wildcat! sysops use WCDRAW, which is included with Wildcat! Lite, to create their menus. WCDRAW reads and writes these codes transparently, making it much easier to use color codes.

These menus display the same commands no matter what the user's security level; of course, the user will still not be able to select commands restricted to a higher access level, but the menu text will be displayed. This is ideal for a profit system, where you would like your callers to see what your BBS offers, but not allow them to actually use any of the pay services until they subscribe!

> **Tip**
>
> Today, it's more important to spend time on your RIP and ANSI menu screens than your ASCII menus. In the early days of bulletin boards, standard ASCII was the only text standard guaranteed to work across any platform; however, over time, terminal programs have come to rely on ANSI as the BBS "common denominator," and even your callers using Macintosh computers can generally make use of ANSI graphics.

You can assign different sets of .BBS, .SCR, and .RIP screens to each of your user security profiles (see table 6.2). Note that any allowable DOS filename character can be used to identify a menu set, but most Wildcat! sysops prefer to use a series of numbers or letters of the alphabet. Each of these static screens displays what you would like that particular security access level to see, making it easy for you to create an entirely different look and feel for different security levels. Some sysops refer to a system with such menus as having a board within a board, because callers with the profile NEWUSER have no idea that users with the FULLUSER profile have different menu screens and a different set of commands.

Table 6.2 The four menu files and examples of their ASCII/ANSI naming conventions

Menu	ASCII Name	ANSI Name
Main	MAIN0.BBS—MAIN9.BBS	MAIN0.SCR-MAIN9.SCR
Message	MSGA.BBS—MSGZ.BBS	MSGA.SCR-MSGZ.SCR
File	FILE0.BBS—FILE9.BBS	FILE0.SCR-FILE9.SCR
Sysop	SYSOPA.BBS—SYSOPZ.BBS	SYSOPA.SCR-SYSOPZ.SCR

There are also two important values you should set within MAKEWILD that control your caller's access to ANSI and RIP menus. If you'll be offering ANSI menus, make sure you've answered Yes to the question "Will you be offering color ANSI menus?" on Part 2 of the General Definition screen. If you've decided to add RIP graphics to your BBS, you should also display Part 3 of the General Definition screen and answer Yes to the question "Enable RIP graphics support?".

Now that you understand how your BBS displays its menus, let's build an example of each for The Digital Mozart BBS to illustrate how you can create your own menu screens.

Building ASCII Files

For our hypothetical BBS devoted to music, we'll modify the existing ASCII Main menu for our FULLUSER profile users. Your Wildcat! Lite default security definition for the FULLUSER profile menu is set to 5; this is determined by the value entered for the question "Menu Display Set" on the Edit Security Profile screen. Therefore, the name of the file will be MAIN5.BBS. We'll use the standard MS-DOS EDIT text editor, but you can use WCDRAW or any editor that saves files in ASCII format—such as the popular QEDIT.

1. Change directories to the \WC30\MENU directory, the location where Wildcat! looks for its menu files.

2. Start EDIT with the file MAIN5.BBS. Type **edit main5.bbs** and press Enter. EDIT displays the screen in figure 6.6.

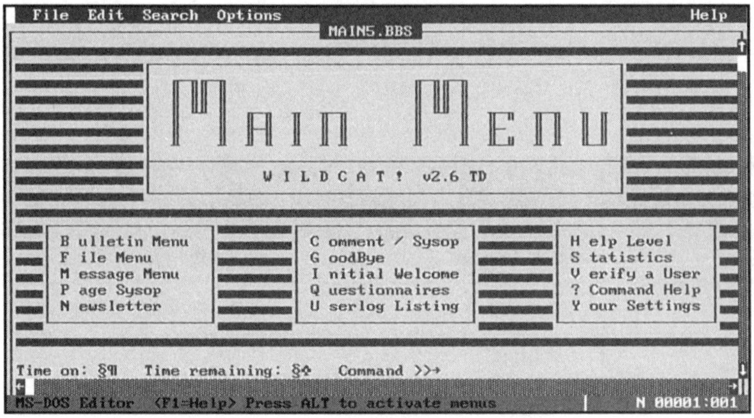

Fig. 6.6
The MAIN5.BBS menu file loaded into the MS-DOS EDIT text editor.

As you can see, this default .BBS menu also includes text color codes, so it will also display correctly for ANSI color users. We'll make four changes on this menu: we'll replace the line "WILDCAT!v.3" with the name of our board, we'll remove the Initial welcome command and we'll change the command prompt. Note that removing the Initial Welcome command from this menu will not disable the function itself, so a user could still select it. We'll disable the actual command later in this chapter.

3. Turn Insert mode off and place the cursor on top of the W in the word "WILDCAT!" Type **The Digital Mozart BBS**.

> **Tip**
>
> Your BBS should only display a maximum of 79 characters per line, so make sure you've turned Insert off to avoid your text falling off the right side of the screen! If you're creating a screen from scratch, simply make sure that no line on your menu is longer than 79 characters.

4. As you can see, the embedded color codes in this menu file have "pushed" the text for *Initial welcome* right off the screen! To reach the right part of the file, move your cursor down and to the right until it's reached line 14 and column 115; it should be resting directly on top of the color code immediately preceding the letter I in Initial welcome. Press the space bar until the words "Initial welcome" are erased and your cursor has reached column 139. If you add a command later, it can take this spot.

Tip

It may be difficult for your users to tell at first glance exactly which key activates each command; that is especially frustrating for callers if you're running a BBS program that uses hotkeys. As a rule, make the command key the first letter in the description; however, you should also clearly separate the command key, so that your users can easily distinguish it. On a color menu, simply use a different color for the key, or use the blinking attribute. On an ASCII menu, use a separator character like the right parenthesis ")" or the right bracket "]".

5. Finally, we'll add a new field to your command prompt on this menu. Remember those control codes we mentioned earlier in this chapter? You can see three of them already embedded in the prompt line at the bottom of the editor screen: the amount of time used, the current conference, and the amount of time remaining. Actually, what you see are the "@" codes that Wildcat! will recognize in your file. Move your cursor to the C in the word "Command" and turn Insert mode on. Type the word **Time:** and hit the space bar once to separate the time display from the word. Now type the code **@TIME@**, which will cause Wildcat! to display the current system time after the word "Time:."

Table 6.3 The Most Commonly Used Embedded Codes Wildcat! Will Recognize in ASCII and ANSI Display Files and Menus

Code	Wildcat! Substitutes...
@TIME@	Current system time (from clock) in format HH:MM.
@DATE@	Current system date in format MM/DD/YY.
@BBS@	Name of the BBS in MAKEWILD.
@TFILE@	Total number of files available on the system.
@PREVON@	Name of last caller.
@TMSG@	Total messages on the system.
@PAUSE@	Displays the "Pause" prompt immediately.
@SYSOP@	Sysop's full name from MAKEWILD.
@TCALLS@	Totals calls received by the system.

(continues)

Table 6.3 Continued

Code	Wildcat! Substitutes...
@TUSER@	Total number of users on the system.
@VER@	WILDCAT! version number.
@BDATE@	User's birth date.
@FROM@	User's "From" field.
@CPU@	User's computer type.
@CALLS@	User's total number of logons.
@COMPANY@	User's company name.
@LEFT@	User's time remaining this call.
@ADDR1@	User's address 1 field.
@ADDR2@	User's address 2 field.
@CITY@	User's city.
@STATE@	User's state.
@ZIP@	User's zipcode.
@UPK@	User's total upload kilobytes.
@DOWNK@	User's total download kilobytes.
@DOWNS@	User's total number of downloads.
@FIRST@	User's first name.
@ALIAS@	User's alias name.
@LASTON@	User's date of last call.
@USER@	User's full name.
@UPS@	User's total number of uploads.
@PHONE@	User's phone number.
@DATA@	User's data number.
@MEMO@	User's Memo date.
@MEMO1@	User's Comment 1 field.
@MEMO2@	User's Comment 2 field.

Code	Wildcat! Substitutes...
@MSGSLEFT@	Total messages left by the user.
@MAXDL@	Maximum downloads possible per day.
@SINCE@	User's date of first call.
@TIMEON@	User's time on system this call.
@LASTNEW@	User's last [N]ew files search date.
@SEC@	User's security level.
@CONF@	User's current message conference.
@EXDATE@	User's expiration date.
@BELL@	Beeps the speaker at the remote terminal only.
@NOSTOP@	Turns off the user's ability to stop screen display.
@NOPAUSE@	Turns off the "Pause" prompt line in display files.
@CLS@	Clears the screen.

6. Your final screen should look something like figure 6.7. Now save the file by selecting Save from the File menu, and then select Exit from the File menu to return to DOS.

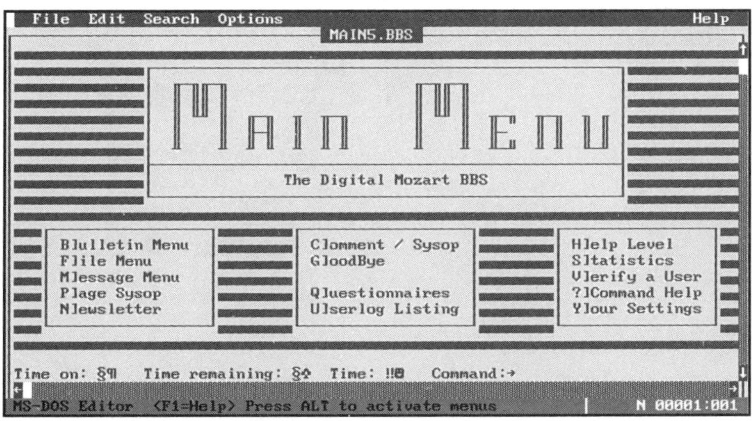

Fig. 6.7
Our new MAIN5.BBS ASCII screen.

Of course, we simply modified this ASCII screen, but your callers will now see your BBS name each time the main menu is displayed, and the current time will always be onscreen. You can use the same methods to create brand new ASCII screens from scratch, or modify the other existing screens.

Building ANSI Files

Color ANSI has been the graphical foundation of PC bulletin boards for more than a decade now, and there are many "art gallery" door programs devoted to displaying the best works of online ANSI art. Most online games written for PC boards require ANSI to play. Although there are improved graphical emulations like RIP and NAPLPS that will almost certainly overtake the "ancient" ANSI standard in popularity some years in the future, the vast majority of PC-based bulletin boards around the world will still depend on color ANSI graphics for years to come.

Many bulletin boards now "auto-detect" that a caller is using ANSI, including your Lite version. Your new users can also select it as a default during the registration sequence, and during future logons the BBS will switch to ANSI as soon as the caller successfully completes the logon process. As you've already learned, you enable support for ANSI color menus by running MAKEWILD and answering Yes to the question "Will you be offering color ANSI menus?" on Part 2 of the General Definition screen.

Like many other aspects of running your own bulletin board system, the complexity and design of your ANSI menus are left completely up to your talent, your taste, and your time. As an example of an advanced menu system with an interesting effect, the author's BBS uses pull-down menus reminiscent of a Windows interface (figure 6.8). Although your possibilities for menu design are more limited with the Lite version of Wildcat! , you can still create a unique look for your system.

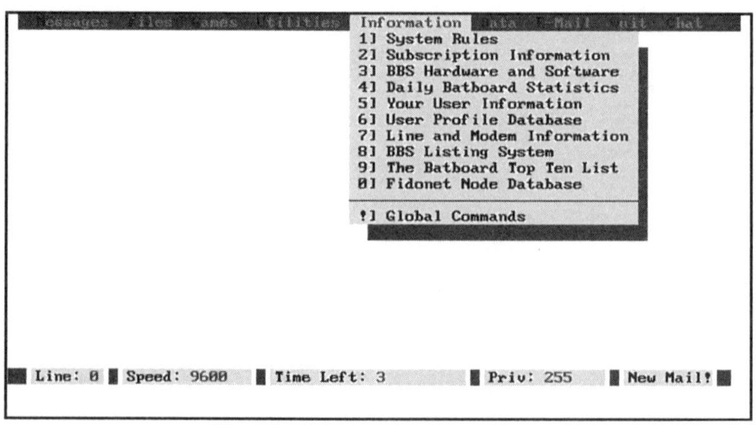

Fig. 6.8
A pull-down ANSI menu from the author's BBS.

In this section, we'll use a utility called THEDRAW to create a new MAIN05.SCR file that reflects the musical theme of our example system.

Tip

Unlike your ASCII menus, you can't use a standard text editor to create or modify ANSI files (unless you've got nothing better to do for the next couple of years). THEDRAW isn't the only ANSI screen creation utility available, of course, but it's generally recognized as the best, and it's used by sysops running every type of PC-based BBS. Whatever drawing program you use, make sure it's been designed to create ANSI screens!

What makes a good ANSI menu? Every sysop has a different opinion, but here are some common mistakes to avoid when creating your ANSI menus:

- **Lack of a common color, layout, or graphic.** Have you ever called a BBS where each menu seemed to have been drawn from a different system, and none of them seemed to flow together? When it comes to a good menu design, variety should be applied cautiously. Your individual menus should provide some sort of unifying common color scheme, command layout, or graphic element with which your callers can identify as they move around your system. The default Wildcat! .BBS ANSI menus are excellent examples of a unified layout, with the colored bars and 3-D drop shadows appearing on each menu.

- **Extensive ANSI animation.** That ANSI "filigree" may be funny or breathtaking the first time a caller sees a particular menu, but if it takes more than one or two seconds to display, your users are going to get very tired of it very quickly. After all, your 2400-baud callers can't use any of the commands on the menu until your software finishes displaying the menu screen; Wildcat! allows you and your callers to abort the display of any file with the spacebar, but that becomes tiring after a short time as well. The best ANSI artwork (especially animation) is simple but striking.

- **Poor color combinations.** Keep in mind that some of your users may be calling you with monochrome or grayscale displays, and, for them, the yellow lettering you use on a white background will simply disappear. Such a color combination will even leave your users with color monitors squinting as they try to read the text. Whenever possible, check your screens by displaying them on a monochrome or grayscale system. Black works well as a background, and each foreground color has a brighter, "highlighted" intensity often used for emphasis.

Once again, we'll use the Main menu for our FULLUSER profile users as an example; the name of the color ANSI file will be MAIN5.SCR. For this example, we'll use THEDRAW from TheSoft Programming Services (which is a favorite of sysops running all types of BBS software), but you can use any ANSI screen design utility. If you'll be using Wildcat! Lite as your BBS program, use the WCDRAW utility provided with Wildcat! Lite.

Tip

WCDRAW, a Wildcat! specific menu-driven drawing program that works similarly to THEDRAW, is located in your \WC30 directory. Since WCDRAW was designed for use exclusively with Wildcat!, it's recommended that non-Wildcat! sysops use THEDRAW instead. WCDRAW generates screens with the specialized color codes recognized by your Wildcat! Lite system, and it also manages Wildcat! menus, display files, bulletins, and help files. A complete discussion of every WCDRAW feature is beyond the scope of this book; however, like MAKEWILD, WCDRAW includes comprehensive online help, which you can display by pressing F1.

THEDRAW is generally available on most large bulletin boards, as well as CompuServe. These steps will introduce you to THEDRAW, but the program does come with a manual of its own that explains all of the powerful drawing and animation features offered. Remember, if you continue to use THEDRAW, you must register it; you'll find an order form within the file THEDRAW.DOC.

1. Change directories to the \WC30\MENU directory, the location where Wildcat! looks for its menu files.

2. Change to your THEDRAW directory and start THEDRAW. Type **thedraw** and press Enter. THEDRAW displays the screen in figure 6.9.

3. We'll use several items on the information line at the bottom of the screen. The numbers in parentheses at the far left are the column and row positions for your current cursor location. The word "Color" is displayed in your current foreground and background color combinations. Finally, the characters next to the numbers 1 through 10 represent the characters that will appear in your file when you press Function keys 1 through 10—these are the Extended IBM graphics you learned about in Chapter 2, and they allow you to create some interesting effects online! To change between the 15 different character sets for the Function keys, press Alt-F and use your up and down arrow keys to highlight the set you want to use. For our example, we'll use set 6.

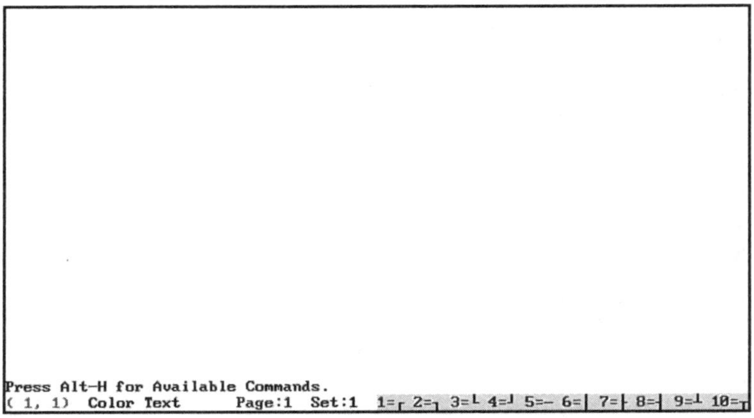

Fig. 6.9
The edit screen from THEDRAW.

Tip

If you get stuck within THEDRAW, press Escape to display the drop-down menu and Alt-H to display the online Help menu. You can even hold down the Alt key by itself for a few seconds to display a list of the Alt-key commands.

4. Right now, you've got a blank screen. Let's create a box to hold your commands on the left side of your menu. With your cursor at the upper-left corner (1,1 on your display), press F4 to place a block character there. Now move your cursor down and to the left with the arrow keys, and press F4 again. Continue this process until you've reached column 1, row 20. Now, press F4 continuously to draw the lower edge of the box; stop at 20,20. Move your cursor to column 20, row 1 and draw the top edge of the box. Finally, draw the right side of the box in the same manner as the left. When you're done, your screen should look like figure 6.10.

5. Now let's add a 3-D effect by drawing a *drop shadow*, a popular effect with sysops. First, we need to change the foreground color to a darker color, so press Alt-A. From the color menu, select a foreground color of 8 and a background color of 0; you'll note that the word "Color" at the bottom of the screen changes to reflect your selection. Place your cursor at 3,21 and press F5 until you reach 21,21 (this is the bottom of your drop shadow). Now move your cursor to 2,21 and use the same technique you used to draw the right side of your box to draw the right side of the shadow.

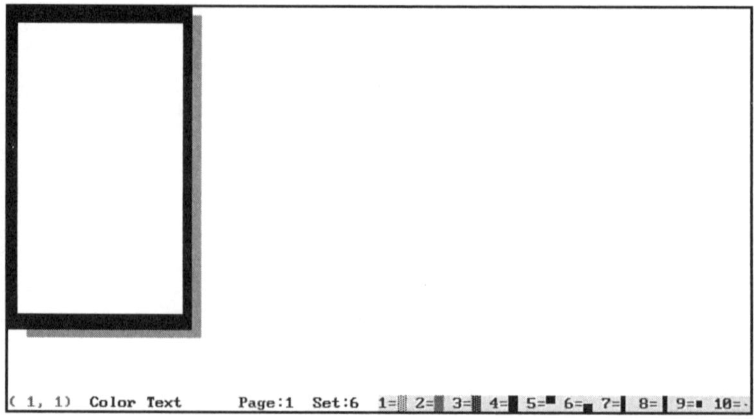

Fig. 6.10
The beginnings of your ANSI menu.

6. For our example main menu, we'll add only the File, Message, and Bulletin commands. First, a menu title is a necessity, so that your users will know their location within your system—so, move your cursor to 6,3 and type **MAIN MENU** in whatever color you like. Move your cursor under the menu title and type **COMMANDS**. Now that you've identified your menu, select a highlight color (like bright yellow) and type **[M]** at 4,6, **[F]** at 4,8, and **[B]** at 4,10. Use another color (like green) to type the rest of the command description; this sets the command key apart, as we mentioned earlier. Note that adding these commands to this menu will not enable the functions themselves; you must make sure the users for this level have access to these three commands in your MAKEWILD configuration. Your screen should now look similar to figure 6.11.

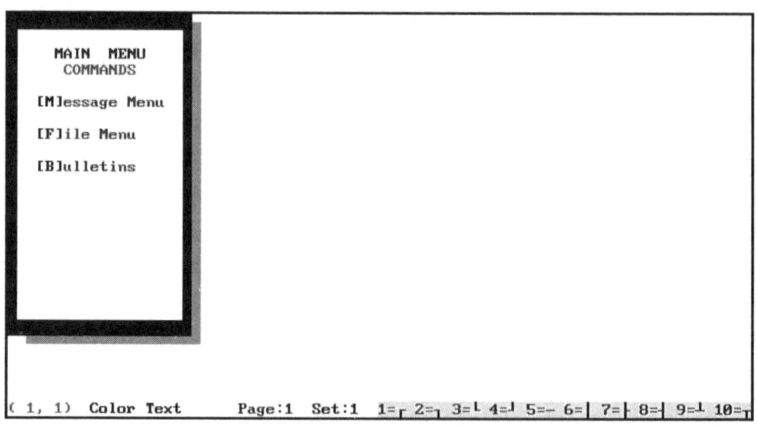

Fig. 6.11
Your ANSI menu with the menu title and commands added.

7. Now we need a strong graphical item for the right side of the menu; perhaps a large musical note to go with the musical theme of our BBS. If you're saying, "There's a problem: I can't draw!", don't worry—this author can't either! THEDRAW also provides several impressive ANSI "fonts" that can provide interesting visual effects. First, change your foreground color to red (or a highlighted color you haven't used before). Then, press Escape to display THEDRAW's menu bar and pull down the Fonts menu. Select the Medieval font, which will help suggest the history of classical music. You're automatically returned to the edit screen, and the word "Text" at the bottom of the screen has changed to "FONT", indicating that the characters you type will now be displayed in the selected font. Move your cursor to 27,3 and type **DIGITAL**. Next, move your cursor to 27,9 and type **MOZART**. Finally, move your cursor to 27,15 and type **BBS**.

8. Lastly, you might notice a little empty space after the title BBS. Our system also concerns compact discs so let's add a colorful representation of the level meters common on stereo components to even out that space with the line above it; this should also pull together classical music and modern technology in the caller's mind. First, change your foreground color to bright green. Now we need to turn the Font feature off—press Escape to display THEDRAW's menu bar, pull down the Fonts menu and select the Standard font. You're automatically returned to the edit screen, and the word "FONT" at the bottom of the screen has changed back to "Text." Use the F9 key to draw three lines of seven box characters each at 51,16, 51,17, and 51,18. Next, switch colors to bright yellow and add more box characters to all three lines. Switch colors to bright red and add a few more box characters to the end of the second line. You've created three level meters in ANSI, and your finished ANSI color menu design should look something like figure 6.12. You can save your screen in ANSI format with the Alt-S command. THEDRAW will prompt you with several questions when you save a file; all of the defaults for the Save questions should work well for most bulletin boards. However, if you're creating screens for Wildcat! Lite, make sure you specify that the screen should not be cleared before displaying the file.

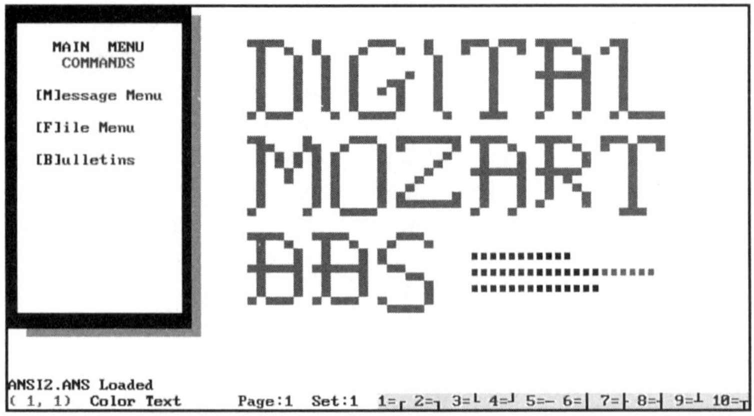

Fig. 6.12
The completed ANSI Main Menu screen.

To provide that critical common layout, your other menus would probably feature the same command box on the left side and the title on the right side. You should also add a command prompt as well, using the same techniques we covered in the previous section on ASCII menus. Wildcat! Lite will place the input cursor for your keystroke after the last text in the menu, so you could add a line at 1,23 that reads:

Time remaining: @LEFT@   Command:

This would show the user the amount of online time remaining each time the menu is displayed.

Remember, this section has only introduced you to the tip of the iceberg when it comes to creating ANSI screens using programs like THEDRAW and WCDRAW—these programs have dozens of other effects, paint and draw modes, and much more. Your menu screens are limited only by the Extended IBM character set. If you'd rather not draw your screens yourself, you can usually contact a well-known local ANSI artist on other bulletin boards to arrange to have them done for you. You might also find ANSI "clip art" that you can add to your menu files on other bulletin boards.

Although WCDRAW is provided for Wildcat! sysops and THEDRAW is probably the best known ANSI screen utility, you'll find others available that handle the task of creating ANSI menus—and many of them also automate much more of the process, because they're designed especially for menu construction.

An example is PROMENU, an excellent menu design tool from HARRIS TECHNOLOGY Associates. PROMENU not only creates ANSI screens for display on just about any BBS with a minimum of hassle, it also creates equivalent screen files in pure text, ASCII graphics, RIP, and NAPLPS! This is particularly helpful for new sysops who would like to maintain the same appearance for their screens no matter what graphics type the caller is using. Figure 6.13 shows an ANSI screen under construction in PROMENU.

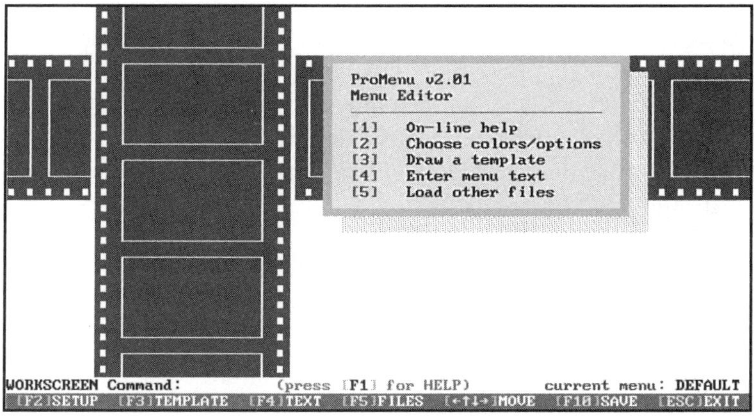

Fig. 6.13
The PROMENU workspace.

If you're not terribly confident of your ANSI talents within WCDRAW or THEDRAW, PROMENU provides a large number of background patterns, pictures, and textures, along with 150 fonts, clip art images, support for different drop shadows and box outlines, a full color palette with configurable defaults, the ability to generate RIP "push buttons" for your command choices, a built-in editor for your menu text, and more. For additional information on PROMENU, contact the author, Randy Harris, at 508/877-5433 (voice).

A Word About GUI Emulations

The online world of PC bulletin boards has been traditionally character-based since its inception. This is understandable because only in the last five years or so have PCs gained the hardware to display high-resolution graphics; until you have the means to use a *graphical user interface* (or GUI, for short) like Windows or a graphical operating system like OS/2, there's no reason to display anything other than ASCII text and ANSI color. Additionally, extra graphics meant extra characters to send, and at 300, 1200, and 2400 baud such additional overhead would slow a communications session to a crawl.

In the last couple of years, however, a handful of innovative terminals and bulletin board programs have appeared that can offer the sysop of a PC bulletin board much more: high-resolution graphics, mouse support for the caller, and even the online display of JPEG (.JPG) format images. All of these emulations require that the caller use a specialized terminal program (some of which are frankly less than acceptable in quality and performance); however, at least one has proven popular enough to warrant the developers of well-known shareware and commercial communications programs to add support for it.

The success of these new graphical terminals mirrors that of Windows and OS/2, along with the graphics offered by Prodigy and America Online. Even CompuServe, which has been an eternal bastion of confusing character-based menus and obscure commands since the day the first user connected, has actively been promoting graphical terminal software that can help new users navigate around the service easier.

Of course, there will always be a contingent of your callers that don't want all the window dressing of graphics, buttons, and scroll bars; for them, you should always provide your ASCII and ANSI menus. The vast majority of your users, however, will welcome the opportunity to point and click their way through your BBS, enjoying the sights (and even sounds!) of cyberspace without pressing a single key. The possible applications for online image display are limitless: electronic matchmaking; online shopping malls where you can see a 24-bit color image of the item you're buying, whether it be a car, a house, or a dog; and online games that stretch the boundaries of the current multiplayer games on CompuServe and GEnie.

At the time of this writing, the "GUI Wars" are still raging, but it certainly appears that the Remote Imaging Protocol (or RIP) emulation from TeleGrafix Communications is the clear winner for now in the PC arena; Macintosh sysops also feature their own GUI terminals, but these are not available at this time for the PC. Of course, your Wildcat! Lite BBS program has RIP support built-in, so you can offer it to your users. Whether RIP will eventually become a standard on the level of ANSI color, no one knows—but the trend toward online graphics is in full swing, and it's certain that you'll need to offer additional graphics in the future to stay competitive. We'll cover the creation of RIP graphics in Chapter 17.

Let's outline RIP and two of the other graphical options available to you right now:

- **RIP.** RIP has several advantages that have made it a clear standout so far: the required terminal program, RIPterm, is offered free of charge, so your users can download it off your board without having to register it. RIPterm is actually a very serviceable package, with many of the features found in commercial programs. The programming *specification* (or guidelines) for displaying RIP is publicly available, so others can incorporate it into their communications software. RIP supports a mouse, so the caller can click a graphical button as well as press a command key. It can display simple animations of a higher resolution than ANSI graphics. RIP uses standard 7-bit ASCII to send graphics, so it can be used over virtually any communications link. TeleGrafix sells both a comprehensive paint program and a simple drawing package. Most importantly, though, the design of the RIP emulation makes it easy to add to **existing** bulletin boards, so that sysops have been able to use it without purchasing special BBS programs. Figures 6.14 and 6.15 show two RIP menus from the author's TBBS system.

Fig. 6.14
An example of the striking graphics possible with RIP.

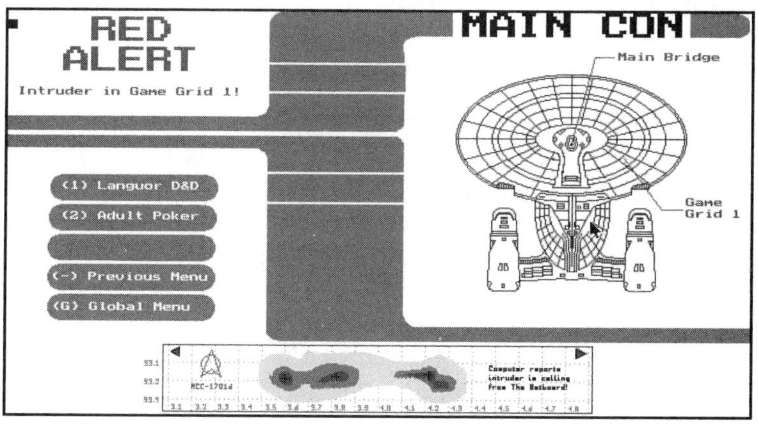

Fig. 6.15
Another example of RIP graphics.

On the downside, the first version of the RIP specification does not include any form of error correction, nor does it offer direct image support for GIF or JPG display, and the draw and paint utilities are fairly expensive. Finally, the terminal has a requirement of EGA or VGA resolution. The second version of the RIP specification (which should be available as you read this) will remedy some of these shortcomings, including support for 24-bit color image transmission and display, support for most major sound cards, and additional resolution choices. For additional information on RIP, contact TeleGrafix at 714/379-2131 (voice). We'll cover RIP in more depth—including a short tutorial on how to use RIPaint to create a RIP welcome screen for the Digital Mozart BBS—in Chapter 17.

- **NAPLPS.** NAPLPS (short for North American Presentation Level Protocol Syntax) is a much older emulation than RIP, but it has certain advantages. First, NAPLPS is an actual ANSI standard, and it is resolution independent (meaning that you can display the same NAPLPS graphic on a PC equipped with CGA video and a PC equipped with VGA video, and the image will be displayed to the full capability of the hardware). NAPLPS also provides support for international languages, a feature that has made it popular for online graphics around the world. If you've ever used the Prodigy online service, you've seen NAPLPS in action.

  However, NAPLPS also has two major disadvantages that have all but removed it from the running for BBS sysops. First (and most damaging), it does not support the caller's mouse, so your callers must still interact with your BBS in the traditional way—no buttons or hotspots to click. The other major problem is the lack of a good terminal program and a good paint program that support NAPLPS; the terminals that do exist are below average in features and performance, and the paint programs offer none of the powerful capabilities of their RIP counterparts.

- **FX Term.** Although it offers several impressive features, the Tel-FX software from Hamilton TeleGraphics is essentially a "closed" terminal program; it offers its proprietary imaging emulation only when calling RoboBOARD FX, the company's BBS package. FX provides online display of JPG graphics, a point and click interface very much like Windows or GeoWorks and resolutions up to 1024x768 256 colors. A simple drawing package is also included.

  Unlike RIP, FX Term has not been well received by most sysops because you must run their BBS program to offer it to your users. RoboBOARD FX offers the basics, but the user interface cannot be customized from the ground up (which a sysop can do with RIP). Sysops will tell you that they selected the bulletin board software they run for various reasons, and no sysop likes to be limited to one particular BBS program. As mentioned before, the new RIP specification will include JPG transfer and additional resolutions, so it will almost certainly overshadow FX Term.

Other packages may not be suitable for use as a full-featured bulletin board, but work well as doors. For instance, Imagen's Fracterm software and Durand Communications' DC NET and DC GENESYS provide online image databases for just about all bulletin boards available today. They still require special terminal programs, but at least they work in the league with the BBS program you're already running.

Using System Questionnaires

With the rules and regulations enforced by any good sysop, a bulletin board system is very rarely a democratic environment—usually, it's referred to more as a monarchy (in polite conversation) or a dictatorship (at user meetings). The analogy also holds true on another level: most sysops don't communicate regularly with each of their users, and the feedback a sysop receives usually applies only to an individual, rarely addressing the BBS as a whole.

You may be wondering how to collect one or more pieces of information from all of your users at once. For instance:

- How can you gauge whether your subscribing users would like you to concentrate on more games, more message bases, or more files? (Actually, the answer is usually all of the above!)
- How can you help build interest in a controversial topic in your message base by providing an anonymous voting booth?
- From a business standpoint, how can you regularly update your user information for mailings and demographic reports?
- Is there a simple method of taking orders for products online, without a custom door program?

All of these needs are answered with a single solution: the online questionnaire.

Wildcat! Lite allows you to configure the number of questionnaires available on each conference in your system through the MAKEWILD Conference Definition screen. With the desired conference highlighted, press Enter to display the Conference Description screen; note that you can also define a separate questionnaire path for the conference from this screen as well.

You describe the questionnaires you offer in the files QUESTION.BBS and QUESTION.SCR, and the actual questionnaire data files are named QUESnnnn.DAT, where the n represents the same number as the description in your QUESTION.BBS file (note that leading zeros are required if your questionnaire name has less than four digits). When a user answers a questionnaire, the responses are stored in the corresponding QUESnnnn.001 answer file, and you can view them from DOS, load them into your text editor, or compile and total the answers with a questionnaire compiler. Mustang provides such a compiler as a part of an additional utility package, WC PRO, but there are third-party utilities available for the same purpose.

Contrary to appearances, the questions you answered at the beginning of your first call were not part of a questionnaire; instead, they're internal to Wildcat!, which actually inserts the information into the caller's userlog record, so you can't change them. If you want to collect additional information about first-time callers during their first logon, however, you can create the special data file QUESNEW.DAT. The answers supplied by your users are stored in QUESNEW.001. You can build additional questionnaires—ranging from simple voting booths to complex order entry programs for online purchases—with the MAKEQUES utility (figure 6.16). Like MAKEWILD, MAKEQUES is run from DOS. It allows full-screen editing of your questionnaire data files, and you can specify branching from one question to another depending on user response.

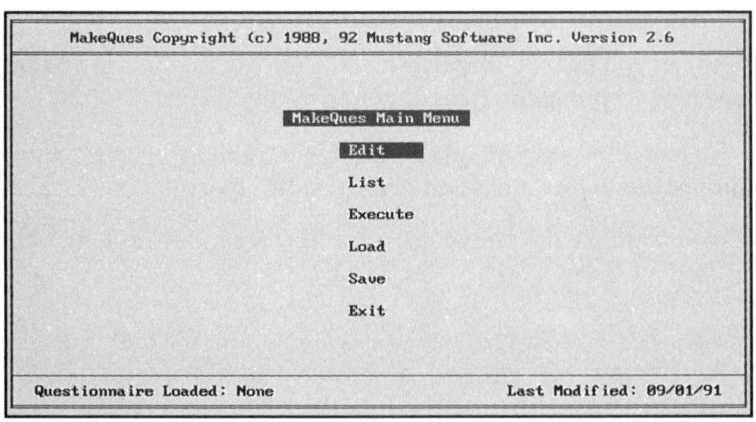

Fig. 6.16
The MAKEQUES menu.

The available commands within MAKEQUES are:

- **Load.** Press F3 to load a questionnaire data file. If necessary, you can move through the different directories on your drive to find the data file.

- **New.** Press F4 to discard the current questionnaire data file and start over.
- **Save.** Press F2 to save the current questionnaire data file. The .DAT extension is not required.
- **Exit.** Press Escape to exit the MAKEQUES utility.
- **Insert.** Press Insert to enter a new line into your questionnaire above the highlighted line.
- **Delete.** Press Delete to delete the current line.
- **Test.** Press F5 to run the current questionnaire without saving any information to disk.
- **Print.** Press F9 to print the current questionnaire in its entirety.

Press F3 and load the example questionnaire QUESNEW.DAT, which is located in your \WC30\QUES directory (so you'll have to select the \QUES directory first). Press Enter to edit any single question; for example, move the highlight to line 5 and press Enter to display the edit screen (figure 6.17).

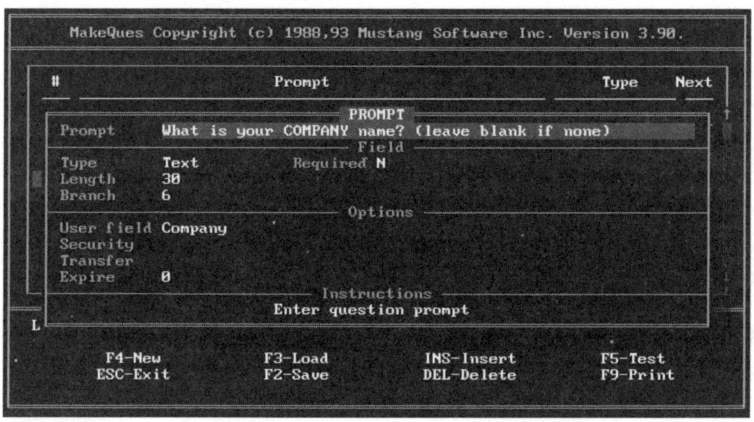

Fig. 6.17
The MAKEQUES edit screen for a questionnaire line.

From the Edit screen, you can specify the following fields:

- **Prompt.** This field holds the question text that will be displayed to the caller. You can also specify a text file to be displayed instead of a single line of text by entering the complete path to the file preceded by a forward slash—for example, /C:\WC30\INTRO.TXT.

- **Type.** This field determines which type of response or action the question will accept; press Enter to select the type. Select None if the line is to be used only to display text (as in the first four lines of this example). Set Required to Y if the user must enter a response before continuing.
- **Length.** This field specifies the maximum length of the caller's response.
- **Branch.** If the questionnaire should "jump" to another line depending on the user's response, press Enter to specify the next question. MAKEQUES allows separate branches for question types like "Yes/No".
- **User field.** If you'd like to import an answer from your questionnaire into the caller's userlog record, press Enter and select the target field. The default setting of None disables the import feature.
- **Security.** This field specifies a security profile name that will be applied to the caller after the question has been answered; for example, a subscription questionnaire could raise or lower a caller's security level.
- **Transfer.** This field allows you to run another questionnaire file after the question has been answered. Specify the questionnaire name, or leave the Transfer field empty to disable this feature.
- **Expire.** This field allows you to change the user's expiration date (as a number of days from the current date). The caller's userlog record is updated and the expiration date will be set to the specified number of days in the future.

To exit the Edit screen, press Escape. Note that your changes are not saved to the questionnaire data file unless you use the Save command.

It's a good idea to use the Test command before saving your changes and exiting MAKEQUES; the program will display the current questionnaire just as the user will see it; however, MAKEQUES will not execute a Transfer to another data file, and text files substituted instead of the prompt will not be displayed.

Modifying Your Menu Commands

In Chapter 5, you made a number of basic changes to your Wildcat! configuration, but we left the default menu commands in place to get you up and running as fast as possible. Of course, Wildcat! also allows you to edit or remove commands and their descriptions from all four of the system menus;

this is usually necessary if you create custom ASCII, ANSI, or RIP menus. In this short section, we'll make a few changes to your system's main menu commands, and you'll see how those changes are reflected in the dynamic menus displayed by Wildcat! Lite. Follow these steps:

1. Run MAKEWILD. From the main menu, use your down arrow key to move the highlight to Menu Definition and press Enter. The screen in figure 6.18 appears.

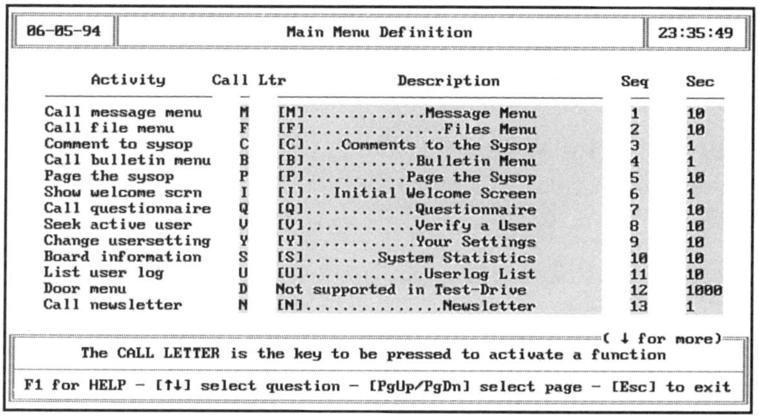

Fig. 6.18
The Menu Definition screen for the Main Menu commands.

The text under "Activity" describes the action Wildcat! will take when you select that command, while the "Call Ltr" field contains the actual keystroke itself. The "Description" field holds the text that is displayed for this command on dynamic menus, while the "Seq" value indicates the sequential order in which the commands will be arranged (both on the dynamic menu and on the command prompt). There should be a unique number in the sequence for each command. Finally, the "Sec" field indicates the minimum security access level necessary to use the command. Note that the possible activities for each menu are *hardcoded*, meaning you cannot change them or move them to another menu—however, all of the other fields can be changed any way you see fit.

2. Let's remove the Initial welcome command. Press the down arrow key until you reach the activity labeled "Show welcome scrn." Although you can't remove the command entirely, you can prevent it from being displayed. Press Enter three times to move to the Sec field, use your Delete key to clear the field and enter **1000**. The Initial welcome command is now invisible to everyone but you.

3. Next, change the command description for the V command, which is currently described as "Verify a User." Press the down arrow key until you reach the activity labeled "Find active user." Press Enter to move to the Description field, use your Delete key to clear the field and enter **[V]........View Active Users** (make sure you maintain the right justification so that the description matches the other entries).

4. Finally, let's change both the view command key and the command description for the L command. Press the down arrow key until you reach the activity labeled "List user log" and press **L**. Press Enter to move to the Description field, use your Delete key to clear the field and enter **[L]........List System Users**.

Figure 6.19 displays the original default dynamic menu for a FULLUSER caller. If you were to save this configuration, the same dynamic menu would now look like figure 6.20.

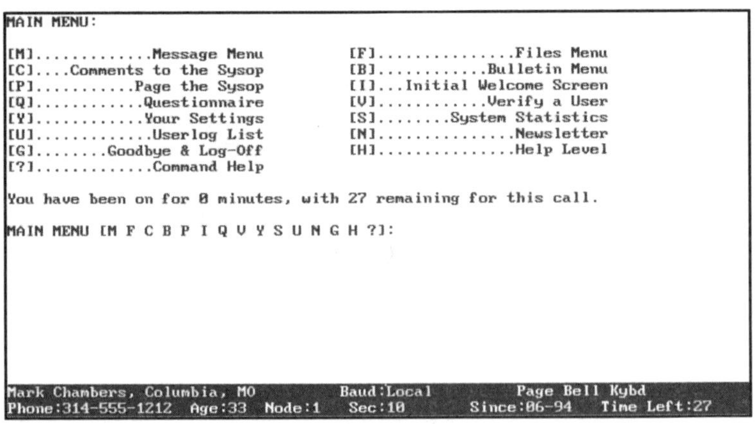

Fig. 6.19
The default dynamic Main Menu commands.

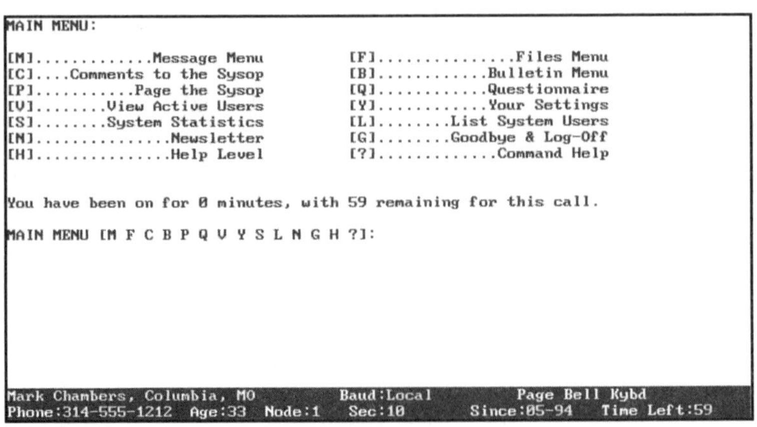

Fig. 6.20
The dynamic Main Menu commands after our changes have been made.

Adding Standard Files

If you're already a regular user of other systems in your area, you've probably noticed that the successful, well-run bulletin boards you've called all provide a number of similar text files and display files—in fact, many experienced sysops maintain that these standard files are a requirement if your BBS is to attract callers. Some of these files are informative, while others lend a professional look, or outline the legal responsibilities taken by the sysop.

In this section, we'll discuss the common files that every sysop should offer to the public.

Your Rules and Regulations

Without a well-designed set of rules, your BBS may not disintegrate into chaos—but it will certainly provide you with a great many more headaches than you can imagine. If you create a set of rules and regulations before the first caller connects, refer to those rules when making decisions on BBS matters, and display them prominently in your bulletins or on your main menu, you'll defuse virtually all of the trouble on your system before it starts.

Some sysops force new callers to agree to abide by the system rules during the registration process by prompting them "Do you agree to follow these rules? (Y/N)", or something similar. Of course, this is no guarantee, but it does provide a certain amount of ammunition on your side if you must lock a user out of your BBS later for multiple infractions of one of your rules.

Here are several fundamental rules you'll probably want to include in your file:

- As you gain experience running your BBS, you'll learn that certain situations can arise that result in friction between personalities. Whether it be between you and one of your callers, between two callers themselves, or between two groups, it's almost certain that you'll eventually see someone launch a personal attack in your message base or chat area. However, we should note that an attack is different than someone expressing an opinion. Your system rules should clearly delineate the definition of a personal attack and explain the punishment for continued abuse.

- Your system rules file is a perfect place to outline your file upload/download ratio policy, if you have one. This will help as you answer countless messages from callers who'd like "just a megabyte more" without subscribing and/or uploading. And, while we're on the topic of file transfers, state your policy on uploading commercial software to your BBS.

- State your policies on deleting messages, files, and users.
- If you won't be allowing foul language, adult messages, or adult files on your system, make that clear in your rules file.
- You'll probably also want to add a series of guidelines that will help your new callers understand the preferences of the majority of your users—for example, most callers dislike reading messages typed in all uppercase, and most of your users would prefer that those leaving messages stay on topic rather than discuss matters that don't relate to the subject of the particular message folder.
- If you have co-sysops, state their powers and responsibilities in your rules file (we'll discuss co-sysops in more detail later in this chapter).
- Finally, it's all-important that your callers know you will keep their personal information completely confidential! Distribution of any information the caller gives you—even a problem caller—is a serious breach of faith on your part, and may even have legal ramifications.

A rules file will help to regulate your users; however, many sysops fail to understand that most of these rules and regulations must apply equally to them. Of course, your system is your property and your responsibility, so you do have the right to enforce whatever rules you think are fitting (and you should). Keep in mind, though, that nothing can ruin the friendly atmosphere of a bulletin board—no matter how many services or features it offers—than a sysop on a power trip. The negative impression it will create among your callers will become a topic of conversation on other boards, and you're likely to find yourself with a reputation as an immature or fickle system operator. Favoritism or bias is just as easy to detect online in a message as it is face-to-face, so the best idea is to follow the same rules you impose on your callers!

Your Disclaimer

A good legal disclaimer is probably the most important standard file you can add to your system! More and more sysops are displaying their disclaimer to all new users as a part of registration, thereby making certain that they can attest that every caller has seen the disclaimer at least once.

If you have the resources, you might consider hiring a lawyer to help you compose your disclaimer (especially if you'll be running a profit or business/ support system). BBS lawsuits and BBS seizures are still very rare, but they are slowly growing in number, and they never fail to attract negative publicity for the hapless sysop and the online community at large. A professionally written disclaimer may help save you both headaches and money.

If you'd rather not hire legal help, read Chapter 7, "Legal Aspects of Operating a Bulletin Board System," closely before writing your own disclaimer, as it centers on legal issues of concern to sysops. *Boardwatch Magazine* also periodically covers BBS legal matters. Finally, call other bulletin boards in your area that display disclaimers and study their language.

You may want to cover these points in your disclaimer:

- The nature of private e-mail on your system. Virtually all BBS programs allow the sysop to view so-called private electronic mail. This should be made clear to your callers.

- Disclaimer of responsibility for files downloaded from your system. Unless you wrote the program and created the archive yourself, you can't be completely sure that a freeware or shareware file downloaded from your system is bug-free. Loss of data through a badly-written program is a rare occurrence, but it does happen, and even a CD-ROM might harbor a Trojan Horse or virus.

- Contents of echomail and newsgroups. Public message echoes on FidoNet are moderated, and are usually much safer for a sysop to carry than Internet, where unmoderated personal attacks (usually called *flame wars* by everyone online) can produce language and invective that may upset some of your callers.

- Proof of age for adult messages and files. If you're offering adult material, it's imperative that you obtain proof of age, and your disclaimer should reflect the fact that you do—as well as the possibility that a minor might supply you with false proof.

- Lastly, you will probably want to add a disclaimer of responsibility for any illegal activity that others may discuss or carry out on your system. This can include swapping phone card numbers, commercial files through attached messages in e-mail, and discussions of illegal subjects like child pornography.

As has been proved recently in several cases, what's legal in one area may not be tolerated in another! It's strongly recommended that you take the time to check your local laws on adult material before you write your disclaimer.

Your Welcome Screen

Enough warnings, cautions, and regulations! The last three standard files we'll discuss in this section are less stressful, but just as necessary—especially this discussion of your system welcome screen. Once again, THEDRAW or ProMenu will be very helpful in creating both the ASCII and ANSI versions of your welcome screens, which are named HELLO1.BBS through HELLO9.BBS (and HELLO1.SCR through HELLO9.SCR for their ANSI color counterparts)—note that the .BBS versions of these files are required, even if you create .SCR versions. If each of your menu levels has a different look, it's worth the time to design a different welcome screen for each; if one level is for subscribers, for instance, your welcome screen for that security level could include the words "Thanks for Supporting Our System!" at the bottom.

Wildcat! Lite also provides a time-sensitive HELLO1N.BBS through HELLO9N.BBS; these files are displayed only if the user's last call date is earlier than the file creation date, so they're displayed only once to a caller.

Although your welcome screen is the perfect place to display your artistic talent, it should also provide the caller with real information, such as:

- The modem speeds you support.
- Your location.
- Your network mail and Internet addresses, if any.
- Your hours of operation, especially if your system will not be up 24 hours a day.

The same general rules apply for ANSI welcome screens as ANSI menus; however, your users are likely to be more tolerant of extensive ANSI animation as a part of the welcome screen, since it's generally displayed only once per call. Again, if you're not an ANSI artist, you might ask someone known for ANSI screens to create your welcome screens for you; alternately, you could announce a contest and give away prizes for the top entries, which not only provides your screens but helps to publicize your system as well!

Figure 6.21 shows one of the welcome screens from the author's system.

Fig. 6.21
An original ANSI welcome screen from the author's BBS.

Your Newsletter

Think of your Newsletter as a press release to all of your callers—it should always contain the latest additions of features and services, along with announcements of particularly popular download files. This is the place to get as enthusiastic as possible about your system! You can also use your newsletter to notify your users of future *downtime* when your BBS will be unavailable (for hardware installation, software upgrades, or similar projects).

Like most other display files within Wildcat!, you have an ASCII version (NEWSLTR.BBS) and an ANSI version (NEWSLTR.SCR). Your BBS will automatically check the date of each user's last call, and if the newsletter was created after that date, WildCat! offers the user the chance to see it during the logon process.

Because your Newsletter will usually contain several pages of information, the ANSI color version shouldn't be created with THEDRAW—instead, you might create a colorful ANSI banner that will appear at the top of the file, taking up only 10 rows or so, and then append plain ASCII text after the banner. Alternately, use one of the utilities specifically written to create ANSI bulletin files—many of these will feature different border effects. A good example is the "computer paper look," as shown in figure 6.22.

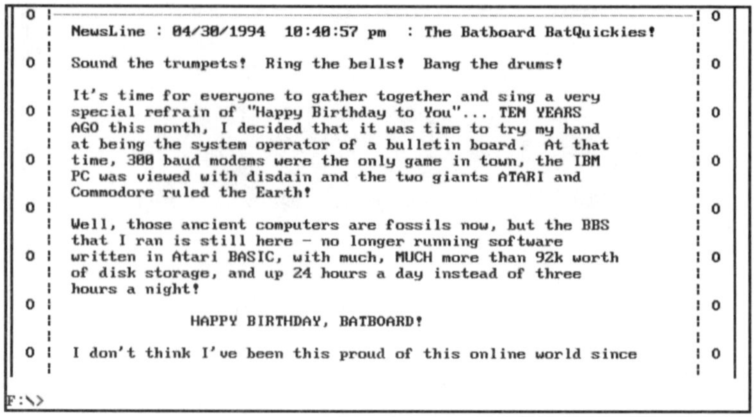

Fig. 6.22
An ANSI Newsletter file created with a bulletin utility.

Usability Testing

Once you've completed your modifications and your bulletin board is ready to go, it's time to begin usability testing. No matter what the scope, the idea behind BBS usability testing is a simple one: find a friend with a modem who's willing to call your system before it officially opens and have that person try every command for each of your security levels (and, if you're going to be running a multiline system, each line should be separately dialed). Just as you did earlier in your first logon, the person testing should write down any immediate impressions he or she has, both good and bad. If possible, you should also be on hand to watch the reactions of your tester—if a particular menu is badly-designed, for instance, your tester might pause for several seconds to try and locate a command description, tipping you off that some measure of redesign might be necessary. Specific areas to cover include:

- If you're going to offer ASCII, ANSI or RIP menus, your tester should try out both for each menu level and make sure that everything looks correct when calling from a popular communications program like PROCOMM PLUS or Qmodem. If your terminal software doesn't display RIP graphics, call the TeleGrafix BBS at 714/379-2133 and download the latest version of RIPterm.

- Error messages of any kind. These are usually generated when your BBS can't find a file where it's supposed to be located, or a particular message area or file section has been misnamed. Have your tester write down any error messages and any accompanying text.

- If you've assigned higher access levels to some menu commands, have your tester display those commands with a lower access level to make sure they're actually hidden; dynamic menus are good for this, because anything meant for the higher access users simply won't be displayed. Pay close attention to the sysop menu—no one should be able to access it except for you and your co-sysops, if any!

- Have your tester try any new questionnaire files you may have created.
- Make sure your tester receives the proper access level after completing the registration process.
- Using your sysop access, try dropping to DOS remotely. Make sure you can restart the BBS again as well.

Do You Need a Co-sysop?

Now that you're familiar with much of what goes on behind the scenes, you may be asking yourself whether you can handle the maintenance required by your system, or whether you can participate at the level necessary to attract new users. As you learned before, your BBS is self-maintaining in many ways, but you'll always have mail to answer and files to approve, as well as public messages to read and chat requests to answer. This usually isn't as much of a problem for single-line systems, but multiline bulletin boards can rapidly turn what started as a pleasant hobby into a source of long hours at the keyboard and a permanent headache! If you're running a large enough profit or business/support system, you can always hire one or more employees to help—but what about a single- or multiline hobby system?

Enter the *co-sysop*: your co-sysop is essentially your second in command, with a subset of your powers and your authority, who can help maintain your BBS, act as a moderator in your message base, and boost interest by participating in every part of your bulletin board. In turn, the co-sysop enjoys a higher status on your system, usually accompanied by extra online time, and is recognized by you throughout your BBS. Being a co-sysop is much like running your own system without the expense, so any reputable BBS usually has several dedicated users who would be happy to perform these duties.

> **Tip**
>
> Many BBS programs also allow you to designate sigops; a sigop acts as a co-sysop for a single message area or file section. Sigops usually have fewer powers than a full co-sysop, but they usually can delete messages and/or files from their area, as well as moderate all user interaction in their area. The suggestions offered in this section apply equally to them.

Selecting and Recognizing a Co-sysop

If you're considering adding a co-sysop, consider these questions:

- Does the person have a history as a user on your system—either good or bad? Problem users very rarely make good co-sysops! Your co-sysop should be someone who is well respected on your system, and has exhibited a sense of fairness and restraint when dealing with other callers.

- Is the person sufficiently mature so as not to damage your system or your reputation? Note that mature in this case does not directly imply age; instead, it refers to the person's ability to understand the responsibilities of helping to run your system. Remember, you will be held accountable for any illegal activity on your system, and you could very well be the target of a lawsuit if personal information or messages are distributed to others.

- Is the potential co-sysop familiar with your bulletin board system menus, message base, file system, and doors? You can train a potential co-sysop if you like, but it's much easier when you have someone on hand who already has that knowledge.

- Is the person in a position where he or she can log in regularly (at least once or twice a day)?

If you decide to ask someone to become a co-sysop, take the time to make it worthwhile for that person! Mention your co-sysop by name in your rules and regulations, and outline what powers he or she has. Add your co-sysop's name to your welcome screen and main menu, so that others will recognize your co-sysop's authority on your system. Allow that person limited access to your sysop menu (usually you must add a new security level), and award your co-sysop additional time online.

Co-sysop Duties

Remember, your co-sysop should be given a limited set of your sysop menu commands, not the same access level that you enjoy as sysop! Unless it's absolutely necessary, do not give your co-sysop access to the following:

- Your drop-to-DOS function (or, in the case of integrated BBS software, your DOS command processor).

- Private e-mail messages not addressed to the co-sysop, including your own. You can always add another message area called "Message to Co-sysop," if users should address requests directly to your co-sysop.

- Your userlog editor. As you'll learn shortly, Wildcat! Lite can allow userlog access without displaying each user's password.

- Any questionnaire output containing personal user information.

Using Wildcat! Lite, this is easy to do if you create a security level lower than your own, but higher than the highest standard user security level. You can then assign the new security level to those commands that your co-sysop should be able to use. Follow these steps for Wildcat! Lite:

1. Run MAKEWILD and select the Security Profile Definition screen.

2. Press Insert to Add a profile. MAKEWILD prompts you for a name for the new security profile; type **COSYSOP** and press Enter. MAKEWILD displays the new profile name.

3. Next, we'll copy the existing values from FULLUSER into COSYSOP. Press F3 to display the Copy Security screen (figure 6.23). Highlight FULLUSER in the From column and select the COSYSOP field in the To column. Press F10 to perform the copy, and then press Escape to return to the Definition screen.

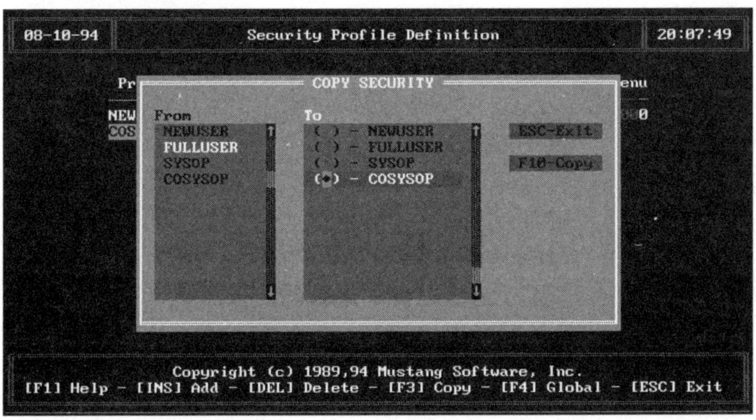

Fig. 6.23
The Copy Security screen from the MAKEWILD utility.

4. With the COSYSOP profile highlighted, press Enter and edit the fields in the profile you'd like to change. If you change the value for Sysop Access to Yes, your co-sysop will be able to use the Sysop menu functions (unless you raise the minimum security access for the Sysop menu commands); however, the co-sysop will still not be able to see the contents of the password field when reviewing users in your database.

Note that we didn't start by copying your SYSOP level security profile to the new COSYSOP profile—although it would have saved you time in editing the new profile, you might have missed a field and accidentally awarded more power to your co-sysop than you actually desired!

Tip

No matter what BBS program you're running, take extra care when you're modifying or creating new access levels, and never allow a caller to use a new access level without logging on locally and thoroughly testing the user's new privileges yourself! For example, this testing can help you avoid accidentally granting minors adult access—or, in this case, accidentally allowing your co-sysop access to your remote DOS shell command!

Typical co-sysop duties include the following:

- Approving new uploads and adding them to the appropriate file section.
- Maintaining your external events.
- Managing any contests or giveaways you may offer. We'll talk more about these later in the book.
- Monitoring your activity log.
- Alerting you of a problem user (after your co-sysop has given that user ample warning).
- Increasing user interest by participating in your message base conversations.
- Answering basic user questions in e-mail.

Summary

In this chapter, we covered many of the options you have in customizing your BBS with your own look and feel. First, you made your initial logon to your Wildcat! Lite system. We discussed the creation of custom menu screens with utilities like THEDRAW and PROMENU, as well as cutting-edge graphical emulations like RIP. You were introduced to the standard text files every sysop needs, and the questionnaire capabilities of Wildcat! Lite. Finally, we discussed usability testing and how you can recruit help in the form of a co-sysop.

Now that you've come this far, you're ready to accept your first callers! Once your system is fully tested and officially online, you may wish to skip ahead, temporarily, to Chapter 11 to learn how to promote and market your system, but make sure you return to the next chapter, where we discuss legal issues that concern every BBS sysop.

Part II

Bulletin Board Issues

Chapter 7

Legal Aspects of Operating a BBS

by John R. Harris

(Special thanks and acknowledgment to Les Bessenger, who assisted the author in his research and drafting)

In this chapter, we endeavor to provide a bulletin board sysop with some general and practical guidance as to the laws most likely to affect BBS operation. Any society that professes to embrace the ideals of equality and justice must endeavor to balance many different competing interests, lest the society devolve into anarchy. Our society attempts to seek this balance through the laws and the courts. Because of the complexity and number of different laws that have arisen from this impossible societal balancing act, it is not possible in the space of 30-odd pages to even come close to identifying all the laws that may affect your BBS.

But there are a few areas of law that you are most likely to encounter—obscenity laws, privacy laws, and copyright laws. You may also encounter computer crime laws, the law of libel and slander (defamation), and trademark laws. There is some overlap within these broad areas of the laws, especially considering how concerns about privacy permeate so many legal considerations. For example, the subject of pornography must be considered both in the context of a person's right to privacy as well as in the context of computer crimes (there are "computer porn" criminal laws in some states).

The most frequently asked questions (okay, FAQs to those in the know) from sysops include the following: When can the authorities seize my equipment?

What procedures do they have to follow to nab my gear? Do I have to monitor uploaded files for copyright infringements, or stolen credit card numbers, or pornography? If I find files or e-mail that might get me in trouble, can I delete them? Can I read my subscribers' e-mail? What issues should my subscriber's agreement cover in it to protect me personally and my equipment?

We will try to give you at least some basic answers to these and some other questions. The main points we will make are as follows:

- If you elect to operate on the boundaries of the law, be prepared to face the consequences—familiarize yourself with the laws that might apply, and try not to direct undue attention of the authorities to yourself by speaking out too much or engaging in outrageous behavior.
- Familiarize yourself with the copyright laws and the privacy laws—they are the laws that are most likely to affect your operations.
- Have a good "user's agreement" that gives you, the sysop, the right to monitor uploads for obscene materials, copyright violations, defamatory messages, and other materials that might threaten your BBS with legal action.
- Enforce your agreement—bar access to those who violate your agreement.
- Cooperate with legal authorities if you are confronted with legal process (that is, you are served with a search warrant, a subpoena, or a seizure order).
- Hire yourself a good, (legally and technically) competent lawyer before you start your BBS.

Disclaimers

Because this chapter deals with legal questions, we (the authors, editors, publishers, and any other contributors to this book) have to provide some legal disclaimers (we do it for good reason—it's too easy to get sued these days, and too many hungry lawyers are looking for lawsuits to file). We have to "read you the fine print." We have to note that this chapter is NOT intended to constitute legal advice from the authors or contributors. You *must* seek your own counsel if you have a legal problem or want more detailed information about running your BBS. If you follow everything we say in this book and in this chapter, you *still* may be sued and you *still* may lose. Thus, we take NO RESPONSIBILITY WHATSOEVER for the accuracy of the information or the viability of any of the laws we discuss. Rather, consider this chapter as a guide for asking further questions of *your* lawyer.

Keep in mind that every state and country has its own laws, and rarely do two lawyers agree on an interpretation of a particular law (which is one reason there are so many lawsuits). If you find that you have a problem or concern about a potential problem that may create a risk of legal liability to you or your business, seek legal help immediately. Try to get advice *before* you do anything big. Prevention is the best cure; you can avoid many legal problems by governing your behavior in an acceptable manner and by attempting to abide by the known laws.

Finally, the views expressed in this chapter are personal opinions held by the author, and in no way constitute the views or opinions of the author's law firm, law partners or associates, or clients, or of the publisher or any other authors of this book. Now, we know that disclaimers are distasteful, but we are finished. Anyway, on to the subject at hand.

New Electronic Media—The Information Shopkeeper

Conventional media (such as newspapers, magazines, television, etc.) often mention the right of free speech and freedom of the press when legal issues arise that might affect their ability to gather and disseminate the news (at least, the news as they perceive it). The right to express oneself openly is often invoked as a defense to a legal wrong. For example, a newspaper has more latitude to criticize a public figure than a private person—untrue and irresponsible statements about a private person that cause damage are a libel.

In many respects, a BBS is merely another form of media, another form of the press. In fact, the very term "bulletin board" indicates a medium of communication. While a BBS is not strictly press, its capability to collect and disseminate information is not all that different from a newspaper in which the readers are allowed to write the stories. If a BBS is treated as press for purposes of certain laws, then certain privileges and defenses may be available. But if a BBS is not treated as press, then those privileges and defense may not be available.

When thinking about the laws and whether a BBS is press, it is useful to put yourself back in time 150 years (pre-telegraph) and pretend that you are a shopkeeper of information, very much like a bookseller. Then, as now, suppliers uploaded information (books) to the shopkeeper, and customers downloaded by buying the book.

Of course, one critical difference is that the "supply"—the information—is inexhaustible in a BBS. A bookseller can run out of books, but a BBS doesn't run out of copies of information—one customer's downloaded copy of a file is as good as another's. Thus, a BBS can serve as a distributor, or a publisher, or a republisher of information. The electronic medium defies classic definition, because there are aspects of distribution and publication.

With a BBS, there is no reason why someone can't be a supplier and a customer, or why the shopkeeper can't take a sealed envelope and "hold" it for someone (e-mail). Although electronic media are a far cry from a nineteenth century shopkeeper, many of the laws have their origins in such a marketplace, and the shopkeeper may be a useful analogy because this (perhaps overly) simplistic view is how many prosecutors, judges, and juries of laypersons will look at it.

The BBS and Free Speech Issues—First Amendment Rights

The press and other forms of media are integral parts of American society. Democratic governments can only exist when information about the functions of the government, and the proper and improper roles of government is freely disseminated, discussed, and debated amongst the governed people. After the American Revolution, when the Founding Fathers wrote the Constitution and the Bill of Rights, these functions were often fulfilled by "pamphleteers." Anyone with an idea and some money could buy or borrow a printing press, and soon be distributing their ideas around the town.[1]

Today, computer bulletin boards and electronic newsgroups are used not only for modern-day pamphleteering, but also for more mundane and commercial purposes. Bulletin boards contain listings of items for sale, notices of meetings, and discussions about matters important as well as trivial. BBS sysops and users are growing increasingly concerned as more and more regulations are imposed upon BBS operations and freedoms.

The First Amendment of the U.S. Constitution is an important source of legal rights for a BBS sysop and user. Within certain limits defined by the courts, it protects speech and the press from undue governmental censorship.

> *"Congress shall make no law ... abridging the freedom of speech, or of the press ... ." (U.S. Const., Amendment I.)*

Whether a particular activity is protected speech or protected press will probably depend on the function of the BBS. Freedom of speech is most likely involved, for example, when a sysop expresses his or her personal views online, or a user participates in an online forum. Expression of one's personal views about topics such as politics, sex, or use of the controversial Clipper chip for governmental access to privately encrypted data, is considered vital in a free society.

On the other hand, freedom of the press relates more to public expression of opinions and ideas in a public medium. It is more likely applicable to a situation where a BBS acts as a publisher or republisher of third party materials online, or exercises editorial control of online remarks. If Congress should pass laws that have the practical effect of stifling expression, for example, imposing special taxes upon BBS operation, or trying to regulate the political content of a BBS, then you might expect First Amendment concerns to be raised.

Limits on First Amendment Rights

The First Amendment probably has no applicability if a user complains about censorship or other controls imposed by a sysop in a private setting. A privately owned BBS is not Congress, and a sysop under most circumstances will have the right to control what goes on the board and what is said on the board—just like a newspaper can print (or omit to print) what it chooses. The First Amendment simply doesn't apply to private censorship in private media.

While the rights of freedom of speech and of the press are deeply rooted in American legal tradition, such rights are not absolute. Take for example the classic prohibited actions—inciting a riot or uttering fighting words. You cannot falsely yell "Fire!" in a crowded theater to watch the masses panic and claim you were merely exercising your right to freedom of speech when you are charged with the misdemeanor of creating a public disturbance. One may not in the name of freedom of speech use a BBS or any other medium to disseminate obscene matter, incite a riot or create a panic, urge or advise the commission of a crime, advocate the overthrow of government by force or violence, or promote fraudulent or deceptive advertising.[2]

There are other limits to the First Amendment rights. In a broad sense, the First Amendment cannot act as a shield for illegal or unlawful activities. In one widely discussed case, *U.S. vs. Riggs,* BBS users were indicted under various federal criminal statutes for allegedly gaining unauthorized access to a telephone company computer system, downloading a copy of a file relating to emergency 911 services of the telephone company, and transferring the file to a BBS.[3] The First Amendment was of no help in getting the indictment dismissed.

On a BBS, unprotected activities include things such as stating or restating defamatory remarks, making unlawful copies of copyrighted software or images, and distributing or displaying obscene or pornographic images. Unprotected activities are not expressly defined in the First Amendment itself—courts determine the applicability of the First Amendment on a case by case basis. For example, a BBS forum that criticizes a particular vendor's computer system should be protected free speech, but a discussion that devolves into libel or a planning session for hacking into the vendor's computer system probably won't enjoy any First Amendment immunity from a civil suit for defamation or criminal prosecution for wire fraud.

Sexually Explicit Materials and the BBS World

One frequently hears mention of the First Amendment in the context of obscenity and pornography. Bulletin boards can be and have been a medium of distribution for pornography. People can upload and download sexually explicit images to a BBS or participate in sexually explicit discussions while online. Most of these are commercial boards, which only allow access for a fee. On the Internet, there are sexually-oriented discussion groups for various sexual "specialties."

But where is the limit as to what is legal or illegal? What is "obscene?" As mentioned earlier, the area of sexually explicit materials is an area where the First Amendment protections can be limited. If you plan to run a BBS that caters to prurient interests—whatever they may be—you should become familiar with the obscenity laws in your state. The government's interest in "smut peddlers" varies with the times, and if you are prosecuted you will want to know how much protection is available under the guise of free speech.

State and Federal Obscenity Laws

Although the U.S. Supreme Court categorizes sexually explicit material into "obscene" and "indecent" material, it is only the "obscene" material that goes unprotected by the First Amendment.[4] Defining what is obscene is not a simple task. It hinges on the ordinary person applying the local "community's standards" to see if the material has a "prurient interest," if it depicts or describes offensive sexual conduct, and if the material has no serious societal value. Each state has its own local statutes on obscenity, each with varying language and varied interpretations of their own local "community standards."

In addition to state laws, there are also federal laws and regulations concerning sexually explicit material that can apply to a sysop. For example, the relatively new federal child pornography statutes are designed to make it illegal for a sysop to knowingly receive, distribute or possess (more than three copies of) graphic depictions involving sexually explicit behavior with anyone under the age of 18.[5]

The key here is the sysop's *knowledge* of the material on the BBS. On the one hand, if you are running a commercial BBS with pornographic QUICKTIME child porn movies or still photos that takes money for each download, you will probably not be able to claim that you had no knowledge that the materials were on your board. On the other hand, if the occasional child porn photo finds its way onto your board, you truly did not know it was there, and you periodically monitor for such materials and remove them when you find them, you should be okay.

One of the difficulties in discussing pornography on the BBS lies in distinguishing the system operator as "victim," that is, the innocent republisher of pornography, from the system operator as "smutmeister." The operator may be, but usually is not, the original publisher of obscene materials.[6] A sysop is more generally a republisher of information and, like a bookseller,[7] should not fairly be held to know in advance the contents of files uploaded to the bulletin board. In a U.S. Supreme Court case involving a bookseller, *Smith vs. California*, the issue was whether the bookseller could be held liable for obscene material in his store absent knowledge of the contents. The Court held that he could not. "Every bookseller would be placed under an obligation to make himself aware of the contents of every book in his shop. It would be altogether unreasonable to demand so near an approach to omniscience...."[8]

The BBS sysop's dilemma is much like that of the bookseller. One must be careful, however, when considering the impact of the *Smith* case. In the circumstances surrounding an "adult" bookstore, a bookseller will more likely than not be inferred to know the contents of his merchandise. Likewise, a BBS with substantial (or majority) adult content that charges fees for downloading pornographic images is far more likely to be the subject of anti-porn criminal prosecution than a commercial BBS that only has pornographic images uploaded occasionally. It clearly is legally riskier to have specially dedicated "adult zones" on the BBS. Thus, the overall factual situation could be dispositive in the context of a bulletin board system.

The big unanswered question raised by the obscenity laws (and for that matter, by many other laws) is, to what extent must a sysop monitor and control the nature of the materials uploaded to the board? In other words, does a sysop have an affirmative duty to prevent child porn from creeping onto a BBS? Any requirement that a person act in a particular manner is called an "affirmative duty," as contrasted with a negative duty or prohibition. It is usually easier to comply with a law that states a prohibition (for example, "Thou shalt not display child porn") than a law that seems to impose an affirmative duty. Few laws actually impose affirmative duties. One obvious example is the affirmative duty to pay taxes.

The simplest answer is—if you want to be on the safe side, periodically monitor your board, for copyright violations, pornography, and stolen credit card numbers. Make sure you have a good user's agreement in place that gives you the right to monitor.

Avoiding Liability Under Obscenity Laws

As will be echoed throughout this chapter, common sense is usually of great help in staying out of trouble. What you, as a sysop, knowingly have on your BBS can get you in trouble under most obscenity statues, which are prohibitive in nature. When in doubt, ask yourself—it is really worth the risk letting this material stay on the board?

Some state obscenity laws have age limits. For example, in Georgia it is unlawful to knowingly sell or otherwise furnish or disseminate to a minor any pictures, motion pictures, books, magazines, etc. which depict sexually explicit nudity, sexual conduct, or sadomasochistic abuse.[9] A "minor" is generally a person under the age of 18, but the age limits can vary in different states. Thus, as an additional safeguard sysops should make efforts to ensure that children cannot get ready access to adult material. While it is physically impossible to watch who is logging in under a given user ID, it is a good idea to impose restrictions in the user's agreement as a condition of board usage. These restrictions can include provision of proof of age. Of course, proof of age identification can be forged, but the key here is, again, how far does the affirmative duty go?

Perhaps the safest course of action is to abide by the Federal Communications Commission (FCC) regulations on obscene or indecent telephone message services (for example, "1-900" numbers). Compliance with these regulations—which do not expressly apply to a BBS—might help establish that the sysop acted as responsibly as possible to keep minors from accessing adult materials. These rules suggest that a sysop should:

- require payment by credit card before transmission of a sexually explicit file; or
- require an authorized access or identification code before transmission of the file, making sure that
  1. the code was issued by mailing it to the applicant after reasonably ascertaining through receipt of a written application that the applicant is not under 18 years of age; and
  2. a procedure is established to immediately cancel the code of any person upon written, telephonic or other notice that the code has been lost, stolen, or used by a person or persons under the age of 18, or that the code is no longer desired; or
- scramble or encrypt the information so that it is unintelligible and incomprehensible to a person without a descrambler or decrypter.[10]

Clearly, if you make reasonable efforts to keep minors off the board, and to keep them out when they are detected, that is about the best a sysop can do and should be enough to get you off the hook for "knowing" violations.

In addition, it is a good idea to display a banner notice to users that log in to adult boards or adult areas in general access boards. For example, a banner notice similar to the following might be considered:

> WARNING—this area contains ADULT material. Persons under the age of 18 are prohibited by law from viewing or downloading materials from this area. In addition, we are prohibited from letting you see them. If you are 18 years of age or under, you MUST LOGOUT of this area immediately. The sysop reserves the right to bar access to this area and materials contained therein to persons under the age of 18, and to revoke user privileges of any person who permits his or her user ID to be used by a minor to access this area or any materials contained herein.

Again, we must provide a disclaimer—the foregoing notice has *not* been tested in court. It is offered only as a suggestion, and we make no guarantees that use of such a banner notice will get you off the hook. But, a notice like this can't hurt!

And, remember that no precautions whatsoever are going to get you off the hook if the materials on the BBS are ultimately judged obscene. If you plan to live (and run your BBS) on the edge of societal propriety, don't be surprised when the police come knocking at your door!

BBS Operation and Privacy Issues

With the now-pervasive use of electronic mail on bulletin boards and the Internet, privacy has become a primary concern. Users want to know, are my messages private? Can the sysop review them? Can the government eavesdrop on my affairs by reading my e-mail? What are my rights to privacy on a bulletin board?

Law abiding citizens generally have little to fear from government eavesdropping or e-mail interception. However, only with vigilance can we prevent our government from moving towards a "Big Brother" state. The laws of privacy are but one step away from the First Amendment. While the First Amendment might protect our right to say what we wish, privacy laws protect our thoughts. If we cannot be left in private to think about what we wish to say in public, we might never have the opportunity to express those thoughts in public. The idea of "prior restraint" has not been lost upon those who wish to impose more and more government control over the private affairs of people.

Surprisingly, there is no general right to privacy written anywhere in the U.S. Constitution. As a result, rights to privacy are generally inferred from a number of areas of the Constitution. While most people believe we all have a right to be left alone in some respects, such a right is not absolute in a society of interacting people. There are times when rights to privacy are secondary to the need for greater societal good.

Basis for the Right to Privacy

One of the Constitutional foundations for privacy comes from the Fourth Amendment right to freedom from unreasonable searches and seizures. The Fourth Amendment to the U.S. Constitution states as follows:

> *The right of the people to be secure in their persons, houses, papers, and effects, against unreasonable searches and seizures, shall not be violated, and no Warrants shall issue, but upon probable cause, supported by Oath or affirmation, and particularly describing the place to be searched, and the persons or things to be seized. (U.S. Const., Amendment IV.)*

In the United States especially, individual privacy is a significant societal value. Where else in the world can one expect, in general, to be let alone? Certainly not in the (present or former) Soviet Union, or in other socialist states. The desire to be let alone, especially in areas of religious freedom, led to the formation of this country.

Most legal scholars agree that individual privacy is protected by constitutional provisions. Many people fail to remember, however, that privacy in any organized society is not absolute, and that privacy protection represents a tradeoff—between the interests of the society in law and order and the interest of the individual to be let alone. Even in civilized society, balancing these interests against each other involves debate and political struggle.

Much of that debate revolves around the extent to which the law should protect individual privacy and balance the need for privacy against societal concerns. The United States probably is unique in drawing the line as close as it does to individuals than to the society. In 1928, Supreme Court Justice Brandeis described the right to privacy as "the right to be let alone—the most comprehensive of rights and the right most valued by civilized men."[11] Privacy may also be defined as the claim of individuals, groups, or institutions to determine for themselves when, how, and to what extent information about them is communicated to others. This aspect of privacy law primarily comes into play in connection with the gathering and selling financial information, a typical credit bureau activity.

Because we live in a society and not on an uninhabited desert island, privacy is not an absolute principle. This observation is even more significant when one realizes that a bulletin board is not always merely a communication between an individual and a computer, but can involve the shared access of a number of different individuals to a limited resource. Thus, users themselves must establish a balance between individual interests in privacy and the interests of society, or find greater government involvement in its use.

Aspects of BBS Privacy

BBS privacy issues manifest themselves in two principal aspects—privacy in telecommunications, and privacy in data collection. The right to privacy in telecommunications generally relates to the content of your communications with others. Does anyone have a right to inspect or monitor your communications with others? This right comes to mind when considering whether the information transmitted pertains to a private business transaction, or whether the information may be judged obscene or seditious. The issue is particularly significant in respect to e-mail.

The second aspect—privacy in data collection—relates to information about the *communicators*, as opposed to the communications themselves. It pertains to the collection of information about individuals. Many people perceive the accumulation and use of data about individuals to be a major threat to individual freedom. It has been reported that an Internet-accessible pornography BBS in the Netherlands collects the Internet addresses of those who logon and "publishes" the addresses as "top 50 of [sic] horny geeks".[12] Once you figure out how to capture log-in addresses, it is not much more effort to compile statistics of the number of log-ins and the areas logged into (for example, heterosexual, homosexual, pedophile). You can readily guess that governments (especially, anti-pornography prosecutors) would like to get its hands on such information, especially information about people who log in to bulletin boards that contain kiddie porn. Unsavory characters might also try to use captured addresses for blackmail purposes.

Fortunately for voyeurs who quickly conclude their business, the Netherlands BBS purportedly publishes its list of "horny geeks" mainly to punish those who spend too much time logged into their site. Excess use of a BBS is a justifiable concern that can be at least partially addressed by legitimate sanctions such as termination or blockage of the log-in privileges of the abusers. BBS abuser identification is thus one legitimate reason for address capture. Now that the Internet and many bulletin boards are (for better or worse) going commercial, there may be other legitimate, but equally unacceptable to some, reasons for capturing addresses of BBS users, such as for marketing purposes.

Capture of "caller ID" information in the telephone networks raises similar issues. Although there are a number of services that provide anonymous remailing service on the Internet, such services are of no protection against caller ID capture equipment in a commercial, telephone dial-in accessed BBS. We'll have more to say about these issues later.

As an aside, you might wonder how concerned you should be about overseas or other foreign callers. Legally, callers outside the United States are not subject to the jurisdiction of the United States courts. It is virtually impossible to prosecute foreign callers for computer crimes, unless there are national security implications associated with the caller and you can convince the appropriate authorities of the seriousness of a problem with access by foreigners. You may want to read about the case of the German Internet hacker described in the book, *The Cuckoo's Egg*.[13] This book tells an excellent and compelling story about the legal frustrations one can encounter when dealing with foreign callers.

Privacy in Telecommunications

First consider privacy of the content of communications. BBS usage involves telecommunications of at least two natures—between user and host, and between user and user via e-mail. These telecommunications are similar in many respects to simple telephone conversations. When a stand-alone BBS operates in a private manner and does not invite or facilitate intrusions, you naturally may expect it to be afforded the same protection given to any other private property.

However, if a BBS is connected to an internetwork such as the Internet, where the whole idea is communications, or offers talk forums or e-mail, different rules apply. In today's society, one is silly to expect that if a door is opened and left wide open, nobody will come in. But that is just what some people try to achieve—they open the door because they want to come and go as they please, and they are not inviting passers-by in just because they leave their door open. Most of us know that this behavior is somewhat unrealistic in a crowded, urban environment—and that perfectly describes modern telecommunications, especially the Internet environment.

Although the "front door" analogy is not strictly applicable, it does illustrate the principle, and it highlights the current movement toward encryption and security in computer communications. Such security measures are designed to allow users to come and go with (hopefully) minimal inconvenience, but to keep unwanted intruders out. Efforts presently are underway to develop and deploy Internet Privacy Enhanced Mail (PEM). If secure e-mail systems such as PEM can be implemented successfully, it will become increasingly difficult for others (including legitimate government investigators with search warrants) to come in the "door." We can expect much more activity on this front in the coming years. The recent discussions on the Clipper encryption technology illustrate this trend.

Most states define unauthorized access to a computer system as a criminal offense. Criminal laws are not, strictly speaking, privacy laws. Nonetheless, such laws often are used to enforce the right of a person to be let alone. Breaking and entering is a crime, regardless of whether you are talking about someone's house or about someone's computer system whose "door" is a telecommunications pathway. With the computer crime laws and a few separate privacy laws, society has established at least the beginnings of a zone of expected privacy and security for computer systems.

Breaking and entering a computer system (for example, obtaining unauthorized access) is, rather clearly, criminal behavior. This criminality would apply whether the burglar is seeking commercial information, trying to plant a virus, or attempting to monitor the communications (e-mail) on a mail server. After a communication leaves the originating computer system and enters the communications networks, it is a different story. The communication has left the expected zone of privacy around the originating computer; the communication is "out in the street." As all urban dwellers know, when you're in the street, you might get mugged.

Fortunately, an electronic mugging is just as unlawful as an actual physical mugging. The operator of the telecommunications provider (Tymnet, AT&T, MCI, Telenet, the local phone company, the local cable company, to name a few) has its own zone of expected privacy and security. The mugger who intercepts an Internet packet from AT&T is just as much a criminal as the mugger who has unauthorized access to the telecommunications line.

Wiretapping is a federal crime. But what about the situation where the interceptor is authorized to be there, for example, the sysop of a bulletin board or e-mail server, or the operator of a commercial service like Prodigy or CompuServe, or a law enforcement officer engaged in a criminal investigation? In some situations, authorized people have legal access to communications on their system, and they may lawfully intercept communications between various entities.

Privacy in Data Collection—Caller ID and Address Capture

The realm of data collection encompasses four principal aspects of individual and societal rights of privacy. First, is the right of the government to collect data about its citizens. Second, is the right of members of society to request and receive the data collected by the government. Third, is the right of private entities, typically businesses such as credit bureaus, to collect data about people. Finally, comes the right of individuals to ensure that privately collected data is accurate (we can't do much to stop private data collection that is lawfully performed).

Obviously, accumulating data about individuals makes little sense unless the information is to be used for some particular purpose. Valuable marketing research information can be captured with the right setup of computer and caller ID equipment, coupled with advertisements or online purchasing services. While none of us particularly cares for the notion of the Internal Revenue Service collecting information about us, society has an interest in insuring that taxes are paid (although many may disagree with this statement). Private data collection is of course different from data collection by government agencies.

Earlier, we mentioned the Internet site that gathers the e-mail addresses of visitors and displays them as "horny geeks." While collections of such data might be merely embarrassing to some people (and devastating to others), the technique has powerful technological implications. Collecting caller ID information or Internet address information about BBS visitors could have significant marketing value. Lists of callers, like lists of mailing addresses, have value to direct marketers and can often be sold for a handsome sum. Such lists are even more valuable if the addresses can be correlated with variables such as personal interests, product purchases, financial net worth, geographical location, and so forth.

Marketing uses of this information may be annoying to some people, but is generally innocuous. Other uses of this information can be more insidious—a list of callers to a pornography BBS has potential for blackmail as well as direct marketing.

The U.S. Supreme Court decided in the case of *Smith vs. Maryland*[14] that devices in telephone lines to record the number called from the line—so-called "pen registers"—did not constitute an invasion of privacy. The Court concluded that callers could have no reasonable expectation in privacy regarding the numbers called, since the numbers are communicated to the telephone company, which had the capability to record them.

Devices that identify a caller's number—sometimes called "trap and trace" and "caller ID" devices —are covered in the Electronic Communications Privacy Act (ECPA), which we discuss in greater detail later on. Federal law prohibits the use of such devices by the government without a search warrant, unless the use (1) relates to the operation and testing of the communication service, (2) records the transaction in order to prevent fraudulent use of the system, or (3) occurs with the consent of the user of the service.[15] The intent of the last exception was to allow people to employ technological means, such as caller identification services or devices, to avoid harassing or obscene calls, or ensure that important calls are not missed.

Absent caller ID, a caller may at his option disclose or decline to disclose his name or telephone number. A system that does not offer to block this disclosure clearly denigrates a sender's right to anonymity, if there is such a right. The cases decided on this privacy issue yield different results.

A case in Pennsylvania, *Barasch vs. Pennsylvania Public Utility Commission,*[16] held that telephone caller ID services violated the state's wiretapping statute, and when operated without a blocking mechanism, also violated privacy rights under federal and state constitutions. In contrast, a South Carolina court in *Southern Bell Telephone & Telegraph Co. vs. Hamm*[17] sustained a caller ID program on the ground that the public benefits of the system outweighed the limited privacy rights in the disclosure of numerical information about telephone numbers.

These two cases illustrate the current policy debate on caller ID, and could have an impact on BBS and Internet caller address gathering. If you as a sysop plan to gather caller ID information or network visitor information, be aware that the law is unsettled in this area. You may find the going easy if the Pennsylvania approach is taken, or the going rough if the South Carolina view prevails.

In addition, be aware that some state public service commissions (PSC), the regulatory bodies that govern public utilities, have regulations concerning caller ID equipment. Contact your local PSC if you plan to gather caller ID information.

Space does not permit a full exploration of these complex issues. However, the United States has several major laws on the books that govern the principal aspects of privacy in data collection. You should seek legal counsel if you have a particular problem in this area.

Expectations of Privacy

The basic constitutional provision relating to intercepted communications, at least in the case of government interceptions, comes from the Fourth Amendment. This amendment relates to the right to be protected against unreasonable searches and seizures. Generally, a governmental authority must have a warrant before it can search. Note, however, that the Fourth Amendment is intended to protect against unwanted *governmental* intrusion, and does not pertain to private action. Of course, no private person has the right to search and seize the property of another (except in certain contractual contexts), but this prohibition says nothing about the mere monitoring of telecommunications—arguably, monitoring does not amount to either a search or a seizure.

Generally, then, courts do not find a reasonable expectation of privacy from the mere use of a communication system. Indeed, there have been cases in which users of cordless and cellular telephones were found not to have a justifiable expectation of privacy for their conversations.[18] These cases are premised on the simple fact that the airwaves are public, and if you use the airwaves, you should expect that others may listen. Those who are installing wireless radio or optical data networks should be aware that it is possible for eavesdroppers to pick up the signals.

In regard to governmental monitoring or listening, two principal federal statutes apply. Both have their origins in the field of wiretapping and surveillance. One of these statutes is the Communications Act of 1934, which prohibits any action to intercept an interstate or foreign communication (by wire or radio) and divulge the communication.[19] The statute has been applied to unauthorized access to an electronic database system.[20]

The Electronic Communications Privacy Act

A second federal statute is the Electronic Communications Privacy Act of 1986 (ECPA).[21] The ECPA amended existing wiretapping laws and made the laws more clearly applicable to electronic data communications, as contrasted with traditional telephone-type wiretapping. The ECPA is not strictly limited to governmental interception. It also applies to private interception. Of all the federal laws that might affect BBS operation, the ECPA is perhaps the most significant to a sysop.

Before the wiretapping laws were amended in 1986 by the ECPA, how the law applied to pure data communications was somewhat uncertain. The 1986 amendments made it clear that the wiretapping laws apply to any form of electronic communications. The ECPA generally prohibits any unauthorized interception or disclosure of wire, oral, or electronic communications. Thus, the ECPA's focus is on data "in transit," as opposed to data that has already reached a destination, either a final destination or an interim destination such as an e-mail server. Again, the key word is "unauthorized," so consent to interception makes a different story. As we discuss later, whether the law prohibits reading e-mail on an interim server is not clear.

Unauthorized Interception of Communications

The civil and criminal liability penalties for unauthorized interception are limited to cases where some effort has been made to restrict access to the system. No criminal or civil liability exists for intercepting an electronic communication made through an electronic communication system that is configured so that such electronic communication is "readily accessible" to the general public.[22] For example, a transmission may be readily accessible if it has not been scrambled or encrypted.[23] This treatment parallels trade secret law and is analogous to the open door situation—if you put a lock on your door (encryption), you intend that the room (the communication) is private; but if you leave the door open, one may come in and browse with impunity (without criminal and civil liability).

What Is "Readily Accessible to the General Public?"

The extent to which the ECPA permits interception or access to an electronic communication on a BBS depends on whether the communication is "readily accessible to the general public."[24] The law does not specifically define what is "readily accessible to the general public" as regards a BBS; the law is defined in terms of radio communications, not BBS services.[25] The extent to which a given BBS is "readily accessible to the general public" is an open legal question. It seems logical to distinguish between a private BBS and a public BBS. An example of a private BBS is one maintained by a private business enterprise for use by its employees and/or customers. Such bulletin boards should have as much expectation of privacy as a telephone call between two people. A public BBS, on the other hand, is one that invites the public to participate, as by advertising its phone number and providing "public" areas. Expectations of privacy are somewhat less for such services.

Thus, to some degree the BBS owner can define a level of expectation of privacy with its users, and thereby defining the extent to which ECPA protections will be available to the users. Expectation of privacy (or the absence thereof) can be expressed with online notices, as well as in a user registration agreement setting out the BBS policies.

If a BBS is set up specifically to be "readily accessible to the general public," then there are fewer restrictions on sysops under the ECPA and fewer user protections. On the other hand, if a BBS is set up as private, then certain ECPA restrictions are more likely to apply.

Unauthorized Interception

The ECPA sets forth criminal and civil penalties for unauthorized interception. In the case of interception of a private satellite video or radio transmission that is not encrypted or scrambled, damages are limited to $500 or $1,000 depending upon whether the violation is a first violation and whether the interception is for tortious or commercial gain. These provisions clearly are intended for the cable and satellite TV "private pirate" situation. In other cases, damages are the greater of either the actual damages to the plaintiff and the wrongdoer's profits, or statutory damages of a maximum of $10,000.[26]

The above penalties relate to private actions against unauthorized interception. In the case of governmental interception, the ECPA places significant procedural hurdles in the way of government agencies who conduct criminal investigations. While such hurdles are consistent with the American notion of privacy under the U.S. Constitution, they do make it harder for the government to enforce the law. Basically, any government agency must obtain a warrant before intercepting a communication, be it aural (telephone) or non-aural (data communications); and to obtain a warrant, must be able to show probable cause supported by oath or affirmation, specifying the place to be searched and the things or persons to be seized. This is straight Fourth Amendment stuff, except that the ECPA may be even more restrictive.

Can They Read My E-mail?

Finally, the answer to the question that you have all been asking. Before turning to the question of how the privacy laws affect e-mail, note again that any privacy right hinges to some degree on consent. Any communication necessarily implies there are at least two parties—a sender and a recipient. Consent by either party to monitoring or wiretapping can negate the protections afforded by law. A sysop of a bulletin board, mail server, or other communications-related service may want to explore the possibility and desirability of a contractual consent to the interception or monitoring of messages that pass through their system. For example, in its User Agreement, Prodigy prohibits certain types of potentially offensive materials, but claims that it will not read your e-mail:

> The Service lets you share information with other Members. You agree not to use the Service to send, or submit for public posting, any abusive, obscene, profane, sexually explicit, threatening, or illegal material, or material containing blatant expressions of bigotry, racism or hate. Prodigy reserves the right (but is not obligated) to review and edit any material submitted for display or placed on the Service, excluding private electronic messages. Prodigy may refuse to display or may remove from the Service any material that Prodigy believes violates this Agreement or any policies or guidelines posted by Prodigy on the Service, or is harmful to other Members, to Merchants or information providers, or to the Service or the business interests of Prodigy.
>
> Prodigy will comply in all respects with the Electronic Communications Privacy Act of 1986, as amended, relating to private electronic messages on the Service. "Private electronic messages" are only those messages sent to a Member for receipt through the Service's Message Center feature. Prodigy will not inspect the contents of private electronic messages, or disclose their contents to anyone other than the writer or an intended recipient, without the consent of either the writer or an intended recipient, except as permitted or required by law.[27]

Although Prodigy did not require consent to inspection of e-mail as a condition of using the service, no apparent legal reason prohibits such a requirement. Even so, it is not clear that an e-mail server can readily circumvent the requirements of the ECPA merely by requiring consent to interception of messages as a condition of usage.

The law appears to offer no clear or consistent protection against government interception of transmissions if there is a contractual consent to interception. More and more commercial e-mail providers may be expected to utilize such consents in their user contracts, following the example of Prodigy (unless, of course, the users revolt). Commercial gateways to the Internet are in a better position than some to impose such a requirement as protection against the usage of their systems for criminal purposes. However, some governmental and educational institutions may not as readily impose contractual conditions upon usage.

Interim E-mail Servers

Based on the ECPA, a BBS user will have a reasonable expectation of privacy—at least some privacy. Any e-mail messages they send are not subject to being inspected by the government without a warrant—at least the messages are not subject to such inspection while "in transit." But what about the situation where the e-mail is stored in an interim server. And what about the e-mail service provider itself? Can these entities access and read the user's e-mail? Probably, yes.

By "interim server" we mean a service that provides "store and forward" messaging. Bulletin boards or anonymous Internet remailers that strip originating address information and replace it with the address of the remailer are serving an interim server function—they receive e-mail from an originator, hold it for a while (and perhaps modify a portion of it, such as the address), and forward it to its intended destination.

There may be no constitutional protection of e-mail messages in an interim server. The issue has yet to be considered in the courts. In most e-mail systems, messages are passed over public network facilities and often stored in a third-party computer for later access. The delayed access nature of computer systems makes the situation very different from traditional telephone or mail systems, because the service provider (the network) is the custodian of the message for at least a limited time.

In this regard, the ECPA has the following provision that appears to relate to telecommunications providers, interim e-mail servers, gateways, and the like:

> It shall not be unlawful under this chapter for an operator of a switchboard, or an officer, employee, or agent of a provider of wire or electronic communication service, whose facilities are used in the transmission of a wire communication, to intercept, disclose, or use that communication in the normal course of his employment while engaged in any activity which is a necessary incident to the rendition of his service or to the protection of the rights or property of the provider of that service, except that a provider of wire communication service to the public shall not utilize service observing or random monitoring except for mechanical or service quality control checks.[28]

This provision is the very first of a long list of exceptions to the general prohibition against unauthorized interception and disclosure of electronic communications. The provision seems to suggest that it's okay for an operator of an interim server, gateway, or other e-mail facility, to intercept communications. The permissibility of the interception is premised on the meaning of "normal course of his employment while engaged in any activity which is a necessary incident to the rendition of his service." As long as the interception occurs somewhat casually, such as while running routine deletion of e-mail messages over 180 days old, or when moving files around while conducting system maintenance, or while troubleshooting a problem, then reading the e-mail of others is probably permitted and not criminal. Thus, users of e-mail cannot have expectations of complete privacy.

Contrast this against another provision of the ECPA:

(a) Offense. Except as provided in subsection (c) of this section whoever

1. intentionally accesses without authorization a facility through which an electronic communication service is provided; or
2. intentionally exceeds an authorization to access that facility; and thereby obtains, alters, or prevents authorized access to a wire or electronic communication while it is in electronic storage in such system shall be punished as provided in subsection (b) of this section.

(c) Exceptions. Subsection (a) of this section does not apply with respect to conduct authorized—

1. by the person or entity providing a wire or electronic communications service;
2. by a user of that service with respect to a communication of or intended for that user; or

3. in section 2703, 2704 or 2518 of this title. [The latter sections relating to government wiretaps.][29]

This portion of the ECPA again is premised on the notion of "authorization," and suggests that system operators, telecommunications providers, and others who have legitimate responsibilities in connection with an "electronic communication service" are permitted to access the contents of the service. But what they can do with such access is another matter.

Another section of the ECPA relates to disclosure of the contents of electronic communications. This section, which is reproduced below, appears to prohibit disclosure of the contents of e-mail messages (or other communication) even if the person accessing the e-mail was authorized to do so:

(a) Prohibitions. Except as provided in subsection (b)

1. a person or entity providing an electronic communication service to the public shall not knowingly divulge to any person or entity the contents of a communication while in electronic storage by that service; and

2. a person or entity providing remote computing service to the public shall not knowingly divulge to any person or entity the contents of any communication which is carried or maintained on that service

   (A) on behalf of, and received by means of electronic transmission from (or created by means of computer processing of communications received by means of electronic transmission from), a subscriber or customer of such service; and

   (B) solely for the purpose of providing storage or computer processing services to such subscriber or customer, if the provider is not authorized to access the contents of any such communications for purposes of providing any services other than storage or computer processing.

(b) Exceptions. A person or entity may divulge the contents of a communications

1. to an addressee or intended recipient of such communication or an agent of such addressee or intended recipient;

2. as otherwise authorized in section 2617, 2511(2)(a), or 2703 of this title;

3. with the lawful consent of the originator or an addressee or intended recipient of such communication, or the subscriber in the case of remote computing service;

4. to a person employed or authorized or whose facilities are used to forward such communication to its destination;

5. as may be necessarily incident to the rendition of the service or to the protection of the rights or property of the provider of that service; or

6. to a law enforcement agency, if such contents

   (A) were inadvertently obtained by the service provider; and

   (B) appear to pertain to the commission of a crime.[30]

Absent specific statutory protection beyond the ECPA, which has its limitations, there is no clearly defined absolute privacy interest in e-mail, especially after it reaches an interim destination. Further, the ECPA clearly indicates that e-mail can be intercepted and read if one of the parties to the communication has consented to the interception,[31] or if the e-mail service provider is looking at the mail in furtherance of the service provider's normal administrative duties.

Some legal commentators believe that, because information on a BBS is essentially on public display, electronic mail and bulletin board systems are subject to routine inspection of their message content by law enforcement agencies without a search warrant.[32] Clearly, not everybody will agree with the conclusions of these commentators. However, it is safe to say that while users may have some privacy, it is not absolute, and that the laws are complex and wordy and in constant change.

Sysops—Delete All Messages Over 180 Days Old!

One final note about the ECPA—180 days is a magic number if you are an e-mail server. If an e-mail message has been in storage less than 180 days, a search warrant is required by a government agency to obtain the message.[33] After 180 days, however, you can be forced to produce any stored or archived messages with only a subpoena. A subpoena is much easier for a government agency to generate than a search warrant—a judge is required to sign a warrant, while a subpoena can be issued by a clerk of court. This fact provides an incentive to delete messages before they become 180 days old.

Because much of the privacy law affecting BBS operation and usage may well come from ECPA, a summary of some of the ECPA's more significant provisions may be helpful to you. The following summary of ECPA provisions affecting system operators comes from the first edition of the popular BBS legal book *SYSLAW—The Sysop's Legal Manual*:[34]

- You have a right to be protected against users who invade your system via tricks or false pretenses and destroy or tamper with messages or data.
- Law enforcement authorities must obtain a search warrant to obtain information on your system under 180 days old.
- You should have no liability to a user for wrongful disclosure as long as you are acting in response to a warrant, subpoena, or court order.
- You must not disclose information on your system that you have promised your users (via their service contracts or otherwise) will be private.
- You must provide user records, user lists, time records, etc. maintained on your system (as opposed to user messages such as e-mail) in response to a subpoena.
- The government can require you to keep a backup copy of user information, but you have to give notice to the individual whose files the government is seeking. This provision is presumably designed to ensure the survival of certain data.
- The government can obtain a gag order prohibiting you from disclosing pending legal proceedings to anyone (presumably including the press and your users). This is to keep you from jeopardizing an ongoing investigation or a trial.

As you may have perceived, the ECPA is perhaps the most dominant law affecting BBS privacy rights. If you are or plan to be a sysop, you are well advised to get a copy of the entire ECPA (we have only reproduced portions of it here).

Also be aware that there is at least one other privacy law that may affect BBS operations, the Privacy Protection Act.[35] There is discussion of this law later in the context of searches and seizures.

We have really only touched the surface of the privacy law concerns. Before shifting to the next most important area of BBS law—copyrights—we leave you with the following reminder. The ECPA is a complicated law, but if you are intelligent enough to set up and run a BBS, you are intelligent enough to read and understand the critical parts of the law. Get a copy of the ECPA and read it! If you still aren't sure what you are supposed to do, seek legal advice before you get into trouble—it's always cheaper to practice preventative legal medicine than curative legal medicine.

Copyrights and the BBS

Aside from privacy law concerns, a sysop is most likely to have copyright law concerns. Questions often asked include, who owns the materials uploaded to my BBS? What can happen if someone uploads infringing software, or images, or other copyrighted materials to my board? Must I actively police the board to remove copyright violations? The answer is usually fairly simple—the copyright owner owns the materials, and all flows from this. The presence of copyrighted materials online available for downloading is one of the classic problems in the BBS world.

While many bulletin boards are legitimate and clean running, from time to time ones hears about pirate boards offering commercial copyrighted software for downloading. In looking at how a BBS sysop can be legally responsible for such activities or even for inactivity under federal copyright law, several recent cases make it clear that a sysop who actively participates in copyright violations can be the subject of an *ex parte* seizure order. ("Ex parte" generally means, with little or no notice of hearing.) Before discussing the recent cases, we will tell you the basics about copyright law.

Basic Copyright Laws

As the name suggests, copyright laws protect against copying. Current U.S. copyright laws evolved from an 18th-century law called the Statute of Anne,[36] which was one of the first parliamentary statutes enacted in England. The statute's primary purpose was to preserve the guild/apprentice system for printers. Centuries passed before computer software was created, and then several decades went by before the copyright laws were applied to protect software. In the United States, the copyright laws did not clearly apply to computer programs until the copyright laws were amended in 1980.

Copyright law is only federal; no valid state copyright laws exist[37] (although they did at one time). The federal copyright laws give authors the right to preclude others from making unauthorized copies of original works of authorship. Copyright does not protect ideas—it only protects expressions of ideas. The distinction between ideas and expressions is not always clear, and much copyright litigation involves a dispute over what is an unprotected idea as opposed to a protected expression. In the software realm, this "idea/expression dichotomy" (a legal term you hear from copyright lawyers) has led to litigation over user interfaces—the idea for a spreadsheet program is not now protectable, but one's particular implementation (and user interface) of a spreadsheet program is, at least to some degree.

Determining the difference between the protected and unprotected aspects of a program isn't always an obvious, intuitive process. For now, suffice it to say that if you sit down and reverse-engineer the user interface of any widely marketed and popular software, instead of sitting down cold without any other programs as a guide—look out. You may well find yourself the subject of a copyright infringement lawsuit if (a) your program is successful enough to attract the attention of the company that put out the popular product, and (b) that company has enough money to pay lawyers to sue you.

This is the dilemma faced by programmers everywhere—they want to enhance the prospects for their own product's success by "emulating" the user interface of successful predecessors, but there is no easy way of knowing which of the predecessor's features are copyright protected and which are not. Legally, one is always safer if one creates new programs and user interfaces, but this approach is riskier business because the marketplace is reluctant to adapt to anything truly new.

There have been many recent court cases involving copyrights for software. A discussion of these cases is beyond the scope of this book. If you are planning a BBS for the purpose of collecting and distributing software, or chunks of reusable code, you should seek the counsel of more detailed books on copyrights, or contact a software copyright lawyer (like the author). Developing all of the themes of copyright protection for software is beyond the scope of this discussion. We will, however, hit the high points.

Elements of Copyright Law

The U.S. Copyright Act lists several basic elements for determining whether a particular work is subject to protection under the Act's provisions: the work must be (1) original, (2) a work of authorship, (3) fixed in a tangible medium of expression, and (4) one that does not extend to any idea, procedure, process, system, method of operation, concept, principle, or discovery.[38] The law gives the owner of the copyright (the owner is always the author, at least in the beginning, subject to the "work for hire" provisions) certain exclusive rights to control reproduction (that is, copying), dissemination, and adaptation of the work (that is, creation of "derivative works").[39] If a work is not copyrighted, it is in the public domain.

As mentioned above, a copyright is really a series of rights. Sysops need especially understand this concept because the existence of "shareware" and "freeware" files on most BBSs. Shareware and freeware files are not necessarily in the public domain, although they can move through a BBS without violating the author's copyright. Notices accompanying shareware and freeware files often include copyright notices and purport to reserve the claim to copyright, and grant a limited license.

Shareware generally denotes that a user can operate the software for a specified trial period after which a fee is legally required for continued use. Also, one in possession of a copy is free to make as many copies as they like, since this will promote distribution (and hopefully lead to more shareware fee income). However, the user is normally not allowed to modify the author's code or distribute the software against the terms of the special licensing agreement.

Freeware is different than shareware in that no fee is required for the user to operate the software. Rights are often purportedly retained by the author and generally noted in the licensing agreement or README file that accompanies the program.

The legal efficacy of the so-called license agreements that often accompany shareware and freeware programs in the README files or elsewhere has yet to be fully tested in the courts. Such "agreements" bear similarities to "shrink wrap" license agreements that generally accompany commercial software. Shrink-wrap contracts or licenses are often used by software vendors to impose "terms" on the sale of computer programs. Such agreements are characterized as "shrink-wrap" because of the manner in which they are a part of the package—a paper containing so-called terms of the agreement is bound up within the shrink-wrapping that often encloses the disks, CD-ROMs, and user manuals.

Shrink-wrap contracts or licenses, as well as online electronic contracts and shareware licenses, raise potential issues associated with the general commercial law doctrine of "unconscionability" and the general reluctance of courts to enforce contracts of adhesion characterized by unequal bargaining power. Unconscionability is an issue primarily arising in consumer purchases, although efforts to apply the doctrine to small businesses have been intermittently successful.[40]

Having said all this, note that we are not advising against use of shareware or freeware licenses. Rather, we are saying that they are subject to some legal doubt, and there are only a few court cases involving them.

Even files that are specifically identified as public domain may actually be copyright infringements; there is no way to tell for sure. In closing out this subject, be aware that the copyright laws are the most widely used tool for protection of computer programs, graphic images such as photos and other artwork, and multimedia. If you become aware that a particular file is an infringement, you are probably best off deleting it rather than risking multiple public downloads, which can compound the problem. Fortunately, most people who want to protect their software use the classic tool to identify the material as copyrighted—the copyright notice.

The Copyright Notice

Until recently, one had to put a copyright notice on one's work in order to flag the work as protected and invoke the copyright law. Prior to March 1989, the U.S. law required that the author of a work place a visible copyright notice (for example, © 1993 Bill Smith) before distributing the work in order to preserve copyright protection. The requirement for use of a copyright notice changed in 1989, when the United States became a signatory to a treaty known as the "Berne Convention."

Note that we said "preserve"—not "create"—copyright protection. Copyright in a work exists and attaches with creation of the work. No legal action is required for the copyright to come into existence. Rather, it used to be that you had to put the copyright notice on the work so as to prevent the work from entering the public domain.

Under the provisions of the U.S. Copyright Act implemented in connection with entry into the Berne Convention, affixation of a copyright notice is no longer required in order to preserve the copyright. Nonetheless, and mark these words keenly, putting the copyright notice on anything that even remotely may be protected by copyright law is still a very good idea. There is no law against putting copyright notice on things that are not protected, and it can't hurt.

Consider, for example, how creators of virtual reality software might display a copyright notice. How on earth can you put a copyright notice in a virtual reality space? Well, what about creating a "virtual billboard" with flashing neon lights? Such a billboard might read, "WELCOME to the COPYRIGHTED VIRTUAL WORLD OF (fill in the blank for your weird space). This virtual reality and all its aspects are © COPYRIGHT 1995 VIRTUAL DIMENSIONS, INC. ALL RIGHTS RESERVED." Or, how about a virtual pop up "copyright policeman" that comes up to you, thrusts a copyright notice and license in front of you, and requires your "virtual signature" before he allows you to pass into the world? Such scenarios are not all that far fetched.

Proper Copyright Notice

A proper copyright notice can defeat a defense that an alleged infringer copied the material innocently. And more importantly, the notice creates a practical deterrent to copying because it gives a clear signal that the owner intends to protect the work. Believe it or not, most of the world is law abiding and tries to do the right thing, so putting a copyright notice on your work helps the law-abiding person know where the line is. Besides, the small percentage of people who are going to rip you off don't pay any attention to copyright notices anyway (or to security barriers), so you don't have anything to lose by affixing a proper notice.

A proper copyright notice contains the symbol © ("c" in a circle) or the word "Copyright," followed by the year of first publication, followed by the name of the owner of the copyright.[41] You often see the follow-up language "All rights reserved," which is acceptable but not required.

Where do you place the notice? The law does make registration of a claim to copyright and deposit of certain material important in enforcing a copyright claim, and affixation of notice in the manner set forth in the copyright rules facilitates registration. Current regulations allow placement of the copyright notice in one or more of the following locations: (1) notice embedded in the copy (for example, in the source or object code), so that it is visible on perceptible printouts, either with or near the title, or at the end of the work; (2) notice displayed on a user's terminal or computer screen at sign up or boot up; (3) notice continuously displayed on the terminal or screen; or (4) labels or printing directly on media or containers for the media.[42] Preferably, if you want to claim copyright you put the copyright notice in some or even all of these areas.

Copywrong? Copyleft?

If you do *not* want to claim copyright, then you may well have to affix a notice to the effect that the work is not copyrighted and may be freely copied. One thing the Berne Convention did to confuse things in the United States was to make it more difficult for authors to communicate that they don't want to treat something as copyrighted. However, this situation does not happen very often in a modern, free-market-based, technological society—most people want all the protection they can get.

If someone wants his or her works to be freely available to all, he or she should say so clearly; use a *non*-copyright notice such as "Not copyrighted—this work is not copyrighted by the author and may be freely copied and distributed without permission." You might want to check out and obtain materials from the Free Software Foundation (FSF),[43] an organization that is philosophically opposed to legal protection for software. The FSF scheme of non-copyright-protection, which some have dubbed "copyleft," has yet to be tested in the courts, but provides a framework for those who are of a like mind with the FSF.

Copyright Registration

Although registration of the claim to copyright is not a condition of obtaining or retaining a valid copyright, registration (like copyright notice) is a good idea if you really are serious about copyright protection. A prior registration is a "ticket to court;" that is, it is a jurisdictional requirement.[44] You must have your ticket before you can invoke the power of the court. After the Berne Convention, however, the registration requirement applies only to works that originated in the United States. For works published in other Berne Convention countries for which enforcement of the copyright is sought, registration is optional. In any case, registration is preferable because it definitely eases the way into court.

Registration serves as *prima facie* (that is, "on its face") proof of the validity of the copyright and of the accuracy of the matters stated in the registration certificate.[45] Facts stated in a registration are rebuttable in a lawsuit at trial, but having the presumption in your favor means that your opponent bears the burden of proof on the particular matter. Presumptions are always preferable in a legal matter, because they guarantee that you automatically win if your opponent does not come up with sufficient evidence to rebut the presumption.

Getting a registration is relatively easy—fill out a form (Form TX for a computer program), pay a $20 filing fee, and submit the filled-out form and filing fee with appropriate deposit materials to the Register of Copyrights. You can generally do it yourself, without the assistance of a lawyer (assuming, of course, that you have figured out what you are doing and are prepared to take the risk of something going wrong).

What "deposit materials" are required? Under current Copyright Office regulations, deposit materials for computer programs in machine readable copies from which the works cannot ordinarily be perceived without the aid of a machine comprise one copy of "identifying portions" of the program.[46] The purpose of such "identifying portions" is nominally to allow the Copyright Office to determine whether the work constitutes copyrightable authorship. In enforcement proceedings, the identifying materials are often used to piece together the whole program as evidence used at trial (because you do not normally deposit the entire program, if you can help it). For software, deposit materials consisting of "identifying portions" typically consist of the first 25 and last 25 pages of a source code printout of the work.

The Copyright Office accepts other types of printouts for deposit material, but you clearly should try to come up with some type of a source code printout. Deposit materials other than the "first and last 25" may result in a registration under the so-called "rule of doubt," which means that you do not get the benefit of the legal presumptions we discussed earlier.

Copyrights and Trade Secrets

As some readers will know, many computer programs are treated as trade secrets. In particular, the source codes of most programs are treated as trade secrets, because skilled programmers can learn a lot about how a program operates by analyzing source code (well, very skilled programmers can learn from object code, but that undertaking is a lot more difficult).

The Copyright rules contain provisions for deposit of "trade secret" material as the identifying material of a program. These provisions allow the deposit of various other types of identifying material, such as the first and last 25 pages of source code with some portions blocked out, the first and last 10 pages of source code with no portions blocked out, the first and last 25 pages of *object* code plus any 10 pages of source code with no portions blocked out, or at least fifty percent of a program whose length is less than 25 pages total.[47] As mentioned earlier, however, using anything other than the "first 25, last 25 pages of source code" rule as deposit materials generally results in a registration under the rule of doubt.

Copyrightability of Databases

One aspect of copyright law that is particularly significant for BBS operators that offer access to proprietary collections of information on databases is the applicability of copyright to such databases. Just because you can access a database does not mean that you may freely download the whole thing. This limitation is true even if a user's modem and communications line is fast enough to do it without attracting attention, and even if the user splits up his online sessions and only downloads a piece of the database at a time. Databases, in short, are copyrightable subject matter. (Well, people generally thought they were copyrightable until recent court cases cast doubt on the extent of the protection; see the BellSouth case following.)

Databases are typically viewed as "compilations" under copyright law. A "compilation" is a "work formed by the collection and assembling of preexisting materials or of data that are selected, coordinated, or arranged in such a way that the resulting work as a whole constitutes an original work of authorship."[48] Copyrightability of a database does not depend upon any one entry in the database being copyrightable. Rather, copyrightability derives from the selection or arrangement of the database items.

Use of the information in a database typically is permitted by the database proprietor, particularly where the user pays a fee to access the database (for example, LEXIS, NEXIS, and DIALOG are three commercially available databases for which the database owner or gateway control system charges a fee to access). On the Internet, many data sources don't, or can't, charge a fee; the lack of a fee, however, does not mean that the database is not legally protected.

Any use of a database must be considered a "fair use" in order to avoid legal liability for copying the information from the database. Under the U.S. Copyright laws, "fair use" of a copyrighted work is not considered an infringement. Determining just what constitutes "fair use," however, is not easy. The copyright law has no specific definition of fair use; rather, there is a legal test for fair use that is intended to be flexible and reflect equitable considerations. The law states a non-exclusive list of factors to be considered in deciding whether a particular use of a copyrighted work is fair. The list includes such factors as (1) the purpose and character of the work (for example, is the work specifically intended for commercial purposes, to make money for the owner?), (2) the nature of the copyrighted work, (3) the amount or proportion of the original work that is used (copying the whole work is much more likely *not* to be fair use), and (4) the effect of the copying on the potential market for or value of the copyrighted work.[49]

As you may discern, these factors do not really tell one how to decide if one's usage is a fair use or not. A number of recent court cases involving the copying of telephone directories have highlighted the difficulty of determining fair use.[50] Telephone directories are essentially databases published in paper media, whereas computer databases are "published" in electronic media. Although certain information in the databases might be public domain (such as the simple name and address, and phone number in YELLOW PAGE listings), the database proprietors have invested enormous sums selecting, coordinating, and arranging the data so that it is usable. Obviously, the database proprietors want to ensure that the data is used in a manner that serves to protect their huge investments. Consequently, people who copy the telephone directories to produce competing directories have had to fight in court over the question as to how much usage of the directory constitutes fair use and how much constitutes unlawful copying.

The recent U.S. Supreme Court case of *Feist Publications vs. Rural Telephone Service*[51] has cast serious doubt on the protectability of databases. Prior to this case, many courts recognized that effort in gathering information and putting it in a database should be protected. Such courts applied what was called the "sweat of the brow" test for copyrightability. The *Feist* case arguably removed the "sweat of the brow" doctrine from the law.

The *Feist* case concerned an alphabetically arranged telephone directory compiled and published by the Rural Telephone Service Company, a state-regulated public utility in Kansas. Feist Publications, a private enterprise, produced an area-wide directory covering a number of different areas, including Rural Telephone's. Feist, since it was a publisher and not a utility, had to get its information from somewhere. Feist offered to buy rights to Rural Telephone's list of subscribers, but Rural Telephone refused. Feist decided to use Rural Telephone's listings in its directory without Rural Telephone's consent. Rural Telephone, after it learned of inclusion of a portion of its listings in the Feist directory (likely because Rural Telephone had planted a number of fictitious listings to detect copying), sued for copyright infringement, and ultimately lost.

The U.S. Supreme Court, in this most recent pronouncement in the realm of copyright law, had to reconcile two well-established but conflicting legal propositions: (i) that facts themselves (e.g. mere names and telephone numbers) are not copyrightable, but (ii) compilations of facts generally are.[52] There is a tension between these two propositions, and, according to the Supreme Court, this tension resulted in the development in some lower courts of an impermissible theory to justify protection of factual compilations. The underlying notion of this theory—the "sweat of the brow" test—was that copyright was a reward for the hard work that went into compiling the facts.

The Supreme Court held that Rural Telephone's directory was a garden-variety white pages directory, devoid of even the slightest trace of creativity. It lacked the "originality" required by the copyright law. Rural did not "select"[53] which names, addresses, and telephone numbers of subscribers to publish, having been required to do so by the Kansas public service commission. Thus, the directory was not copyrightable, and Feist was free to copy it.

The current stated test for copyrightability is "originality"—however it is determined—and not the effort expended in creating the compilation. In order to be protected under the recent court decisions, a work must demonstrate some "minimal degree of creativity." What constitutes a "minimal degree of creativity" may be difficult to figure out; the use of headings and other arrangement organizers were held not to meet the test in later circuit court cases.[54]

The implication of the *Feist* case for database suppliers is that fact-based databases, and much of the information in them as well as much of the format or arrangement of the information (for example, selection of which fields to put in which order, and so on) may not be protectable. More litigation concerning the protectability of databases is likely in the near future.

After all the recent cases, it stills seems that the more of a work that a user copies or uses, the more likely will the use not be considered a fair use. Downloading an entire database, unless that database is clearly marked as unprotected (which is rare), in all likelihood will not be a fair use.

Derivative Works

Another copyright issue that users may face when obtaining and using information downloaded from a BBS is the right to modify that work. Let us suppose that a BBS host contains a shared software area containing lots of C++ routines. Let us further suppose that there is no clear marking that any of the routines are copyrighted, or that anything on that BBS (except for obvious things such as the operating system and commercial software that you can access) is copyrighted. Can subscribers use the routines "as is?" Can they modify the routines and use them?

We have already answered the first of these questions. Even without a copyright notice the routines are copyrightable subject matter under post-Berne Convention law. If users want to use the routines in a commercial product, they'd better obtain permission from the author or other owner. Otherwise, they (and you as the sysop) may be subject to a lawsuit for copyright infringement.

The question of modifying the works raises slightly different problems, but many of the same considerations apply. In a nutshell, one needs permission from the author to modify, then use the routines. The copyright law gives the owner of the copyright the exclusive right to prepare "derivative works."[55] A derivative work is a work that is based upon one or more preexisting works.[56] For example, the screenplay for a movie based on a popular novel is a derivative work, as are the publication of a Spanish-language translation of the novel and the publication of an abridged paperback edition. Creation of a series of prints from an original oil painting is also a derivative work. Software modules and objects that can be modified and reused are likely going to be considered derivative works.

One curious thing about derivative works is that they can have plural authors, and more than one copyright can attach to the work. A derivative work qualifies as a separate, copyrightable work with respect to the new material and expression it contains. If the author of a copyrighted first work gives a second author permission to prepare a derivative work of a computer program by copying the first work and by adding to or modifying it, the resultant second work becomes a work of authorship copyrightable by the second author. Further, because the first work is copyrighted, the copyrights of both the first author and the second author attach to the work.

Note

You need permission of the first author before you can prepare a derivative work. Programmers have no legal right to modify another's copyrighted software, whether or not they have any commercial purpose in mind.

Technically speaking, you don't even have the right to modify a copyrighted program for your own private purpose. The law recognizes that the author's ability to benefit from the market for enhancements and updates may be diminished if users are free to make modifications in the author's original work.

Even so, the fair use provisions should excuse most modifications made entirely for personal non-commercial use. For example, if you add or delete certain program functions, or make changes to enhance the speed of performance or minimize storage requirements, you have made a derivative work. If you don't have permission from the copyright owner to make the modifications, you are technically a copyright infringer. Even though the likelihood of a legal problem is relatively small if you keep your modifications private, you are technically in violation of the law unless your usage is excused under one or more of the fair use exceptions.

Backups

Assuming that you are legally permitted to download copyrighted material (a program, graphics, data from a database, and so on), you have certain rights to use that material. No discussion of copyrights relating to the computer area would be complete without a consideration of the copyright implications of backups. The copyright laws grant the owner of a copy of a computer program rights to additional copies under certain conditions. The law presupposes you are an "owner" of a copy. The law's protection does not apply if you have obtained a copy unlawfully.

Section 117 of the Copyright Act grants the owner of a copy of a computer program a limited right to make an additional archival copy and to adapt the program notwithstanding the exclusive rights of the author. You are entitled to prepare a copy of the program as an "essential step" in using the program on a computer—after all, when you load a program from disk into RAM, you have made another copy! You then have two copies in existence at the same time. Without Section 117, you would be an infringer for making the second copy, but it is impractical (no—**impossible** with present day computers) to run the program without loading at least some of it in RAM.

You can also make a copy for "archival purposes" (that is, make a backup). Under the law, you technically cannot make multiple backups, although doing so is purportedly a widespread practice. Again, the likelihood of a legal problem with multiple backups is low, as long as the number of backups is small and the backup media are placed in safe storage and are not used. The practice adopted by some computer installations of rotating backups for each day of the week (with five different disk cartridges used on a rotating basis, with one or two cartridges used for weekly and monthly backups) is not strictly legal under current copyright laws. While the practice is acceptable (and recommended) for data backups, it is on the borderline between copyright infringement and fair use respecting copyrighted application and operating system software.

Copies made pursuant to the provisions of Section 117 may be transferred without permission of the copyright owner as long as all rights in the copy are transferred to another person. In these circumstances, you are supposed to destroy the backup when you transfer your copy to another person. The common practice of selling used personal computers "loaded with lots of software" is unlawful unless the seller also parts with all the original disks, manuals, and so on and does not retain any part of the original works.

Works For Hire

The final subject for our copyright discussion is that of "works made for hire." This issue comes up often in discussions of ownership of programs that are created on a contract basis. A contract programmer who is *not* an employee of the people for whom he or she works needs to know about the work-for-hire provisions of the copyright law. We can expect that as BBS usage expands, and people use them to telecommute (in particular, by creating copyrightable works on their own computer systems, communicating via e-mail with those who hire them, and even distributing the resultant works via file transfers), work-for-hire questions will come up.

In short, if you are an independent contractor, *not an employee*, and you create a copyrighted work for another, even if you are paid for the work, you are the owner of the work. An independent contractor owns the rights in his or her work. If you are an employee and you create a work within the scope of your employment, your employer owns the work as a "work made for hire."[57] In these circumstances, the employer is deemed the author, even though you as the programmer actually wrote the work.

If the indicia of an employment relationship are not present, then the relationship is probably that of an independent contractor. The common law concept of an independent contractor relationship is one in which the hiring party does not control the details of the work performance and has only the right to accept or reject the finished product. In contrast, an employee relationship is one in which the employer directs and controls the manner in which the work is performed.

The working relationship between an employer and employee is much closer than that between a hiring party and an independent contractor. If you are the proverbial programmer who writes code from the mountain top, based only on the spec provided by the hiring party, you pay your own medical and workers' compensation insurance, you pay estimated taxes instead of having them withheld by another, and so on, then you probably are an independent contractor. Recent court cases have elaborated on the types of factors considered in determining whether a work is one made for hire.[58] You should consult the cases or your lawyer if you need more guidance.

As mentioned, the U.S. Copyright Act treats the employer as the author of works created by its employees within the scope of their employment. In addition, the law defines certain types of specially commissioned works as work for hire.[59] These specially commissioned works, such as contributions to a collective work, parts of a motion picture or audiovisual work, compilations, translations, supplementary works, instructional texts, tests, answer materials for tests, and atlases can be works for hire and owned (and authored) by the hiring party only if a written agreement specifically states that the works are expressly agreed to be works for hire.

Oddly, the list does *not* include computer programs *per se*, which are one of the most widely commissioned types of copyrightable subjects today. However, several of the items in the list may be parts of multimedia works, for example, contributions to a collective CD-ROM comprising a number of different scenarios, parts of a motion picture on the CD-ROM, and so on. People involved with multimedia projects thus should pay particular attention to the work-for-hire provisions.

Because computer programs are not automatically works for hire, they are owned by an independent contractor, absent an outright assignment to the hiring party. In case of any doubt, the independent contractor probably owns the program. Legal agreements involving computer programs and other works not on the list often include language to clarify that particular works are works made for hire and owned by the hiring party, and if for some reason such works are not considered works made for hire, the creating party/hired party assigns all of his or her right, title, and interest in and to the work to the hiring party in perpetuity. Legal agreements include such language to make it clear that the hiring party intends to be the owner and legal author (if not the actual author) of the work.

Thus, if you are a hiring party and want to own rights in the works you pay for, you'd better get an agreement that includes copyright assignment language. If you are an independent contractor and want to retain ownership of your works, you'd better make sure you are not assigning title to your works to the hiring party. Remember, just because someone paid for the work does not mean that he or she owns it! The copyright laws govern on this issue.

Direct Copyright Infringement

Now that we know how copyrights are created, let us consider how copyrights are enforced. Copyright infringement occurs when someone violates the exclusive rights of the copyright owner. Infringement can be "direct" or "indirect." Direct copyright infringement occurs when one actively participates in the unlawful copying. Indirect copyright infringement is usually referred to as "contributory" infringement. The law says that one who with knowledge of the infringing activity of another, induces, causes or materially contributes to the infringing conduct, may be held liable as a contributory infringer.[60] Sysops who turn a blind eye to copying can get in trouble here.

Recently, a Sega games BBS sysop was the subject of a preliminary injunction for being a contributory infringer of Sega video games uploaded to his BBS. In this case, *Sega Enterprises vs. Maphia,*[61] the sysop operated a BBS where Sega games were uploaded by certain users, after which the games could be downloaded to any number of other users. We will have more about this case later, since it directly affects sysops.

To show copyright infringement, one must prove (1) ownership of a valid copyright in the infringed work, and (2) copying.[62] Downloading to make more copies is unauthorized copying; downloading copyrighted computer programs has been held to be fundamentally an infringement of the copyright.[63]

A good example comes from the recent case of *Playboy Enterprises, Inc. vs. Frena.*[64] In this case, a sysop was held to have knowingly distributed unauthorized copies of copyrighted images that were scanned from *Playboy* magazine and then uploaded onto the sysop's BBS. The court held that the sysop violated *Playboy's* copyright by distributing the unauthorized copies and by allowing unauthorized display of the copyrighted images to subscribers as a public display.

The Defense of Fair Use

A common defense in copyright infringement suits is "fair use." Saying that the copying was "fair use" is admission of copying, except that the defendant takes the position that the copying is allowed under certain circumstances. The Copyright Act does not specifically define what a "fair use" is, but it specifies four statutory factors to be considered, on a case-by-case basis:[65]

- *The purpose and character of the use.* The first factor is the purpose and character of the use. The principal aspect of this factor is whether the use is for commercial or non-profit purposes. BBS access for a fee or in exchange for buying products was found to be for profit in the *Playboy Enterprises* case, even though users made personal use of the material.
- *Nature of the copyrighted work.* The second factor is the nature of the copyrighted work. Copyright protection is greater for works of fiction or fantasy (like Playboy images or game software), as opposed to factual works.
- *Amount of copying.* The third factor is the amount and substantiality of the portion copied in relation to the copyrighted work as a whole. What this amounts to is that a small degree of taking may be excused, but copying the whole is not.
- *Effect of the copying on the market.* The last factor is the effect of the use on the potential market for or value of work. This is the most important factor and weighs heaviest in determining if the use if fair or not.

Lack of Intent to Infringe Is Not a Defense

Simply stated, one's lack of intent to infringe a copyright is not a defense against liability, although it may help in reducing damages. Intent is not an element of copyright infringement; even an innocent infringer can be liable. Innocence (that is, lack of intent) is only significant to a trial court when it fixes statutory damages,[66] which are a type of damages that can be imposed by a court when actual damages for copyright infringement cannot readily be proven. This fact came as quite a shock to the sysop in the *Playboy Enterprises* case, who raised the defense unsuccessfully.

How To Avoid Liability for Copyright Infringement

Avoiding liability for direct infringement is pretty easy—don't make unauthorized copies of copyrighted software. Generally, honest sysops should have little to worry about because only their direct activities constitute direct copyright infringement. Contributory infringement is a different story. The *Playboy* and *Sega* cases might be interpreted to create a possible affirmative duty for sysops to look for and delete unauthorized copies of copyrighted works from their BBS.

The extent of the affirmative duty is not clear in the law. In the *Playboy* case the sysop knew there were copyrighted works available for downloading; the sysop even edited the images and put them back on the BBS. Likewise in the *Sega* case—the sysop was involved with other people selling copiers that permitted game play from a diskette without a Sega cartridge. Free download time was offered to subscribers who purchased game copiers, and this indicated knowledge of the infringing activity.

Thus, aside from the common sense advise of "don't copy a copyrighted work," sysops who want to steer clear of copyright trouble may want to consider posting warnings for users at sign-on and during user registration that no copyrighted software will be allowed to be uploaded. Should a sysop find unauthorized copies of copyrighted works, he or she may want to go the next step—take the material off the BBS and contact the user. If such activity continues, the sysop may want to consider revocation of the offender's access to the BBS.

A charge of contributory copyright infringement is a greater risk for an honest sysop than a charge of direct infringement. In the *Sega* case, a preliminary injunction and seizure order was issued. During the pendency of the action, the software, programs, data, memory, duplicating and decoding and computer machines, and other infringing merchandise were impounded, and the sysops were enjoined from a number of activities. In short, they were put out of business. Theoretically, they can get their stuff back—if they win the case. Practically, issuance of a preliminary injunction is most often the end of the matter. Once your equipment is gone and you are prohibited from the work to which you have become accustomed, you are going to have to find something else to do to make a living.

The facts of the *Sega* case suggest that a BBS that tries to avoid trouble, as opposed to walk a fine line, is at little risk. The BBS offering downloadable video games was linked to another BBS that sold "copiers" designed specifically to copy Sega game software from the ROMs in the games cartridge onto a normal computer disk. The BBS, perhaps unwisely named "MAPHIA," charged users a fee or bundled online time with the sale of a "copier." The sysops also specifically solicited copying and uploading of illicitly copied games so that others could download them. The following is an excerpt from the case which shows what the court viewed as evidence of inducement:

> Thank you for purchasing a Console Back Up Unit [copier] from PARSEC TRADING. As a free bonus for ordering from Dark Age, you receive a COMPLEMENTARY Free Download Ratio on our Customer Support BBS. This is if you cannot get ahold of SuperNintendo or Sega Genesis games. You can download up to 10 megabytes, which is equal to approximately 20 normal sized SuperNintendo or Genesis Games. After your 10 megabytes is used, you can purchase full months of credit for only $35/month. You can also prepay and order either 1 year of free downloads for $200/year, or a lifetime of free downloads for only $500.

It is apparent from reading the court decision that the sysop's participation in the scheme was so pervasive that contributory infringement was easy to find. Operators of bulletin boards that wish to operate close to the line may expect to be "at risk" of seizure, and should not be surprised when the marshal comes knocking on the door.

Most importantly, sysops should use some common sense. Knowledge of infringing activity plus inducing or contributing to the infringement does not normally occur by accident. The key for a sysop who wants to run a clean board is to act upon any glimmer of infringing activity. A sysop should not just sit idly by if unauthorized copies of copyrighted works are found on the BBS. A copyright owner is halfway to nailing the sysop for contributory copyright infringement once the sysop has knowledge of infringing activities.

However, knowledge alone should not make the sysop liable—there is still the "contribute" part of the equation. Knowledge of occasional infringements plus mere inactivity alone should not subject a sysop to copyright infringement liability—as long as the sysop does not participate in the infringing scheme. There was clear evidence of the sysop's participation in the scheme in the *Sega* case—Sega easily convinced the court that the MAPHIA sysop was wearing the "black hat" of the bad guy. However, the extent to which there is participation amounting to "inducing, causing or materially contributing to the infringing conduct" will be determined on a case-by-case basis. It can be expensive to find out in court just how much (or little) participation is required.

We expect that copyright owners will continue to press cases that seemingly involve little evidence of participation by sysops. The next step beyond the *Sega* case will be the charge of contributory infringement against a sysop who knows that unauthorized copies are being uploaded and downloaded, but does nothing to prevent it, thereby (so the argument will go) "materially contributing" to the infringing activity. If this next legal step is taken in the courts, the legal effect will be the creation of an affirmative duty on the part of the sysop to monitor the board and delete infringing materials—effectively making a sysop a "copyright owner's policeman." While this is not yet the law, it may well be some day.

Copyright Summary

To be on the safe side, sysops should periodically review the contents of their BBS for what looks like unauthorized copies of copyrighted material. This is not currently required by law and is controversial—we are suggesting "should," not "must." However, activist sysops who keep their boards clean are far less likely to get in trouble than those who turn a blind eye to suspicious activity. Again, the users should be warned of the sysop's rights to review and inspect by means of the user registration agreement. It does not hurt to wear the good guy's white hat!

Liabilities from Other Areas of Law

Although copyright is perhaps the main area of interest to BBS sysops as regards to illegal or illicit materials on their BBS (aside from pornography), a few other legal topics are worthy of mention. Trademark law and unfair competition laws have recently surfaced in these BBS sysops cases, and are frequently seen together in the same lawsuits with copyright law actions.

Most of the BBS cases involving trademark issues appear to have trademark infringement added as an afterthought—a plaintiff (like Sega Enterprises) throws in a trademark infringement count to the lawsuit just in case a more important count (like copyright infringement) runs into trouble. This is exactly what happened in the *Sega* case. Cautious sysops should take certain precautions regarding the trademark rights of others.

Trademark Infringement and Unfair Competition

On occasion, sysops may encounter the trademark laws and the related legal area of unfair competition. These areas of the law are not as likely to be a problem as other areas such as copyright, defamation, and obscenity, but problems do occur from time to time. Often, a trademark infringement complaint is coupled with a copyright infringement complaint to provide a "backup" legal theory for a lawsuit. We will explore these areas of the law briefly.

Trademark Law and Trademark Infringement Basics

Trademarks are distinctive words or phrases used to distinguish a trademark owner's goods from the goods of others in the marketplace. Trademarks serve to inform consumers of the source of the goods and also function as an advertisement. Many companies invest a great deal of time and money building up "good will" in their trademarks and consequently will defend them vigorously against any infringement.

A trademark needs to be distinctive in order to be valid. The U.S. Supreme Court has held there to be varying categories of distinctiveness.[67] These categories are as follows, in increasing order of distinctiveness: (1) generic, (2) descriptive, (3) suggestive, and (4) arbitrary or fanciful. Distinctiveness inheres when the trademark can be considered suggestive, arbitrary, or fanciful. It can also rise to the level of distinctiveness when a descriptive trademark gains "secondary meaning" in the marketplace. "Secondary meaning" is an abstract legal concept that means that the mark has come to be recognized as a trademark, even though it might otherwise be viewed as somewhat (or entirely) descriptive.

As examples, the trademark SPLORK for a soft drink (a name which we just made up) would be distinctive because it is a coined and therefore arbitrary term. Likewise, APPLE for computers is distinctive because it is arbitrary—what does an apple have to do with a computer? The term DOWNY for a fabric softener is considered suggestive, while QUICKOILCHANGE for a motor oil changing service would probably be considered merely descriptive (and unprotectable). Finally, a term such as BEEF for hamburgers goes all the way to the generic and totally unprotectable end of the spectrum—it doesn't merely *describe* the stuff, it *is* the stuff!

As an aside, even highly distinctive trademarks like the famous coined words XEROX, NYLON, and ASPIRIN can lose their distinctiveness and become generic. XEROX has probably been saved as a trademark for photocopiers—you have probably seen the XEROX ads that urge people not to use the word in a generic fashion (e.g., they don't want you to say "please xerox this paper"). NYLON and ASPIRIN were lost to the public domain long ago because of widespread and uncontrolled generic use.

In order to find trademark infringement, a court must find there to be a "likelihood of confusion" between the source of goods in the marketplace. A *prima facie* (that is, "on its face") case for trademark infringement under the federal laws is established by showing (1) that a trademark is owned by or associated with a particular plaintiff, and (2) that a defendant's use of the mark is likely to cause confusion or mistake among the public.[68] There is no need for a plaintiff to prove any actual mistake or confusion; all that is required is the ephemeral "likelihood of confusion."

Courts have established factors that are relevant to a determination of the likelihood of confusion. Not all the factors are required, and the importance of each factor varies with jurisdiction.[69] The factors include: (1) the type of trademark at issue, (2) the similarity of the trademarks, (3) the similarity of products or services, (4) the identity of purchasers and the similarity of retail outlets, (5) the defendant's intent, and (6) any actual confusion in the marketplace of the source of goods. "Actual confusion" is just what it sounds like—a person is actually confused by the marks of two different companies and exhibits that confusion by purchasing one product thinking it was another product, or (as more often happens) trying to return a product or ask questions about a product to the wrong company. Such "actual confusion" evidence can be compelling in a trademark infringement lawsuit.

Recent BBS Cases Involving Alleged Trademark Infringement

In the *Playboy* case previously mentioned, the words "Playboy" and "Playmate," which happen to be federally registered trademarks, were used on the BBS as file descriptors to identify files containing certain images (scanned and often edited images from *Playboy* magazine). The defendant sysop contended that he himself never placed the words Playboy or Playmate onto the BBS; rather, people who uploaded the materials used the terms as file descriptors. He further claimed that he innocently and without malice allowed subscribers to upload whatever they wanted onto his BBS. Needless to say, the court was not persuaded by his proclaimed innocence.

In the *Sega* case, the court stretched a bit to find a likelihood of confusion. It seems more likely that Sega threw in a trademark infringement count just in case its copyright infringement case ran into problems. Games copied from the MAPHIA BBS displayed Sega's registered trademark SEGA and the Sega logo on the screen when the games were played, but were no longer in their original game cartridges. The court found a likelihood of confusion by holding that confusion, if not on the part of the BBS users, was inevitable on the part of third parties who may see the copied game after it entered commerce.

The upshot of these cases is as follows—the mere display of the trademark of another in association with something that does not originate with the trademark owner (which usually occurs when the trademark owner does not receive a financial benefit) is trademark infringement. Although the uploaded images and games originated with the trademark owners (who happened to be copyright owners as well), Sega and Playboy did not get money from the further promulgation of the games and images. Needless to say, they did not like this.

Although the copyright law would have been sufficient to reach the desired result—shutting down the BBS—trademark theories are often used as an adjunct theory.

Unfair Competition

Unfair competition is closely related to trademark law. It uses the same test as trademark law—likelihood of confusion—but unfair competition protects against a broader range of deceptive or unfair trade practices than simple trademark infringement. Section 43(a) of the Lanham Act defines the federal unfair competition law to be violated when making false statements or creating a false impression of a product including false designation of origin.[70] There are several court-made species of unfair competition activities—common law trademark infringement (that is, when there is no federal trademark registration involved), false advertising, trade dress infringement (for example, emulating product or package appearance), character rights, passing off, palming off, and reverse palming off. Some of these activities were found in the *Playboy* and *Sega* cases.

Recent BBS Applications of Unfair Competition

In the *Playboy* case, the sysop edited the scanned images by putting his BBS name, logo, and BBS phone number on certain images after removing some text and the *Playboy* trademark from the image. According to the court, the altered images made it look like the sysop was attempting to take credit for *Playboy's* work, and denied *Playboy* the right to public credit for the success and quality of its goods. This was found to constitute falsely inferring and describing the origin of the images. Removal of *Playboy's* trademarks from the scanned photos was found to constitute "reverse passing off," which is a species of unfair competition.

In the *Sega* case, the court found that Sega established a *prima facie* case of federal unfair competition and false designation of origin, based on the same facts giving rise to the federal trademark infringement.

Defamation

Libel and slander, which are both species of defamation, are state laws. Many people associate this kind of private or civil wrong with just newspaper tabloids, yet the scope of the law is broader. A libelous statement is a printed, injurious falsehood. A slander is an injurious falsehood that is spoken. On a BBS, for example, defamatory statements may be found in the public message areas or even in electronic newsletters. Generally, the media (newspapers and television) are not liable for publishing false statements about "public figures" (famous people), unless they act recklessly or maliciously in publishing the statements. BBS sysops should be entitled to the same immunity, especially when the defamatory statements are made by callers and not by the sysop. The media is liable, however, for publishing false statements about private individuals.

As in the case of pornography, one of the difficulties in discussing defamation lies in distinguishing a system operator as an innocent republisher of a defamation from a system operator as initial defamer. The operator may be, but usually is not, the original publisher of an alleged defamation. As discussed in connection with obscene materials, a BBS sysop's dilemma is much like that of the bookseller, whether we are talking about obscene material or defamatory material. Again, it gives rise to the question of whether the sysop has an affirmative duty to police the board, in this context for defamatory material.

As a publisher, a sysop faces the same risk of a lawsuit for defamation as any other speaker or publisher, due to the greater amount of editorial control of what actually gets published. This can be in the form of a sysop electronic newsletter or even a compilation of edited comments from BBS message logs.

As republisher, a sysop distributes or promulgates previously published materials, such as electronic mail, discussion forums, or text files. Depending on the particular state laws, a repeater or republisher of defamatory matter can be liable as well.

The case of *Cubby, Inc. vs. CompuServe Inc.*[71] involved an action against the well-known computer service CompuServe for alleged libel, business disparagement, and unfair competition. Fortunately for CompuServe, the court held, in granting a motion for summary judgment, that CompuServe was a mere "distributor" of information, and could not be held liable for defamatory statements made in news publications, absent a showing that it knew or had reason to know of the defamation. The court stated the general rule (in New York, where the case was tried) that one who repeats or otherwise republishes defamatory matter is subject to liability for defamation as if he had originally published it. With respect to entities such as news vendors, bookstores, and libraries, New York courts have long held that vendors and distributors of defamatory publications are not liable if they neither know nor have reason to know of the defamation.

The reason for excusing those who do not know and have no reason to know of the defamation is attributed to the First Amendment, and the bookseller case discussed previously, *Smith vs. California*. CompuServe merely offered the allegedly defaming news as a service to its readers; it had no more editorial control over the publication than does a bookseller, library, or newsstand. Since the plaintiff Cubby was unable to come up with any specific facts suggesting that CompuServe knew or had reason to know of the defamatory materials, summary judgment in favor of CompuServe was granted on the libel claim.

The key to avoiding liability for defamation is likely to hinge on knowledge. The more information sources that are offered on a BBS, the more difficult it is to monitor the contents, and the more likely the "did not know and had no reason to know" defense will be available to the sysop. However, if your board is small, offers but a few informational services, or the sysop is actively engaged in editing or providing a news service, the more risk there is for defamation if untrue statements about people get published. In cases where the sysop's role is a mixture of publisher and distributor, it may be trickier to sort out. Evidence of active participation in writing or editing a news forum will likely be a determining factor.

Other Illegal Materials on the BBS

Besides pornography and defamatory materials, sysops need to be aware of their potential liability for other illegal materials on their BBS, such as stolen credit card numbers, hacking information (phone phreaks, satellite decoder pirates), computer viruses, or other dangerous codes. There can be legal problems, criminal and civil, if a sysop knowingly places illegal materials on the BBS or knowingly runs their BBS in a fashion to encourage illegal uploads.

The same old question comes up again in this regard—what is the affirmative duty to watch for illegal material? Again, there is no specific requirement, but the more pro-active the sysop, the more likely he can wear the good guy's white hat when trouble emerges. With apologies for sounding like the proverbial broken record, we repeat—user registration agreements can help avoid problems by informing BBS subscriber and users that illegal materials will not be permitted and that the sysop has the right to take them off.

Computer Crime Laws

A popular perception is that computer crime is a major social concern. Just how widespread computer crime has become is not clear. By their very nature, computer crimes often are difficult to detect and difficult to prove. One particular aspect of computer crime that comes up in connection with BBS usage is the question of unauthorized access to and use of computer systems owned by another. Although all bulletin boards are, to some degree, like open doors to a store, people generally have no right to go "behind the counter." Logging onto a BBS is very similar to walking into a store—you can look around and inspect the merchandise and buy it, if it's for sale. However, as in a store, you cannot legally poke into the cash register and take money, or go in the back room and pilfer the goods.

The Internet Worm and the Federal Computer Crime Act

The most celebrated case to date involving computer crimes was the case of *United States vs. Morris.*[72] Robert Morris, Jr., the defendant in that case, was ironically the son of the computer security guru Bob Morris, Sr., chief scientist at the National Computer Security Center of the National Security Agency (NSA). In 1988, the junior Morris introduced a virus program (which some characterized as a "worm") that affected UNIX computers into the Internet.[73] The worm, transmitted by the Internet, rapidly multiplied out of control and caused many computer systems (estimated in the thousands) to shut down or become temporarily unusable. It took several days to figure out the program and disable it.

Morris was prosecuted under a major federal law called the Computer Fraud and Abuse Act[74] (also called the Computer Crime Act). This law deals with several forms of computer abuse involving computers operated by the United States government or computer systems that cross state lines. There are several prohibited activities set forth in this law, too many to list here. Most of the prohibited acts include the word "accessing" prefaced by terms such as "knowingly," "intentionally," "with intent to defraud," "without authorization or exceeding authorized access," or similar language. Thus, mere use of the computer by authorized users is permitted (as it should be), but exceeding one's boundaries can get one in trouble.

It is important that system operators make their access policies clear up front, so that if problems from unauthorized access occur, proving that perpetrators exceeded their authorization will not be difficult.

By the way, Morris defended himself on the ground that he did not have the required intent to cause damage or deny others access to their computers. His conviction was upheld on appeal,[75] and he was sentenced to three years' probation, 400 hours of community services, and a fine of $10,000[76].

Wiretapping and the Electronic Communications Privacy Act

Several of the provisions of the Computer Crime Act clearly show that Congress was concerned with privacy issues when it passed the law. The discussion on privacy earlier in this chapter gives further consideration to this area of the law. Here, however, we need to make mention of the other principal federal statute that applies to computer crime. The ECPA extended the wiretapping laws to data communications and prohibits various nonaural interceptions of private communications. Basically, the law created a new federal crime of unauthorized access to stored communications. The crime consists of the following types of activities: intentionally accessing without authorization a facility through which an electronic communication service is provided; and intentionally exceeding an authorization to access that facility.

Summarized, the meaning of this law is that someone who logs onto a computer system under someone else's name and password without the individual's consent, or who figures out a way to hack in through a back door without authorization, commits a federal crime. Likewise, one who intercepts another's e-mail messages without authorization (for example, a valid search warrant) also commits a federal crime.

The ECPA, because it was born from federal wiretapping laws, was primarily intended to force government agencies to obtain warrants for wiretaps in connection with criminal investigations. The law also was intended to close a gap in the wiretap laws that were ambiguous as to their application to data communications. The ECPA's principal focus is on data in transit, rather than on information that has already reached its destination and is merely being stored. However, in the Internet e-mail context, messages that are being routed from one system to the next, with interim storage in a way station, may be subject to the law.

Arguably, if either the sender or recipient of an e-mail message consents to the wiretap, the wiretap is not a violation of this law. On the other hand, the viewing of others' e-mail messages passing through your system may be subject to the law. No law requires that e-mail facilities be provided on anybody's system anywhere. Arguably, however, the ECPA requires that if you undertake to pass private messages, you must abide by these regulations, because reading the e-mail of others technically violates the law.

Considering these laws, sysops may want to consider posting a banner to e-mail users that their mail is not private and that the system operator and others may read and inspect the content of any unencrypted messages.

Computer Fraud and Embezzlement

Aside from viruses and the breaking and entering paradigm, various types of acts attain a criminal aspect when implemented through a computer. For example, an embezzlement scheme might be more lucrative by virtue of high-speed data transmissions—one can transfer a lot more money a lot more quickly by a wire transfer than by carrying cash. Cash is easy to spot and more difficult to launder, and banks are required to report cash transactions of more than $10,000. Wire transfers are fairly tightly controlled, but in some senses, credit card account numbers are like cash. "Postings" and other communications of stolen credit card numbers have been reported.[77]

As we mentioned earlier, computer crimes are difficult to detect and prove. Of course, problems of detection and proof are exacerbated by electronic media; the evidence itself is somewhat transient unless it is made tangible by printouts or by storage on a tangible medium. Because electronic storage is by nature changeable, the probative value of electronically stored evidence is questionable. Reportedly, the case of the California BBS sysop who posted stolen credit card numbers was dropped because the prosecutor anticipated difficulty proving that the sysop knew that stolen credit card numbers were posted on his system.

State Computer Crime Laws

The federal laws relating to computer crime typically require some type of federal or interstate involvement. However, individual states have an interest in controlling computer crime within their jurisdictions. Most states have their own computer crime legislation. Each state's law is slightly different. The federal government does not have a specific "computer crime" statute that can be generally applied, but it has long recognized various types of computer-related activities as being criminal. As long ago as 1976 (a veritable eternity in computer time), the federal government classified four basic categories of activities as types of computer crime:

1. introduction of false data into a system,
2. unauthorized use of computer facilities,
3. altering or destroying data, and
4. taking money or services through a computer.[78]

These activities also are generally the same types of activities that are on the books of various states as state computer crimes. The federal government did not implement a specific computer-crime-related law until the Computer Crime Act. The various types of activities classified as "computer crime" in many states include other types of behavior. Georgia's computer crime law[79] addresses subjects such as computer theft, computer trespass, computer invasion of privacy, computer forgery, and computer password disclosure.

The Georgia law includes provisions relating to criminal modification of data. These laws probably would relate to data vandalism, where someone modifies or corrupts the data of others. Introduction of a virus can involve these laws, because a virus often causes the modification or corruption of key security files or other critical system functions. One obvious threat is that an unauthorized user may intentionally or negligently destroy or alter data in the system, causing harm to someone. Over 15 states have direct criminal sanctions for unauthorized alteration, modification or destruction of computer data, including computer programs.

Other state laws are similar. For example, New York's laws prohibit unauthorized use of a computer service; computer trespass (which goes beyond mere unauthorized access or use, and involves intent to commit a felony or gain access to confidential information); computer tampering (which involves altering data or programs, and probably introducing a virus); unlawful duplication of computer-related material (which may be unconstitutional by virtue of the operation of the preemption provisions of the Copyright Act[80]); and knowing possession of programs or data that were unlawfully copied.

Some older state laws (pre-computer age) that pertain to various types of crimes may also be applicable to BBS operation. Thus, certain types of activities are "criminal" whether or not they involve the use of a computer. Nonetheless, the term "computer crime" often is invoked when a computer is used in conjunction with such crimes. In such cases, traditional theft crimes, computer fraud, information theft, trade secret theft, criminal access to a computer, criminal modification of data, all are lumped together with computer crime, although the elements of each of these crimes vary widely from state to state.

In regard to traditional theft crimes, financial fraud involving computers can be prosecuted under state laws by applying traditional theft-related criminal statutes. Traditional theft crimes include larceny, embezzlement, false pretenses, forgery, and similar crimes. General financial fraud cases do not require any new thinking about the application of criminal law on fraud and theft.

Because each state has different laws, sysops need to check out what the laws are in their state. Be on the lookout particularly for statutes that pertain specifically to computers.

Use of Notices Can Help Prove Unauthorized Access

As we discussed earlier, many computer crime laws are premised on someone exceeding their authorization, or accessing a system without any authorization whatsoever. In the Robert Morris case, Mr. Morris defended (unsuccessfully, we might add) on the ground that he was authorized to be on all those systems he shut down. Clearly, it is trickier to pin the blame for a computer trespass on someone who has lawful access to your system. The Georgia law uses the language, "without authority," which arguably (but not expressly) covers the situation where one either exceeds one's authority or operates with no authorization at all. Proof that someone accessed your system "without authority" would help your case when the criminal is tried in court.

Under New York's laws, unauthorized use of a computer service by an otherwise authorized user can be proven more easily if users are provided with notice not to go beyond a certain point. If you run a BBS or data files accessible on the Internet, you may want to consider displaying a notice similar to this:

> IMPORTANT NOTICE—Only users pre-authorized by the system operator are permitted to access, download, or upload files in this area. If somehow you have obtained access to this notice and this area of the system without express authorization by the system operator, please logoff immediately or return to an area in which you are authorized. You are hereby notified that persons accessing the files, programs or other information in this section without authorization will be subject to prosecution to the full extent of the law.[81]

The Prodigy user agreement includes the following language, which (one could argue) at least puts users on notice of authorization to access:

> Unauthorized access to the Service, to restricted portions of the Service, or to the telecommunications or computer facilities used to deliver the Service, is a breach of this Agreement and a violation of law.[82]

The legal effect of such an "authorization notice" has not yet been fully tested in the courts. However, such a notice may prove instrumental in proving lack of authorization, and sysops may want to consider adopting such a notice in their subscriber agreements.

In closing out our discussion on computer crime, we remind that sysops should familiarize themselves with the computer crime laws in the states in which they plan to conduct activities, to get an idea as to the types of activities to be on the lookout for. If a hacker or other person is discovered engaging in unauthorized access, tampering, is in possession of unlawful materials, and so on, you will have a firmer grasp of the situation if you already know which state laws apply. Prosecutors in state courts probably will be less computer literate than you are, and you will find it easier to attract their interest in a case if you already know the laws that apply and have a start on gathering information that might serve as evidence. Keep a paper trail of the events that lead to your discovery of the problem. Read Cliff Stoll's book, *The Cuckoo's Egg,* [83] for a good overview of the type of data that needs to be kept, preferably in paper form for ultimate introduction as documentary evidence in a court proceeding.

Responsible sysops must take action if they know their BBS is being used for a crime, else they risk becoming accessories to the crime by turning a "willfully blind" eye. Even though it may be tough to prove that the sysop had the requisite knowledge or intent to be convicted of a crime, most people will want to ask themselves if the risk is worth it.

Searches and Seizures of BBS Hardware and Software

Up to now, we have discussed the substantive legal causes for searches and possible seizure of BBS equipment—violations of copyright law, trademark laws, obscenity laws, criminal investigations, etc. Now, we will consider the actual mechanics of a search and seizure, and consider what protections might be available against an unreasonable search or seizure. These matters should be of particular importance to a sysop, especially in light of some recent cases showing examples of both proper and improper searches and seizures of BBS computer hardware and software.

U.S. Constitutional Protections

In the U.S. Constitution, the Fourth Amendment prohibits unreasonable searches and seizures by the government. This is comforting, but it does not prohibit all searches and seizures, just unreasonable ones. The government is allowed to search and seize if it is reasonable and a search warrant is obtained because of probable cause. But the Fourth Amendment does not apply to non-governmental entities! Copyright and trademark infringements are civil wrongs, and a complaining plaintiff can seize an infringer's equipment under certain circumstances.

Supplementing the Fourth Amendment is the Fifth Amendment, which says that citizens are not to be deprived of "life, liberty or property, without due process of law." The Fifth Amendment applies to government searches and seizures, as well as to civil searches and seizures. Thus, for any type of search or seizure, there are specific procedures—due process—that must be followed.

In simple terms, for a legal search there must be some kind of evidentiary basis shown to a judge giving probable cause of wrongdoing for issuing a warrant.[84] For a seizure, in addition to the probable cause, the warrant must describe the place and thing searched and seized with particularity. This prevents the police or other governmental entities from obtaining a generic warrant and going on a "fishing trip" through a BBS computer and file system.

Recent Cases of BBS Search and Seizures

Searches and seizures can adversely affect a BBS business like any other business, and sometimes worse. If the BBS computer equipment is seized, then the BBS is out of business until the equipment can be retrieved or other equipment can be set up. Needless to say, a search and seizure can be frightening and humiliating. The case of *Steve Jackson Games, Inc. vs. United States Secret Service*[85] illustrates just how horrible it can be.

Criminal Searches and Seizures

Usually in the criminal context, any type of search or seizure will be pursuant to a search warrant. In the *Steve Jackson Games* case, federal agents with a warrant seized a customer support, BBS-operated business that published books, magazines, box games, and related products. Jackson also operated a BBS called "Illuminati" that posted information about Jackson's products and activities, a discussion forum for game enthusiasts, and provided an e-mail service.

Federal authorities believed that the Steve Jackson Games customer support BBS contained illegal material in the form of a stolen document from Southern Bell relating to "emergency 911" telephone service. A federal agent had found the 911 document on a BBS called "Phoenix", which happened to be run by an employee of Steve Jackson Games and co-sysop of the Steve Jackson Games BBS. During the investigation, the agents found they could no longer access the Phoenix BBS to further their investigation. The agents thought that, because "Phoenix" and "Illuminati" had a sysop in common, *perhaps* the Illuminati BBS would have the 911 document on it. However, the agents made no effort to contact Steve Jackson Games or solicit their cooperation in the investigation.

The federal authorities got a warrant for a search and seizure, but kept the seized computer, disk drives, and printers for over three months. The computer was not returned until Steve Jackson Games resorted to pressure exerted from two Texas senators along with a suit for damages against the government.

Steve Jackson Games eventually won its suit against the government. The government's behavior in the case was reprehensible. Not only did the federal agents fail to investigate whether Steve Jackson Games BBS was properly a target for investigation, they "seized" the equipment when a mere "disclosure" would have sufficed to protect the government interest, and they kept the equipment far too long, causing financial damage to Steve Jackson Games.

As far as the search and seizure of the BBS, essentially the federal agents failed to return the equipment in a reasonably timely manner after being requested to do so numerous times. The agents could have easily made backups of the memory and disks and returned the equipment to its rightful owner, but agents were not cooperative. The federal judge that heard the *Steve Jackson Games* case came down pretty hard on the agents for their abusive conduct.

A final privacy note on the *Steve Jackson Games* case—seizure of the BBS equipment was found to a violation of the Privacy Protection Act.[86] Under this law, it is unlawful for a government officer or employee, in connection with the investigation of a criminal offense, to search for or seize any "work product materials" possessed by a person reasonably believed to have a purpose to disseminate to the public a newspaper, broadcast, or other similar form of public communication. The Secret Service's refusal to return information and property requested by Steve Jackson and his lawyers was held to be a violation of the statute. The agents could have taken measures to ensure no destruction, alteration, or concealment of information contained in the computers, but they did not do so. These actions led to an award of damages against the government of over $50,000.

The government should have made a reasonable inquiry into the background of Steve Jackson Games to see if the Privacy Protection Act's work product immunity applied. The federal agents wrongly assumed that the BBS was one for hackers and was not involved with publishing based solely on their interpretation of specific (and unfortunate) language of an on-screen notice. However, Steve Jackson Games' BBS was used for customer support as well as employee electronic mail. As a result, the federal court faulted the federal agents for not knowing the Privacy Protection Act statute at all and further explained that a reasonable investigation should have taken place.

Civil Searches and Seizures

As we have mentioned elsewhere, a search and seizure order can arise in the context of a civil lawsuit, for example, a copyright infringement or trademark infringement lawsuit. The *Sega* case, mentioned earlier, involved a civil court seizure order to search and seize a BBS for illegal copies of copyrighted games software. Sega was able to show the court how the sysop had actively encouraged the uploading of Sega's copyrighted game software. After seizing the BBS computer hardware and software, Sega made a backup of the seized memory and disks and promptly returned the hardware and software, minus the illegal copies of software.

In the civil law context, a search and seizure typically goes like this—temporary restraining order, preliminary injunction, permanent injunction. A plaintiff files a lawsuit on some substantive ground for a civil wrong (such as copyright infringement), together with a motion for a temporary restraining order (TRO). A motion for a TRO is supposed to contain a showing that the plaintiff is entitled to temporary relief, and typically contains allegations that if the defendant gets wind of the proceedings, the evidence will be destroyed. A date is set for a hearing on the TRO. Often, a motion for a preliminary injunction is filed at the same time.

In the copyright and trademark realm, it is fairly well established that a plaintiff can go to court and enjoin the sale of infringing goods *without notice*, because of the likelihood that a less-than-honorable defendant will hide or dump the counterfeit (or infringing) goods as soon as they learn of the TRO proceedings. So, usually the hearing is set *without notice to the defendant!* These "no notice" procedures, also called *ex parte* procedures, have classic potential for lack of due process.

Not all courts allow ex parte proceedings. But there are plenty of courts that do. In many courts, the proceedings are not totally without notice, but the notice is very short. For example, you might receive a notice of a TRO hearing in the morning, with the hearing set down for 2:00 p.m. that afternoon. It's not much notice, but some notice is better than none.

If you operate your BBS in a jurisdiction where ex parte proceedings are permitted and you are subjected to one, nothing we tell you here can brace you adequately for the shock of the knock on the door. All we can say is, call a lawyer quick! Complain vociferously about lack of due process, politely and calmly of course, but complain nonetheless. Take careful notes of everything that was taken, everything that was said, everything that happened, and everyone's name. Demand, preferably in the presence of witnesses, that your equipment be left. Offer to allow an expert beholden to the plaintiff to make copies of your disks drives on a removable medium of their choice, but please, leave the equipment here. If it is taken, demand it back promptly, and follow up all complaints and demands immediately in writing.

If you can create circumstances where there is no risk that you could destroy any evidence, as by offering to assist in copying the disks, any seizure of your equipment and software (except of course of truly infringing materials) should be improper. You won't be able to block a proper search, but if you have tried to operate a clean BBS, you might can ward off a seizure.

Seizures Under the Stored Wire and Electronic Communications and Transactional Records Access

There is a chapter of the ECPA called the "Stored Wire and Electronic Communications and Transactional Records Access"[87] covering disclosure of the contents of electronic communications, as previously mentioned. The law gives the government the right to require a provider of a remote computer service (such as a BBS) to "disclose" the contents of any electronic communication without notice to the service's customers, if the government gets a warrant. There is no provision for a "seizure," however. The government has the authority to force disclosure and review of electronic communications only if there is reason to believe the contents are relevant to a legitimate law enforcement inquiry. This is far less traumatic than *seizure*, and a request for disclosure should have been attempted by the agents in the *Steve Jackson Games* case (but of course was not).

The government can also require sysops to make a backup copy of their files to preserve communications as a safeguard.[88] There are several specific requirements if you as a sysop are presented with a backup preservation subpoena or court order. Mainly, the sysop must create the backup copy as soon as practicable, consistent with its regular business practices, and must confirm to the government that the backup copy has been made. The backup must be created within two business days after receipt of the subpoena or court order.

While the subpoena ought to advise you what specifically is required, it might not. Moreover, it might seem to require you to do things not within the law. We suggest that you obtain and review a copy of the law, and not take the word of anyone as to what the law requires you to do—except of course your own lawyer, who is supposed to advise you how to protect your interest.

Search and Seizure Summary

As a sysop, we hope you never have the opportunity to experience a search or seizure of your BBS. If you use some common sense and run a clean system, the odds are in your favor. However, in the off chance you are, as in the Steve Jackson Games case, there are several things you, as the sysop, should keep in mind. Probably the best thing to keep in mind is cooperate with the authorities and get a good lawyer as soon as possible. The lawyer may be able to assess whether the warrant is valid, whether the authorities understand the law, and can generally guard your rights. Most importantly, if you are the sysop of a BBS involved with any type of publishing efforts (which most bulletin boards are), inform the authorities you "have the purpose of disseminating to the public a form of public communication" and are protected by the Privacy Protection Act. This may not work getting the search or seizure called off, but hopefully it will at least force the authorities to "go by the book."

Recent Legal Developments Relating to BBS Operation

At press time, there were a number of BBS cases working their way through the courts. Space does not permit a full discussion or analysis of these cases, and besides, some of the cases might be dismissed, settled, or wind up being legally insignificant. We will briefly discuss one recent case of particular note, and list a few others you may want to monitor.

The *Amateur Action* case[89] involved a California couple, Robert and Carleen Thomas, that was convicted in July 1994 of sending pornography to Tennessee using a BBS. Their BBS advertised sexually explicit video tapes for sale, and also offered sexually explicit graphic images (GIF files) for downloading. The case got started when citizens from Tennessee complained to postal inspectors about the BBS.

A Tennessee federal jury found the couple guilty of distributing obscene material through their bulletin board system. The conviction covers obscene videotapes the couple sent by United Parcel Service (UPS) to callers who responded to BBS advertisements, many of which were extremely graphic. At press time the couple had not been sentenced, and their attorney announced (of course) that his clients planned to appeal the verdict.

There was a federal search and seizure warrant involved in that case. According to a motion filed by the Thomas's attorney to recover the seized computer equipment, the federal agents seized (and held for a time) a number of items including backup tapes, UPS records, electronic mail on the BBS at the time of the seizure, and other information that revealed members' names and passwords. In the motion, the Thomas's attorney stated his belief that the federal agents wanted illegal access to names and passwords for purposes of entrapment.

An interesting obscenity issue raised in the *Amateur Action* case relates to "community standards" when a BBS is involved. Material could be considered obscene and not protected in one part of the country (such as rural Tennessee), but not obscene and protected in another part of the country (such as kinky California). Since a California pornography BBS can easily be accessed by a Tennessee citizen, which "community standard" applies when an obscenity charge is concerned? Stay tuned for more developments on this front...

If you are interested in monitoring legal developments on the BBS front, we suggest you check in with the Electronic Frontier Foundation Internet site, especially the Computer underground Digest (CuD), available at ftp.eff.org. Their ftp site contains subdirectories of various legal cases, and you can often track the progress of a case by inspecting these files. At press time, the CuD had files for several pending cases involving BBS operations, including:

- the *Tony Davis* case—involving a pornography BBS in Oklahoma,
- the *Alcor Life Extension Foundation* case—involving the ECPA and a bizarre story of people in cryonic suspension,
- the *Suarez v. Meeks* case—involving defamation, criticism of Internet marketing practices, and a free-lance writer for *Wired* magazine who publishes an opinionated online newsletter called CyberWire Dispatch,
- the *MTV v. Curry* case—involving trademark and copyright claims; MTV is seeking an injunction to force a former MTV host, Adam Curry, to quit using the Internet address "mtv.com,"

- the *Skwarla v. Tandy* case—involving a Radio Shack employee who was fired for running a BBS, purportedly on her own time and with her own money, that was said to be a conflict of interest with her job at Radio Shack, and
- the *United States v. David LaMacchia* case—involving a student at MIT who was indicted for conspiring to commit wire fraud; the student allegedly used a computer in the MIT Student Center to set up and run an Internet-accessible BBS to which people around the world could freely upload and download copyrighted commercial software.

You might want to watch the news—or your favorite BBS news service—for developments in these cases.

Subscriber and User Agreements

Now that you are better informed of your rights, you are ready to start the process of creating your notice banners and your user or subscriber agreements. We have already suggested some banner notices elsewhere.

User registration agreements are essentially contracts between the sysop and the users. As unpleasant as it may sound to most users and sysop, a good agreement can be extremely useful and steer your BBS clear of trouble. A well drawn agreement will clearly state the rules and policies of the BBS, and define the scope of a user's privacy expectations.

Electronic Contracts

It is best to get user agreements in writing, but an "online sign-up" or "electronic contract" is better than nothing. Be aware, however, of the potential legal problems with electronic contracts.

Contract laws in most states require a signed writing to be effective. A purely electronic contract has no provision for receiving a signature and involves no permanent "writing" in the sense of a written paper document. Certain kinds of agreements by law must be evidenced by a writing signed by the parties sought to be bound. For example, in some states a contract that cannot be performed in a year must be in writing. Also, a promise for the sale of goods of $500 or more is not enforceable unless evidenced by a writing.[90]

It can be argued that a contract—an offer and an acceptance—can be created during an interactive online session. The legal efficacy of electronic interactive contracts has yet to be fully tested in the courts. Some of the difficulties associated with "shrink-wrap" license agreements often used with massmarketed software apply here. An electronic online contract bears many similarities to a "contract of adhesion," which is unenforceable in some jurisdictions.[91] A contract of adhesion is a contract of specified form and not actually negotiated.

At least two factors make electronic contracts questionable. The first relates to the manner in which the transaction occurs. The terms of such contracts are seldom negotiated, but are always unilaterally imposed by the vendor. If you don't agree with the terms of a so-called "contract" or "license," why, you can package up the whole thing, send or take it back, and get a refund! These are the terms, take them or leave them—there is nothing to negotiate!

A second questionable aspect of electronic contracts relates to timing. For most commercial PC software, you don't even see the terms until you have paid the money and opened the package. Repackaging the program and sending it back is inconvenient. And, the vendor does not exercise the classic contractual control of withholding, which is that either you agree to the terms ahead of time, or you don't get the goods. In a mass-market context, it is unreasonable to expect that merchants will withhold goods from sale pending execution of a written agreement on behalf of the manufacturer of those goods.

The same holds true for an electronic contract. If a user answers the questions in the online "contract" they may be allowed access. But if the sysop never withholds the services for failure to get a written contract signed by the customer, was there ever truly a contract?

It makes sense, both practical and legal, that a vendor may legally condition a transaction on acceptance of terms. It seems logical that a sysop would want to legally condition an electronic transaction with acceptance of terms in an electronic contract. If you cannot get a signed, written contract, then by all means get an electronic contract. As you probably have noticed, however, in a real-time online environment, there are legal difficulties with electronic contracts that the laws do not readily and conveniently handle.

Some online BBS and service vendors (Delphi, for example) have tried the following solution to the problem of questionable legality of electronic contracts: (1) allow initial but limited access if satisfactory answers are given to certain online questions provided during an initial "sign-up" session, and (2) condition further access on satisfactory follow-up—receipt of a signed, written agreement. This solution can be called an "interactive sign-up/written follow-up" approach. This approach has become extremely popular, and it does not scare away many customers. It is relatively easy, but its ultimate legal efficacy may depend upon whether sysops exercise the terms by cutting off access to those who fail to follow up.

Terms of the Agreement

There are many different terms you may want to consider including in your user agreement. It would go beyond the scope of this book to try to cover them all. We could not possibly give you a subscriber agreement that is exactly right for your situation. We will, however, list some of the main issues that you will want to consider including. Discuss these with your attorney before you settle on any particular language:

- Condition access to your BBS (beyond initial exploration and marketing) on having an agreement in place. A signed, written agreement is best, but an electronic contract is better than nothing.
- List the services that you will provide to the users. Don't promise more than you can deliver—this is a breach of contract!
- Advise the user that you may change or discontinue certain access or services from time to time. You could offer to give notice of intent to discontinue.
- Tell the users how they will be billed for services. One of the biggest customer complaints about BBS services is that the charges (typically to a credit card) are not easy to sort out. Users want to know how the charges accrue so they can control their expenditures. Many popular larger boards have a fixed fee charge, with premium services billed extra.
- Set out the rules of the road. Advise the users that the rules are set forth in part in the contract, but that users are also expected to abide by any rules set forth in banner notices posted in the system.
- Tell users not to use the system for defamation, illegal activity, and the like. If you want, you can spell out what you think is "illegal" by listing things you don't want to see on the board—illegal drugs, gambling, pornography, prostitution, child pornography, sedition, robbery, computer viruses, hacking, cracking, phone phreaking, copyright infringement, stolen credit cards, or whatever else you think is illegal.
- Specify who owns the materials uploaded to your board. Generally, you could assure users that they may retain rights to any original messages they post and original files they upload. It is appropriate to remind users that materials owned by others (for example unauthorized copies of software) should not be uploaded. Notification that shareware and

freeware is copyrighted and owned by others may also help your users avoid infringements.

- Inform users that attempts to break in or obtain access beyond the listed areas are a violation of the agreement and will result in termination of access.
- Specify the expectations of privacy. If you plan to offer private e-mail, you must endeavor under the ECPA to keep it private, except to protect you as sysop and the system. If you do not offer private e-mail, say so clearly.
- Include a limitation on your liability and a disclaimer of warranties. Provisions relating to limitations of liability and disclaimers seem like a lot of lawyer boilerplate, but they can be important.

Perhaps the best way to start assembling your user agreement is to collect and study the user agreements of others, especially the big ones such as CompuServe, Delphi, America Online, eWorld, etc. These agreements have all been prepared by lawyers, and are about as good as any you will find. While their terms may not exactly fit your needs, by studying them you can identify the issues and help your lawyer draft language that suits your needs.

Summary

If the number of bulletin boards is any indication, there has been a great recent increase in the public's awareness and interest in electronic media. There is an increasing amount of information available online that grows every day. Subscriptions to the large commercial boards like CompuServe, America Online, and Prodigy have skyrocketed recently, and figures of over 50,000 are being used to describe the number of smaller boards. With such a proliferation of boards comes a proliferation of legal problems.

If you are interested in following legal developments and have Internet access, we recommend you check out the Electronic Frontier Foundation (EFF). This private organization, which maintains an ftp site at ftp.eff.org, collects legal research and articles on issues affecting bulletin boards and Internet usage. The EFF also helps people such as Steve Jackson Games and some on the electronic legal borders with their legal proceedings.

We expect more and more cases like those involving *Steve Jackson Games*, *Sega vs. MAPHIA*, and *Playboy vs. Frena*. These cases will establish new rules and boundaries. We hope that this overview will help you identify and manage the main legal issues you will face as a sysop.

[1] Pamphleteers were pervasive during the time and, according to legal commentators, almost certainly within the intended coverage of the First Amendment's "Freedom of the Press" Clause. Lange, The Speech and Debate Clauses, 23 U.C.L.A. L.Rev. 77 (1975).

[2] See *U.S. v. Peace Information Center*, 97 F.Supp. 255 (D.C.D.C. 1951).

[3] *U.S. v. Riggs*, 743 F. Supp. 556, 559_560 (N.D. Ill. 1990).

[4] *Miller v. California*, 413 U.S. 15, 24, 93 S.Ct. 2607, 2614 (1973).

[5] 18 U.S.C. § 2252.

[6] Comment, An Electronic Soapbox: Computer Bulletin Boards and the First Amendment, 39 Fed. Comm. L.J. 217 (1987) (authored by Eric L. Jensen).

[7] *Smith v. California*, 361 U.S. 147, 80 S.Ct. 215, 4 L.Ed.2d 205 (1959).

[8] *Smith v. California*, 361 U.S. at 153-4.

[9] O.C.G.A. § 16-12-103.

[10] See 47 C.F.R. § 64.201 for exact wording of rules.

[11] *Olmstead v. United States*, 277 U.S. 438, 478 (1928) (Brandeis, J., dissenting).

[12] Jared Sandberg, "Wasted in Cyberspace", *The Wall Street Journal*, June 27, 1994, Special Supplement "Technology", p. R10.

[13] Cliff Stoll, *The Cuckoo's Egg*, Pocket Books/Simon & Schuster Inc. (1990).

[14] *Smith v. Maryland*, 442 U.S. 735 (1979).

[15] 18 U.S.C. § 3121(b).

[16] *Barasch v. Pennsylvania Public Utility Commission*, 576 A.2d 79 (Pa. Commw. Ct. 1990).

[17] *Southern Bell Telephone & Telegraph Co. v. Hamm*, 409 S.E.2d 775 (SC 1991).

[18] See *Tyler v. Berodt*, 877 F.2d 705 (8th Cir. 1989); *Edwards v. State Farm Ins. Co.*, 833 F.2d 535 (5th Cir. 1987). However, New York apparently has an anti-eavesdropping statute, see *People v. Fata*, 159 AD2d 180, 559 NYS2d 348 (App. Div. 1990).

[19] 7 U.S.C. § 605 (as amended in 1988).

[20] *Telerate Systems, Inc. v. Caro*, 689 F.Supp. 221 (S.D.N.Y. 1988) (In its user agreement, an investment information database supplier only allowed access to its database via its own software.)

[21] 18 U.S.C. § 2510 et seq.

[22] 18 U.S.C. § 2511(g)(i).

[23] 18 U.S.C. § 2510(16)(A).

[24] 18 U.S.C. § 2511(2)(g)(i).

[25] 18 U.S.C. § 2510(16).

[26] 18 U.S.C. § 2520.

[27] PRODIGY User Agreement, Prodigy Services Company (Sept. 1993).

[28] 18 U.S.C. § 2511(2)(a)(i).

[29] 18 U.S.C. § 2701.

[30] 18 U.S.C. § 2702.

[31] 18 U.S.C. § 2511(2)(c) - (d).

[32] Cf. Haynes, The Envelope Please: Problems and Proposals for Electronic Mail Surveillance, 14 Hastings Const. L. Q. 421 (1987).

[33] 18 U.S.C. § 2703.

[34] See Wallace & Morrison, *SYSLAW—The Sysop's Legal Manual*, LLM Press, New York, New York (1988). NOTE—this is the "first edition" of SYSLAW and is believed to be out of print.

[35] Privacy Protection Act, 42 U.S.C. § 2000aa.

[36] 8 Anne, c. 19 (circa 1710)(English laws).

[37] The preemption provisions of 17 U.S.C. § 301 did away with common law copyright.

[38] 17 U.S.C. § 102.

[39] 17 U.S.C. § 106.

[40] See White & Summers, *Uniform Commercial Code* 170 (2d Ed. 1980).

[41] 17 U.S.C. § 401.

[42] 37 C.F.R. § 201.20(g).

[43] The Free Software Foundation (Cambridge, MA), is responsible for creating and distributing a UNIX-compatible software system called "GNU", which stands for "Gnu's Not Unix." The stated intent of the FSF is to eliminate restrictions on copying, redistribution, understanding, and modification of computer programs.

[44] 17 U.S.C. § 411(a).

[45] 17 U.S.C. § 410(c).

[46] 37 C.F.R. § 202.20(c)(vii).

[47] 37 C.F.R. § 202.20(c)(vii)(A)(2).

[48] 17 U.S.C. § 101.

[49] 17 U.S.C. § 107.

[50] *Feist Publications, Inc. v. Rural Telephone Service Co.*, 111 S.Ct. 1282 (1991); *BellSouth Advertising and Publishing Co. v. Donnelley Information Publishing, Inc.*, 999 F.2d 1436 (11th Cir. 1993)(en banc).

[51] *Id.*

[52] 17 U.S.C. § 101. ("A 'compilation' is a work formed by the collection and assembling of preexisting materials or of data that are selected, coordinated, or arranged in such a way that the resulting work as a whole constitutes an original work of authorship.")

[53] *Id.*

[54] *BellSouth v. Donnelley, supra* note 50.

[55] 17 U.S.C. § 106(2)

[56] 17 U.S.C. § 101.

[57] 17 U.S.C. § 201(b).

[58] *Community for Creative Non-Violence v. Reid*, 490 U.S. 730, 109 S.Ct. 2166 (1989).

[59] 17 U.S.C. § 101. (Definition of "work made for hire.")

[60] *Casella v. Morris*, 820 F.2d 362, 365 (11th Cir. 1987).

[61] *Sega Enterprises v. MAPHIA*, No. C93-4262CW, 1994 U.S. Dist. LEXIS 5266, (N.D. Cal., March 28, 1994), at p. **18.

[62] See *Sid & Marty Krofft Television Productions, Inc. v. McDonald's Corp.*, 562 F.2d 1157, 1162 (9th Cir. 1977).

[63] See *MAI Systems Corp. v. Peak Computer, Inc.*, 991 F.2d 511, 518 (9th Cir. 1993), *cert. dismissed*, 114 S.Ct. 671 (1994).

[64] *Playboy Enterprises, Inc. v. Frena*, 839 F. Supp. 1552 (M.D. Fla. 1993).

[65] 17 U.S.C. § 107.

[66] 17 U.S.C. § 504(c)(2); See *D.C. Comics Inc. v. Mini Gift Shop*, 912 F.2d 29 (2d Cir. 1990).

[67] *Two Pesos, Inc. v. Taco Cabana, Inc.*, 112 S.Ct. 2753, 932 F.2d 113, 23 U.S.P.Q. 2d 1081, 1083 (1992).

[68] See *Jockey Club, Inc. v. Jockey Club of Las Vegas*, 595 F.2d 1167 (9th Cir. 1979).

[69] *In re E.I. duPont de Nemours & Co.*, 476 F.2d 1357, 1361, 177 U.S.P.Q. 563 (CCPA 1973).

[70] 15 U.S.C. § 1125(a); *Playboy Enterprises, Inc. v. Frena*, 839 F. Supp. at 1562.

[71] *Cubby, Inc. v. CompUServe Inc.*, 776 F. Supp. 135, 139 (S.D.N.Y. 1991).

[72] *United States v. Morris*, 928 F.2d 504 (2d Cir. 1991).

[73] A good discussion of the events leading to the discovery and neutralization of the virus is contained in the Epilogue of Cliff Stoll's book, *The Cuckoo's Egg.*

[74] 18 U.S.C. § 1030. This law was enacted in 1984, and primarily pertains to computer systems having some "federal interest" involved. The prohibited activities include:

> accessing a computer that falls within specified security categories with intent or reason to know that the information is to be used to the injury of the United States or to the advantage of a foreign nation;
>
> accessing a computer to obtain information in a financial record of a financial institution, or a card issuer, or contained in a file of a consumer credit reporting agency on a consumer, as such terms are defined in the Fair Credit Reporting Act;
>
> accessing a computer system without authority or beyond authorized access in a system that is operated exclusively for the government or, where the access affects government use of the system;
>
> accessing a federal interest computer with intent to defraud or to obtain anything of value other than the mere use of the computer;
>
> intentionally and without authorization accessing a federal interest computer to alter, damage, or destroy information, or to prevent authorized use of the information or the computer; and
>
> accessing information regarding passwords or similar access information that affects interstate or foreign commerce.

[75] *United States v. Morris*, 928 F.2d 504 (2d Cir. 1991).

[76] See Johnson, Dell, "The Future of Electronic Educational Networks: Some Ethical Issues," U.S. Dept. of Education, Office of Educational Research and Improvement, Document No. ED 332 689 (May 1991).

[77] See the book *SYSLAW* for the story of Tom Tcimpidis, a California BBS operator who was prosecuted for posting stolen credit card numbers on his BBS.

[78] See "Computer Related Crimes in Federal Programs," Government Accounting Office (GAO) (1976).

[79] O.C.G.A. § 16-9-93. Computer crimes defined; exclusivity of article; civil remedies; criminal penalties.

(a) *Computer Theft.* Any person who uses a computer or computer network with knowledge that such use is without authority and with the intention of:

(1) Taking or appropriating any property of another, whether or not with the intention of depriving the owner of possession;

(2) Obtaining property by any deceitful means or artful practice; or

(3) Converting property to such person's use in violation of an agreement or other known legal obligation to make a specified application or disposition of such property

shall be guilty of the crime of computer theft.

(b) *Computer Trespass.* Any person who uses a computer or computer network with knowledge that such use is without authority and with the intention of:

(1) Deleting or in any way removing, either temporarily or permanently, any computer program or data from a computer or computer network;

(2) Obstructing, interrupting, or in any way interfering with the use of a computer program or data; or

(3) Altering, damaging, or in any way causing the malfunction of a computer, computer network, or computer program, regardless of how long the alteration, damage, or malfunction persists

shall be guilty of the crime of computer trespass.

(c) *Computer Invasion of Privacy.* Any person who uses a computer or computer network with the intention of examining any employment, medical, salary, credit, or any other financial or personal data relating to any other person with knowledge that such examination is without authority shall be guilty of the crime of computer invasion of privacy.

(d) *Computer Forgery.* Any person who creates, alters, or deletes any data contained in any computer or computer network, who, if such person had created, altered, or deleted a tangible document or instrument would have committed forgery under Article 1 of this chapter shall be guilty of the crime of computer forgery. The absence of a tangible writing directly created or altered by the offender shall not be a defense to the crime of computer forgery if a creation, alteration, or deletion of data was involved in lieu of a tangible document or instrument.

(e) *Computer Password Disclosure.* Any person who discloses a number, code, password, or other means of access to a computer or computer network knowing that such disclosure is without authority and which results in damages (including the fair market value of any services used and victim expenditure) to the owner of the computer or computer network in excess of $500.00 shall be guilty of the crime of computer password disclosure.

(f) *Article not Exclusive.* The provisions of this article shall not be construed to preclude the applicability of any other law which presently applies or may in the future apply to any transaction or course of conduct which violates this article.

(g) *Civil Relief; Damages.*

(1) Any person whose property or person is injured by reason of a violation of any provision of this article may sue therefore and recover for any damages sustained and the costs of suit. Without limiting the generality of the term, "damages" shall include loss of profits and victim expenditure.

(2) At the request of any party to an action brought pursuant to this Code section, the court shall by reasonable means conduct all legal proceedings in such a way as to protect the secrecy and security of any computer, computer network, data, or computer program involved in order to prevent possible recurrence of the same or a similar act by another person and to protect any trade secrets of any party.

(3) The provisions of this article shall not be construed to limit any person's right to pursue any additional civil remedy otherwise allowed by law.

(4) A civil action under this Code section must be brought within four years after the violation is discovered or by exercise of reasonable diligence should have been discovered. For purposes of this article, a continuing violation of any one subsection of this Code section by any person constitutes a single violation by such person.

(h) *Criminal Penalties.*

(1) Any person convicted of the crime of computer theft, computer trespass, computer invasion of privacy, or computer forgery shall be fined not more than $50,000.00 or imprisoned not more than 15 years, or both.

(2) Any person convicted of computer password disclosure shall be fined not more than $5,000.00 or incarcerated for a period not to exceed one year, or both.

[80] 17 U.S.C. § 301.

[81] See *SYSLAW*, 1st Ed., p. 67 for an exemplary notice. Consult with counsel before you adopt any particular legal notice language.

[82] PRODIGY User Agreement, Prodigy Services Co., Sept. 1993.

[83] Cliff Stoll, *The Cuckoo's Egg*, Pocket Books/Simon & Schuster Inc. (1990).

[84] Cleary, Edward W., et al., *McCormick's Handbook of the Law of Evidence* § 164, at 364 (2d Ed. 1978).

[85] *Steve Jackson Games, Inc. v. United States Secret Service*, 816 F.Supp. 432 (W.D.Tex. 1993).

[86] 42 U.S.C. § 2000aa. "Notwithstanding any other law, it shall be unlawful for a government officer or employee, in connection with the investigation ... of a criminal offense to search for or seize any work product materials possessed by a person reasonably believed to have a purpose to disseminate to the public, a newspaper, broadcast, or other similar form of public communication...."

[87] 18 U.S.C. § 2701 *et seq.*

[88] 18 U.S.C. § 2704(a).

[89] *State of Tennessee v. Robert & Carleen Thomas* (estimated case name), discussed in the *Wall Street Journal*, July 29, 1994, p. B8; certain details about the case are available online from the Electronic Frontier Foundation, Computer underground Digest (CuD), ftp.eff.org.

[90] Uniform Commercial Code (UCC) § 2-201(1).

[91] See *Vault Corp. v. Quaid Software Ltd.*, 655 F.Supp. 750 (E.D. La. 1987), aff'd 847 F.2d 255 (5th Cir. 1988). (Shrink wrap license form not enforceable since it constituted a contract of adhesion.)

Chapter 8

Protecting Your BBS

by Mark L. Chambers

Since we discussed some of the legal issues that concern sysops in the previous chapter, it's appropriate to familiarize you with three of the potential sources of damage to your system. You'll see that these three dangers not only threaten your BBS hardware and software, but your system's reputation and your peace of mind as well:

- **Viruses and Trojan Horses.** This section begins by defining the two terms *virus* and *Trojan Horse,* which you may have heard much about without really knowing the difference. We'll explore the great myth surrounding viruses and bulletin boards. You'll learn how viruses can infect your system, and how you can regularly check your BBS and your download files for infection. Finally, you'll learn how you can remove them.

- **Problem Users.** You'll be introduced to the immature flamers and hackers that take perverse pleasure in disrupting your BBS (instead of participating in it), as well as the more dangerous users that sometimes try to use a BBS for illegal activities. You'll also learn when and how you should lock out a user.

- **Copyrights—Yours and Others.** Finally, we'll cover the dangers inherent in offering commercial or copyrighted programs and images to the public—as well as how to protect your copyrighted work.

Of course, we'll also discuss how you can take measures to protect the time, money, and hard work you've invested in your BBS!

Virus Protection

Because of extensive—and somewhat undeserved—attention in recent years, the computer virus has been elevated to Public Enemy No. 1 on the computer user's list (even above hard drive failure and lightning strikes). The fear of virus infection has become so prevalent that scanning functions have been built into DOS, while some communications and file backup software check for viruses as they save files to disk or tape.

Indeed, viruses and Trojan Horse programs are a very real threat, especially because there are so many different types; some of them are perfectly harmless, while others can render a hard drive unusable. Others can slow down your PC, or cause symptoms that make your hardware appear faulty. Today's viruses even attack at different times; some go to work immediately, while others may interfere with your PC only at random times or certain dates.

Before you panic, however, it's important to recognize the truth behind the virus myth—and that's what we'll do in this section! You'll learn the steps you can take to ensure that your BBS will remain virus-free, including the files available to your callers.

What Is a Trojan Horse?

A *Trojan Horse* is a simple destructive program that is represented as being a genuine application or utility, often complete with documentation that promises the program will perform some beneficial task. As soon as you run the program, however, it will format your hard drive, erase your file allocation table, or delete your data.

Trojan Horses were the predecessors of today's modern viruses, but they are not viruses themselves. The Trojan Horse does not infect your PC or reproduce itself within other files—it simply causes as much damage as possible as quickly as possible. The author of a Trojan Horse takes no steps to hide the effects of the program; in fact, some Trojan Horses actually display a screen informing you that you've been duped after they complete their destructive tasks.

Although Trojan Horses are much rarer than viruses, they're actually more dangerous in some ways. Unlike many viruses, a Trojan Horse usually attempts to cause the maximum amount of damage to your data. Plus, Trojan Horses cannot be uncovered with virus detection software, because they simply use standard DOS programming calls to format your drive or erase your files.

> **Tip**
>
> How can you protect yourself against a Trojan Horse uploaded by one of your users or included on a CD-ROM? Many shareware and commercial virus protection packages offer a TSR (short for *terminate-and-stay resident*) program that constantly monitors other programs you run and prevents them from writing and deleting files or formatting your drive. It's not recommended that you run such a monitor simultaneously with your system, because your BBS must constantly write to disk. You can run it while your BBS is down, however, especially before running any programs for the first time.

What Is a Virus?

Like any other program, a *virus* is simply a set of instructions that your computer follows when you run it—however, instead of performing some kind of worthwhile task, the virus has been created by its author to disrupt the operation of your PC. The results of a virus can be so minor as to be unnoticeable for as long as it remains on your computer, or it could have an immediate and disastrous effect upon your data or your hardware.

Contrary to popular opinion, a program need not cause any damage to your PC or your data at all to be considered a virus! A virus program must meet two requirements:

- **Replication.** A computer virus grows by reproducing itself within your PC's files, memory, or floppy and hard drive boot sectors. For instance, some strains originally infect one file and then replicate themselves within many different files on your disk while you use your PC.

> **Tip**
>
> Floppy disks are one of the primary carriers of virus infection. A single infected file can spread to an entire PC user group or office from a single disk! Because it takes much less time to scan a floppy than it does an entire hard drive, you may want to scan floppies you receive from your users or coworkers before copying any files from them.

- **Concealment**. Remember, the moment you've detected a virus, it's easy to remove—therefore, authors of virus code go to great lengths to make it difficult to identify their programs, and most viruses do not signal their existence even after they've started to wreak havoc on your computer. There are a few exceptions that print a message on the screen or disrupt your display, but most viruses rely on stealth so that you'll continue to use your PC and continue to infect other computers.

As you learned earlier, Trojan Horses have been around longer than true viral programs. The first virus is considered to have originated at Jerusalem's Hebrew University in July 1987; the "Friday the 13th" virus (sometimes also called the "Israeli" strain) destroys every program you run on any Friday the 13th, slows down your PC, and draws a characteristic black box at the left edge of the screen.

There are three major divisions of PC viruses:

- **Those hidden in programs.** A virus of this type overwrites the first two or three thousand bytes of the target program with a copy of itself, which is loaded back into memory each time you run the program (which is why the virus isn't removed when you turn off your PC). These are the most common viruses.
- **Those occupying the boot sector.** These viruses copy themselves into the reserved area called the boot sector, which is found on all IBM PC-compatible floppy and hard disks. Because this data area is loaded into memory each time you turn on your PC, viruses of this type constantly infect any floppy disk you use on that computer. Even worse, many of these boot sector viruses move your original boot sector data or your disk File Allocation Table to another location on your drive, which complicates the process of removing the virus. This type of virus is much rarer than those hidden in programs.
- **Those that are created in programs.** These programs actually load viruses, which then lie dormant for some period of time before attacking the system. Viruses created by loader programs are the rarest of the three types.

Table 8.1 describes some common viruses and their symptoms.

Table 8.1 A List of Common Viruses

Name	Type	Symptom
Datacrime	Program	Formats your hard drive on any October 12
Keypress	Program	Randomly repeats keystrokes you type
Vienna	Program	Destroys files, randomly reboots your PC

Name	Type	Symptom
Whale	Program	Slows system, damages files, display flickers
Stoned	Boot	Damages data, displays a pro-marijuana screen
Ping Pong	Boot	Displays a bouncing ball on your screen
Joshi	Boot	Forces you to type "Happy Birthday Joshi"
Disk Killer	Boot	Formats hard drive after infecting floppies
AIDS	Loader	Displays an infection warning, locks your PC
Strain 403	Loader	Changes all letter "O" characters to zeros
Burger	Loader	Destroys data by copying itself over files
Leprosy	Loader	Deletes all files in a specific directory

The Great BBS Virus Myth

How are viruses transferred from PC to PC? There are three specific methods of transmitting a computer virus. They are:

- Copying, installing, or running a program from an infected floppy disk.

> **Tip**
>
> Remember, commercial software is just as susceptible to viral infection as other PC programs, so never consider a shrink-wrapped package as a guarantee that the disks inside are virus-free! There have been many cases reported in the last few years of commercial programs carrying viruses, so it's just as important to scan even if you don't use shareware programs.

- Running programs from a network.
- Running programs downloaded from a bulletin board.

Naturally, it's the last of these that will be of the most concern to you as a sysop! Unfortunately, one of the common perceptions of computer users everywhere is that bulletin boards harbor countless virus strains, and downloading a file from a BBS is asking for trouble—a myth that was reported constantly by the media during the "Michaelangelo" virus scare, and one that also surfaces often concerning the Internet as well.

This misconception couldn't be more incorrect! The vast majority of BBS callers have never been exposed to a virus, and have regularly downloaded software from bulletin boards for **years**. As a matter of fact, this same statement is true of PC owners as a whole; although computer viruses are big news as a hi-tech danger, the PC community as a whole hasn't been affected by them to any great degree. Most casual PC owners scan their systems for viruses even less frequently than they backup their hard drives, all without losing a single byte of data to a viral infection.

Well-run bulletin boards check their uploads for viruses before they're offered to callers—some even perform the scanning operation in real-time, immediately after the upload has completed. Other sysops run virus scan utilities as a part of their regular maintenance event. If you do find a virus within an uploaded file, alert the uploader immediately!

Tip

Before you purchase a CD-ROM disc for your BBS, check to make sure it's virus-free. Reputable BBS CD-ROM manufacturers scan their files before the disc is manufactured, and usually note this in their advertising.

Checking Your System

The first step in protecting your BBS from viral infection is to regularly scan your own hard disk with a virus detection program. Note that this measure has nothing to do with passing a virus to a caller through a download file: you're simply protecting your own PC and ensuring that your BBS is not a target.

The most popular virus detection program available today is a well-known shareware success story in itself: VIRUSCAN, by McAfee Associates, is both fast and comprehensive, and it's updated often to detect the latest viral strains. Plus, you're free to try VIRUSCAN and distribute it to your users in its shareware form; if you continue to use it, make sure you register it.

VIRUSCAN does not decompress files archived with utilities like PKZIP, so it shouldn't be used to scan uploads unless they've been unarchived to a separate directory (or your RAM disk). Additionally, VIRUSCAN does not attempt to repair an infected file; instead, it offers the safest (and recommended) option of simply overwriting and deleting the infected file. The only guaranteed method of removing viruses from your PC is to overwrite and delete the infected file! This is another reason to back up your system often. Figure 8.1 shows the results of a typical VIRUSCAN session across multiple drives.

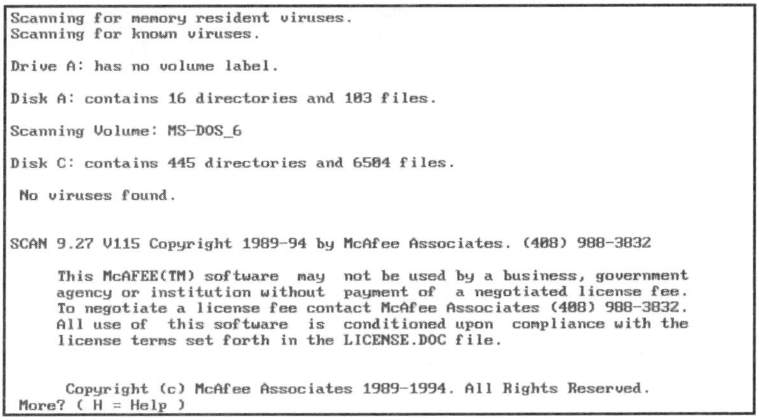

Fig. 8.1
Status messages displayed by VIRUSCAN as it searches for viruses.

You can download the latest version of VIRUSCAN from the McAfee Support BBS at 408/988-5190 (or via the Internet at ftp.mcafee.com).

Checking Uploaded Files

As we mentioned earlier, you can scan new files immediately after they've been uploaded; some BBS programs now support this internally, while most others run one of several external door utilities specifically written for this purpose. The archive file is uncompressed into its component files, which are then scanned individually for viruses. One of the most popular of these online scanner utilities is TranScan, written by Craig Dunstan (see fig. 8.2).

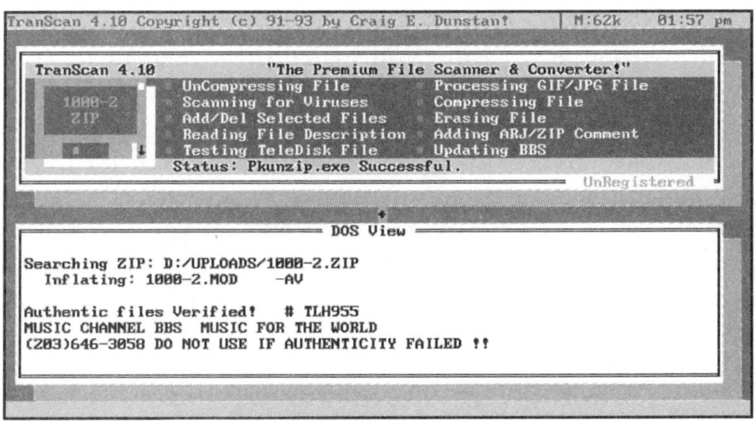

Fig. 8.2
The local console display from the virus scanner utility TranScan.

For details on how to add doors to your system, refer to Chapter 15. You can also run most of these same doors in batch mode from DOS, so you can make them a part of your midnight maintenance event.

Tip

As we did in Chapter 4, make sure you limit access to your upload file section to only you and your co-sysops; you can then move the files manually after they've been automatically checked.

Problem Users

No one operates a BBS with services so singular that callers can't go elsewhere to find them; therefore, you must control your system as fairly and equitably as possible, and you should treat your callers as any business treats its customers. For this reason, it should be rare that a caller is locked out of your system (or even publicly punished for that matter).

Unfortunately, every sysop has to deal with problem users from time to time, and you may even be forced to lock out a few of them to maintain order on your system. In this section, we'll discuss three types of problem users—flamers, hackers, and criminals. You'll learn how to identify each one, as well as a general plan of action for dealing with problem users.

Flamers

Flamers form the largest contingent of problem users, and are often found participating in FidoNet and Internet messages as well. These callers are known for:

- Launching one personal attack after another at a user or group of users in your message base. Often hiding behind the guise of free speech, flamers delight in belittling and insulting other users in direct defiance of your system rules, often with no concrete reason. Their attacks usually last long after the original message topic has run its course, and flamers have long memories: if you reply in kind, you'll often become their prime target in future flame wars. Unfortunately, flamers often single out new users who're simply trying to learn their way around your BBS.
- Quoting portions of private e-mail messages in a public message area.
- Constantly criticizing the sysop, co-sysop, or sigop in public messages. As in any endeavor, constructive criticism is a positive form of feedback, and you should welcome it; however, a flamer with a grudge against an authority figure on your BBS will continue to bait you in an attempt to make you lose your composure.

- Flagrantly ignoring your system rules by continuing use of foul language in areas where such language is not allowed.

Although it's not much, there is one positive angle in dealing with a flamer on your system: that person is almost invariably disliked to a high degree by every other user on your BBS! Because the flamer will undoubtedly complain loudly in public messages if you interfere in his or her fun, the trick is in maintaining your poise and your sense of humor. As with any problem user, handle as much of the problem in private e-mail as possible.

Hackers

Hackers are much more dangerous to your BBS than flamers, as they often attempt to sidestep your system security or disrupt your board's operation (even to the point of damaging your system data). Typical hacker tactics include:

- Attempting to crash your BBS. If you've never heard the term *crash*, it refers to a caller using certain techniques to cause your BBS to generate errors, lock up your PC, or (in the worst case imaginable) drop to DOS. Hackers were much more successful crashing bulletin boards in years past because today's BBS software is much more secure, reliable, and resistant to tampering. Many older BBS programs written for 8-bit machines also had well-known back doors (codes or sequences that allowed the program's author to use the BBS remotely with no restrictions)—such a program feature is unthinkable in today's BBS community.

Tip

Interested in maintaining a secure system? Remember, each time you add an external door program, you're also adding the potential for a BBS lockup or one of your callers suddenly being presented with a DOS prompt. If a door program is not well written and well tested before being released to the public, it'll probably be prone to failures that will keep your BBS from answering until you can return home and reboot the system. Whenever possible, wait until a door program has earned a solid reputation before you add it to your BBS. Note that game doors aren't as much of a problem with integrated bulletin board software like TBBS and Major BBS, because these BBS programs run doors internally and never shell to DOS; they usually recover from door errors without a lockup.

- Logging on to your system under different names—even to the point of masquerading as you by using the word "sysop" somewhere in their logon name!
- Demon dialing. This is a hacker term for making repeated calls to one or more systems, much like the dialing queue feature of communications programs like PROCOMM PLUS. However, a hacker uses a demon-dialing utility as a weapon by programming it to call your system every two to three minutes, tying up your telephone lines.

Actually, the term hacker has taken on two meanings in the last five years or so, the problem users we've just discussed have become known as hackers, so the name has a negative connotation. However, the term hacker has a much older meaning with a very positive connotation that stretches back 15 or 20 years—it used to refer to someone with a high level of computer and electrical experience who could build (or hack) computer hardware from basic components. Therefore, the first sysops were hackers, and if your system is lucky enough to attract BBS "old-timers," they may refer to themselves as hackers (much to the surprise of your other users).

Many bulletin boards have methods of helping you maintain tighter security over your userlog information. As an example, most BBS programs allow you to specify whether your system should be *open* or *closed*. An open system adds new users to the userlog and leads them through the registration process, just as we did earlier in this book. This is the default access method for your Wildcat! system. However, if you're setting up a business/support system and you wish to limit your userlog to certain individuals within your company, you can run a closed system and add each user manually. Any caller that doesn't already exist within your userlog cannot logon to a closed system.

Another common security feature involves prompting each user for a personal piece of information that the BBS stores as a part of the userlog: for instance, the caller's birthdate, phone number, or even the caller's mother's name! After a certain period of time has elapsed or a certain number of logons have been made, the user is prompted to re-enter the information during logon as a form of verification. If the caller enters the same information, the logon procedure continues normally—if the caller cannot enter the correct information, the BBS alerts the sysop of a possible security breach and either logs the user off or reduces the user's access level. The sysop can then call the user directly by voice and investigate the problem.

Criminals

The third type of problem user is undoubtedly the worst. Even if you don't participate in any criminal activity on your system, allowing such activity to continue is an invitation for you, the sysop responsible for your system, to visit your local courthouse. Criminal activities that have taken place on bulletin boards include:

- Distributing credit card and telephone calling card numbers. If the parties are intelligent, they'll limit this activity to e-mail.
- Distributing pornographic material. Again, the definition of pornography varies with location, but images of children performing sexual acts have led to the seizure of several bulletin boards, while the sysops of these systems are charged under criminal law. For a complete discussion of the community standards that differentiate between pornographic and obscene, refer to Chapter 7.

> **Tip**
>
> If your system will feature adult material, make sure you allow access to all restricted areas—including adult messages and multiline chat mode—only to those adults who have sent you a copy of their state driver's license. This is an extra step for your users to take, and it may cost you a certain small percentage of your adult callers; however, the legal advantages clearly outweigh the loss of a few callers.

- Distributing commercial software or images. We'll cover this problem in the next section.
- Discussing acts of violence online. Many sysops don't consider a user threatening another with violent harm to be dangerous, but the possibility still exists that the threat could be carried out. In any case, such negative message traffic will almost certainly result in you losing a fair number of users, so it's not a good idea to allow it to continue.

In years past, many criminals considered bulletin boards to be a safe haven because police departments and the media were less aware of the existence of the online community. Today, however, a staggering number of new callers enter cyberspace every year, and it's a good bet that both your local media and your local police department are well aware of bulletin boards in your area. If any of your users are engaging in criminal activities online, lock them out immediately!

Handling Problem Users

Finally, let's discuss a simple plan of action you can use to handle flamers and hackers on your system. It's a good idea to publicize this process in your system regulations so that both you and your callers can refer to it.

1. As soon as you become aware of a problem user (either through your own observations or a report from another caller), leave an e-mail message to the offending caller. This letter should be short and to the point, stating that you've noticed that the person has been engaging in an activity that's specifically prohibited in your system rules file. Further, your message must make it clear that the problem user is receiving a first warning—in private—and that you'll be watching closely for further infractions.

   Luckily, most of your problem users will heed your private warning, and nothing further will be required. If the problem caller has received your mail and the activity continues, move to the next level.

2. Leave a public message addressed to the offending caller. This message should note that the problem user has already ignored a private message and has continued the offending activity. Once again, warn the user that you're watching his or her conduct—but this time, the user will be locked out of the system (temporarily or permanently) if the activity continues.

   If you are indeed forced to lock the user out, post a final public message announcing that fact to the rest of your users.

The process of locking a user out is quite simple for bulletin board programs using security levels to control access. Simply reserve your lowest security level for problem users. Change the access level for the problem user to this level, which should severely curtail both the user's online time and the number of system features that person can access. For example, your security level 5 might provide only five minutes of online time, and it might allow a problem user to only download utilities and logoff. Whether you allow the user back on with full privileges eventually is your decision, and really depends upon the particular person and the severity of the infraction.

Tip

Even if you lock out a problem user permanently from your system, don't delete that person's record from your userlog; this prevents the person from rejoining your system under the same name, and it also prevents another caller from joining your system and posing as the original problem user!

Additionally, you'll find these guidelines to be helpful in dealing with problem users:

- Keep an archive file containing your complete system logs for at least the previous year; this will help you track the activities of a problem user.
- Use a registration questionnaire to permanently record complete information on every user. You can use this data later if you need to contact a problem user in person.
- If your bulletin board program supports caller ID (either internally or through a door), subscribe to the service if your telephone company offers it. The knowledge that your BBS has recorded the actual number where a call originated works wonders in discouraging hackers and criminals from using your system.
- Monitor the electronic mail traffic on your bulletin board. Although some sysops consider this a breach of ethics, it really isn't (as long as you don't join in an e-mail conversation or intercept messages from either side). If you don't monitor your mail by reading it and two or more of your users are engaging in criminal activity, you'll have no way of knowing there's a problem before your BBS is raided by the police.
- If the problem user is underage (as most are), don't hesitate to place a voice call and speak to the child's parents—they can do wonders in solving a problem! Even if the user is an adult, the personal contact of a voice call may solve your differences (as long as you practice the same restraint and control you've shown that person on your BBS).
- Above all, never lose your composure and respond in kind to a problem user! If you return a flamer's attack in your message base, you're being manipulated, and you'll lose respect in the eyes of the rest of your callers. Your image on your system is too valuable to tarnish.

Instead, follow the steps we discussed earlier in this section, handle the problem maturely and you and your BBS may even benefit from the situation! Well-run systems with friendly sysops are always in demand.

Copyrights and Your BBS

As a sysop, you should closely monitor the programs, images, and text files offered on your BBS—both those created by others and those you've created yourself. Operating a busy bulletin board is much like taking the editor's job at a daily newspaper: you filter through the news you receive, you decide what your reading public will see, and you make sure credit is given where it's due.

Unfortunately, it isn't always easy to determine whether a program or image is copyrighted or not, especially when you consider GIF pictures. In this section, we'll discuss how you can recognize copyrighted material you receive and how it should be handled on your system. You'll also learn how to copyright the materials you create to publicize and market your system.

Using Copyrighted Material

To the large majority of your callers, copyrighted information on your BBS means one particular type of files—commercial software—and they know it's illegal for you to offer such software for downloading. Of course, some software you'll recognize as pirated as soon as you investigate it, but other programs may be harder to identify as commercial software. Usually, commercial software will arrive on your system with some sort of *crack* applied; some cracks remove the documentation check used by most game programmers, while others remove the original purchaser's name or enable features in shareware that should only be available to registered owners. Another sign of a potential pirated commercial program is a lack of a comprehensive manual, or the inclusion of a rough list of command keys—some pirate organizations even include READ.ME files describing how the game was cracked!

Tip

Although cracks and so-called trainer programs for commercial games are not illegal for you to offer to your callers, it's illegal for anyone other than the original purchaser to apply them. If you're worried about your board's image, it's best not to allow such files on your system, either within your hard drive file sections or any CD-ROMs you may use on your BBS.

However, there are two other different types of copyrighted material that you must avoid:

- **Copyrighted images**. No matter what the format, if an uploaded image is copyrighted and no authorization appears on it allowing for free distribution, think twice before adding it as a download. Of course, if you downloaded it from a source that allows distribution, you're free to provide it to your callers. Many GIF files carry embedded text comments that you can read within popular picture viewers like VPIC; the text isn't displayed as part of the image, so the viewer displays such a comment separately. These comments may allow or disallow distribution, so make sure you check them if your hardware allows (see fig. 8.3). Images on BBS CD-ROMs can be usually be considered safe for distribution.

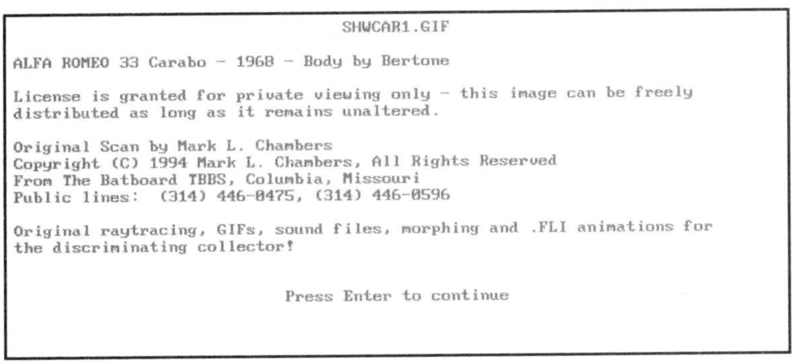

Fig. 8.3
A GIF comment reserving distribution rights.

- **Copyrighted books and periodicals**. Just as you cannot duplicate a copyrighted book and sell it, you also cannot provide electronic copies of any book or periodical without permission from the publisher. This includes electronic editions of *USA Today*, *Boardwatch*, and *Newsbytes*.

Copyrighting Your Material

Your original images, programs, and text files are also protected if you copyright them before releasing them to the public, but they must be completely yours; for example, you can't scan a picture from a magazine and distribute that image because the original picture wasn't your property.

Tip

We'll cover how you can publicize your BBS with your own original GIF files in Chapter 11—for now, though, it's worth noting that you can hire an artist or photographer to create images for you.

Your original images, programs and text files are also protected if you copyright them before releasing them to the public, but they must be completely yours; for example, you can't scan a picture from a magazine and distribute that image, since the original picture wasn't your property.

All that's required for a general copyright is the following line, which should appear at the beginning of any original text file, on the title screen of any program you write, or as a part of any image you create:

> **Copyright© 1994 (your name or business name), All Rights Reserved.**

The copyright line should appear somewhere in every GIF file you create as well; your scanning software probably has a paint program that allows you to overlay text on top of the picture. The copyright line should be large enough to see without spoiling your image.

Summary

In this chapter, we detailed how to protect your system from viruses, problem users, and copyright infringement. You learned the basics of scanning for viruses, how to lock out problem users, and how to copyright material you've created for distribution on your system.

Next, we'll return to your Wildcat! Lite system to learn more about user and file maintenance tasks, including how to add, modify, and delete both users and files. We'll also set up a maintenance event and update our CAT.BAT batch file to allow your BBS to automatically take care of itself.

Chapter 9

Sysop Maintenance and Administration

by Mark L. Chambers

In this chapter, we'll explore how you can control several features of your BBS with automated events. *Internal* events can restrict callers by baud rate, toggle your Sysop page function on and off, purge your deleted mail, and even force your system to shut down when the current caller logs off. *External* events can run utilities that process BBS reports, game turns, and other daily tasks automatically. Events like these can be a big help in keeping your BBS manageable because they greatly reduce the tasks you'd otherwise have to perform manually.

We'll also cover the Sysop menu, demonstrating step-by-step how you can make changes to your userlog and file databases, manage events, purge deleted mail, and view your system activity log.

Finally, we'll discuss how you can use DOS commands and run programs remotely by dialing in yourself—this comes in handy when you're away on vacation or on a business trip.

Scheduling Internal and External Events

Wouldn't it be great if you could somehow stay by your BBS console 24 hours a day? For example, you could prevent 300 and 1200 baud callers from tying up your phone lines during the busiest hours of the day (a common problem when you're running a single-line BBS), while allowing users connecting at

2400 baud or faster to logon normally. Or, perhaps you'd like to dial other boards every morning at 8:00 a.m.—you could shut the BBS down as soon as the last caller logged off at 7:45 a.m.!

Of course, sysops are dedicated people, but no one has the stamina required to monitor a BBS 24 hours a day! Besides, modern bulletin board software is sophisticated enough to perform tasks like these automatically through the use of events. As we mentioned, internal events perform system functions just as if you were initiating them from the keyboard. Internal events that apply to your single-line Wildcat! system include:

- Toggle 300 baud access ON or OFF. This event either allows or rejects any 300 baud connection; Wildcat! remains in the current state until the opposite event of the same type occurs.
- Toggle 1200 baud access ON or OFF. Allows or rejects any 1200 baud connection; Wildcat! remains in the current state until the opposite event of the same type occurs.
- Toggle 2400 baud access ON or OFF. Allows or rejects any 2400 baud connection; Wildcat! remains in the current state until the opposite event of the same type occurs.
- Toggle the Sysop page function ON or OFF. Enables or disables the Sysop page function, a useful feature if your BBS is located in your bedroom.
- Reset the idle screen Quick Statistics display. Resets the Quick Statistics displayed by Wildcat! while it's waiting for a caller. This function is also available from the console.
- Set DOS Next. Wildcat! will shut down and exit to DOS as soon as the current caller disconnects.
- Kill deleted messages. This event purges deleted messages from all conferences within your message base.

External events are a common feature of all bulletin board programs, including network and integrated systems. During an external event, the BBS shuts down and runs a DOS batch file that you specify; most sysops schedule an external batch procedure at midnight or very early in the morning. Typically, this maintenance batch file runs several third-party utilities to generate file listings, process activity file listings, perform game processing, and anything else that requires execution once daily.

Most multiline network BBS packages allow each node on a LAN to drop to DOS separately, which provides you with additional flexibility in executing external events. Depending on the external program you're running, you can even perform tasks such as processing new uploads for viruses or connecting with your FidoNet host without shutting down your BBS.

Although integrated BBS programs can't drop directly to DOS, they can perform some of the same functions without shutting down the BBS. For example, an integrated multiline bulletin board package like TBBS can dial and connect with a FidoNet or Internet host over one of the system's telephone lines while the other lines continue to accept callers as usual.

Wildcat!'s event handling is extremely flexible—a feature that any sysop will appreciate, because most bulletin board programs simply force the caller off the system, or restrict the amount of online time available to the caller to match the event. Events can be executed every day of the week or just on the days you specify. There are also three methods of event execution, which determine whether your BBS will force a caller off for an event or allow the user to log off normally:

- **Flexible.** Wildcat! will execute the event anytime during the scheduled day after the amount of time specified in the field, "Inactivity before flexible events," on Part 2 of the MAKEWILD General Definition screen (by default, five minutes). If the required amount of inactivity doesn't occur, Wildcat! automatically upgrades the event to a soft execution at the time you've entered for the question, "Time to start forcing flexible events," on the same MAKEWILD screen. Events with this execution method need not be run at any particular time during the scheduled day, but they will be run as soft events if necessary.

- **Soft.** Wildcat! executes the event as closely as possible to the time you've indicated. If someone is online at the time, the user will be allowed to finish the call normally, and then the event will execute.

- **Hard.** Your BBS will cut short a caller's time and ensure that the event is processed at the time you've specified.

Now that you know how Wildcat! processes events, we'll go through the scheduling process and set up an internal and an external event.

Using the Event Manager

Wildcat! BBS events are scheduled from the Sysop menu. We'll create two events: your primary event that will handle all of your daily maintenance chores (we'll schedule it to run every night at one minute past midnight), and a secondary event that purges deleted mail at 2:00 a.m. every Monday, Wednesday, and Friday.

> **Tip**
>
> Always perform as much event processing as possible in the early morning, which will maximize the amount of time available for users trying to reach your system during regular business hours! There are callers that will frequent your BBS at 3 a.m., but they'll quickly learn when your events usually begin and end, so they'll call before or after the event. If your BBS program supports internal events that won't force the BBS to shut down, check to see whether an internal event can perform some or all of the functions instead.

First, start your BBS and log on locally from the console, then follow these steps:

1. At the Main menu screen, press **1** to display the Sysop menu (see fig. 9.1). Note that if you have hotkeys enabled, there's no need to press Enter at most of these prompts.

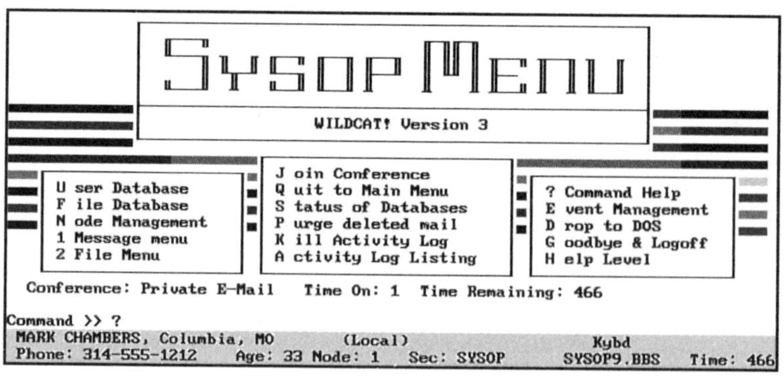

Fig. 9.1
The Sysop menu, as seen from the local console.

2. Next, press **E** at the Sysop menu to display the Event Manager (see fig. 9.2). Because your system currently has no events scheduled, the list is empty.

3. Press **A** to add an event. Wildcat! displays a list of available events, if you've added any (see fig. 9.3).

4. Enter the number **6** and press Enter to indicate you'd like to add an external event that runs a batch file. Wildcat! displays the event date selection screen (see fig. 9.4).

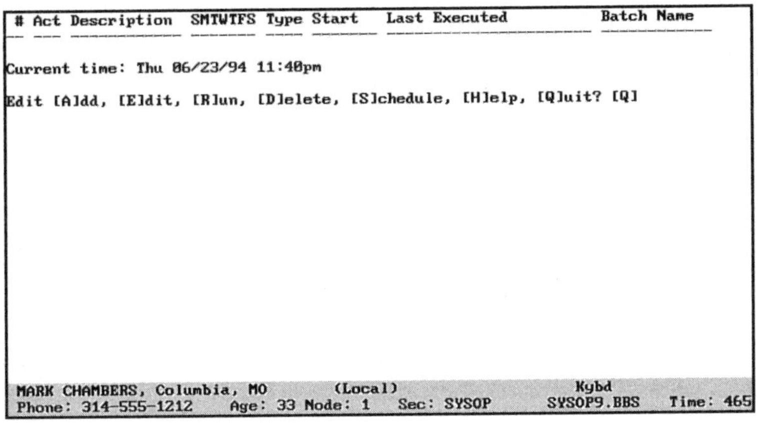

Fig. 9.2
The Event Manager screen.

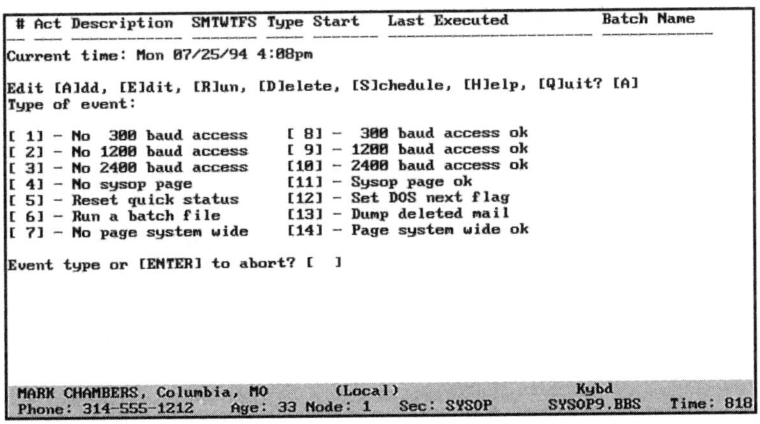

Fig. 9.3
The list of event types displayed when adding an event.

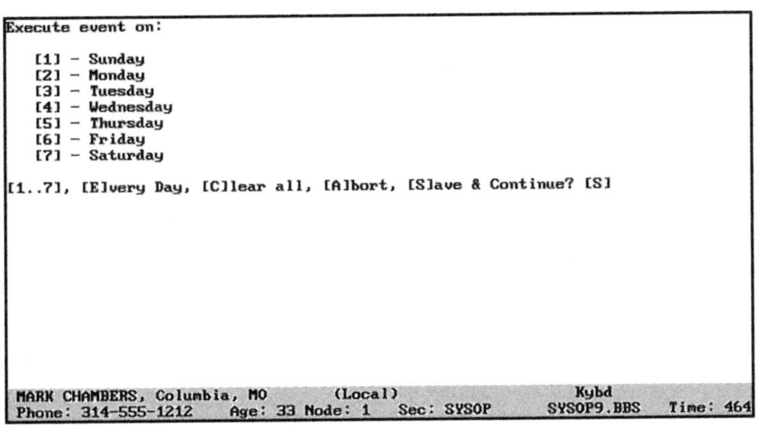

Fig. 9.4
Selecting the days to execute an event in the Event Manager.

5. Press **E** to denote that our external event should run every day of the week. Wildcat! flags each day with an asterisk, indicating the event will run daily. You can toggle days individually as well.

6. Press **S** to save and continue. Wildcat! prompts you to select an execution method.

7. Press **S** again to specify the soft execution method. Wildcat! will allow any user currently online at 12:01 a.m. to complete the call normally before running our external event.

8. Wildcat! now requests the time for our event. Enter **00:01** (24 hour format for 12:01 a.m.) and press Enter.

9. Because we've selected an external event, Wildcat! needs to know whether it should shell to DOS (with some of the BBS program remaining in memory) and execute the batch file, or exit completely to DOS and run the batch file. Press **S** to shell—this method is preferred, as it requires no changes to your CAT.BAT file.

10. Wildcat! now requests the DOS path and name of the batch file to run (see fig. 9.5). We'll assume that the batch file you want to execute is called MIDNIGHT.BAT, and it resides in your Wildcat! home directory; type **C:\WC30\MIDNIGHT.BAT** and press Enter.

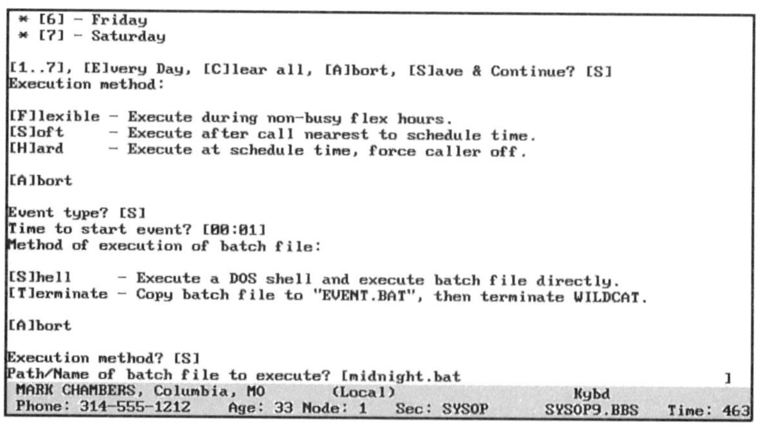

Fig. 9.5
Specifying a batch file name for an external event.

11. That's it! Wildcat! returns you to the Event Manager screen, where you'll see the details of your external event now displayed (fig. 9.6).

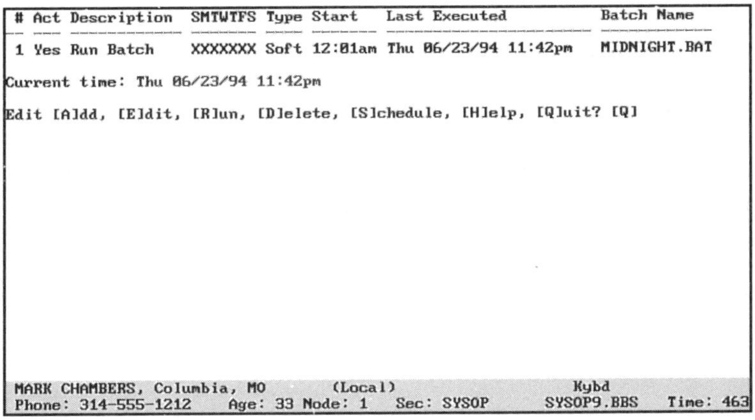

Fig. 9.6
The completed external event as displayed within the Event Manager.

Now let's schedule your secondary internal event that purges deleted mail at 2:00 a.m. every Monday, Wednesday, and Friday.

1. Press **A** to add an event.
2. Enter the number **13** and press Enter to indicate that you'd like to purge all deleted mail. Wildcat! displays the event date selection screen.
3. Press **2**, **4**, and **6**. Wildcat! flags Monday, Wednesday, and Friday as scheduled days for this event.
4. Press **S** to save and continue. Wildcat! prompts you to select an execution method.
5. Press **F** (or just hit Enter) to specify the flexible execution method. Because this isn't a critical event, Wildcat! will try to process it in a period of inactivity, but it's still guaranteed to run on each scheduled day. This also means we won't need to specify a start time, as we did with the soft method used for our external event.
6. Wildcat! returns you to the Event Manager screen, where you'll see the details of both events are now displayed (see fig. 9.7).

In addition to adding events, you can also perform the following functions from the Event Manager:

- Delete existing events.
- Edit existing events.

- Toggle the display between the next scheduled event and the last time the event was executed.
- Run a selected event immediately.

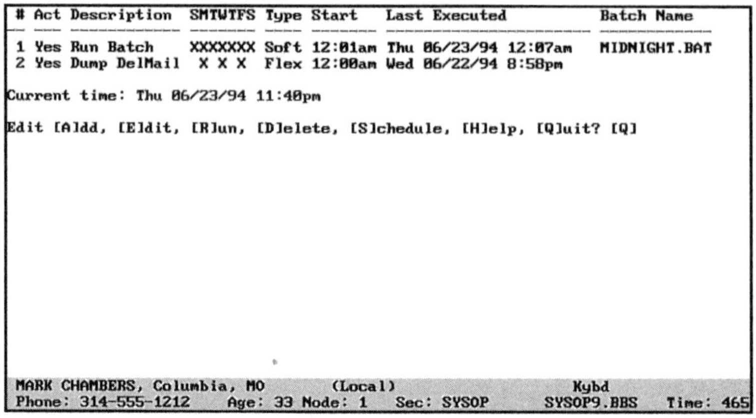

Fig. 9.7
The completed events (one internal, one external) displayed within the Event Manager.

Writing a Scheduled Batch File

Although writing a DOS batch file is a simple operation, you'll still have to test it thoroughly before you allow it to run unattended, and you should provide plenty of comments throughout to help you keep track of which programs are being executed and what they're doing.

If you're running Wildcat! Lite, always use the "shell to DOS" method for your external batch files when possible, which allows a small portion of Wildcat! to remain in memory. If you use this method, do not add the line CAT or WILDCAT to the end of your batch file, because the BBS program will automatically reload itself after the batch file exits to DOS.

Although detailed instructions on writing a batch file are beyond the scope of this book, there are a number of guidelines that particularly apply to sysops:

- Keep in mind that your batch file must change directories to the proper location before attempting to run a program (unless you've added the directory where the utility is located to your DOS path, in which case you can run it from any directory). Failing to change directories is a common mistake among new sysops writing their first batch files.
- If a program generates messages to the screen while it's running and you want to record them, you can use the DOS redirection command to send the text to a file; because most of your batch files will run

unattended, this is a good way of checking program status and error messages the next morning. A typical redirection command would appear like this:

```
utility1.exe > utility1.txt
```

If you'll be using the redirection command on a continuing basis, don't forget to delete the existing file first before running the program; or, you can append text to the file by using two redirection symbols, like this:

```
utility1.exe >> utility1.txt
```

- Remember, you can't run programs from your batch file that pause for a keystroke or require typed input! However, depending on the program, you may be able to use the DOS pipe command to supply keystrokes from a file. A typical pipe command would appear like this:

```
keypress.txt ¦ utility1.exe
```


Using the Sysop Menu

Your Sysop menu acts as the command center for your entire bulletin board system—therefore, it bears repeating again that you and your co-sysop should be the only people with security levels high enough to see this menu! In this section, we'll discuss the commands available from the Sysop menu, as well as how you'll use them to view and manage your system files.

We'll also cover one of the most useful functions available on your system—the drop to DOS command, which you can use to access DOS and run programs on your system while connected with a modem.

Managing Your System Files

Warning: We're now entering an area that every sysop would rather forget about—or at least ignore as long as possible! No matter what BBS program you choose, maintaining your system files is probably the least glamorous part of running a bulletin board, and unfortunately no BBS utility can possibly perform it for you. Whether you're upgrading users, verifying uploaded files, or simply calling up a user's record to retrieve a forgotten password, much of your online time will be spent adding or editing records in your userlog or your download file directories.

> **Tip**
>
> Time to say it again: Backup your hard drive regularly (at least once every two weeks)! The data we'll be discussing in this section is a sysop's most prized possession. Ask any sysop who's lost an entire userlog or a complete file library's worth of descriptions to a hard drive crash—your BBS will likely take many months to recover from a catastrophic hardware failure without a backup.

Adding, Editing, and Deleting Users

Wildcat! Lite provides three methods of accessing the User Maintenance screen (see fig. 9.8). The most obvious entry point is from the Sysop menu (with the U command). You can also display the user record for the sender or receiver of a message you've just read by pressing **S**. Finally, you can display the record for the user who uploaded a file from the file database by pressing **U**.

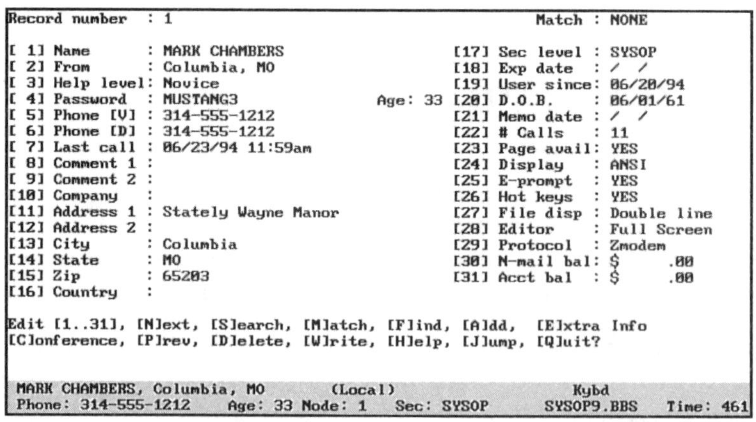

Fig. 9.8
The User Maintenance screen.

> **Tip**
>
> Many BBS programs provide external programs to allow you to make changes to your userlog from the DOS prompt. If your BBS package has such a program (or you're using a third-party utility), see if it can run unattended within your external event batch file—if so, you can adjust items such as security levels and flags automatically every day.

Let's briefly describe each of the commands that are available from this screen:

- **Next.** Displays the next userlog record in the database. If you've used the Match function to set display criteria, Next displays the next record that matches the specified criteria.
- **Search.** Searches your entire userlog file for a specific name or portion of a name.
- **Match.** Displays all records with a security access level or expiration date matching the value you specify. Once you've displayed the last matching record, the match criteria is reset to NONE.
- **Find.** Searches your entire userlog file for a specific full name.
- **Add.** Allows you to manually add a user to your userlog, which you must do if you elect to run a "closed" system. Make sure the user knows the password you assign!
- **Extra Info.** Displays a second screen of userlog data for the current record.
- **Conference.** Allows you to assign the user as a co-sysop for a message conference or lock the user temporarily out of a conference.
- **Prev.** Displays the next userlog record in the database. If you've used the Match function to set display criteria, Prev displays the previous record that matches the specified criteria.
- **Delete.** Removes the current record from your userlog file.
- **Write.** Allows you to compose and send a message to the user currently displayed.
- **Help.** Displays online help for these commands.
- **Jump.** Skips to the record with a last name closest to the string you enter.
- **Quit.** Exits the User Maintenance screen and returns you to the Sysop menu, saving any changes you've made.

To illustrate how you'll use the User Maintenance screen, let's add a caller, modify his userlog data, and then delete him. To add a user, follow these steps:

1. Press **A** to add a user and press Enter.
2. Wildcat! prompts you for the name of the new caller. Type **Mark Twain** and press Enter.
3. Next, assign the caller a security level; in this case, press **2** for standard user access and press Enter.
4. Type the caller's location—in this example, your city and state—and press Enter.
5. Wildcat! prompts you for a password for the new caller. Type the word **password** and press Enter. Make sure the caller knows the password you assign!

You're done—Wildcat! displays the new user record (see fig. 9.9). You'll notice that most of the fields are still blank; rather than force the sysop to enter all of the information for a caller, the Add function requires only a minimum of data. The new caller you've added should use the Your Settings command on the Main menu during his or her first logon to fill out the remainder of the questions in the user record.

Fig. 9.9
A partial new user record created with the Add function.

```
Record number  : 2                                         Match : NONE

[ 1] Name       : MARK TWAIN                    [17] Sec level : FULLUSER
[ 2] From       : Columbia, MO                  [18] Exp date  : /  /
[ 3] Help level: Novice                         [19] User since: 06/23/94
[ 4] Password   : PASSWORD              Age: ?? [20] D.O.B.    : /  /
[ 5] Phone [V] :                                [21] Memo date : /  /
[ 6] Phone [D] :                                [22] # Calls   : 0
[ 7] Last call : 06/23/94 11:45pm               [23] Page avail: NO
[ 8] Comment 1 :                                [24] Display   : No color
[ 9] Comment 2 :                                [25] E-prompt  : YES
[10] Company    :                               [26] Hot keys  : NO
[11] Address 1 :                                [27] File disp : Double line
[12] Address 2 :                                [28] Editor    : No default
[13] City       :                               [29] Protocol  : No default
[14] State      :                               [30] N-mail bal: $      .00
[15] Zip        :                               [31] Acct bal  : $      .00
[16] Country    :

Edit [1..31], [N]ext, [S]earch, [M]atch, [F]ind, [A]dd,  [E]xtra Info
[C]onference, [P]rev, [D]elete, [W]rite, [H]elp, [J]ump, [Q]uit?

 MARK CHAMBERS, Columbia, MO          (Local)                  Kybd
 Phone: 314-555-1212     Age: 33 Node: 1    Sec: SYSOP    SYSOP9.BBS    Time: 460
```

Next, we'll edit the user record we just created. From the Sysop menu, follow these steps:

1. Press **U** to display the User Maintenance screen. Because we exited and reentered this screen, we must search for Mark Twain's user record.

2. Because we know the complete name and the correct spelling, press **F** to find the record. If we had not known the exact spelling or the last name, we could have used the Search function—or, if we had known only the first few characters of the last name, we could have used the Jump command. Wildcat! prompts us for the complete user name; type **Mark Twain** and press Enter.

3. Wildcat! displays the record. We'll change the password and provide the birthdate. First, press **4** to change the password. Wildcat! prompts you to enter a new password (note that you must backspace over the existing password, which is provided as a default). Type **steamboat** and press Enter.

4. Now press **20** to edit the date of birth (DOB) field. Wildcat! will automatically format the date, so no slashes or hyphens are necessary. Type today's date and press Enter.

5. Finally, press **Q** to quit and press Enter. Wildcat! automatically saves your changes to the caller's record, as well as any other changes you made to other records during the same session.

Finally, let's delete this example record. From the Sysop menu, follow these steps:

1. Press **U** to display the User Maintenance screen.

2. Once again, press **F** to find the record. Wildcat! prompts us for the complete user name; type **Mark Twain** and press Enter.

3. Wildcat! displays the record. Press **D** to indicate you wish to delete this user and press Enter.

4. The BBS prompts you for confirmation. Press **Y** to confirm your choice and press Enter.

5. Wildcat! displays a status message confirming that the record has been deleted.

Adding, Editing, and Deleting Files

Wildcat! provides two methods of accessing the File Maintenance screen (see fig. 9.10). The most obvious entry point is from the Sysop menu (with the F command). You can also display the maintenance screen while reading messages by pressing **S**.

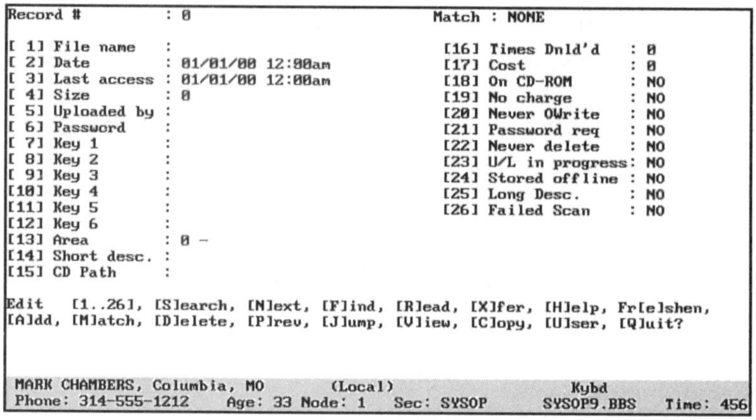

Fig. 9.10
The File Maintenance screen.

Tip

Unlike Wildcat!, most bulletin board programs maintain separate "directory" files within each download section. A directory file holds the ASCII text description of each download file in that section. The Wildcat! database approach places all these descriptions in a central database. If you're using another BBS program, it should still allow you some method of adding files without shutting down your system.

Let's briefly describe each of the commands that are available from this screen:

- **Search.** Searches your entire file database for a specific filename or portion of a filename.
- **Next.** Displays the next file record in the database. If you've used the Match function to set display criteria, Next displays the next record that matches the specified criteria.
- **Find.** Searches your entire file database for a specific full filename.
- **Read.** Displays the contents of the file corresponding to the current record. The file must be in ASCII text format.
- **Xfer.** Allows you to move a file from one file section to another. The file's date stamp is automatically updated, marking it as a new file.
- **Help.** Displays online help for these commands.
- **Freshen.** Updates a record's date and time stamp to match the file's current stamp.

- **Add.** Allows you to manually add one or more files to your file database. A subdirectory of files can be added by specifying the DOS filename wildcard *.* instead of a single filename.
- **Match.** Displays all file records in a file area, all file records with a particular keyword, or all files uploaded by a specified caller. Once you've displayed the last matching record, the match criteria is reset to NONE.
- **Delete.** Removes the current file record from your file database. You can elect to erase the corresponding file from your drive, or simply delete the record and leave the file on your drive.
- **Prev.** Displays the next file record in the database. If you've used the Match function to set display criteria, Prev displays the previous record that matches the specified criteria.
- **Jump.** Skips to the record with a filename closest to the string you enter.
- **View.** Displays the contents of a compressed archive file—for example, a ZIP or ARJ archive.
- **Copy.** Copies the file corresponding to the current record to the location you specify. Note that this does not delete either the existing record or the original file.
- **User.** Displays the User Maintenance screen, with the user record of the file's uploader displayed as the current record. Once you select Quit, Wildcat! returns to the File Maintenance screen.
- **Quit.** Exits the File Maintenance screen and returns you to the Sysop menu, saving any changes you've made.

To illustrate how you'll use the File Maintenance screen, let's add a file, move it to another file section (as you might move uploaded files to their proper section), and finally delete the file. First, however, we'll need to create a file in your \WC30\UPLOADS directory. For this example, simply copy the file CAT.BAT from your Wildcat! home directory into your upload directory.

To add a file, follow these steps:

1. From the Sysop menu, press **F** for File Database. Wildcat! displays the File Maintenance screen—it will be empty unless you've already added files.
2. Press **A** to add a file and press Enter.

3. Wildcat! prompts you for the name of the new file. Type **CAT.BAT** and press Enter.

4. Next, you must tell the BBS where the file is located; select area 6 (Uploads) and press Enter.

5. Wildcat! prompts you for confirmation that you wish to add CAT.BAT to the database. Press **Y**.

6. You now have a chance to assign a password to this file; if you use this security feature, any user attempting to download this file must provide the correct password before the download can begin. For our example, no password is necessary (and most sysops don't use them for downloads because passwords are easily forgotten), so press **N**.

7. Wildcat! requests that you enter a file description, which will be displayed to your callers. Type **An example file** and press Enter.

8. Finally, you're asked to enter one or more keywords that your callers can use as search criteria. Type **test** and press Enter.

Wildcat! confirms that the file has been added to area 6 of your database and displays the new file record (see fig. 9.11).

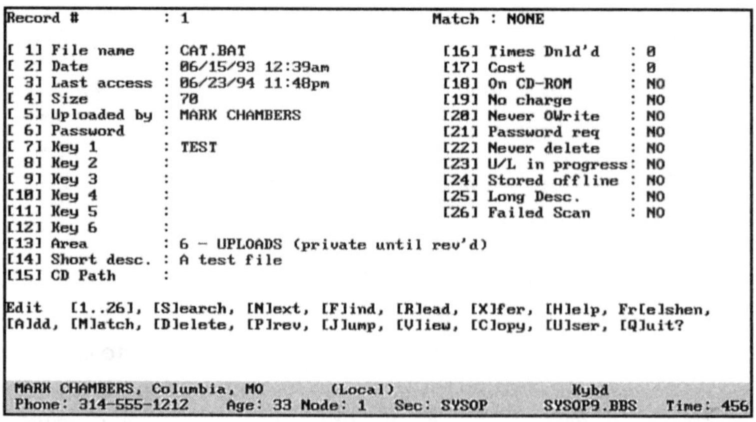

Fig. 9.11
A file database record created with the Add function.

Next, we'll move both the file record we just created and its corresponding file to the proper area; this will probably be one of your most common chores. From the File Maintenance screen, follow these steps:

1. Press **X** to transfer a file. Wildcat! prompts you for the destination file area—if you're unsure which area is which, press **L** to list all of your areas. For this example, let's move CAT.BAT to area 1 (Utilities).

2. Press **2** to indicate file area 1 and press Enter. Wildcat! should display a status message indicating that the transfer was successful. Press Enter to update the record display, and you'll note that field 13 now reflects Utilities as the file area.

Finally, let's delete this example file record. From the Sysop menu, follow these steps:

1. Press **F** to display the File Maintenance screen.

2. We only have a single file in our database so there's no reason to use the Find function. Press **D** to indicate you wish to delete this file and press Enter.

3. The BBS prompts you for confirmation. Press **Y** to confirm your choice and press Enter.

4. Wildcat! displays a status message affirming that the record has been deleted, then asks if you'd like to delete the file CAT.BAT from the Utilities file area.

5. We do wish to delete the spare copy of CAT.BAT; press **Y** and press Enter.

Purging Your Message Database

The Sysop menu command Purge Deleted Mail removes deleted mail from your message base, freeing the space it occupied for additional messages. Although a message is marked deleted, it's not actually removed until you use this function (or run the Purge Messages internal event); therefore, callers with access levels high enough to read deleted mail can still read deleted messages. For security, this access level should be restricted to you, the sysop.

Unlike the Purge Messages event, this command allows you to selectively purge deleted messages from either your current conference or the entire message base.

Note that you can always check on how many active and deleted messages you have in your message base by using the Status of Databases command from the Sysop menu.

Viewing and Killing the System Activity Log

Your system activity log is your online record of everything that occurs on your BBS, including who calls and when they connected, the commands they used, any errors encountered by the BBS program, and any scheduled events that were processed (fig. 9.12). For a Wildcat! system, you can view the log online from the Sysop menu with the Activity Log Listing command; the BBS displays the log starting with the most recent entries and works backward. The BBS will ask you which node log you wish to view; because your Wildcat! system is a single-line BBS, always reply 1 to this question.

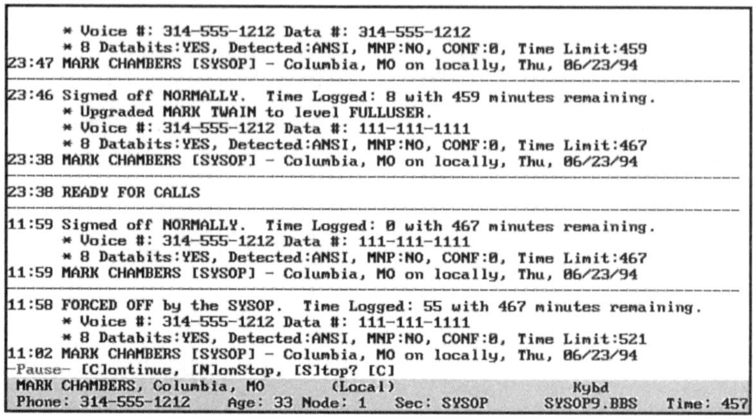

Fig. 9.12
A typical excerpt from the BBS activity log.

Of course, your activity log is likely to grow quickly on a busy system, so you'll have to delete it from time to time to conserve space. You can use the Kill Activity Log command on the Sysop menu to delete your activity log; Wildcat! will prompt for confirmation before erasing the file. Another empty log is automatically created, ready for new entries.

> **Tip**
>
> If you have the space (either on your hard drive or on floppies), it's a good idea to save your old activity logs before you delete them! You can use these records to track a user's activities over time, as well as track down errors that may have occurred some time ago. At a minimum, you should keep the last log file; however, some sysops keep log files going back a year or more! To create a backup, copy the log file (in this case, ACTIVITY.001) with an extension of .BAK in your BBS directory or to a floppy disk. You can then erase the file and regain the space.

Using the Node Manager

The Sysop menu Node Manager (see fig. 9.13) allows you to toggle many system functions on or off, modify the access level or time for the current caller, and display additional status information on the current and previous caller. If you're running a multiline system, you can use the Jump command to display the same information for each node in your system; with a single-line system like ours, however, we can still use it to control Node 1.

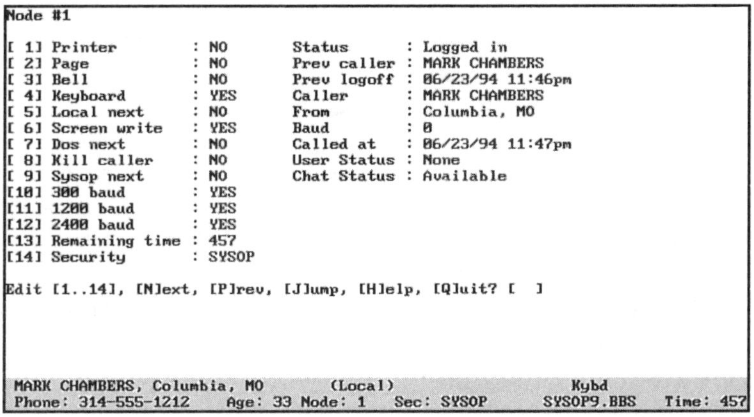

Fig. 9.13
The Node Manager screen.

From this screen, you can control the system printer, keyboard, and screen, enable or disable paging or the page bell, and restrict logons by baud rate.

The Local Next, DOS Next, and Sysop Next switches determine the action Wildcat! will take when the current user logs off. Set Local Next to Yes to initiate a local logon. Set DOS Next to Yes to exit Wildcat! and return to DOS. Set Sysop Next to Yes to initiate a sysop local logon.

You can also control the current caller's session. Change the value for field 13 to modify the caller's remaining online time; change the value of field 14 to raise or lower the caller's security level (much like the sysop console F9 key). You can even kill the current caller's session, which logs the user off immediately—take care, this switch controls your local logons as well!

Using the Remote Drop to DOS Command

Nothing is more convenient for a sysop away from home than the ability to drop to DOS remotely, especially when an error has occurred (such as the BBS hard drive running out of space); as we mentioned earlier in the book, it's one of the luxuries of running a network BBS program instead of an integrated program. From the DOS prompt, you can use the familiar DOS commands you already know to copy, rename, and move files, type files to the screen, run automated batch files and—if you invoke the program DOORWAY as a part of the process—you can even use well-behaved DOS applications that display ANSI graphics!

Tip

Although you can provide your co-sysop or other users with access to your Drop to DOS command, most sysops do not—and those sysops who do invariably come to regret it sooner or later! Even if your co-sysop is trustworthy to a fault, online accidents can happen. This command effectively puts your PC in the control of the remote caller, so restrict it to yourself!

In practice, the remote drop to DOS function is much like an external event. You once again have the option of shelling to DOS (with some of the BBS program remaining in memory) or terminating Wildcat! completely and exiting to DOS. As before, the shell method is highly recommended; it allows you to return quickly to Wildcat! by typing **Exit** and pressing Enter (just like the DOS Shell command on the Waiting for Calls screen), and doesn't require any changes to your CAT.BAT file.

Whenever you select the Drop to DOS command from the Sysop menu, Wildcat! first searches your Wildcat! home directory for a file called DROPDOS.BAT, which you can create with your text editor. If this file is found, Wildcat! executes any DOS batch file commands in DROPDOS.BAT automatically.

How does your BBS send the characters that are normally displayed on your console screen through the modem connection? This job is handled by a redirection program, which is required. DOS comes with an internal redirection command, CTTY, that will do in a pinch. However, it's highly recommended that you route characters with software created especially for BBS use, like the shareware redirection program DOORWAY. If you're running Wildcat! Lite, you can use the DROPDOS.BAT file to load DOORWAY automatically each time you drop to DOS remotely. The typical command is:

```
DOORWAY COM1 /C:DOS
```

where your BBS is using COM1. You can download DOORWAY and its documentation from the Mustang BBS.

Summary

In this chapter, you learned many of the features Wildcat! offers you behind the scenes on the Sysop menu. You added, modified, and deleted example records from your userlog and file databases. We discussed how to schedule automatic events that can help you maintain your system. You also learned more about using the Drop to DOS command for remote maintenance.

Chapter 10

Expanding Your BBS

by Mark L. Chambers

Here's a scenario that's familiar to thousands of sysops around the world: your hobby BBS is now a couple of years old, and it's been steadily growing in popularity and services (even though you're not charging your users for access). You also find it's taking more of your time and money to maintain your system and add improvements, much less participate in the messages and games as you once did. Perhaps you've enlisted the help of a co-sysop to assist you in answering system mail or adding files. Suddenly, one of your users begins complaining about the busy signals in a public message, and a wave of replies appears out of nowhere—each agreeing that your BBS needs additional phone lines and a faster modem!

At this point, you'll have to make a number of important decisions. First, should you expand your system, and how? If you do decide to upgrade to a multiline BBS, should you continue to offer your users free access? Is it time your callers started sharing the cost of your bulletin board? Finally, if you do decide to charge your users, how will you do it? In this chapter, we'll address each of these questions in turn, and provide the guidelines you'll need to answer them for yourself.

Note that expansion in this case refers to additional phone lines or the addition of major services, not just a larger hard drive or a faster modem. Purchasing a single piece of hardware is usually more of a requirement for your system to operate instead of a fundamental expansion of your BBS.

It's also important to note that this chapter applies to every hobby and profit bulletin board, no matter what BBS software it uses, how many lines it currently offers, or the services it provides. Even if you're currently running a multiline system for profit, expansion is a continuing process, and you'll have to ask yourself the same questions whenever you must decide if your BBS should grow.

Reasons for Expansion

Of course, it's up to you whether you should expand your system—however, the signs that your BBS has reached its limit with your current PC, services, or phone lines are usually obvious to everyone, so you're likely to hear complaints from your users long before your system reaches critical mass! Reasons for expansion include:

- **Telephone line bottlenecks.** If your phone line (or lines) are busy at least 75 percent of your peak hours, it's time to consider adding additional lines. Peak hours typically fall between 7 a.m. and midnight, which yields 17 hours (or 1020 minutes). Why peak hours? Usage on most boards drops dramatically after midnight, so we can obtain a more accurate reading if we factor in only those hours where a user would have a hard time connecting to your BBS (if you have statistics for only a full 24-hour period, you can still use them, but peak hours are preferred). To calculate the percentage, multiply the number of calls your system receives on an average day during this time period by the number of minutes allowed for your standard access level; then, multiply 1020 by the number of lines you have. As an example, let's say your system has two lines and handles an average of 30 calls during those 17 hours. Figure 10.1 shows the calculation you would perform to arrive at 44 percent usage, which is well below our bottleneck figure of 75 percent usage.

Fig. 10.1
Calculating usage for a two line BBS.

$$\frac{\text{30 minutes x 30 calls}}{\text{2 lines x 1020}} = \frac{900}{2040} = 44\%$$

- **Sluggish system response.** TBBS, one of the two commercial integrated BBS packages we've mentioned, features real-time performance meters that display the amount of system resources used by both your CPU and your hard drive. Even if you don't have the luxury of performance meters, though, you and your users will be able to tell when your BBS is taxing your PC to its limits. Message retrieval slows to a crawl, or perhaps the BBS takes a noticeable amount of time loading even the smallest external door. Keep in mind that system response problems like these are rarely solved with a single component like a faster hard drive or extra RAM—instead, your BBS is telling you that it's time for a major PC upgrade, probably to the next processor level or a higher speed processor of the same type.

- **Consistent user comments.** Although they may or may not be phrased in the form of complaints, a consistent series of comments on the lack of a particular service from your users can often point out holes in your BBS feature list. For example, you might have a good collection of doors and an excellent file library, but you haven't added a message network on your BBS. As time passes, you might notice that your users always leave your system to read and post FidoNet messages on other boards, or several users might ask how they can access the FidoNet area on your system.

> **Tip**
>
> A targeted online questionnaire can also provide this kind of information; simply ask your users, "In what areas does this BBS need improvement?" Usually you'll get at least one area that's consistent among most of the users who answered the questionnaire.

Although the reasons for expansion that we've just listed are all practical, there's one intangible reason we haven't listed yet, and it's just as important: if you're excited by the prospect of improving your BBS, count that as a point in favor as well. It will take considerable enthusiasm on your part to install the hardware, configure the software, and perform all the testing necessary to add extra lines and services—if you're not feeling positive that you can do the work or that your BBS will benefit from the expansion, don't start!

Adding Lines

If you've determined that you need to add lines (which implies you'll be adding nodes to your Wildcat! system), the expense is worth it. Whether you're charging your users or not, they like your services and you're marketing and maintaining your BBS correctly. Expanding your line count is a very positive event, one that warrants a press release and all the advertising you can muster.

Adding extra lines involves additional decisions on your part as well. For example:

- **Subscriber-only or public lines?** If you're running a subscription hobby board or a profit system, consider offering at least one of your new lines as a subscriber-only number. If you're running a hunt group, this number should be separate, so that it returns a busy signal whenever a caller is online. These exclusive lines are a primary attraction, and they can generate quite a few subscriptions. Naturally, subscriber lines deserve the fastest modems on your system. If you do offer subscriber-only lines, make sure that fact appears somewhere during your new user registration process.

- **Restrict baud rates?** As you learned in the last chapter, most bulletin boards (including Wildcat!) provide a method of selectively restricting callers who connect at 300, 1200, and 2400 baud from using one or more of your lines. If your system concentrates on providing download files, these users are probably creating bottlenecks for callers who would otherwise have time to connect.

- **Business line rates?** Most telephone companies charge higher rates for more than two or three lines entering your home, even if your system is not operated as a business. Make sure you consider the rates for business lines in your local area before ordering those additional lines.

- **Upgrade your BBS software?** Your additional lines may force you to upgrade your BBS software. Most bulletin board programs are offered in a step system, where you purchase a version of the program that will operate a certain maximum number of lines. If you're adding more than one or two lines and your proposed line count will force you to upgrade your software, consider adding only the necessary number of lines to reach the maximum (thus avoiding an expensive upgrade).

The equipment you'll require to upgrade is dependent upon the following:

- **The type of BBS you're running.** If you're running a multiline network system like Wildcat!, you may require an additional workstation PC for each line you add. Integrated systems like TBBS and Major BBS may need additional multiport serial cards.

- **The response time and system loading displayed by your current BBS computer.** If you can add lines to your current system and your PC is easily handling your BBS at full load (when all lines are busy), it's a safe bet that you can add one or two extra lines without compromising your system's performance.

Adding Services

Adding major services is a more difficult decision than adding new lines, which are a basic requirement if your BBS is to continue to grow. Although the requests may be frequent and the demand may seem heavy initially, your users will probably take some time before they use the full potential of expensive services. For instance, the addition of Internet services to a BBS typically involves the purchase of a front-end program, a deposit and continuing membership with an Internet UUCP provider, and a large amount of disk space—yet a month after a difficult installation, you may find that your system has only received a handful of Internet e-mail messages!

Which services are most often added after a BBS goes online? In general, sysops either select major services that they decided to postpone during the original planning of their system, or they select a service that will generate direct profit. Typically, such services include:

- **Message networking.** Most sysops—the author included—feel it's much easier to add FidoNet or Internet connections after a BBS is running smoothly, because joining a network involves interaction with others and possible delays while your connections are finalized. For example, it may take some time for your FidoNet Regional Coordinator to assign you a FidoNet node ID and submit your system for incorporation into the international nodelist. Additionally, you'll find that connecting to one of these networks is rarely a trouble-free process, so it's better to make sure that your BBS is running well before digging in to a message network installation!

- **Graphical support.** Even though today's BBS programs offer much better built-in support for graphical emulations like RIP and NAPLPS, it still takes time to truly customize your new graphical menu system with unique images and menus that match your theme. Once again, most sysops wait until their systems are operating smoothly before undertaking the graphical challenge.

- **Merchandise sales.** If you have a business license, you're eligible to open an entirely new source of potential profit by offering an online shopping service to your callers. For instance, our example BBS might sell new and used classical CDs, with an online catalog available to callers 24 hours a day.

- **Subscription access.** A majority of systems start out as completely free—perhaps the sysop wants to gain experience before accepting subscriptions, or the sysop feels the BBS doesn't offer enough yet to warrant financial help from callers.

When you do add a major service, take the time to test it thoroughly before you allow your users access to it. The temptation to begin advertising a message network connection, subscriber access, or a fancy RIP menu system can be strong, but it's a good idea to use the new service several times a day for a week or so; you can also enlist the aid of your co-sysop or a couple of trusted users to help.

Selecting a Subscription Method

If you've been running a free hobby system, it's a big step to begin charging for access—both for you and your users! This is certainly not something to be done lightly, because you'll be making a commitment to your callers as customers rather than visitors, and you must be prepared to spend additional time, money, and effort in improving your BBS to attract them into a subscription (and keep them returning to resubscribe).

> **Tip**
>
> To avoid publicizing your home address, consider obtaining a post office box for your subscription mail.

Similarly, it's also a big step to move from a hobby system that charges for higher access to a true profit BBS. You should obtain a business license before opening your system to the public. You'll no longer be offering your new callers a standard free access level; instead, they should be given a trial period of partial or full subscriber services so that they can judge for themselves whether they should join your system. Callers who don't subscribe should receive a minimum of services.

In this section, we'll discuss the following two subscription models that you can apply to your system:

- A *hobby subscription* model, where you accept contributions for your system and provide higher access levels (while still maintaining a level of free access).

- A *pure profit subscription* model, where new users are allowed a glimpse of your system and then subscribe to receive full access. There are several methods of providing a brief look at your BBS for your new users, and we'll discuss these as well.

The Hobby Subscription Model

The hobby subscription model is quite popular among hobby sysops who really don't want to dedicate the time required to make their bulletin boards a profitable venture, but still want to add improvements. If you feel that your users should share just a part of the cost involved in operating your BBS, this is a good plan to implement. Hobby subscription boards rarely break even financially, so skip forward to the next section if you'd like to make a profit from your system.

This subscription model requires that you set up a rate chart for your callers. You'll use this rate chart in your subscription bulletin, a permanent text file that provides users with complete information on how to subscribe to your system. Your chart should look something like table 10.1.

Table 10.1 A BBS Subscription Rate Chart

Plan	Daily Time	Daily Bytes	Subscriber Line	Cost
A	30 min.	1,024,000	no	$10.00
B	45 min.	2,048,000	yes	$20.00
C	60 min.	unlimited	yes	$30.00

Notice that this chart offers several subscriber access levels, each of which provides the caller with additional time and a higher download limit per day. Each step on this chart is clearly defined, and each offers a clear advantage over the levels below it. A single flat rate subscriber access level wouldn't be nearly as popular as this system, because your callers will appreciate the opportunity to choose the access level they want. For instance, if a caller knows that a megabyte of files will be more than sufficient each day, the lower cost of subscription plan A will be highly attractive; if you had offered only plan C, however, that user would probably have decided not to subscribe at all.

At a minimum, your rates should be available in six month and one year plans; again, the more flexibility you provide, the better the chances that your customers will subscribe, so you may even wish to provide a three month subscription rate! As we mentioned earlier in the book, you should still include a standard access level that's free for all users; subscribers will fall back to this level when they reach their expiration date.

Your Wildcat! BBS has basic built-in support for a subscription system based on expiration dates, and it's more than adequate for most hobby boards. To prepare this system, follow these steps:

1. First, run MAKEWILD and display the Security Profile Definition screen.
2. For each of the subscription access levels you add, highlight the profile name and press Enter to display the Edit screen (see fig. 10.2). Note the field close to the bottom of the screen called "Expire profile name"—change this field to the name of your free profile level, so that once the caller's expiration date arrives, he or she returns to standard user access level.

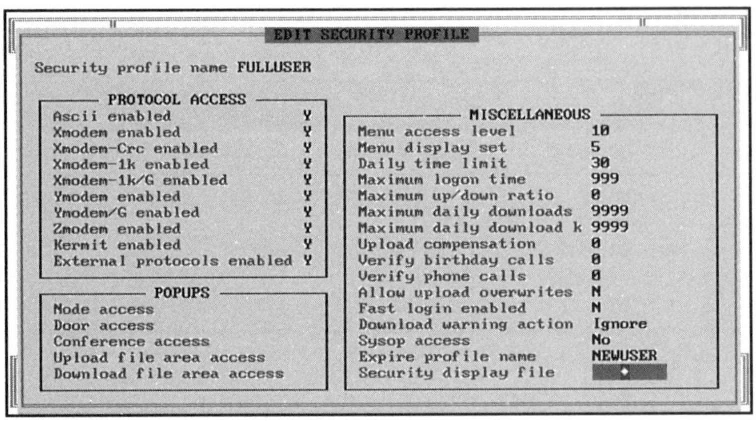

Fig. 10.2 The MAKEWILD Security Profile Edit screen, where you should specify the access level subscribers receive on their expiration date.

3. Next, create four files in your Wildcat! home directory: WARN60.BBS, WARN45.BBS, WARN30.BBS, and WARN15.BBS. These files are displayed to your subscribers during logon when their subscriptions are 60, 45, 30, and 15 days from expiring. Your warning files can include display variables, so you can personalize them automatically. Don't forget to inform the caller how to re-subscribe and how many days remain until expiration!

Now you're ready to accept subscriptions! When you receive subscription money from a caller, assign that caller the corresponding subscriber access level, and set the expiration date in the caller's user record to the correct number of days in the future. Wildcat! will take care of the rest by warning the caller of the approaching expiration date—if the user doesn't resubscribe, your BBS will automatically reset the user record to the standard free access level.

If you accept funds for your bulletin board, don't forget that you're taking on some or all of these additional responsibilities:

- You'll need to report any income for your tax return. If you're uncertain how to handle this, consult a professional tax preparer on your next return.
- Even though your hobby BBS may not make a profit, your city and county government may require you to obtain a business license and charge sales tax anyway. If you're running a profit BBS, these will probably become necessities. To learn the requirements in your area, contact your local Better Business Bureau or the Department of Revenue.
- As we mentioned earlier, your telephone company may require you to pay business rates for your lines if you accept money for subscriptions.
- Naturally, you should maintain complete records of each transaction—both income and expenses—for tax purposes. If you decide to treat your BBS as a home business, you'll be able to claim business expenses, and those records will be worth their weight in gold at tax time. Store your original receipts in a well-ordered fashion; if you use a personal financial program like Microsoft Money, create a separate set of records for your BBS.

The Pure Profit Subscription Model

Many profit boards use the idea of time credits, which the caller can purchase to use online. This method is roughly equivalent to the system used by theme parks—the customer pays money up front to buy online time, and then all of your services from that point are provided free. The advantage to the credits system is that your users can apply them toward any online service you offer and use them as they see fit. New users on credit boards typically receive a number of credits up front—you decide the amount you feel is fair.

Some boards apply the credit method to a particular part of the board—for example, netmail access, games, a fax service, or download time—and offer the remainder of the BBS for free. Under this plan, callers would be able to read messages and scan file descriptions for free, but downloading or playing games would cost them credits; the new user on this type of board still has a form of free access, but is restricted from enjoying all the benefits of your system without subscribing.

Your profit board can use the same expiration system that we described for hobby subscription boards, but remember to provide an expired access level that allows your callers at least a few options after their subscriptions have run out! For example, this access could allow a caller to read public messages, leave you feedback, and download general utility files like PKZIP and VIRUSCAN. As you learned earlier in the book, if you don't provide a minimum access level, you're sending the wrong message to your users and they're likely to subscribe only once.

If you use an expiration system, new users should either receive a trial subscription level (perhaps a week) or be provided with a new user access level (complete with bulletins describing all the services you offer).

As a sysop of a profit BBS, you should immediately obtain a third-party user management/accounting system especially written for your BBS. Many of these are online programs that you can use without taking down your system; they can print demographic reports, handle automatic subscription expiration and sales taxes, print mailing labels, and track subscription renewals. Figure 10.3 shows the main screen from a popular user management system. Ask the opinions of other sysops running your BBS program for their recommendations on which user management package is best—a good place to do this is on the BBS manufacturer's support system.

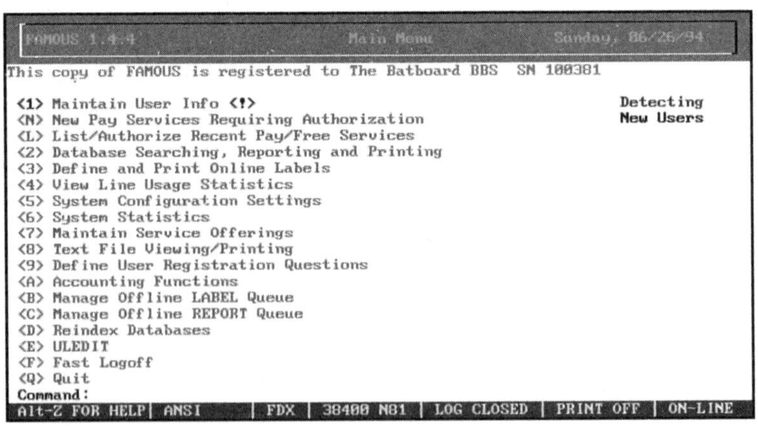

Fig. 10.3
A user management/accounting system tailored for subscription and profit bulletin boards.

No matter what subscription method you choose, keep one important fact in mind: your BBS has crossed over the line and has become a business (even if it's still not your livelihood). You must provide the best services and maintain them daily, or your service is doomed to fail! Take the time to add new files daily and participate as much as possible in every area of your BBS. You should also answer feedback messages and process user requests as soon as possible.

Tip

If you're committed to making your BBS your primary source of income, consider the possibility of creating a corporation instead of remaining the sole proprietor of your system. Corporations provide many tax and legal liability advantages, and they're relatively inexpensive to create. The requirements for creating a corporation vary from state to state, so contact an accountant or attorney for information on what's necessary in your area.

Expanding Your Charging Methods

If you've been accepting money from subscribers for higher access to your hobby system, it's likely that you've been receiving that money in two forms: personal checks and money orders. At times, many sysops also accept hardware donations in exchange for higher access, which sometimes can result in substantial upgrades for your BBS computer.

However, accepting only checks and money orders imposes limits on your subscribers that are guaranteed to limit the size and growth of your BBS as well. Your users are less likely to take the time to write a check or buy a money order, address an envelope, and mail it to you as they are to provide a credit card number online and receive immediate credit (in effect, credit cards allow online impulse purchases)! Certainly, obtaining a credit card merchant account for a BBS is a hassle, and it opens your system to fraudulent credit card charges—but the potential benefit to your profit BBS is so substantial, it's worth these problems.

Until recently, there was no alternative to credit card purchases for online subscriptions, but the arrival of 1-900 billing has provided another route of charging your callers for online time.

In this section, we'll discuss how you can put one of these two online subscription methods into practice on your profit BBS.

Adding Credit Cards

Why is it such a headache for a BBS sysop to get a credit card merchant account for a BBS? In essence, it's because of the nature of bulletin boards themselves. To illustrate, let's pretend you're running a software store instead of a BBS. When you approach your banker for a merchant account, you could point to your building and your software stock as assets; you'd be the owner of a conventional business, familiar to your banker, and you'd be accorded the respect deserved by any business owner.

Now imagine the banker's position as a sysop arrives to discuss a credit card merchant account. Where's the storefront? Where's the stock, the goods that customers will purchase? It's not the banker's fault that bulletin boards aren't well known as profitable business ventures; instead, if your banker has heard of bulletin boards at all, he or she has probably heard that they're purveyors of pornography or hangouts for software pirates. Remember, your banker is responsible for any charges that you cannot repay.

The secret to obtaining a local merchant account for a BBS is to prepare yourself beforehand—not only with proof that your BBS will make money, but with the real facts about cyberspace! It's important not to appear technically condescending while you're talking with your banker; instead, do your best to paint your BBS as a conventional business that uses high-tech equipment. Keep these guidelines in mind:

- Your banker will expect a formal business plan, which describes your current business structure and lays out the possibilities for future growth. Although many books purport to provide instructions for preparing a plan on your own, it's highly recommended that you recruit the services of an accountant or professional business consultant to help you build a comprehensive business plan.

- Plan on presenting complete statistics from your BBS that prove how popular it really is and explain the common technology behind a bulletin board—if you have a laptop with a modem or you can borrow one, prepare a short demonstration of just what services you do provide. A hands-on demonstration can go far in proving that your system is a legitimate, prospering online business.

- Make sure to bring examples of the credit-card processing features and accounting reports available within your BBS user management software. This can include printouts of your cash flow information (as long as the data is positive!), statistics on the number of subscribers to your system and positive demographic data.

- Finally, appeal to your banker's interest in making a profit—present examples of successful bulletin boards that are already taking credit cards. Possible sources of information include Chapter 12 of this book, a copy of *Boardwatch Magazine*, and even testimonials from local computer stores.

Is there a way to avoid all this hassle? As long as you stay on a local level, the answer is no—however, one of the most popular card account providers is not even a bank, and you won't be required to explain what a BBS is in order to be considered! Teleflora CreditLine is a national organization that provides merchant accounts to high-risk clients, and they've provided sysops with accounts for several years; you can contact them at 800/325-4849.

Adding 1-900 Services

As mentioned earlier, the 1-900 charge method offers another avenue for collecting subscription money from your users. In this system, a caller wishing to subscribe to your system calls a 1-900 number you provide, which results in a flat rate being charged to the user's telephone bill. In return, the subscribing user receives a password or code to enter in a special door you offer on your system, which updates the user's security access or credit balance with the equivalent subscription access.

This system is not without its problems as well because minors can abuse the subscription system. If you use a 1-900 charge method, you must make certain that your BBS displays the appropriate warnings and legal disclaimer to avoid potential problems with minors overcharging their parent's telephone bill. You'll also need the door software to process codes so that your BBS can supply higher access to subscribers.

Contrary to popular belief, it's not economically feasible for an individual bulletin board to add a 1-900 number. Of course, users would accumulate tremendous bills calling your BBS directly through such a number, even for the shortest online session. At the same time, the number isn't used enough by callers obtaining codes to warrant the expense of maintaining it.

Because a sysop really can't afford to maintain the phone line, how can you offer a 1-900 charge system on your BBS? The answer is a 1-900 service provider—for example, True Media Inc. offers the Telephone Access Billing System (or TABS for short), complete with free door software for members. Callers who subscribe to a TABS system call the company's 1-900 number, and True Media issues them the code for subscriber credit on that BBS. The sysop of a BBS using TABS receives a check each month, with no additional processing or work required. In return, True Media withholds 25 percent of the profit—that may seem high when compared to a credit card merchant account, but the convenience may be worth it. For more information, contact True Media at 800/755-8227.

Summary

In this chapter, we explored how you can expand your BBS to meet increased demand from your users, and how you can recognize that demand. You learned the details of adding additional lines and services to your BBS, as well as two popular methods of charging subscribers for access to your system. Finally, we covered the most important addition you can make to your profit system: the ability to charge by credit card or 1-900 billing.

In Chapter 11, you'll learn how to market and advertise your system to generate additional interest in both your new users and your current callers!

Chapter 11

Marketing Your BBS

by Mark L. Chambers

One of the keys to cultivating a thriving BBS is often overlooked by inexperienced sysops: it's the process of *marketing your system*, using the same approach employed by other types of businesses to build and expand their customer base. Without marketing savvy on the sysop's part, even the best of bulletin boards will never be well known beyond its local calling area. No matter whether your system is designed as a hobby BBS or a profitable online service, it will benefit from a few hours of your time spent on promotional tasks.

This chapter will help you attract the all-important long-distance new user, as well as build the popularity of your BBS among your existing callers. You'll learn the proven techniques and resources available to publicize your system in a professional manner. We'll also explore methods of increasing interest in your BBS through your own copyrighted promotional materials and demonstration software.

Publicizing Your BBS

Since the early days of bulletin boards, the online community has relied on the simplest and easiest method of disseminating BBS data: the BBS list, which can be printed and displayed on the wall at a software store, uploaded to local and long-distance boards, handed out at user meetings, or offered as an online database door for callers. Typically, original BBS lists offered only the numbers for boards in a local area or those boards with a specific theme, with perhaps a mention of the fastest modem speed supported by each system; the caller had to connect with each bulletin board to learn more about it.

Only in the past few years have such bulletin board lists attained national status, listing hundreds (and even thousands) of BBS numbers. Some of these expanded lists include the number of megabytes of file storage and incoming telephone lines, the theme of the BBS, and much more. With the advent of specialized magazines, newsletters, and message bases dedicated to bulletin boards, you now have many more avenues for publicizing your system by posting your system's number.

How can you tell which of your publicity methods is working? Simply add a question to your registration questionnaire that asks your new users where they learned of the existence of your system. If your promotional efforts are successful, you'll be surprised at the response you receive in calls from around the country, and sometimes even around the world.

In this section, we'll start by discussing BBS listings and continue to other methods—most of which are free or very inexpensive—of getting the word out to the rest of the world about your new BBS!

BBS Lists

Once you've announced the opening of your bulletin board with public messages on other local systems, check to see if there's a local bulletin board listing and who maintains it. You're likely to find this information somewhere within the list itself; if the list is available as a download file, there may also be instructions on how to add your system in a READ.ME or .DOC file. Listings may also be posted at local computer stores, or distributed at PC user group meetings.

> **Tip**
>
> If no one in your area maintains a local BBS list, consider creating one yourself. As an author of a BBS list, you're always kept up to date on your local online community, and your bulletin board can serve as the central point for others to submit updates and corrections. To create a format, study the regional and national listings mentioned later and select the features you want to include in your list. Make sure that others know where to send updates and additions. It's a fun project, and makes you very visible in your area of cyberspace.

Many systems also offer bulletin board databases or BBS list doors, where both sysops and users can post BBS numbers for other callers to search and download. If you're calling a system and notice this feature, it's well worth a few minutes to add your BBS name and number; callers who are new to data communications are always hungry for more numbers, and yours should be included in the list. In addition, ask your users to post your BBS name and number in the same manner on every BBS they call!

Bulletin board listings with national recognition include:

- **The Computer Shopper BBS Listing.** *Computer Shopper* magazine offers one of the most comprehensive BBS lists available; each entry includes the date the BBS was established, the number of lines, the amount of storage space online, whether or not the BBS charges a fee, the sysop's name, and much more. Listings are free of charge. Your system must operate 24 hours a day to be included. To add your BBS to the list, call the publisher's BBS at 913/478-3088.

- **The Online Access List.** *Online Access* magazine periodically publishes a huge listing of bulletin boards. This listing offers the name and number for each system.

- **The USBBS List.** Editor Bob Breedlove updates this well-known listing of PC-based bulletin boards often, and the USBBS listing now contains well over 3,000 systems; it's the best national listing that's not connected with a magazine. Figure 11.1 shows the first page of the USBBS list. The list includes details like the number of lines and the storage space for each system. The USBBS is a favorite upload on any BBS, and it's widely distributed, so make sure to call Breedlove's BBS at 916/929-7511 to add your board.

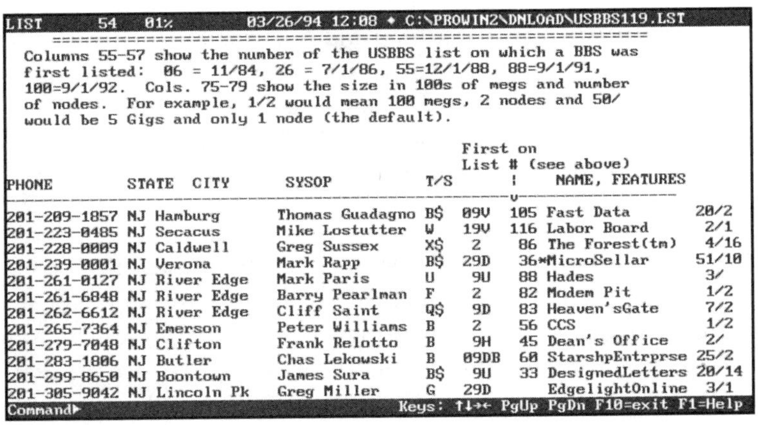

```
LIST        54   01%        03/26/94 12:08 ♦ C:\PROWIN2\DNLOAD\USBBS119.LST
    ==================================================================
  Columns 55-57 show the number of the USBBS list on which a BBS was
  first listed:  06 = 11/84, 26 = 7/1/86, 55=12/1/88, 88=9/1/91,
  100=9/1/92.  Cols. 75-79 show the size in 100s of megs and number
  of nodes.  For example, 1/2 would mean 100 megs, 2 nodes and 50/
  would be 5 Gigs and only 1 node (the default).

                                                 First on
                                                 List # (see above)
PHONE           STATE  CITY        SYSOP             T/S        !    NAME, FEATURES
------------------------------------------------------------------v--------------------
201-209-1857 NJ Hamburg        Thomas Guadagno B$  09V  105 Fast Data        20/2
201-223-0485 NJ Secacus        Mike Lostutter  W   19V  116 Labor Board       2/1
201-228-0009 NJ Caldwell       Greg Sussex     X$   2    86 The Forest(tm)    4/16
201-239-0001 NJ Verona         Mark Rapp       B$  29D   36*MicroSellar      51/10
201-261-0127 NJ River Edge     Mark Paris      U    9U   88 Hades             3/
201-261-6848 NJ River Edge     Barry Pearlman  F    2    82 Modem Pit         1/2
201-262-6612 NJ River Edge     Cliff Saint     Q$   9D   83 Heaven'sGate      7/2
201-265-7364 NJ Emerson        Peter Williams  B    2    56 CCS               1/2
201-279-7048 NJ Clifton        Frank Relotto   B    9H   45 Dean's Office     2/
201-283-1806 NJ Butler         Chas Lekowski   B   09DB  60 StarshpEntrprse  25/2
201-299-8650 NJ Boontown       James Sura      B$   9U   33 DesignedLetters  20/14
201-305-9042 NJ Lincoln Pk     Greg Miller     G   29D      EdgelightOnline   3/1
Command▸                                  Keys: ↑↓→← PgUp PgDn F10=exit F1=Help
```

Fig. 11.1
The first page from the national USBBS List.

- **The Boardwatch List.** *Boardwatch Magazine* maintains a popular, growing listing of bulletin boards called The Big List, where sysops can advertise their systems inexpensively on a monthly basis with a paragraph of text. *Boardwatch* also prints a different BBS listing each month that centers on one area, which often includes international bulletin boards in a particular country.

User Mailing Lists

If you've called many large multiline bulletin boards, you've probably received a postcard or brochure from at least one system—these *user mailings* (often called *follow-up mailings*) serve as a hook to remind you of the services offered by that BBS, and they're a proven method of enticing new callers to visit the system a second time. If you've made that critical second call, the BBS has made an impression on you, and you're more likely to subscribe. Mailings provide your callers with tangible evidence that you're running a business or a serious hobby system.

"Aren't mailings expensive?" you may be wondering. That depends, of course, upon the target audience (or the size of your userlog) and the type of mailing. A mailing targeted toward your new users will usually require a somewhat predictable amount of money each month, while a bulk mailing to over 2,000 users is going to cost considerably more. Postcards qualify for an inexpensive rate, but they don't offer much space for your introductory message or your feature list—on the other hand, multipage mailings are more expensive to mail and produce. A good compromise between the two is a single standard sheet of paper, folded in thirds.

Depending on your desktop publishing and layout skills, you may wish to design your own new user document, or you might ask a friend or one of your callers for help. Commercial programs like Print Shop or its shareware cousins can also create a simple one-page layout. Whatever tools you use, make sure your new user mailing includes the following information at a minimum:

- **Your BBS telephone number.** This may sound strange, but most callers type new numbers from a BBS list directly within their communications program, without creating a directory entry—unless your BBS makes a very favorable impression, there's a good chance the user would have to look up your number again before calling your bulletin board.

- **Your network and Internet addresses.** If your BBS has network or Internet connections, let your callers know where they can reach you.

- **Your most popular services.** Naturally, there's less room to do this on a postcard, so select the best, most impressive and most popular services offered on your system. Alternately, you may want to mention your board's theme.

- **How to subscribe.** If you're running a profit BBS or your hobby system takes subscriptions, let the caller know where to find your subscription bulletin—or, if you have room, give full details on your subscription setup.

User mailings aren't restricted just to your new callers, however. Sysops often announce important additions, improvements, or changes to their systems with a mailing (along with a bulletin or series of bulletins); for example, the addition of a new line, a change in access numbers, or a contest would probably warrant extra publicity. A mailing also makes it more certain that each of your callers will see your announcement, because some users may not log on during the period that a standard bulletin appears.

If you're running a profit system, you should also send a mailing to your paying users when their subscription is about to expire. This mailing should take another angle: you've already proven the value of the services and features of your BBS (or else these callers wouldn't have subscribed in the first place), so stress future improvements and how easy it is to renew a subscription on your BBS. Don't forget to thank your subscribers for helping to support your system, either; even if they don't renew their subscription immediately, they may do so in the near future!

Holidays and events may also provide you with opportunities for a mailing. Christmas postcards featuring your bulletin board logo make an excellent mailing, as do birthday announcements on your system's anniversaries. Another event worth a mailing might be your 1,000th or 10,000th caller, or a BBS party you're throwing (we'll discuss BBS parties later in this chapter).

Where do you find this address data on your callers? They'll provide it during the registration process, and most bulletin boards store it as a part of the userlog record. Many third-party utilities allow you to generate mailing labels from this data, ready to be added to your follow-up letter or postcard. It's a good idea to maintain periodic backups of your mailing list database, so that you can recover from catastrophic error.

Another type of user mailing never reaches the Post Office—this is an online *mass mailing*, where a sysop leaves the same electronic mail message for all users in the userlog (or a defined group of users). The advantages to mass mailing are obvious—there's no expense involved, and each user on your board receives a personal message. Many bulletin boards offer this feature built-in, while others may require a door or utility to perform the same function.

Although the mass mailing feature works differently on each BBS, the general steps are the same:

1. Write your mailing text. If your BBS allows you to "import" text into a message, use your text editor to create an ASCII file with your mailing information. Remember, your mailing should be written as if you were addressing an e-mail message directly to the individual caller; use a personal style, and use display variables to insert the caller's first name at one or two points in the text (if your BBS supports them). Also, unless you're specifically requesting feedback of some sort, phrase your message so that no reply is needed—this can save you from reading 50 replies to the same mass mailing!

> **Tip**
>
> If you're creating a text file to import, note that some BBS programs do not perform automatic "word wrap" while the caller reads messages—this feature automatically formats message text to match the number of columns displayed by the user's terminal program. If your BBS package doesn't have word wrap, use a right margin at column 39 so the message will display correctly to those callers using computers that display 40 columns.

2. Determine which group of users should receive your mailing. If your BBS uses a list of user names as a "template" for mass mailing, create the list as a file with your text editor.

3. Logon your system locally and begin the process of posting an e-mail message. Depending on your BBS software, you'll address the message in different ways to perform a mass mailing: the recipient field may contain more than one name or a particular code, you might specify the list template from step 2, or you might use a "carbon copy" field. Check your BBS documentation. If your BBS allows text import, you can load the text file you created in step 1 containing the message.

4. Save the message in the normal fashion.

Message Bases Devoted to BBS Advertisements

You'll find that many bulletin board systems you call will have a message section devoted to general discussions about BBS topics, while others have sections specifically provided for BBS advertisements. Take advantage of services like this and post an advertisement for your BBS every time you connect to a new system, whether it be local or long distance.

You can prepare for this in advance if you create an ASCII text advertisement for your BBS that's suitable for uploading. Most bulletin board programs allow the caller to upload the text of a message, which allows you to upload your advertisement directly instead of typing it each time. You can also upload your advertisement to the file section (some sysops frown on this, so check beforehand).

You can also distribute your ASCII text advertisement among your users by making it a download file. Encourage your users to post your advertisement in the same manner on every BBS they call—this kind of free publicity can result in a sharp increase of new users on your system!

Online services like CompuServe and networks like FidoNet and the Internet also provide message and file areas set aside for bulletin board advertising. On CompuServe, type **GO IBMBBS** at any ! prompt and upload your advertisement to the BBS Notices library section. On Internet, you can post advertisements on the alt.bbs Usenet newsgroup.

Press Releases

As a whole, the sysop community has only recently begun distributing press releases to the media; previously, bulletin boards weren't hot news for existing computer magazines and journals, and BBS-specific publications simply didn't exist. Today, there are a growing number of publications—both traditional and electronic—that have published press releases from larger bulletin boards.

Of course, the larger the BBS or service, the better your chances that your press release will be printed. If you run a smaller system, however, don't despair; the international message areas on CompuServe, FidoNet, and the Internet that we just discussed allow you to post announcements, so even a brand-new system can issue a press release that will be seen by thousands of bulletin board callers.

Like a user mailing, a press release should always contain your BBS number, network addresses, and a short description of your most popular services. Additionally, the format for a press release you distribute to BBS publications should follow these guidelines:

- Keep the length down to two pages or less. If a press release is too long, the editor will probably discard it rather than take the extra time necessary to trim it down to size.
- Don't be concerned with the layout of your release; if it's accepted, the text you've provided on disk will be formatted according to the style of the publication. Press releases are designed to be read quickly, so appearance isn't as important as correct spelling and punctuation.
- If you have a business card for your bulletin board, make sure you include it; even if your release is rejected, your card may result in a feature story or interview later.
- Begin your text with one or two paragraphs stating the reason for your release; it should be an important event worthy of mention. For example, if you're adding a CD-ROM jukebox for your file library, open your release with the date the hardware will be online, the capacity of the jukebox in gigabytes, and some of the CD-ROM titles it will offer. These facts are what will be interesting to readers, not the history of your BBS or the number of calls you receive a month (which are more suited for the ending of the release).
- Provide the text of your printed release on disk, as well as images in TIF or PCX format (if applicable).

Press releases should be addressed to the publication's editor; it's also a good idea to write "Dated Material—Press Release" on the envelope.

Signs

Another method of advertising is a sign promoting your BBS. Once again, you can use Print Shop or a similar program to create a one-page layout with your BBS name, number, and a short list of features and services you provide; if you have a clip art library, add an appropriate graphic or two to catch the reader's eye. Once your layout is complete, take the master page and have it copied onto colored paper.

Of course, you should post these signs at computer and software stores, but don't forget other businesses with customers that might be interested in your BBS; for example, we might post signs for our hypothetical Digital Mozart BBS at music stores or used CD shops. If your BBS specializes in online games, post a sign at your local fantasy gaming store. If there's a college or university nearby, you're likely to attract a surprising number of callers by posting a sign within the student union.

Figure 11.2 shows an example sign advertising our Digital Mozart BBS.

Fig. 11.2
An example sign publicizing The Digital Mozart BBS.

Demo Programs (Sound, Graphics, and Animation)

Demonstration programs are a fun way of promoting your BBS, and often you'll find they're accepted as upload files on systems that won't allow you to upload press releases. Additionally, a good demonstration program, image, or sound file will be distributed even further by other callers who've downloaded and enjoyed them.

There are only two rules to creating your own demonstration software: first, your program should perform some sort of worthwhile function for the person who spends the time (and quite possibly the money) to download it. Second, any original work you create should not violate an existing copyright (as we discussed in Chapter 8); in fact, you should copyright your demonstration before releasing it to the public.

If you're already experienced in some form of computer art or computer programming—as many sysops are—put that talent to work! Examples of BBS promotional files include:

- **Raytraced art and animations.** *Raytracing* involves the creation of lifelike, computer-generated 3-D images, and it has become one of the most popular types of computer artwork in a very short time. Although commercial raytracing applications are typically very expensive, several shareware and freeware programs are readily available on CompuServe and many bulletin boards, some with a surprising range of powerful features. Figure 11.3 shows a raytraced image promoting the author's bulletin board. You'll note that the BBS number is prominently displayed, while the image itself reflects the theme of the BBS; however, the picture can stand alone as an interesting example of raytracing, so it's also worth downloading. Raytraced animation (much like that used by television networks) is also a proven winner for demonstration programs.

Fig. 11.3 An example of a raytraced promotional image.

- **Simple freeware programs.** Although shareware authors rarely tie their programs directly to their bulletin boards, some sysops have created useful freeware utilities that display a simple advertisement for their bulletin board. Because the program is not shareware, you should avoid adding *nag* screens (display screens that pop up before, after, or even during operation) to advertise your system; rather, add a couple of lines with your BBS name, number, and a brief description that will display when the program returns to DOS.

- **Morphing animations.** *Morphing*—the process of slowly changing the contents of one image into the contents of another—is a fascinating visual effect being used in film and television. Like raytracing, morphing has attracted many would-be Hollywood special effects technicians to create their own animations on their home PCs. You'll find several shareware morphing programs available for downloading on CompuServe and larger bulletin board systems.

Tip

Both raytracing and morphing require fast PCs and a considerable amount of time, so you certainly shouldn't attempt to build (or render) either type of image on your BBS computer. However, if you're using a slower machine or you have to take your BBS down to design an image, you can still prepare the required files; once you're ready to go, ask a friend with a faster system to perform the actual rendering.

- **Hand-drawn images.** If you have freehand talent, grab a paint program and start drawing! Original hand-drawn art is comparatively rare on bulletin boards, and any good promotional image you create has a good chance of being well received. Of course, if you can pattern your image around the theme of your BBS, you'll tie the picture even closer to your system. As always, make sure you copyright your work within the image itself.

- **ANSI art and animations.** Because most PCs can display ANSI characters if the ANSI.SYS driver is loaded, ANSI animations have long been a favored form of BBS advertising. You're likely to find at least one or two in the file library of every BBS you call. Often, these animations are nothing more than the BBS welcome screen with simple added animation, but some sysops prefer to create long, detailed animations that tell a story in ANSI and last for a minute or more! THEDRAW makes the perfect tool for creating ANSI animations, with fancy dissolves, layering tools, and even controls for the display speed.

- **RIP art and animations.** With the growing popularity and availability of RIP graphics, some sysops have created high-resolution RIP images and animations as advertisements; these are sure to be popular, since well-done RIP artwork is still hard to find. To create a RIP graphic or animation, you can purchase either of the TeleGrafix drawing packages (RIPdraw, an inexpensive paint program, or RIPaint, a much more sophisticated package with a higher price). Alternately, you can use a shareware RIP drawing program.

- **Video animation.** Although it takes a certain level of expertise and the proper hardware, some sysops have created AVI or MPG-format video BBS advertisements, which usually include a view of the BBS hardware and a few words from the sysop. These animations can be viewed after downloading with the Video for Windows runtime module. Other bulletin boards create these animations and offer them to subscribers for downloading, but the subjects are usually adult.

- **MIDI music files.** If you're a musician who can create MIDI music files, consider releasing some of your work to the public, accompanied by a READ.ME file advertising your BBS.

- **WAV format sound files.** Finally, those sysops with sound cards installed in their PCs may want to record a collection of sound files in Windows WAV format, once again for distribution with a READ.ME file advertising their systems. Again, keep in mind that copyrighted material from any CD or tape should never be distributed; this includes clips from films, TV shows, and music CDs.

Once you've completed your project and you're ready to distribute it, make sure you add a short READ.ME file containing your copyright message and information about your BBS. You may also want to provide background information on how you created your demonstration file, including what tools you used and any special techniques you used.

When the READ.ME has been prepared, archive the files with a utility like PKZIP or ARJ and start uploading to your favorite systems. Your description of your demonstration file should be both enthusiastic and specific; let the caller know as much about the file as possible.

Custom Scanning

The rapid drop in scanner prices have brought the cost of a good handheld color scanner below $400. With a little practice, a sysop can put a scanner to use in applications like these:

- **Advertising.** You can create your own GIF and BMP pictures, and these images make great advertisements. If you find it hard to locate material that's free of an existing copyright, you can always scan photographs you've taken yourself; if one of your callers is an experienced photographer, you may even be able to arrange a commission for a series of pictures. Figure 11.4 shows a GIF advertisement scanned by the author. This image was taken from a "royalty-free" image collection (meaning that the manufacturer expressly allows owners of the collection to redistribute the images in advertising).

Fig. 11.4
An example of a scanned promotional GIF, complete with BBS logo.

Tip

Although it's not a requirement, your promotional pictures will be even more effective if you create a clip art version of your BBS logo and add it to the image. If you're running Windows, copy your clip art (in BMP format) into the Windows Clipboard, and then use Paintbrush to load a BMP version of your picture. Select a spot where your logo will not obstruct the subject of the picture, yet keep it close enough to the subject so that it can't be easily cropped. Paste the clip art image into your picture and move it to the right location, and then save your work. You've now added a custom logo to your image! As mentioned in Chapter 7, you can only add your BBS information to an image if you hold the copyright, or if the owner of the image has released it "royalty-free." If you're unsure whether you can use an image, check the legal information accompanying the source image.

- **Caller images.** Ask your users to send in a picture of themselves for a free scan, and then ask if you can place the image online in a file section set apart specifically for user pictures! Because almost all personal contact in cyberspace is through words and text, callers like to browse through pictures of other users to match faces with names.
- **Scanning images for profit.** If you're particularly skilled in the use of your scanner, advertise your scanning services on your system. Computer users often need photographs or text scanned, and you may discover it's a sideline that helps support your BBS.

> **Tip**
>
> If you've scanned your BBS logo, you can use it to create inexpensive business cards that you can hand out to potential callers (especially at user meetings and conventions). A custom business card projects a much more professional image than a hastily-written number on a scrap of paper! Figure 11.5 illustrates an example of a BBS business card.

Fig. 11.5
An example of a bulletin board business card.

Media Advertising

Generally, advertising your BBS in your local newspaper or a local magazine is not an effective method of publicizing your system. This doesn't mean that bulletin boards as a whole aren't gaining in popularity and recognition—rather, readers of these general publications simply aren't focused or prepared to see an advertisement for a bulletin board, and they're likely to gloss over it.

Additionally, once you've added your system to the local BBS list and posted free advertisements on other local boards, callers in your area will almost certainly try your BBS anyway, so you're essentially wasting money.

For a business or support system, advertising is never a problem. If you're running a business BBS, simply ask everyone with customer contacts at your company to distribute the BBS number, and make sure it appears on any print advertising and the company letterhead. In fact, your BBS number should appear anywhere that the company fax number is displayed.

For a hobby or profit system, however, the only BBS advertising space worth paying for is the space offered in magazines and periodicals devoted to bulletin boards, and the wider the distribution the better. Why? Because you can be assured that your audience is truly interested in what your system has to offer. The wider the coverage, the more likely your advertisement is to attract the long-distance caller. Publications like *Boardwatch* and *Online Access* offer targeted advertising that will reach readers with modems, ready to call. Certainly, even a small advertisement in one of these publications will cost a considerable amount, so it's wise to explore the other methods of promoting your BBS first.

If you do decide to spend the money on a national advertisement, no matter what the size, make sure you stress a single service or your board's theme (rather than trying to cover every feature of your system in a few inches). If possible, your advertising should also be designed by a professional. If you're lucky, one of your users may have experience in print advertising or graphic design; otherwise, ask the sales representative at the publication to help you with design ideas.

Increasing User Interest

So far, we've been examining methods of attracting new users to your BBS through promotional materials and advertising—but what about your existing callers? How can you tempt them into subscribing to your system or renewing an existing subscription? How can you build interest and interaction between your users? In this section, we'll discuss various methods of increasing activity and participation among your current callers.

Even though your BBS may largely run unattended, it's important to remember that your callers are human beings who will grow impatient if your system isn't updated often with new attractions like the latest files and online games. Of course, this doesn't mean you must add a feature or service every day, but a BBS that doesn't provide something new on a regular basis will never be successful, especially if the sysop charges for access. This continuing quest for new attractions is part of the reason why a busy hobby system is hard work, and a profit bulletin board that's earning money is a full-time career.

Let's review some of the techniques used by experienced sysops to provide something new for their callers:

- **Contests and prizes.** Everyone loves a contest, and the more you hold, the more popular your BBS. If your BBS specializes in games, *high-score competitions* are a natural, and you should consider running them on a monthly basis; offer a box of disks for the winner of each contest, or buy a popular commercial game as the prize. This is a great way of highlighting a new online game, or renewing interest in an old favorite.

  Promotional prizes are another good idea. Take your BBS logo to a screen printing shop and have T-shirts or hats made especially for your system; these can also represent a nice profit if you sell them directly.

  To generate even more interest, you can offer a single large prize (perhaps a subscription to your system) for the winner of an *activity contest.* These contests reward the user with the highest amount of uploaded bytes or the greatest number of public messages within a certain time period. As you might guess, the benefits for your system from such a contest can be quite impressive—make sure you have adequate hard drive space for all those messages and file uploads!

- **Voting booths and opinion polls.** If your system has its share of opinionated callers—and most do—you can generate a surprising amount of interest in your message bases by creating voting booths and opinion polls on topics of current interest. Questions should be open-ended whenever possible, and give your users several lines of space for each answer. Once you've started a debate within your message base, don't hesitate to jump in with your own opinion! As long as you allow everyone the same rights, your BBS will benefit from your participation in your message base.

- **BBS parties.** BBS parties are wonderful social events. If you hold a party, you'll have plenty of opportunity to observe as your callers meet each other face-to-face for the first time—the results can be a lot of fun, and your callers are likely to continue talking about your party for months! Make sure your party is held at a place and time convenient for everyone, including your teenage callers; you might reserve a separate room at a restaurant, for example, or hold a picnic. Provide a map or directions for those that need them, and start publicizing your party at least a month or two in advance. If you have a scanner, bring a camera along and record the event on film, and then create a series of GIF pictures that you can add to your download library.

- **User meetings.** Although the same people may appear at both functions, a user meeting is radically different from a BBS party. User meetings are more like serious town meetings; a sysop holds one to hear user opinions firsthand (rather than through an online voting booth) on an important change to the bulletin board. User meetings are often held when a sysop is considering moving from a no-fee system to a subscription-only format. Like a BBS party, you should announce your user meeting a month or two early to allow all interested parties plenty of notice.

- **Chat links.** With bulletin board programs like Wildcat!, TBBS, and the Major BBS, it's not necessary to add 16 or 32 lines to your system in order to offer a huge teleconference! These programs allow one BBS to link its multiline function to another system with the same software. Users from one BBS can talk with each other, just as if everyone had dialed into the same system (in fact, new users are often surprised to find the person they're chatting with lives several hundred miles away). Each board must reserve a single line for the connection to the other system, however, so you must have a multiline system to offer this feature.

ONE BBSCON

The BBS world changed significantly in 1992 with the arrival of the ONE BBSCON, the first national convention truly devoted to bulletin board sysops and their callers. Sysops from around the world met and discussed online issues, attended seminars focusing on different topics of interest to the online community, and saw firsthand the latest advances in technology in the vendor area. In fact, the RIP graphical emulation from TeleGrafix received a huge boost from its appearance at ONE BBSCON, as did the manufacturers of several shareware CD-ROMs. At the 1993 convention, well over 100 vendors sold over a million dollars worth of BBS merchandise! Although there are other shows that have appeared after the success of ONE BBSCON, the original convention is the largest and the most prestigious by far.

If you're truly serious about turning your BBS into a profitable enterprise, don't miss the annual BBSCON, which is usually held sometime in August. The contacts you'll make and the information you'll take home are invaluable. Seminar topics range from "how to" classes to open forums on the future of bulletin boards, including several sessions that center on how to run a profit BBS. There are also separate seminar tracks that focus on each of the most popular commercial and shareware bulletin board programs.

For complete information on an upcoming ONE BBSCON, check *Boardwatch Magazine*. The magazine's editor, Jack Rickard, is a co-founder of ONE, Inc., which sponsors the convention.

Summary

In this chapter, we discussed how you can promote your BBS for little or no money, plus several inexpensive methods of generating interest in both new callers and your existing users. As with any other facet of running a BBS, your results are in step with the amount of effort you apply to marketing; whenever possible, ask your co-sysop and your favorite callers to mention your BBS on other systems, and never miss a chance to promote your bulletin board.

In the next chapter, "BBS Success Stories," we'll examine several successful profit systems to see what features and services they offer, as well as some of the techniques the sysops use to market and promote their systems.

Chapter 12

BBS Success Stories

by Dave Gibbons

At this point, you should have a good idea what you want to do in the BBS world. You know how BBSs work, how you can set one up, and the basics of running it. This chapter shows you a little of what's possible for a well-run BBS. It goes straight to the source for advice and information about operating a successful BBS—and what better source than some of the most prominent sysops in the industry? In this chapter, you'll learn the histories behind four very successful BBSs and some of the lessons their sysops learned on the way.

Each story starts with an overview of the BBS's current offerings, including special features, online hardware, and pricing structure. The sysops then talk about technical, management, and marketing issues, and each concludes with advice to present and potential sysops. At the end of the chapter you'll see the points where the sysops' advice overlaps.

Aquila

Aquila BBS

Sysops:	Kevin Behrens, Kent Behrens, Steve Williams 4430 East New York Street, Ste. #201 Aurora, IL 60504
Voice:	708/820-0480
Fax:	708/820-8813
BBS:	708/820-8344
Features:	Over 120,000 files Online Publications (*USA Today*, *Boardwatch*, PcCatalog, Local Weather) Internet mail (including 2,000 message conferences)

(continues)

Aquila BBS (continued)

	Free trial membership	
	28.8KB and 14.4KB lines, ISDN access available	
Charges:	$8.95	Monthly Subscription. 30MB total shareware downloads, 30 hours total online time (up to 16 hours in one call).
	$25.00	3-Month Subscription. 90MB total shareware downloads, 90 hours total online time (up to 16 hours in one call).
	$60.00	12-Month Subscription. 360MB total shareware downloads, 360 hours total online time (up to 16 hours in one call).
	All rates are current as of this writing, but may change at any time. Contact Aquila for current rates.	
Hardware:	42 incoming lines, 30 386- and 486-class PCs networked with Novell, 12GB storage on file server, 6 CD-ROM drives	

AQUILA BBS™

4430 East New York St. Ste. #201 Aurora, IL 60504

Fig. 12.1
The Aquila BBS Logo.

When Kevin Behrens decided to start a PC-based bulletin board system, his wife suggested the name Aquila (ah-KEE-la, Spanish for "eagle") because of the Aquila constellation. He had seen some of the commercial BBSs in the Commodore community, but no BBSs geared to PC users. They went online with an XT and a single 1200 baud modem in 1987, and have since grown to the largest BBS in Chicago (42 lines) and one of the most popular shareware boards in the country. Like all BBSs of the time, it started out as a hobby. "We never thought this was going to be a business," Behrens said. "I had no concept that other people were doing this."

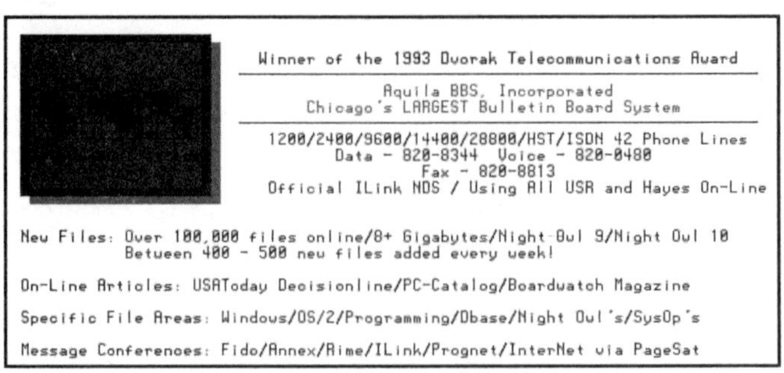

Fig. 12.2
Aquila's log-in screen advertises their industry accolades and features.

Like two of the other three BBSs in this chapter, Aquila is primarily a shareware BBS. It offers many other services, but Behrens said shareware is the main draw for their users. Aquila is so popular with shareware authors, their staff adds from 400 to 500 new shareware files to its libraries each week. "What our callers look for is shareware that's new every day," Behrens said. "Some days we have to limit how many we post, because it gets to be too many for the users to look through."

Among the other services Aquila offers is Internet mail and Usenet news. Behrens said they may offer more Internet services like FTP and Telnet someday, but will probably stick with mail and Usenet in the short term because it makes the most sense from a business standpoint. Like the other sysops in this chapter, Behrens emphasizes the need to treat the BBS as a business, paying attention to profitability and customer requests. "Eighty percent of what people want to use on the Internet is mail and Usenet," Behrens said, "and that's only 20 percent of the cost." He said the other services are expensive to implement and not very popular, so they're not very profitable.

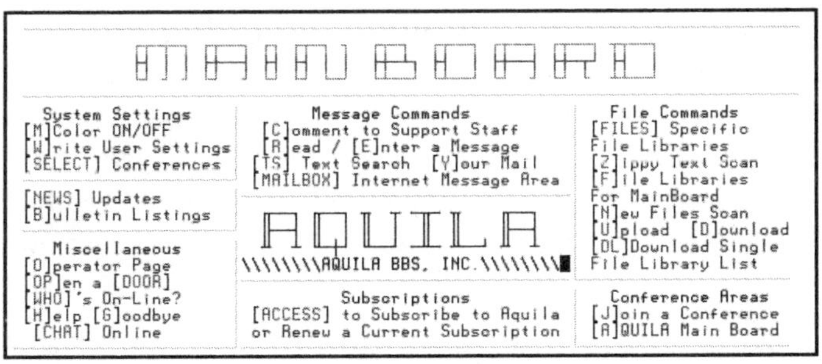

Fig. 12.3
The Aquila main menu has a wide variety of options.

In a somewhat daring move, Aquila has recently removed all adult material from their file libraries. "It bothered me," said Behrens, "and I didn't want to be associated with that section of the industry." He admits to a few problems with some users over the decision, but says it hasn't impacted the business too much. "It makes us work a little harder, but I think you end up with a better product," he said.

Behrens said one of the elements that made Aquila a success was geography. "The larger, more profitable BBSs are in the North," he said. "As sysops say, this is definitely a winter sport." According to Behrens, caller statistics across the BBS industry follow a predictable pattern with the change of seasons. Aquila gets from 1,000 to 1,500 calls a day in the summer, and as many as 3,000 other times of the year. "The biggest time is from about Christmas to early May," he said. "Summer is when we actually get work done. Sometimes we can shut down a bank of incoming lines in the summer, but we run the full 42 lines when it's cold."

A development that has benefited the entire industry, said Behrens, is the low price of 9600 and 14.4KB baud modems. Just two years ago, the majority of callers used 2400 baud modems, but now "maybe 1 in 100 calls is at 2400 baud." He said because the higher speeds quadruple (at least) throughput, BBSing has gotten a lot more efficient. "People download more, but it takes less time. It's like a huge bottleneck broken by the industry itself."

Behrens said the future of the BBS community is wide open. "Consumers tend to run to something," he said. "Everyone will understand how BBSs work, and once they get easier to use we'll probably have a shortage of online services." He said this would be a boon for specialized boards, which will grow radically. "There will be a lot of 40-line boards and fewer 4-line boards."

Every year, Behrens speaks to other sysops at the ONE BBSCON round table. He and other top sysops answer a broad range of questions. For potential sysops, his advice focuses on fundamentals. "Look at your BBS software," he said. "Users don't like change—they just despise it. Make sure the package you use is the best for *them*, not necessarily what you want from the sysop level. A package can have 10,000 tools for the sysop, but it doesn't mean anything if your callers can't use it." Aquila uses PCBoard, which Behrens said is a good choice. "It's probably the most popular, so it gets the add-ons quicker. It's also a very open architecture, so you can write your own modules."

He also said it's important to accept mistakes. "Sysops tend to get afraid to make a mistake and therefore do nothing," he said. "BAD. If we're not doing something wrong, we're not doing something. You can't learn without doing things—wrong and right. Do something, even if it's wrong. Most of the time if it's the right thing to do, it'll feel right." He said callers are quick to point out problems, but don't hold grudges. "Things can get fouled up on the system and as soon as they're happy, it's all forgotten—they don't even remember it anymore. They're very forgiving people, and I hope they stay that way."

The Westside

The Westside BBS

Sysop:	Dave Harrison	
BBS:	213/933-4050	
Features:	100 chat areas	
	Online magazines (15 including daily news, Inside TREK, and *Boardwatch*)	
	High-speed, Tymenet, and packet network access	
Charges:	$50/yr.	2 hrs./day or unlimited access during business hours
	$249/yr.	Unlimited access
	$10/mo.	Introductory offer, 1 month normal access after signing up through TABS 900 service
	Outdial services and adult areas carry an additional charge.	
	All rates are current as of this writing, but may change at any time.	
	Contact The Westside for current rates.	
Hardware:	132 incoming lines, 10 486-class PCs, 8GB storage on file server, 12 CD-ROM drives	

Fig. 12.4
The Westside BBS Logo.

The Westside is the only BBS in this chapter that doesn't focus primarily on shareware. "File transfers are maybe 20 to 30 percent of the system use," said The Westside sysop Dave Harrison. "We're an adult social place." While other sysops are investing in gathering files from other boards, he dedicates his resources to monthly mixers.

Of the BBSs in this chapter, The Westside started out the most technologically advanced. It had two 2400-baud lines on a Turbo XT. Harrison launched The Westside in April 1987, which was in the earliest days of entertainment-oriented BBSs. His was one of the first successful chat systems. Two years after The Westside went online, it became his full-time job ("consumed me," as he puts it).

A trip through The Westside is like walking into an incredibly diverse cocktail party, with discussions on almost any subject. During "prime time" (about 8 p.m. to midnight) you can count on more than 100 members being online with you.

Harrison says it's important to advertise, but word of mouth is much more valuable. The best way to generate that, he said, is to "treat your customers right and don't get in their face." He said many sysops try to control their members too much with unnecessary rules. "We have a very open system, and for the most part people stick to the rules on their own."

Harrison said the industry's big buzzword, the Infobahn, is more fad than fact now, but will change when the BBS community links in. "Right now it's just information, like a library" he said. "They need destinations like The Westside to make it fun." With this in mind, Harrison said he might hook The Westside into an Internet Relay Chat channel.

His best advice for potential sysops is "Don't do it. It's not just an adventure, it's a job." He said the biggest mistake new sysops make is believing the sales literature that comes with their BBS software. "It's an awful lot of work, and it basically has to be a labor of love—don't expect to make a lot of money very quickly." But the BBS market still has opportunities, he said, if you approach it right. "Don't try to do everything at once. Fill a niche. Don't expect to take over the file transfer market or the chat market, aim more for one specific thing." He also recommended testing the waters before diving in. "Set up a one-line system and have fun."

Software Creations

Software Creations BBS	
Sysop:	Glenn Brensinger 26 Harris Street Clinton, MA 01510
BBS:	508/368-7036
Features:	40,000 downloadable files High speed and SprintNet access Home board (main support and distribution point) for over a dozen software companies, including Apogee Online software store Internet access

Charges:	$30/6 mos.	60 min./day
	$45/yr.	60 min./day
	$60/yr.	90 min./day
	$80/yr.	120 min./day
	All rates are current as of this writing, but may change at any time. Contact Software Creations for current rates.	
Hardware:	85 incoming lines, 70 386-based PCs networked with Novell, SLC-96 switching box from AT&T	

As the home board for more than a dozen software companies, Software Creations is able to make new games and enhancements available to its users before any other bulletin board. The games make their way around to other online services fairly quickly, but sysops know Software Creations is the first place to look for new games.

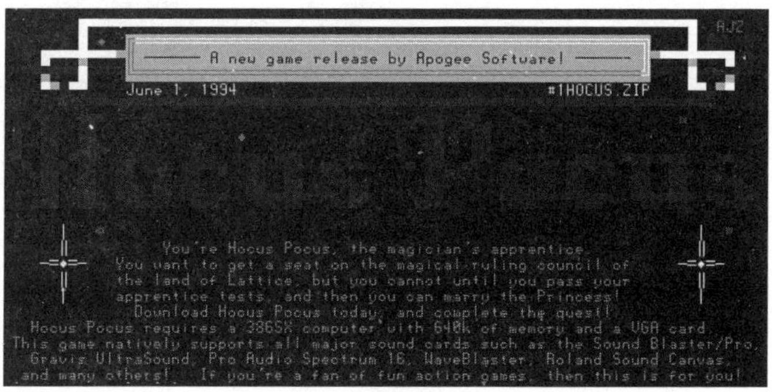

Fig. 12.5
Sofware Creations offers up-to-the-minute releases of new games.

Sysop Glenn Brensinger has taken over for Dan Linton, who built up the system from the start and is still president of its parent company, Linton Enterprises. As of this writing, the BBS operates out of Linton's basement, but it will soon move into an office building. The BBS was almost moved out of Linton's house a few years ago when it overloaded the Clinton, Massachusetts phone system, but Linton decided to get his own switching system and a direct, high-speed connection to a larger phone company instead.

Brensinger says marketing and quality have been the main keys to Software Creations' success. The marketing strategy they use is relatively inexpensive, based in part on the barter system. They have been very successful at forming partnerships with other software companies, publicizing and supporting their partners' games on the BBS in exchange for publicity in the games' packaging. The partnerships help maintain Software Creations' high quality standards as well, providing the most up-to-date games and enhancements possible. Quality of files, says Brensinger, is much more important to a BBS than quantity. "We're not really interested in impressing anybody with the number of files we offer," he said. "We'd rather carry the quality and the clean files."

By "clean files," Brensinger means virus-free and legal. As users upload files to the BBS, the files are automatically virus-scanned and checked for duplication against the current library. A team of file sorters then checks out each file to make sure it is shareware rather than commercial software, and its quality is high enough to be released on the BBS. Some BBSs, by contrast, use duplicates and substandard files to pad their file listings, making it appear as if they have more files to offer than they really do.

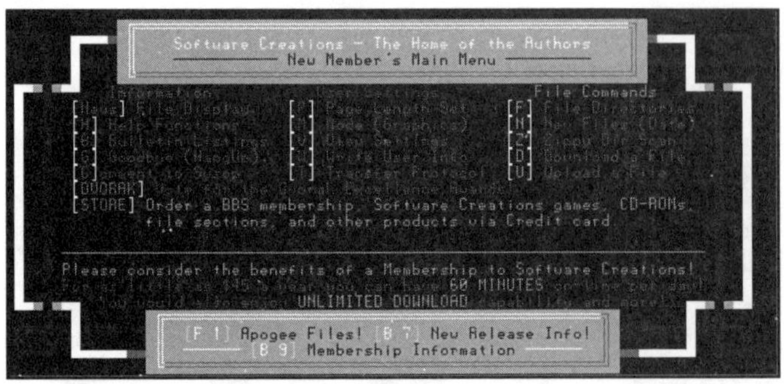

Fig. 12.6 Software Creations' large file area is its main draw.

The main source of income for BBSs is the sale of memberships, but it's not easy to get users to pay. Software Creations has thousands of paying members, even though you don't have to be a paying member to download their files. One reason users become members is for easier access—non-paying users must maintain a 5:1 download/upload ratio (uploading 1KB of data for each 5KB they download). Also, only paying members can access the Internet areas of the BBS, which are becoming very popular. Another way Software Creations has encouraged callers to become paying members is with special members-only phone lines that are much less busy than the public lines used by non-paying users.

Like most others in the communications industry, Brensinger sees the Internet as a big part of the BBS future. He said he hopes the popularity of the Net will help clear away some of the myths about BBSing. "The general public sees BBSs and thinks, 'Oh, adult graphics! Pornography!'" he said. "It would be nice if people knew more about the real world of BBSs."

Potential sysops, said Brensinger, need to be aware of these public perceptions and some common new-sysop mistakes. "There are two big things I usually run into," he said. "The first is time commitment. If you're going to run a bulletin board, it has to be something you want to continue running, not just a summer project. You've got to be committed to your customers. The other big one is over-estimating a BBS's potential. It really helps if the board has a theme instead of trying to cover the spectrum of what's out there. Lots of sysops buy a ton of hardware and spend lots of money but nobody calls. Start small and work your way up."

Brensinger says the BBS never stops growing. When they add enough new incoming phone lines to meet the increased demand, he said, they know they'll have to add more in about two months. The rapid changes don't bother him, though. "The ideal bulletin board," he said, "is one that doesn't stay static."

Exec-PC

Exec-PC BBS		
Sysop:	Bob Mahoney	
	PO Box 57	
	Elm Grove, WI 53122	
BBS:	414/789-4210	
Features:	350,000 files	
	Hyperscan(r) search engine, which searches the entire file library in about two seconds	
	Over 15 online magazines	
	Online shopping	
	Online job search	
	Full Internet access	
	Local access through any CompuServe node	
Charges:	$25	3-month membership
	$75	1-year membership
	$4/hr	through any local CompuServe access node
	SLIP or PPP access (up to 28.8KB), $20 for the first 30 hrs., $1/hr above 30.	
	All rates are current as of this writing, but may change at any time. Contact Exec-PC for current rates.	
Hardware:	Over 280 incoming lines, 100Mbit/sec fiber optic backbone for the Novell network, 55GB storage	

When Bob Mahoney started Exec-PC in November 1983, he said he was in "hardware heaven." After a consulting project for a large company, he was allowed to keep the hardware they had supplied him with: a 30MB hard drive (worth $7,000) and a high-speed 1200-baud Hayes modem (worth $700). He spent some time collecting business software from the few other BBSs that existed at the time, and dedicated his 4.77Mhz XT to the first all-business BBS in the country. Access was free, and the board gained popularity quickly. "I dreamed of having two lines," Mahoney said. Nine months later, he was able to add that second line, and he said "I thought, 'that's it, boy, I'll just sit back and enjoy....'" A lot has changed since then.

Exec-PC is now the largest LAN-based BBS in the world, with over 350,000 files, over 15 online magazines, full Internet access (including SLIP and PPP up to 28.8KB), 5,000 callers a day from over 50 countries, online doors and games, and over 150 Exec-PC-specific message conferences (in addition to more than 100 FidoNet and more than 3,000 Usenet message conferences). Exec-PC is in a class by itself, not really comparable to other BBSs or online services. Mahoney cites the example of a new shareware program posted simultaneously to Exec-PC, CompuServe, GEnie, Delphi, and BIX. Within the first week, it was downloaded from Exec-PC almost as many times as all the other services combined (122 times on Exec-PC, 130 on all the others combined), and the nearest competitors, CompuServe and GEnie, showed less than half as many downloads as Exec-PC.

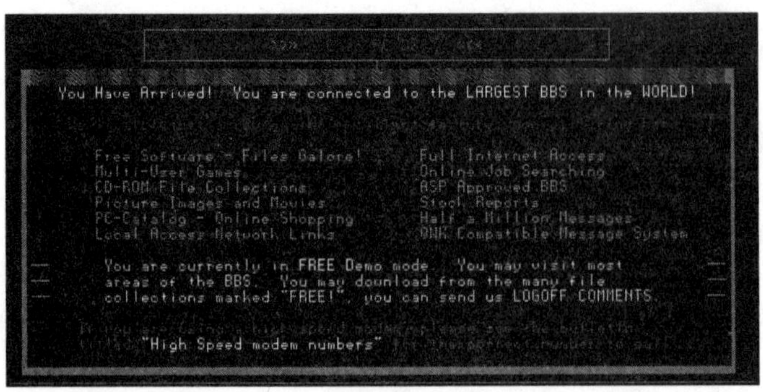

Fig. 12.7
Exec-PC's initial screens advertise the BBS's tremendous size and features.

Like the other BBSs in this chapter, Exec-PC started out as a hobby. As it grew, however, it consumed Mahoney's life savings within about 18 months. He resisted charging for the service because he thought people would stop calling, but in March 1985, he reluctantly announced a $35/year access charge. A few days later, he found his mailbox stuffed with $35 checks. Now the BBS is more than self-supporting, allowing Mahoney to hire some people to help manage it, and move it out of his basement into an 8,000 square foot office building.

After Exec-PC's success with a business-only focus, Mahoney decided to broaden the service. Two years ago, he hired some people to polish the board's interface and add new non-business services like games and doors, and Exec-PC continued to grow in popularity. Today, he even helps organize tournaments for the DOOM video game players. "When I started, I never thought I'd be helping people set up tournaments where they're shooting lasers at each other," he said.

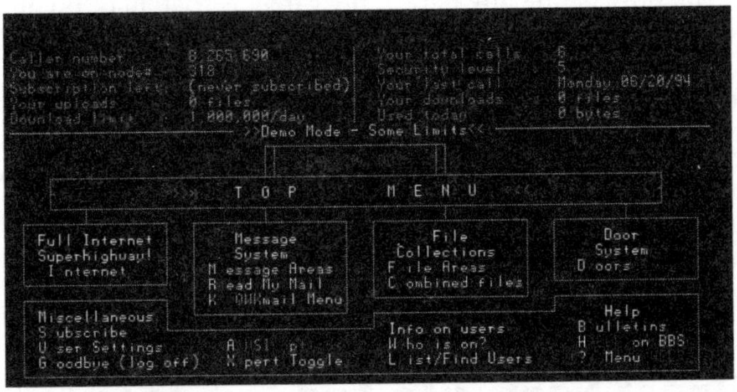

Fig. 12.8
From the main menu, Exec-PC callers can access the Internet in addition to the wealth of files, messages, and doors.

Bob Mahoney truly enjoys his work, he says, but it is work. The board absorbs so much of his time, he hasn't even been able to attend industry conferences like One BBSCON, and he and his wife Tracey have only managed two vacations since Exec-PC started. "That's part of the glamour of the BBS," he said. "You'd better be ready to give up vacations for about five years."

Much of the new work being done on Exec-PC involves the Internet. The new building has two T.1 and one T.3 connection to the Net, which will allow members free Telnet access into Exec-PC. "This will make Exec-PC a direct presence on desktops all over the world," Mahoney said. In the earliest days of Exec-PC, he imagined the ultimate BBS would be a free call from anywhere in the country. When the phone companies were deregulated, he thought that might do it, but it's the Internet that is finally making that dream possible. "We've been in the right place for ten years," he said. "Finally, it's the right time."

Mahoney has a lot of advice for other sysops. Even if it's a hobby, he said, manage it as a business. "Take some basic accounting courses. Learn what happens to your money, how to analyze investments and ROI, do growth projections." He stressed the importance of paying attention to copyright infringement—and that people who don't, often get their BBSs sued or shut down.

Another point Mahoney touched on relates to sysops' attitudes. "Don't let the power go to your head," he said. "I think that's the biggest mistake sysops make. You're in a service industry—you have to be nice to those people or you'll scare them away." He cites BBSs with screens full of warnings and rules as the worst offenders. "Enforce the rules *after* somebody breaks them, not before," he said.

He jokes, "The only depressing part of my career is that all of my life's work can fit on four 8mm backup tapes."

A user who voted for Exec-PC in the Boardwatch BBS contest wrote this letter: "I believe the casual professionalism that Exec-PC demonstrates in both online and voice contact had more to do with my vote than the number of modems operating or files available. I get the impression that the people at Exec-PC are dead serious about running the BBS as a business yet have a great time doing just that."

The Pros' Formula for Success

Though each BBS in this chapter has its own unique history, there are a few common threads running through the stories:

- Each of these BBSs started as a hobby, but the sysops utilized good business practices in serving their members.
- Each board started very small (one line in most cases) and grew as the needs of its membership changed.
- The sysops spent countless 16-hour days working through technical problems, answering members' questions, and managing file libraries and chat areas, all before making any profit.

Clearly, if you want to run a BBS, you can't jump straight into success—especially monetary success. It has to be something you honestly enjoy enough to maintain and support financially. Even if you're committed to the BBS and the BBS community, you're safer starting with a small amount of hardware and adding more if you need it than starting with a large, expensive setup and hoping the board will grow into it.

The successful sysops in this chapter were all asked to give advice to potential sysops. The advice varied a little, but mostly followed these lines:

- Start your BBS as a hobby—don't expect to make big bucks right away.
- Start small. Expand only as your needs grow.
- BBSing is a winter sport, so be prepared for lulls in the summer.
- Adding new phone lines is a non-exact science, but you generally need one extra phone line for each 40-50 paid customers on a file board, each 30 paid customers on a chat board. Add an extra channel of Internet access for each 10-15 new Internet-only callers.
- Virus-scan everything, no matter how harmless it may look.
- Make the interface as unobtrusive and intuitive as possible.
- Use good business practices in dealing with subscribers.
- Pay attention to the quality of your offerings; don't think padding your file lists will draw new users.
- Be very aware of potential copyright violations. Don't post software that isn't clearly labeled as shareware, freeware, or public domain, and don't post pictures scanned from magazines.
- Remember to serve your customers, the callers, above all else. They're the ones who do the real advertising, and determine your success or failure.

Call the BBSs in this chapter to see how it's done. Read the comments from the callers, and pay attention to the systems' interfaces.

Summary

This chapter profiles four of the most successful BBSs in the country: Aquila, The Westside, Software Creations, and Exec-PC. The main sysop for each board tells its history and offers advice to new sysops. Among the most common pieces of advice are: pay attention to copyright infringement, don't start out with dreams of big money, and serve the callers above all else.

Part III

Adding Value to Your BBS

13

Chapter 13

Shareware

by Markus Pope

In this chapter you learn about the concept of shareware. You get to take a look at how it differs from other methods of software distribution and how it affects your BBS. In short, this chapter:

- Explains the concept of shareware and describes the programs that are distributed as shareware.
- Describes the passion that users have for the shareware concept and why you want to provide it on your BBS.
- Gets you started by telling you where to get shareware programs and what to watch out for.

The chapter begins by explaining the shareware concept, giving you the differences among shareware, commercial, and public domain software. To give you an idea of how companies can start out as shareware and end up commercial, you're shown examples of at least one shareware program that's gone commercial. In addition, we tell you about the two major types of shareware programs and list what is usually found in a shareware package.

After learning to recognize shareware programs, you learn what to look for—what makes a good shareware program. We suggest some simple guidelines that you can build upon to govern the programs that you make available in your download libraries. In addition, you're given justification for the hard work that goes into maintaining a good shareware library.

When you have a good understanding of what shareware is and why you want to make it available on your BBS, we'll tell you where to get it. You learn about several shareware distribution channels and are given a few excellent sources. In addition, we give you some things to watch out for when you're collecting your shareware library. Let's start by examining the shareware concept.

What Exactly Is Shareware?

Shareware is a concept that originated in the 1980s. It provides users with software that they can try before forking out cash to pay for it. In addition, it provides software authors with an extremely cheap way to distribute their programs. A standard shareware package includes software, documentation, and a registration text file (documentation and registration are usually provided in electronic format as opposed to a bound manual).

Registration is what makes your copy of a software package legal. Most shareware authors let you to use their software for a period of 15 to 30 days—after which, you send them anywhere from $5 to $50 (average cost). The period of time you're allowed to use shareware before registering is referred to as the *grace period*. During the grace period, you're encouraged to explore a piece of software and decide whether or not it meets your needs. If you choose to keep the software, you send in fees outlined by the registration file. Upon receiving payment for their software, authors consider you registered and legal. If you're not keeping the software, it's standard practice to delete it and pass it along to someone else.

Shareware is passed around by users and sysops. This is a very inexpensive way for authors to spread their software around and make it successful because they aren't spending cash on advertising, pretty boxes, and printed documentation (some authors do promise a printed manual if you register). Users and sysops spread shareware around by downloading it from some online systems and uploading it to others. Since it's transported from computer to computer by modem, authors don't spend a whole lot of money on shipping and handling. One drawback to using shareware as a distribution method is that users aren't always willing to pay for the software they have. We cover the legal aspects of shareware only slightly in this chapter. For a more in-depth look at the legal side of things, refer back to the discussion on shareware in Chapter 7.

Tip

If you have the time, the know how, and the means to write your own shareware applications, do so. Typically, you don't make a lot of money releasing shareware programs, but you do make a name for yourself—as a result, your BBS becomes more popular.

Shareware vs. Public Domain

Shareware is often confused with *public domain* or *freeware*. Public domain is free software that is not copyrighted by the author. It's free because the author doesn't want to support it, feels that it may not be worth charging for, or is just an all-around nice person. Freeware differs from public domain only slightly. Freeware programs are free but a copyright is maintained by the author. Distribution of public domain and freeware is handled exactly like shareware—you find it in the download libraries of most bulletin boards. The funny thing about public domain and freeware is that it's often of very high quality and it typically holds its own against shareware and commercial programs.

Shareware vs. Commercial

Commercial software are the programs that you buy off-the-shelf at Egghead Software, Software Etc., through a mail order distributor, or some other software retail outlet. It differs from shareware and public domain in its medium of distribution. You can sometimes find commercial software for download on BBSs, but that's highly illegal and you can get into major legal trouble by downloading it and putting it on your BBS. Commercial software comes in a box that contains manuals, diskettes, and registration cards. In addition, most commercial software companies provide excellent technical support via telephone, fax, or BBS (the kind of support that you don't usually find with shareware authors). The quality of most shareware programs is surprisingly comparable to commercial titles; in fact, a lot of commercial authors start out by writing and distributing popular shareware programs. Let's take the shareware program shown in figure 13.1 as an example.

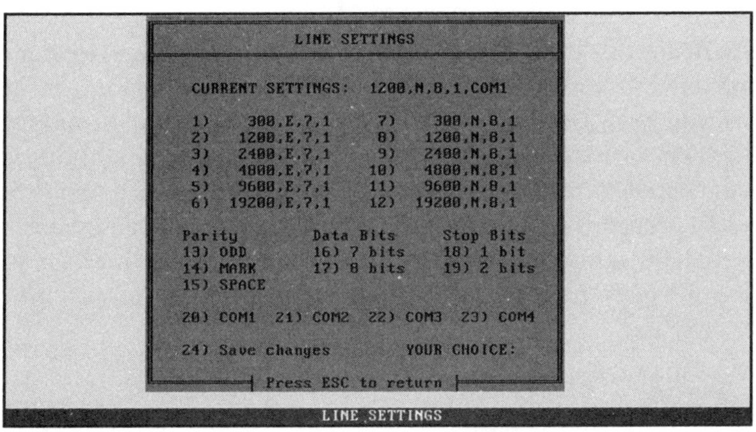

Fig. 13.1
Procomm is a very popular shareware program designed for use with modems, created and distributed by Datastorm Technologies, Inc.

Procomm was written and distributed during the mid-1980s. It's a telecommunications program for IBM personal computers. Released originally as shareware, Procomm gained in popularity so much that in 1988, Datastorm Technologies released a commercial version called PROCOMM PLUS. Later, Datastorm moved into the Windows arena and released a commercial version for Microsoft Windows. Today, Procomm, PROCOMM PLUS, and PROCOMM PLUS for Windows are the standard telecomm programs used worldwide. Take a look at figure 13.2 and see how a shareware program like Procomm can grow up to become an excellent commercial product!

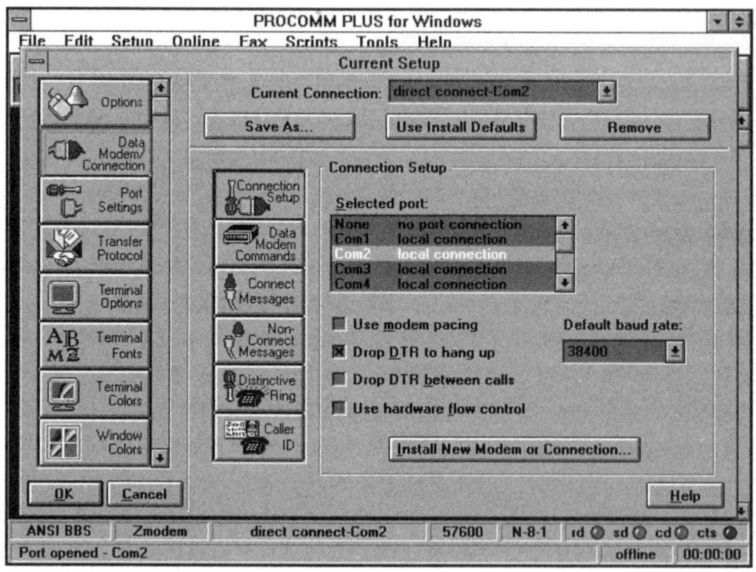

Fig. 13.2
PROCOMM PLUS for Windows 2.0 appears to be the final solution for anyone wanting to use high speed modems, fax modems, or direct connections.

Notice in figure 13.2 that PROCOMM PLUS for Windows has a really nice graphical interface with easy-to-see buttons and hundreds of features. Also included with PROCOMM PLUS for Windows are two bound manuals, one detailing their software package and the other detailing their scripting language, and excellent technical support (some of those things that distinguish commercial programs from shareware). Of course, this company shares its glory with many other commercial software companies that got their start in the shareware market. Utilities like Procomm aren't, by any means, the only popular programs.

Types of Shareware to Offer

There are two major types of shareware programs—utilities and games. Utilities are programs like word processing, spreadsheet, accounting, communications, and file management programs. On the other hand, games are programs that provide entertainment. While you can find many useful shareware utilities in the download libraries of your favorite BBSs, games are by far the most popular.

Good shareware games boast high speed graphics that are both creative and humorous. Most are arcade-style games that offer combat with multiple levels, complex puzzles, or little fuzzy creatures that spit things. These types of games are the most popular. Slower paced games are at the opposite end of the spectrum. They are patterned after board and card games like Othello, Checkers, Poker, and even Scrabble. Though board-type games aren't as popular as action packed arcade-style games, they're just as fun. Utilities, on the other hand, sport very few graphics and no little fuzzy creatures (unless, of course, you're referring to your mouse driver).

Utilities are useful programs that are centered more toward functional uses such as word processing, file maintenance and communication. Good shareware utilities are not only useful, they show off excellent interface design and informative documentation. Documentation for games isn't important because the object is usually simple—you move through a maze and shoot stuff. The manuals for utilities are extremely important because utilities typically perform more than one complex task that requires at least some knowledge of the parts of the computer involved (topics usually covered in manuals).

Now that we've taken a look at the two major types of shareware found in download libraries, let's formulate some basic criteria that you can use when searching for good games and utilities. Keep these five things in mind when you're looking for good shareware programs for your libraries:

- Good graphics and/or user interface (arcade-style action in games).
- Decent manuals and supporting documentation.
- Author's name and some sort of contact address.
- Software that you enjoy or can be familiar with.
- Still supported by the authors or is in the public domain and is documented accordingly.

Let's expand upon these five criteria. We mentioned earlier that good shareware games have arcade-style graphics, a good plot, and (the more popular ones) fast action. Also mentioned earlier is the importance of manuals that accompany utilities. If you tie these concepts together, you can come up with some general rules that you can use while choosing software for your libraries. Choose wisely because you can end up supporting software that's of poor quality (software that doesn't work). For example, let's say that someone downloads a copy of ZARP 1.0 from the Digital Mozart BBS.

ZARP 1.0 is a make-believe utility that we're inventing for this example. It's a file management program that you downloaded from a BBS and put into your download libraries without reviewing its quality. When users download and run ZARP, it works most of the time. Sometimes, though, ZARP unintentionally messes up files. In addition, the interface is so hard to use that it's really easy for users to accidentally format their hard disk drives. Although you're not technically responsible for damages caused by ZARP, because of your disclaimer, you could have prevented this problem by reviewing it before making it available. Upon reviewing ZARP, you would have found that the author's intentions were good, but that it has a few major bugs.

From all of this, what can we say about good and bad shareware? Good shareware programs include easy to understand instructions, intuitive interfaces, and, if you're looking for games, excellent graphics. Bad shareware programs have bad documentation, are hard to use, and show off bad graphics. Figure 13.3 shows what a good shareware program looks like. Notice the arcade-style graphics. Decent manuals and graphics aren't the only criteria that you can apply while searching online systems for utilities and games.

Fig. 13.3
Shareware programs like Cosmo's Cosmic Adventure intrigue users with awesome arcade-style graphics.

If you want to be a bit more strict, you can add other criteria to your list. For example, not only do you want to make sure programs have good manuals and graphics, but also that the author's name and some kind of address are included. This lets you forward any questions or technical problems regarding the software to the authors—so you don't spend time and money supporting someone else's product line. This isn't to say that if your users are having problems with a program you shouldn't help them. You should try to provide the best service possible, especially if you're running your board for profit or business; however, try to draw a dotted line between user support and technical support.

This leads us to another piece of criteria that we can add to the list—try to collect software that you enjoy just as much as your users or that you can at least become familiar with. When you provide software that you're familiar with, it's a lot easier to answer users' questions and draw that dotted line. Also, if you are not able to figure out how to use a particular shareware program, it's a pretty safe bet that your users aren't going to either. With user support in mind, sticking to software that's still supported by the authors is a no-brainer.

Many shareware authors write utilities and games as a hobby. When they run out of time and more important things come up, they often leave their software out on the market unsupported. Don't add software to your libraries that are unsupported by authors unless you're willing to provide at least some support yourself (support may just appear as a CompuServe or Internet account to send messages to, or a telephone number). The exception to this rule is software that has been released into the public domain by authors. It's okay to post these programs as long as there is adequate documentation to that effect and it fits within the boundaries of your theme.

Note

Keep in mind that even "supported" shareware may not have the level of support you are accustomed to from commercial products. Most shareware products require you to register and pay for the software before receiving support. Shareware authors do not have the resources for 24-hour, 7-day a week telephone support either. Support may be an e-mail address you can report problems to or a phone number with an answering machine.

Now that you know what makes up a good shareware product, you can start collecting utilities and games for your download libraries. Be sure to ask your users specifically what type of files they want. The basics are provided in this chapter, but tastes change from town to town and from day to day. So, where do you go to get the shareware your users want?

Shareware Sources

Obtaining shareware for your download libraries is a time-consuming venture. To make your libraries work, you need to find two or three good sources. Finding sources for shareware isn't quite as simple as it sounds. It's going to cost you money, so the first thing you should do is figure out how much cash you want to fork out for collecting software each month. After deciding how much money to invest in your libraries, search BBS lists looking for various sites around the world (or at least within your own country or state). Then comes the task of signing onto multiple BBSs to look for and download interesting titles. While looking for titles, you need to bear in mind that there are good sources and bad sources.

Good and Bad Sources

Good sources are obvious—they're high profile BBS systems, online services, and software vendors that offer a wide range of excellent games and utilities. Bad sources, though, aren't as easy to recognize. Bad sources are often hot spots for software piracy. Their download libraries are filled with commercial programs that are paraded as shareware and public domain titles. Sometimes, a source may show off a lot of good shareware titles, but closer examination reveals modified version numbers and patched files. These sources are bad because they use disguised software to trap innocent users who don't know that downloading these materials is illegal.

Shareware vendors can be bad sources too, though this is very rarely the case. Bad vendor sources may sell commercial software packages wearing shareware or public domain masks (users don't know that they're buying commercial packages). Like bad BBS sources, bad vendor sources promote bad business practices. Vendors are allowed to charge for the distribution of shareware but they're not actually allowed to sell it—users must still send in the registration fee for the software.

Vendors are given a license, by shareware authors, to distribute shareware programs. There's nothing wrong with charging for the distribution of the software. It's bad business practice, though, when a shareware vendor doesn't make it clear that the customer must pay the author when they decide that they want to keep the software. It's much worse when vendors discourage the registration of shareware! Steer clear of BBSs that provide commercial software for download and shareware vendors that promote bad business practices.

Where Do You Get Shareware?

What are some good sources for shareware? There are three different types of sources for shareware programs—BBSs, online services, and shareware vendors. BBSs are the most commonly used sources and usually distribute the newest and best stuff. Online services, like CompuServe, devote entire forums to shareware titles. Shareware vendors are a good source for shareware CD-ROMs which are loaded with hundreds of programs. Let's talk about some good sources.

When you look through BBS lists, like the USBBS list put out by Darwin Systems, Inc., they contain hundreds and thousands of entries. If you're lucky, your list flags or highlights good shareware sites. Sadly, the USBBS list doesn't, but to get into the list sysops must have a pretty large chunk of space allocated to file download areas. It's a sure bet that one out of every 10 BBSs on a USBBS list is an excellent source of shareware games and utilities. You can download the USBBS list from the Darwin BBS. Their telephone number is 301/251-9206, 24 hours a day, 7 days a week.

Apogee is an excellent shareware source and the games they represent are phenomenal. Their download libraries are filled with the latest in high-speed action games (arcade-style) that amaze users with awesome graphics and twisted plots! Becoming a member of the Apogee BBS (aka Software Creations) is very easy. Simply call their BBS and sign on. After they verify your account, you're given access to their wonderful collection of shareware games—titles like DOOM, Duke Nukem and Cosmo—like those that you typically find for home entertainment systems such as Nintendo and Sega. To contact the folks at Apogee, write or call:

> Apogee Software Productions
> P.O. Box 496389
> Garland, TX 75049-6389
> 214/271-2137 Business telephone
> 508/368-4137 Software Creations BBS

Good sources aren't, by any means, limited to bulletin boards. Online services like CompuServe, America Online, and Prodigy often have forums devoted to shareware. In addition, you can find shareware utilities in just about all the forums you sign onto. CompuServe, for example, provides a forum that's run by the Association of Shareware Professionals (we talk about the ASP later in this chapter). All you have to do to get access to the shareware forum is to type **GO SHAREWARE** at the CompuServe prompt and select the Join option from the Forum menu.

In the shareware forum's libraries you find tons of shareware programs, plus information about other sources. There's a file in Library 3 of this forum called "WWIS.ZIP" (Library 3 is called Shareware!). WWIS is a file containing lists of BBSs, online services, and vendors that are approved by the ASP—they're excellent sources! You can become a member of CompuServe by calling Customer Service at 800/848-8199. CompuServe's membership fees vary but you can easily spend $100 a month downloading new titles. Another source we classify as an online service is the Internet—the Information Superhighway as it's being called by the media these days.

The Internet is a humongous network of PCs and mainframes that span the globe, all interconnected. Using the Internet, you can sign onto thousands of systems around the world through local nodes (if available in your area). It's a shareware and public domain gold mine that's just sitting there waiting for you to come along with your sifting pan in one hand and your laptop in the other. But seriously, the Internet is a superb source of download library material. Listed below are the node addresses for some decent shareware sites:

- FTP.CICA.INDIANA.EDU
- FTP.UWP.EDU
- WUARCHIVE.WUSTL.EDU
- FTP.MARCAM.COM

Tip

If you're not familiar with the Internet and don't have an account, you can usually get information, access numbers for local nodes, and accounts from libraries and universities. Give your local library or university a call and find out how to get online with the Internet.

A good way to build a good solid foundation for your shareware libraries, and fast, is to add a CD-ROM drive to your system. CD-ROMs can provide virtually limitless libraries of shareware programs. *Boardwatch Magazine*, a monthly carried by most book stores, contains countless advertisements for CD-ROMs containing hundreds of megabytes of shareware programs. Some boast over 5000 programs on a disk—that's probably less than five cents per program! CD-ROMs can save you some bucks when it comes to building massive libraries. One disadvantage is that you can put only one CD-ROM in a CD-ROM drive, but you can get around that by installing multiple drives (if you have that kind of money) or by rotating them every week or so. The Marketplace!—they advertise in *Boardwatch*—is a superb source for shareware CD-ROMs. They offer a nice selection of software for a reasonable price and are extremely helpful when contacted by telephone. Contact The Marketplace! at:

The Marketplace!
P.O. Box 10925
St. Louis, MO 63135
800/289-1766 Business telephone

Note

Incidentally, *Boardwatch* magazine includes a large list of bulletin boards with their locations and telephone numbers. If your local book store doesn't carry *Boardwatch,* you can get subscription information by calling 800/933-6038.

CD-ROM vendors aren't the only good vendor sources. Some vendors, like Public Brand Software, in Indianapolis, IN, offer entire catalogs filled with every type of program you can imagine: Windows programs, DOS programs, spreadsheets, communication programs, you name it! Public Brand's catalogs are outstanding. They not only list programs to choose from, they describe and rate them as well—extremely handy for picking out just the good stuff for your libraries. Contact Public Brand Software by calling or writing:

Public Brand Software
P.O. Box 51315
Indianapolis, IN 46251
317/856-4144 Business telephone
317/856-2085 Support BBS

Once you've established a good foundation, you can start building up your shareware libraries. The sources covered in this section are just a few—there are many more out there in the online world. Explore and find new sources to use and pass along to other sysops. If you share your sources with other sysops, they're likely to be just as kind and share their sources with you.

(You may also pick up some good tips along the way!) Also, be sure to encourage your users to spread your collection around and upload what they've collected from other sources. Soon you'll have a thriving shareware library that's almost alive!

Giving Shareware to Your Users

So, what do I need to know about giving shareware to my users? Well, there are two issues involved in obtaining shareware and putting it on your system. First of all, is it legal to distribute shareware on your BBS; and second, why would you want to. Let's take a minute to discuss the first of these two issues.

Is It Legal for Me to Distribute Shareware?

Since the general concept of shareware involves distribution of programs through BBSs and online services, you're free to put just about all shareware programs in your libraries for users to download. There are some companies however, that ask you to let them know before making their programs available. They want to be positive that your users know that the programs are shareware, not freeware, and that they understand what that means. Companies that want you to ask before posting their stuff usually include distribution instructions with their products. If you're ever unsure about whether or not to post something in your libraries for download, hold off on posting and give the company a call.

When you call a shareware company about distribution rights, save yourself some time and first try the sales department—customer service will refer you to sales anyway. Technical support can give you the answer you're looking for, but you get gray hair and start foaming at the mouth while trying to get in touch with them. If you have trouble reaching the target company by telephone, try some of their other forms of customer support, such as fax, their BBS, or an online service like CompuServe (some companies offer support forums on CompuServe). If all else fails, send them a letter—but don't post a program for download if you have any doubts whatsoever! Refer back to Chapter 7 for an in-depth discussion regarding the legalities of distributing shareware programs.

Why You Want Shareware on Your BBS

So far we've told you about the two major types of shareware programs, the legalities of distributing shareware, and where to get it. What we haven't covered yet is why you want it on your board in the first place. File transfer libraries are the most often accessed part of a BBS. Users are crazy about collecting new programs, games and utilities both, to show their friends and make their work easier. Everyone's playing a big game of who can collect the most toys and they're willing to pay to win!

If you run your own business or work in a retail store, you know that the markets of the world are driven by supply and demand. People see something they want or something that someone else has, and they must have it. Let's take the hula hoop for example. The hula hoop came out in the early 1960s. Shortly after its release, the hula hoop became a national craze, sweeping the nation with hula fever. Now, everyone knows what a hula hoop is.

The shareware market is no different from other markets. People want it because it's a low cost solution for software needs and the quality is often just as good as software that you buy off-the-shelf. In fact, shareware is so popular that you can buy CD-ROMs containing hundreds of titles. If you're running your BBS for profit, adding lots and lots of shareware to your download libraries makes your BBS irresistible. Many hobbyist sysops boast that their BBSs support gigabytes of shareware online and make hundreds of dollars a month in subscription fees!

Note

A gigabyte is about a billion bytes, or 1,000,000 KB.

Note

Of course, there is more to making your BBS popular than just providing shareware in your download libraries! In order to be popular, your BBS should also be easy to use and follow some sort of theme as described in previous chapters.

So why do you want to make shareware available for download on your BBS when your BBS is for user support and not-for-profit? Recall what we said earlier in this section about why people want shareware: it's a low-cost solution to their software needs. While you don't need to provide games in order to provide user support, utilities are a different story. Some utilities are vital for support of your BBS or even your own products and services.

PKZIP, for example, is a shareware archive and compression utility used commonly by offline mail systems. It's used to compress mail packets so that they're easier and faster to transfer. Providing PKZIP for download in your libraries saves your users time and money—money they can spend buying more of your products and services instead of paying telephone service tolls. Also, think about what they're going to say to other people about the quality of your support. Word-of-mouth is a very strong advertising tool in the business world! PKZIP is just one example—there are thousands of other shareware utilities out there that can make things better for your users. If you're not running a BBS for profit or business, consider what type of reputation you can develop by giving users what they really want.

Types of Shareware Users Want

Users have different tastes and like different kinds of software. Some people enjoy fast action games like those distributed by Apogee Software, while others are more likely to want board and card-style games. Other users are just out there trying to find cool utilities that utilize their hardware. It's hard to say what users like from one day to the next, but we can come up with some generalizations that may make it easier for you to maintain a shareware library.

First of all, games tend to live very short lives. They're popular one minute, and the next, everyone has played them. The fast turnover of games makes shareware game libraries difficult to maintain. When you get a good game and make it available for download, it's popular for a few months and then its popularity diminishes. You're then left with the task of removing it and replacing it with something new and improved.

Games are a funny form of addiction for most users. It seems the level of game addiction varies depending upon the number of levels, the intensity of the graphics, and the number of creatures there are to shoot at. Games containing graphic violence are extremely popular and the more violent they become, the more popular they are (sometimes the popularity of these games grows exponentially). Of course, graphic violence isn't the only source of attraction to games.

Games like Duke Nukem by Apogee Software, shown in figure 13.4, contain cute little creatures that spit slime on you. The object is to save the world from the dreaded Dr. Doom—which brings us to another point. Not only do the popular games employ superb graphics, numerous levels, and spitting creatures, but they have a hero. The object of the game is usually to save something from the evil grip of something else, and people just love the enticement of good vs. evil. But, this isn't to say that the only popular games are the shoot- 'em-up style games.

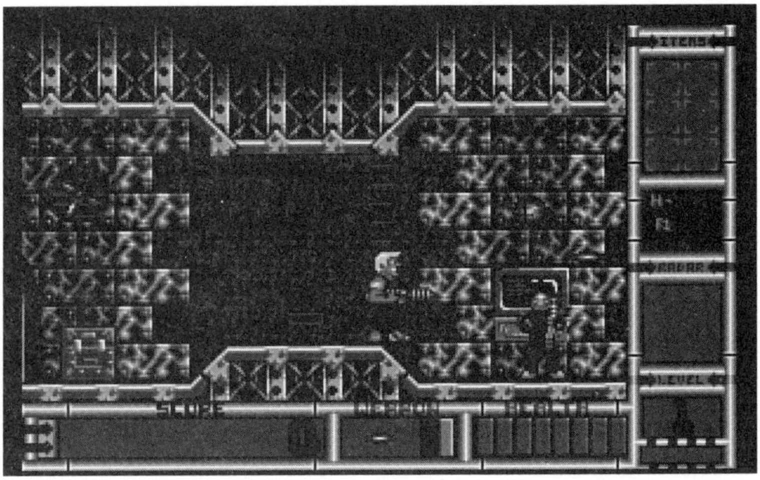

Fig. 13.4
Duke Nukem is a very popular game written and distributed by Apogee Software.

There's an occasional wave of board and card-style games hitting the shareware market that are just as addicting as games like Duke Nukem. Games that aren't fast paced with maze-like levels maintain their addictiveness by testing you with complex puzzles and opposition to the effect that you must think two or three moves in advance in order to win. Hexxagon by Software Creations, shown in figure 13.5, is a game that's similar to Checkers in design but much more complex. You place your pieces by clicking on the piece to move and then clicking on the hexagon you want to move it to. When your piece lands next to any of your opponent's pieces, your opponent's pieces are given to you (changed to your color). The object of the game is to *own* most of the playing board when there's no place left to put pieces.

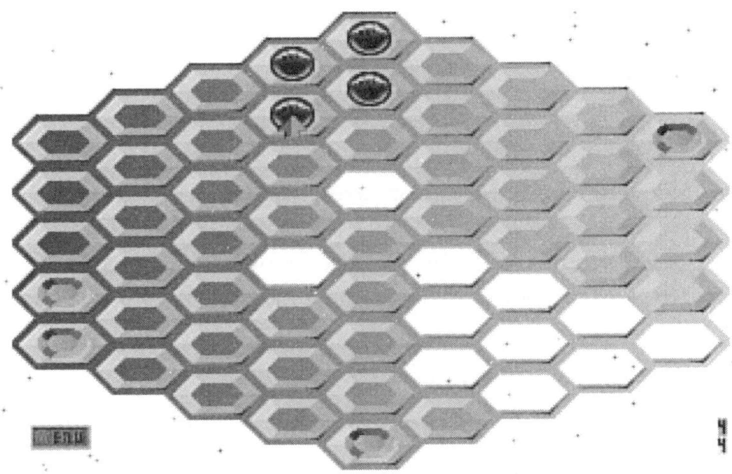

Fig. 13.5
This is an excellent game called Hexxagon, by Software Creations.

Other board and card-style games include versions of Checkers, Scrabble, Poker, Hearts and Mahjongg. The style of board and card-style games is different than the fast-paced action games. Notice though that board and card-style shareware games have something in common with the fast-paced action games—good graphics. If a game has good graphics and at least a small plot to it, it's bound to be successful on the shareware market and in your download libraries. On the other hand, utilities are popular for other reasons (they're not typically popular because of good graphics).

Popular shareware utilities are those that offer the best interfaces, features, and documentation. Although some may provide graphical interfaces, they're not any more popular than those that display DOS text screens. Among the most downloaded shareware utilities are offline mail readers, archive and compression utilities, clocks, screen-savers, and text editors. Figure 13.6 shows QEDIT, a shareware text editor written and distributed by Semware, Inc.

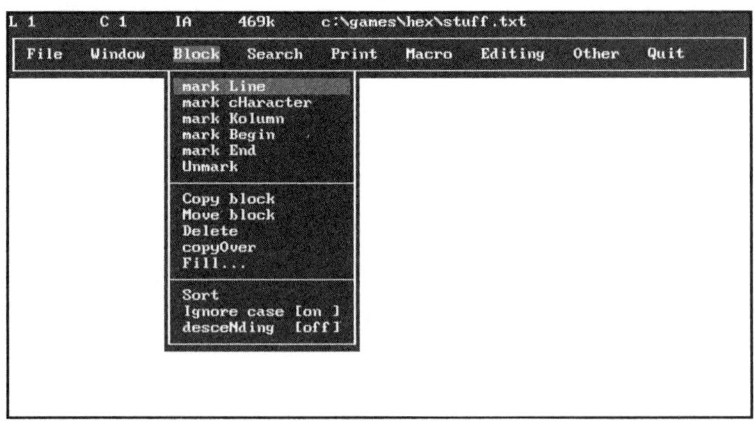

Fig. 13.6
QEDIT is a text editor that provides some specialized features that are extremely useful for DOS and Windows programmers.

QEDIT is especially handy for programming. It gives you a well-designed and intuitive interface plus some features that you can't live without! For C and C++ programmers it provides some auto-indention options that aren't even supported by commercial editors. For example, let's say that you're coding along and you enter a **{** ("{" and "}" are used to delimit function blocks in C and C++), QEDIT automatically indents the following line by three or four spaces. Of course, a utility like QEDIT isn't complete with good documentation.

The manual for QEDIT is a text file in a format ready for printing. It includes page numbers and page breaks at page sizes that fit almost any printer. Its documentation is extremely well done and includes textual pictures and diagrams of the software. Although the shareware version of the QEDIT manual is not indexed, it contains a very helpful table of contents. Also included with the documentation is a text file containing helpful hints and commonly asked questions. Just as users expect good graphics in shareware games, they expect to see good documentation included with utilities.

Association of Shareware Professionals

The Association of Shareware Professionals (ASP) is an organization made up of bulletin boards and shareware authors. ASP *approval* is like the ISO9000 of the shareware world. They're devoted to setting standards for programs marketed with the shareware concept. Some of their standards include good documentation, professional interface, and fair business practices. To become a member of the ASP means that you either author or provide high quality shareware programs for general computer users.

Note

ISO9000 is a set of production standards given by the International Standards Organization. It guarantees quality by defining the way companies make their products. An ISO900-compliant company's products and production processes are reviewed by government-appointed agencies to ensure the highest level of quality.

Boards that are ASP approved are often more visible than those that aren't. Users that sign onto an ASP approved board know that they're going to find programs that they want and programs that are worth paying for. If you want to make your BBS popular by offering loads of high-quality shareware utilities and games, strive to meet the standards of the ASP and become a member—you have nothing to lose! Besides, having the ASP's stamp of approval is like having an Intel Inside sticker tattooed to your forehead. Get information about the Association of Shareware Professionals by writing to:

ASP Ombudsman
545 Grover Road
Muskegon, MI 49442-9427

In addition to writing the ombudsman, you can contact the ASP through CompuServe mail by sending a message to 70007,3536.

Summary

In this chapter, you learned what shareware is, where to get it, and why you want it. We covered the two major types of shareware programs, utilities and games, and taught you how to recognize the good stuff and the bad. You can tell the differences between shareware, freeware, and commercial software packages, and you know what organization to look to for high-quality shareware (ASP). And, finally, you know what's legal about distributing shareware and the type of programs that users look for.

It's now your turn to take all of this information and create a successful and profitable BBS. Be sure to include some of the awesome utilities and games distributed by the talented authors represented by Apogee Software and other shareware distributors. All of these people are working their tails off trying to entertain the ever-expanding world of computer users. As long as we keep them going, we'll have low-priced high-quality software to last for lifetimes to come—so, urge your users to register their software!

Chapter 14

Using Offline Mail

by Markus Pope

Offline mail is a way for users to read and respond to their messages while they're not signed onto your system. It's implemented in several different ways: Blue Wave, UUCP, and QWK Mail. The most common offline mail system used by BBS sysops is the QWK Mail standard. In this chapter, you will learn:

- What QWK Mail is and how it works.
- Advantages to providing offline mail on your BBS.
- QWK Mail readers, what they look like, and what they are used for.
- Instructions on how to install offline mail using Wildcat! BBS Software. Unfortunately, QWK Mail is not included with the version of Wildcat! Lite accompanying this reference. We urge you to upgrade to the full-featured commercial version to take advantage of the features not included in Wildcat! Lite.
- Tips on how offline mail is installed on other BBS systems.
- Disadvantages and limitations of offline mail systems.
- Commonly asked questions and problems regarding QWK Mail systems.

First, we will talk about what makes up the QWK Mail system, the components of the system, how those components work together, and why you need it. Next, we give you examples of offline mail readers, show you some screens from some of the more popular ones, and list and describe some of their features. After we show you the components of the QWK Mail system, we walk you through step-by-step instructions on how to install the Tomcat QWK Mail system that's supplied by Mustang, the makers of WildCat!. In case you're not using the Wildcat! software included with this book, we give you tips regarding the installation of offline mail using other popular BBS software packages. Finally, we give you the disadvantages to using offline mail (there aren't many), the limitations, and some commonly asked questions and problems.

What Is QWK Mail?

QWK Mail is a standard that defines how messages are read and responded to offline—while not connected to your BBS. It allows users to sign onto a system, download waiting messages, respond to them and then upload their responses at a later time. The ability to read and respond to messages offline provides BBS users with several advantages:

- Messages are read and responded to at the user's convenience. There's more time for users to think about the messages they're reading and writing.
- QWK Mail saves money invested in long-distance telephone calls placed to systems outside of the user's local calling area.
- Online editors are often slow and hard to use. QWK Mail readers typically provide excellent message editing features. Some even give you the ability to use more elaborate viewers and editors rather than those built into the QWK Mail reader.
- Most QWK Mail utilities (on the BBS side of the fence) allow users to choose which message conferences they want to look at and respond to.

Similarly, you also benefit from the services that QWK Mail provides (other than those advantages you get as a user of QWK Mail):

- Since users have more time to think about the messages that they're writing, your BBS looks more professional; messages have more heart and much clearer meaning; they may contain less spelling and grammar errors; and there are no garbage characters resulting from communication problems that occur while users are online.
- Your BBS can support more users because they spend less time online. They spend a few minutes signing onto the system, downloading and/or uploading messages, and then the line is free for other callers.

Note

More important for sysops who are running bulletin boards for profit—you save money in hardware costs when you increase the number of users that can access your system without expanding your system's hardware.

- QWK Mail is another add-on utility that makes your BBS more attractive for new and seasoned users—the more attractive bulletin board systems are the most successful.

Basic Components

Five components make up the QWK Mail system: conferences, services, QWK packets, message file compression, and the offline reader. Conferences and services are messages and bulletins provided by the BBS. QWK packets, message file compression, and the offline reader are the tools used to present conferences and services to the users. Once you understand the basic building blocks of the QWK Mail system, implementing QWK Mail on your BBS is a snap!

Conferences

Conferences is just a fancy word for message bases or message areas. The conferences that you provide in the QWK Mail system are those that are defined in the configuration for your BBS. For example, if you create a message base in the Digital Mozart BBS called "Famous Fifths" you can also create a QWK Mail conference that relates directly to that new message base. When users request messages from the "Famous Fifths" conference using QWK Mail, they're actually receiving messages from the "Famous Fifths" message base in the Digital Mozart BBS.

Setting up conferences in QWK Mail, however, isn't as easy as just telling it to look at your BBS message bases. QWK Mail limits conference names to 12 characters—a limit that is not often imposed on BBS message base names. In our example for the Digital Mozart BBS, the name "Famous Fifths" is one character too large. Luckily, this doesn't mean that we must change the name of our message base in order to use it with the QWK Mail system.

In the QWK Mail configuration, you can specify the name of a conference as it's referenced by the offline reader and by the name of the BBS message base to which it corresponds. It's this cross-referencing that allows us to provide message bases with names longer than 12 characters as QWK Mail conferences. Let's revisit our previous Digital Mozart BBS example. Since "Famous Fifths" is one character too large, we can simply configure QWK Mail to reference this message base as "FAM_FIFTHS". "FAM_FIFTHS" is a legal QWK Mail conference name because its length doesn't exceed 12 characters. Notice also that we use "_" instead of space in the conference name. Some QWK Mail implementations don't allow imbedded blanks within conference names. Using "_" is a good way to make conference names readable while still maintaining compatibility with the wealth of QWK Mail readers on the BBS market today.

The QWK Mail "standard" is a *de facto* standard and in the BBS world there is only a modicum of documentation on the specification. It's changing every day, so it's tough to say what features are and are not supported by the many implementations. Fortunately, most new implementations of QWK Mail are backward compatible with the old.

Tip

Use descriptive conference names so that users who are new to your system can determine what conferences their messages belong in. Remember that users are reading your conferences offline and may not know what message bases they're referencing.

Access to QWK Mail conferences can be limited just like message bases on a BBS. If a user doesn't have the privilege level required for a conference, then he/she isn't permitted to access the messages in the corresponding message base. Privilege level refers to the access rights granted to users by the sysop. Let's imagine that we want to restrict the use of the "Famous Fifths" message base, so you use the QWK Mail configuration to restrict access for the "FAM_FIFTHS" conference to users with privilege levels greater than five. Unless a user has adequate access, he/she isn't allowed to download or upload messages to and from the "Famous Fifths" message base.

Newer QWK Mail systems allow conferences to have special features such as enclosed files, carbon copy mail, and return receipts; however, there's no guarantee that your QWK Mail system supports these features because they weren't provided for in the original QWK Mail specification. Similar to setting access restrictions, these special features are enabled by specifying flags or options when you configure the conferences for your BBS.

Enclosed files are files that are attached to messages. An enclosed file is uploaded to a BBS at the message editing prompt before a message is saved. A line is usually included in the message indicating that a file is attached and stating the file's original name. The names of enclosed files are changed to avoid conflict with existing files. Your QWK Mail utility may or may not rename enclosed files when they're included in a QWK message download.

Carbon copy mail allows users to send a copy of a mail message to more than one user without including more than one copy of the mail message in their QWK message upload. When the BBS receives a mail message that's addressed to more than one user, it sends the mail message to its primary destination and routes copies of the message to users specified to receive carbon copies. Typically, the BBS stores a separate copy of the mail message for each user.

Return receipts are messages, sent to the message sender, indicating that a user has received a specific mail message. They provide a way of determining whether or not a user has read his or her mail. A similar analogy is that of a registered letter. You know that someone's read a registered letter because you get a receipt from the postal service containing the addressee's signature. When a user reads a mail message that is sent with a return receipt request, the BBS sends the requester a message saying that the mail has been read.

Services

File lists and bulletins are services that you can provide using QWK Mail as a medium. They're included in QWK Mail message downloads, but aren't read like messages. While some offline readers provide a way to view these files, most are read manually using a text file viewer or reader. If the offline reader does provide bulletin support, there's a chance that the user sees bulletins automatically when he or she starts the reader.

File lists are text files containing names, dates, and descriptions of files available for download. Your QWK Mail system may even keep track of the last time a user is online and provide lists of only those files that are added since the user's last login. Either way, QWK Mail is a fast and easy way to distribute your most current file lists to your users.

Bulletins are text files that may contain any information you want to make available to your users. Most often, bulletins are used to relay welcome messages, good-bye messages, and news. For instance, let's say that we're going to have a party to promote the Digital Mozart BBS. Along with the news files that users see when they're online, we can also tell the QWK Mail system to include the news files in QWK Mail message downloads. QWK Mail then bundles the news files along with users' packets when they download messages. If their offline reader provides a way to view bulletins, users can read about the party before or after they read and respond to messages.

In addition to file lists and bulletins, services may also include binary files (data files or executables). Binary files provided as services are normally those that change often and have value to a majority of the people that use the QWK Mail system. While QWK Mail doesn't limit services to text and binary files that are volatile and useful, it's still a good idea to restrict use of services to these criteria.

QWK Packets

Although not at the heart of the QWK Mail system, the QWK packet is an essential building block. QWK packets contain the conferences and services that are downloaded by users. Once downloaded, the QWK packet is used by the offline reader to present messages and bulletins to the user. When the user is finished reading and responding to messages, the QWK packet is used again to transport the user's replies back to the BBS message bases. When a packet is downloaded from the QWK Mail system, it's referred to as a QWK message packet. When a packet is uploaded, it's known as a QWK reply packet.

When a QWK message packet is downloaded, its name consists of a BBS identifier and an extension of ".QWK". The BBS identifier is an abbreviated name that you give your BBS. It's limited to eight characters in length so that it can be used to as a valid DOS file name. If we configure the BBS identifier on the Digital Mozart BBS as "DMOZART", for instance, message packets downloaded from the QWK Mail system are called "DMOZART.QWK".

Optionally, the BBS may change the name of message packets if more than one is downloaded by the same user within the same day or online session. Message packets are renamed by changing the "K" in the extensions to a number between 0 and 9. For example, if you download two QWK message packets from the Digital Mozart BBS in the same day, the second message packet may be called "DMOZART.QW0". Typically this is done so that users can download more than one message packet without overwriting existing ones. QWK reply packets are handled in basically the same manner. We'll cover the reply packet later on in this section. First, let's take an in-depth look at the QWK message packet.

QWK message packets are essentially made up of a message file, index files, a control file, welcome messages, bulletins, and enclosed files. We've already talked about welcome messages, bulletins, and enclosed files, so we won't spend too much time on those items right now. Index and control files give the offline reader information about the BBS system and the message file. The message file contains the conferences requested by the user.

If we look at the message file under a microscope, we find detailed information about each message and the messages themselves. Messages are stored in the file with a message header followed by the message body text. The message header is made up of the message type and status (public or private, read or unread, for example), the message number, its date and time, who the message is for, who it's from, its subject, the number of the message it's in reference to, the message's size and the conference in which it's posted. As stated above, following the message header is the actual body text of the message.

The message file contains a header and body text for each message requested by the user. It's created by the QWK Mail system when the system is preparing the QWK message packet for download. The file name given to the message file is always MESSAGES.DAT. Index files may accompany the message file in the QWK message packet.

Index files contain references that tell the offline reader where to find messages within the message file. There is one index file for each of the conferences included in a QWK message packet; however, offline readers do not require indexes, so many QWK Mail utilities include them at the user's discretion. The references themselves are very simple. They're composed of only the message's location within the message file followed by the number of the conference in which the message is located.

If included in the QWK message packet, the names of index files consist of the numbers of the conferences for which they're referencing and extensions of ".NDX". The conference numbers are right-justified on three zeros. Let's revisit the "Famous Fifths" message base example, but this time let's say that the number of the "Famous Fifths" conference is 1. When a user downloads a QWK message packet that contains messages from the "Famous Fifths" conference, an index file called "001.NDX" is most likely included, which points to messages within the message file belonging to the "Famous Fifths" conference.

Similar in function to index files, control files provide information about the BBS system to the offline reader. The control file is a plain text file that gives the offline reader the name, location, and identifier of the BBS system that produced the QWK message packet. It also includes the sysop's name, the caller's name, the date and time that the QWK message packet was created, and a list of conferences included in the message packet. Other data, such as the user's voice phone number, number of calls and total bytes downloaded, may be included in the control file but is often ignored by the offline reader (and left out of the file by the QWK Mail system).

When the QWK message packet is created by the QWK Mail system, the Control file is given the name of "CONTROL.DAT". This file is required by the offline reader and is always included in the QWK message packet. Typically, this file is used by the offline reader only to obtain the list of conferences included in the message packet and their respective numbers.

Welcome files are optional files that are in the same classification as services—they provide general information about the BBSs that create the message packets. Each message packet contains one welcome file and it's given the name of "WELCOME.TXT". This file is likely to be a copy of the file that's displayed to users when they sign onto your BBS and may contain either straight text or ANSI sequences. Typically, you can specify the file to include "WELCOME.TXT" in the configuration for the QWK Mail system.

Note

Since quite a few offline readers display the contents of the welcome file when opening a QWK message packet, it's handy to use as an advertising tool for your BBS. In the case of the Digital Mozart BBS, you can display a banner describing the billions of sound files that you have made available in your download areas.

As described previously, QWK message packets may also contain bulletins. Since we discussed bulletins in the services section of this chapter, we won't cover them in much detail here. In review, bulletins are usually news files that describe upcoming events related to the BBS or that provide other types of general information. Bulletins are given file names that consist of "BLT-" and a number that uniquely identifies each. For example, if you create a bulletin to include with QWK message packets downloaded from your BBS, it may be called "BLT-1".

Enclosed files are thrown into QWK message packets when the packets are created by the QWK Mail system. Unfortunately, there is no provision for files attached to messages in the specification for QWK Mail. Offline readers ignore enclosed files and leave this level of handling to the user because there's no way to link together the enclosed files and the messages to which they're attached. Another shortcoming regarding enclosed files is that the QWK Mail system on the BBS may not rename the files to their original file names (remember, their names are usually changed to avoid conflicts with existing files), so users may not be able to tell what file a message is referencing.

Files other than those we've talked about thus far may be included in message packets created with new implementations of the QWK specification. These files are optional and are outside the scope of this discussion; however, if you're interested in learning about these optional files, check the manuals for your QWK Mail system for a list and descriptions of all files contained within its message packets.

Now that we've taken a very close look at the files included in the QWK message packet, let's talk a little bit about the QWK reply packet. The only file that's included in the QWK reply packet is the message file, except that its name consists of the BBS's identifier with an extension of ".MSG". Recall that the BBS's identifier is a name given to your BBS that is less than eight characters (so that it can be used as part of a valid DOS file name). Message files for the Digital Mozart BBS, for example, may be called "DMOZART.MSG".

The new message file is created by the offline reader. It contains replies written by the user to messages in the QWK message packet. The format of this file is identical to that of the message file in the message packet with one exception—each reply's message number is replaced with the conference in which the message is posted.

Similar to the message files contained within them, QWK reply packets are given a name that consists of the BBS identifier and an extension of ".REP". "DMOZART.MSG" from our example above, for instance, is included in a QWK reply packet called "DMOZART.REP". This may seem like trivial information, but quite a few QWK Mail utilities reject QWK reply packets if they're named incorrectly.

Message File Compression

So far we've covered the components of QWK message and reply packets and you probably noticed that we hinted around about the message and reply packets "containing" other files, but we haven't been specific about what we mean by this. Message and reply packets are archive files that are usually compressed.

Archive files are simply files that contain other files. Archiving was developed to make transmission and storage of multiple files easier. With an archive utility, you can create a file that contains 10 or 11 other files and upload them to a BBS in one fell swoop. In such a case of multiple files making up a complete system, it's much less time consuming to download one archive file than to fumble with downloading multiple files.

After the invention of archiving came compression. File compression is a technique used to shorten the length of files in an archive. The first form of compression was a simple concept called *run-length encoding*. Run-length encoding is a process that replaces redundant information in a file with a prefix indicating that information is repeated followed by a character representing the number of occurrences and one copy of the text that is redundant. For example, a utility that uses run-length encoding may change "AAAAAAA" to "&7A", because "A" is repeated seven times. We use "&" in our example to indicate that the following characters represent run-length encoded information.

Actually, a run-length encoding utility is more likely to replace the seven characters in our example with a prefix followed by a character with an ASCII value equivalent to the number of times that the text is repeated. Rather than a literal seven in our example, you're more likely to see a Ctrl-G (character 7 of the ASCII character set)—also known as the bell character.

Nowadays, compression is not that straightforward. Newer compression techniques are based upon complex mathematical expressions and error-detection algorithms. Error-detection, as the name implies, alerts the compression utility of problems that occurred during compression of a file when the file is restored to its original state. While run-length encoding programs do a fair job of compressing data in text files, the newer and more complex compression utilities are much better suited for compression of binary files and QWK packets!

Now that you have some idea of what archive and compression utilities are and what they do, we can get on to a more important topic—using file compression utilities with QWK Mail. File compression utilities are used by both the QWK Mail system and the offline reader. Some QWK Mail systems have compression utilities built into them, such as QSO by eSoft, Inc., while others require the use of third-party compression utilities like ARC, LHA, and PKZIP.

If your QWK Mail system has built-in compression, it probably doesn't allow you to use an external utility. Usually though, the system does let you specify whether or not you want the QWK message packets compressed. Some of the more integrated QWK Mail systems can determine whether a caller is using a high-speed modem (one that supports compression internally) and turn compression on or off based upon the capabilities of the caller's modem. Compressing and decompressing data when it enters a modem is more efficient than transferring data that's already compressed. Even if compression is off, however, QWK message files are still transferred as archive files.

If your QWK Mail system lets you specify the compression utility to use when compressing and decompressing packets, you should pick a utility that:

1. Most of your users already have and are familiar with.
2. Is available for download somewhere on your BBS.
3. Can be used from a DOS command line.

Choosing a compression utility that most users already have and are familiar with saves you the trouble of explaining how to use it. It's a fair bet that your users' offline readers have this utility set up and ready to go. Also, users tend to help other users with the more common utilities, giving you time to concentrate on making your BBS more popular.

Since you can't guarantee that your users already have the compression utility you're going to use with the QWK Mail system, it's a good idea to provide it for download somewhere in your file download areas. Optionally, you can provide it as a selection on the same menu where the QWK Mail system is located, or include it in the file download area that contains your offline readers.

It's very important that you choose a compression utility that can be executed from the DOS command line; at least, there should be a DOS command line version available for those users still using the DOS operating system. For users who are not using the DOS operating system, make sure that the utility can still be called using command line parameters. Offline readers provide a command line interface to compression utilities even in Windows, so a utility that can't be executed from a command line is painful to use with an offline reader.

Previously, we mentioned three archive and compression utilities: ARC, LHA and PKZIP. ARC was one of the first archive utilities developed in the early 1980s and was widely used until the introduction of ZIP compression around 1984 or 1985. It's not used much anymore but is still supported by most offline readers.

LHA is an extension of and is based upon ARC archive and compression techniques. It provides the ability to distribute archives in self-extracting format. Self-extracting archives exist in the form of executable programs. When you execute a self-extracting archive, it expands files that are contained within its own data area (within the executable). There's not much advantage to using LHA over ARC in the QWK Mail arena; however, because there's no need to provide message and reply packets in self-extracting format, extraction and creation of archive files is handled by the offline reader. Its biggest benefit is that it's in the public domain, which means that it's free for non-commercial use without payment.

ZIP is the most widely used archive and compression technique—specifically, PKZIP by Phil Katz. Katz released the first version of PKZIP back in February of 1989. Today, PKZIP is so popular that you can find it in the download libraries of just about any BBS or online service you call. It supports all of the features available in ARC and LHA, including self-extracting archives.

There are two versions of PKZIP: version 1 and version 2. Version 1 is directly compatible with other utilities that support ZIP compression. Archives created with version 2's default settings, however, can't be decompressed using ZIP utilities compatible with version 1. Since most users have converted to PKZIP 2.0, this isn't a major problem unless your QWK Mail system has built-in ZIP compression. If your QWK Mail system has built-in ZIP compression, it's most likely not compatible with the default settings of PKZIP 2.0.

Tip

Notice that we use the term "default settings" when stating incompatibilities between PKZIP 1.0 and 2.0—users can make archive files, created with PKZIP 2.0, compatible with 1.0 by setting their offline reader to call PKZIP 2.0 with the "-e0" option. The option is only necessary when creating the QWK reply packet.

QWK Offline Readers

Offline readers are used to read and respond to messages in QWK message packets. Additionally, they may provide support for bulletins, welcome and good-bye files, news files, and new files lists. After you read and respond to message packets, offline readers create reply packets that you upload to the BBS. The QWK Mail system takes messages from QWK reply packets and imports them into the BBS message bases.

Since you're providing QWK Mail support for your users, it's a good idea to make a few offline mail readers available for download in your file download areas or at least tell your users where to get them. Also, you may find it handy to familiarize yourself with the offline readers that you provide, so that you can confidently answer questions regarding their use. Provide at least one offline reader for DOS and one for Windows to satisfy both your DOS users and your Windows users.

There are a lot of good commercial, public domain, and shareware QWK offline readers that we can talk about; but, to keep this discussion relatively short, we'll briefly cover only the most popular. Among the most popular of the offline readers are Blue Wave, OLX, CmpQWK and WinQWK. Blue Wave and OLX are DOS applications while CmpQWK and WinQWK are Windows applications. First, let's take a look at the Blue Wave mail reader.

Blue Wave

Blue Wave is a shareware offline reader created and distributed by Cutting Edge Computing, in Burton, Michigan. When you run the Blue Wave offline reader, the first feature that you notice is the beautiful blue, sea-colored, exploding windows. The interface is very well designed and very clean. And, like OLXTD, which is discussed later, the program is packed full with every feature imaginable. Blue Wave is shown in figure 14.1.

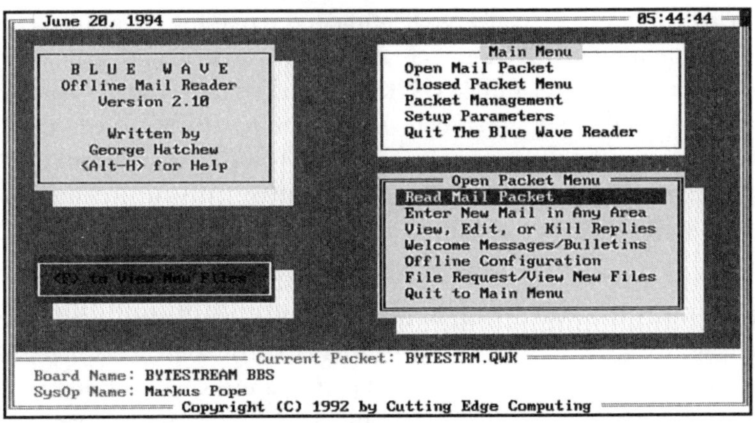

Fig. 14.1
Blue Wave benefits from good design and ease of use.

Included in the setup for Blue Wave, we find the same options found in other offline readers: global toggles (including an on-screen clock), message read options, reply options, tagline settings, and memory and color control. Blue Wave's setup, however, also contains settings not seen in typical offline readers. These options are printer and video control. Also included in the setup for Blue Wave are the familiar path, archive, and compression and quote options. On top of the well-designed, very pretty interface of Blue Wave, you'll notice that the status line at the bottom of the screen displays help messages about each item highlighted in the setup!

Global toggles contain options such as on-screen clock, mouse support, and exploding windows. In the read options, we find features like automatic personal message scanning, beep on personal messages, and delete message packets after reading. Automatic personal message scanning finds messages addressed to you based on your name rather than using index files. Since index files are optional and may not be included in a QWK message packet, personal scanning is an invaluable feature. Continuing on to reply options, there's quoting, reply subject, and network mail settings. You can set whether or not you want taglines, and if so, you can specify the order in which they're chosen—randomly, sequentially, or prompted. Both extended and expanded memory are supported in the memory settings. In the printer and video options you can change settings like what port your printer is on, whether a form-feed is sent after each message, and the number of lines supported by your video display. Compression utilities supported are ZIP, ARC, LZH (LHA), PAK, and ARJ. In addition to the five archive and compression utilities supported internally, Blue Wave also allows you to specify your own choice.

Complementing Blue Wave's treasure of setup features is the ability to open, close, delete, and rename packets. Deleting and renaming are available from a file management menu; open and close allow you to read and respond to message packets. After opening a QWK Mail packet, Blue Wave prompts you with message handling options such as read, compose, view or edit mail, view new files list, the welcome message, and offline configuration. If your QWK Mail system supports it, offline configuration lets you to change your QWK Mail setup while you're offline and include setup commands in reply packets.

When you select the read option in Blue Wave, a menu is displayed showing conferences included in the message packet. Unfortunately, personal is not included if you're not using the internal personal message scanning feature—even when the appropriate index file is included in the message packet. After choosing a conference, Blue Wave gives you a list of messages from that conference. In the message viewer that appears when you select a message to read, you can select from the usual options of reply, next, and previous.

Blue Wave doesn't highlight the letters that activate commands in the message viewer, so it's difficult to tell what keys to press to move next, previous, and to start replies. Luckily, there's a well-formatted help screen available at the touch of a function key. Blue Wave is feature packed and extremely easy to use.

Offline Xpress Test Drive

Offline Xpress (also known as OLX) is an offline mail reader created by Mustang Software, Inc. OLX is a commercial software package but Mustang distributes a *Test Drive* version called OLXTD. Test Drive means that you can try it out before you buy it. Mustang provides a very flexible license which allows you to use OLXTD for an unlimited time, provided that it's not used in a commercial application. You can also put OLXTD on your BBS for downloading as long as you don't modify the contents of the OLXTD archive or charge for the program. You can download Offline Xpress Test Drive from just about any bulletin board service.

OLXTD provides a wide variety of options for reading and responding to messages and manipulating QWK packets. When you first start Offline Xpress, you're prompted with a screen similar to DOS shell programs. From the opening screen, you're given the ability to delete, rename and sort packets. In addition, you can compose a message and create a QWK reply packet from scratch—without downloading a QWK message packet. This screen also provides direct access to the configuration and even an option to shell to DOS.

In the configuration menu, you'll find a gold mine of options including paths, general options, toggles, editor settings, reply options, archive and compression utility setup, colors, and function and ALT key options. The General options menu contains items such as left mouse support, extended and expanded memory options, and the sort orders for messages and conferences. Included in the toggles menu are options such as scroll bars, exploding windows, and whether the program beeps on personal messages (messages addressed to the user). Editor settings allow you to change your message editor so that you can use the text editor you're most acquainted with. Reply options lets you specify what quoting style to use, all lines, single lines, or no lines at all. And in the function and ALT key options, you can set OLXTD to execute a menu item or program operation when you press specific keys.

Once you choose a QWK message packet to read, OLXTD gives you the choice of viewing bulletins, the news file, reading mail, or viewing a list of new files. Bulletins displays a list of bulletins included in the chosen message packet; selecting news opens the viewer and displays the news file; selecting the files option displays the new files list; and messages opens the gate to the BBS message bases.

When you select the mail option to view and respond to messages in the packet, you can choose from the conferences included in the packet. In addition, you can choose a personal conference which contains messages addressed to you specifically, or a replies conference which contains all of the replies you write for the chosen packet. After you choose a conference, OLXTD displays the first message appearing in the conference and gives you another wide range of options to choose from.

In the message viewer, you can select a next or previous option to move forward or backward through the message packet, or compose replies. An index option provides a list of all messages contained within the current conference. To read a specific message, simply highlight the message and press Enter. On a miscellaneous menu in the message viewer, OLXTD provides search, mark message, and animate options (for ANSI messages), and lots more! OLXTD spoils you in features and has excellent mouse support. For keyboard users, however, the menu options in the message viewer are less than intuitive—OLXTD doesn't highlight characters that activate menu items.

Figure 14.2 shows some of the options that are available in OLXTD's message viewer.

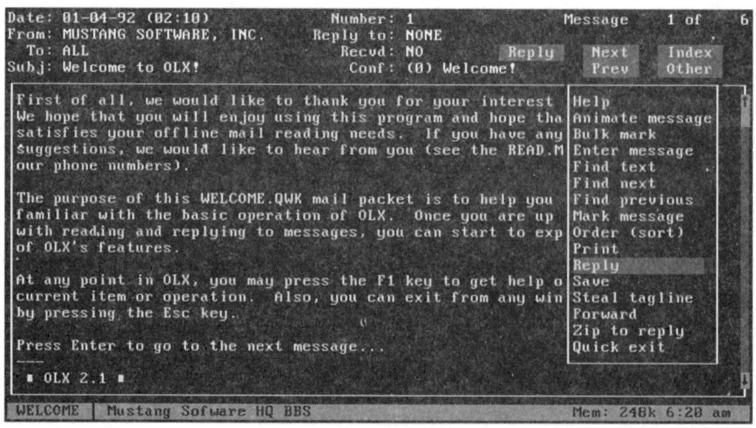

Fig. 14.2 Offline Xpress Test Drive provides many useful features just off of the message viewer.

CmpQWK for Windows

CmpQWK, by Derek Backus, is a full-featured Windows application disguised as an offline reader. CmpQWK presents a very clean and easy to use interface that seems to follow the Microsoft Windows guidelines to the letter. It displays a button bar for access to the most often used features, such as next message, previous message, and reply. In addition, you can select a button with the mouse that moves to the next conference included in the QWK message packet.

Upon entering the CmpQWK offline mail reader, a file selection dialog box is displayed containing a list of message packets. Included in the dialog box are options for deleting, renaming, and opening packets. Once you open a QWK Mail packet, the scenery gets even better. A list of conferences appears on the right side of the screen and when you select a message conference to read, CmpQWK displays the first message in that conference in its application workspace. Figure 14.3 shows off the message viewer and the button bar.

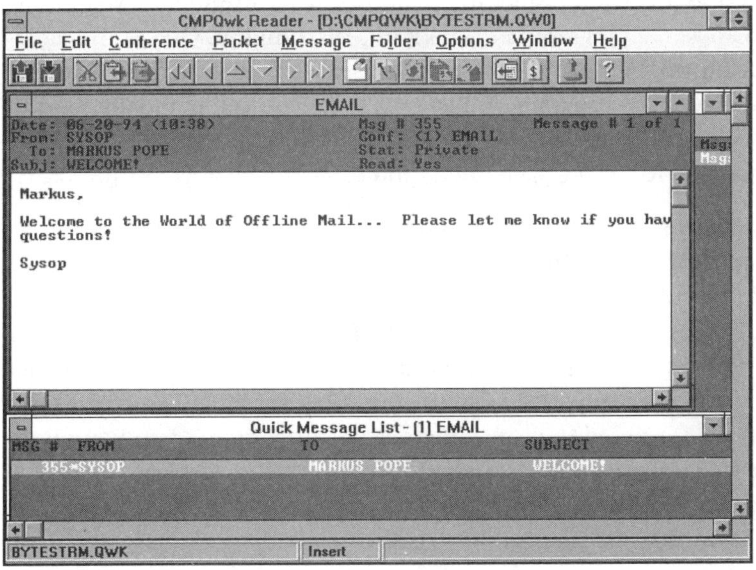

Fig. 14.3
CmpQWK is a masterpiece of usability and features usually exhibited only by large companies.

Notice the icon with the pencil and paper. You click on this icon to compose a reply to the currently active message. We say "currently active message" because you can display as many messages as you wish, and from any conference. In packets from the Digital Mozart BBS, for example, you can view messages from the Electronic Mail conference while you're viewing messages from the Famous Fifths message base.

Setup options include paths, general options, configuration of the message viewer, a separate configuration for the reply window, and packet management settings. In the paths options, we find support for internal ZIP, external ZIP, ARJ, LHA, WUNA, and external archive and compression utilities. General options include the ability to change the size of icons on the button bar, window startup position, and the viewer used to view ANSI messages. In the message viewer settings, we uncover options to start windows maximized, warn when re-reading messages, and sort by subject, window colors and Windows WAV file options. Reply window settings include quoting and spell-check options. And, finally, CmpQWK's packet management provisions include renaming packets after they're opened and an option to set the number of days after which to delete old message packets. Renaming lets you keep message packets that you've already read (recall that new packets downloaded from a specific system are always given the same name).

WinQWK for Windows

WinQWK is an offline reader for Windows. It's distributed as shareware by Doug Crocker, a programmer from Kent, Washington. One of the most notable features of WinQWK is that it walks you through configuration the first time you start the program, unlike OLXTD where you manually select setup. Setup options include archive and compression utilities, paths, file names of internal files, fonts, message filters, and some miscellaneous options.

WinQWK supports five archive and compression utilities, ZIP, ARC, ZOO, LHA, and ARJ, shown in figure 14.4; and you can change the command line used to execute each one—both for expanding message packets and creating them. In files setup, you can change the files used for tag lines, saved messages, viewing ANSI files, pick lists, and dictionaries. Tag lines are signatures that are automatically appended to your messages by offline readers. In fonts, you set the font used to display messages. This feature is handy for users that have a tough time reading standard Windows fonts. Message filters help you to "weed out" unwanted messages. You can make WinQWK display messages to and from specific users or messages with specific subjects.

Miscellaneous options include header and prefixes used when quoting messages in replies, quote strings, the default sort method, and tab stops. Other miscellaneous options (available from the menu only, and not from the setup dialogs) include confirm deletes, beep on personal mail, and disable hi-bit characters.

Unlike other offline readers, WinQWK features a spell-checker with both stock and custom dictionary support! WinQWK also provides a nice button bar with descriptive icons. All in all, WinQWK is a fairly decent Windows based offline reader but, like OLX, its interface appears to be centered toward mouse users. If you're using a laptop without a mouse, WinQWK is still usable but much more difficult.

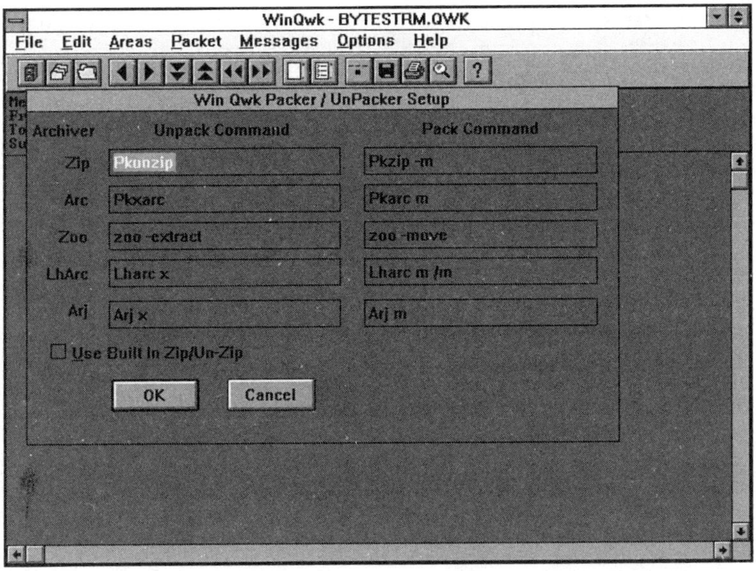

Fig. 14.4
WinQWK supports five archive and compression utilities while some other offline readers support just four.

We've given just an overview of the features of these popular offline mail readers. We didn't attempt to cover the many other useful features included by their creators. We suggest that you play around with these and other offline readers before making your final choices. Use the information provided here and the information that you collect while experimenting with other readers to make at least two offline readers available for download on your system—one for DOS users and one for Windows users.

How It All Works

In "Basic Components" we took a look at the inner workings of the QWK Mail system. You learned what each component of the system is and how it works. Now let's step back and take a look at what happens, both from the user's perspective and the BBS's perspective, when all of the components work together during a QWK Mail session. You can use this information when answering users' questions about QWK Mail.

Selection of Conferences and Services

Before users can download and upload messages using the QWK Mail system, they must select the conferences and services to which they want to subscribe. Subscribing in this sense means that they select the conferences containing messages they want to read and services they want included in the

QWK message packet. Typically the QWK Mail system knows when a call is a user's first visit. On a caller's first visit, most QWK Mail systems present the conferences and services selection menu automatically. Figure 14.5 shows a list of conferences that users can choose from. This particular user has a security level on the BBS that's high enough only to give him access to the electronic mail message base; therefore, only one conference shows up in the list (Private E-Mail).

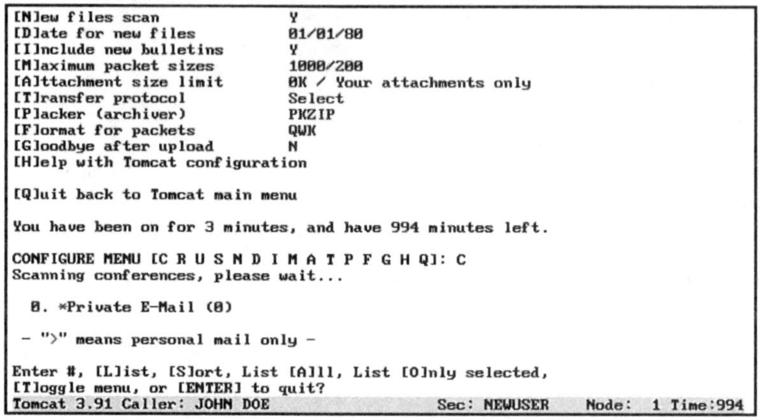

Fig. 14.5
Displayed is the conference selection screen for Mustang's full-featured commercial version of Wildcat!.

Conferences and services presented on the selection menu, as we've discussed in previous sections, are those that you tell QWK Mail to make available to your users. This is done during the installation of your QWK Mail system and is part of the configuration phase. In review, conferences are BBS message bases and services provide users with general information (such as file lists) or binary files.

In most QWK Mail selection menus, conferences are listed in the order in which they appear in the configuration for the BBS—the electronic mail message base shown in figure 14.5 is the first message base that appears in the BBS configuration file. Message bases are usually numbered starting with 1 and continuing up to the total number of message bases in the BBS. Your QWK Mail system may, however, use a numbering system similar to an alpha-numeric numbering scheme. Alpha-numeric numbering schemes commonly start with 1 and continue to the letter 'z' ("1,2,3...9,A,B...z", for example). These schemes allow users to select and deselect conferences using single key presses. Figure 14.5 shows that Tomcat displays a list of conferences starting at 0 instead of 1. Services are presented in much the same manner, but may be included on a separate menu.

Let's take a look at figure 14.5 again. Notice the asterisk next to the "Private E-Mail" conference. As a user selects conferences or services to include in QWK message packets, asterisks or some other characters are displayed next to them to indicate that they're included. Likewise, when they're deselected, the asterisks are removed to indicate that they're not included in the QWK message packets. If a user doesn't select a conference, messages from the corresponding message base are not included in subsequent QWK message packet downloads. In addition, some offline readers don't allow you to compose and post messages in conferences that aren't included in a message packet.

Selection of conferences and services is not limited to the first time someone uses the QWK Mail system. The selection menu is always available from the main menu or the configuration menu of the QWK Mail system.

Downloading QWK Message Packets

After the user selects conferences and services to include in QWK message packets, the QWK Mail system is ready to collect messages and send them to the user's computer. When a user selects the download option from the main QWK Mail menu, as in figure 14.6, the QWK Mail system searches the selected conferences for new messages. New messages are those posted since the date and time of the last message read by the user. The "last message read pointer", as it's commonly referred to by sysops, is based on message numbers—the BBS stores the highest message number read by each caller (message numbers are assigned to messages sequentially). Upon finding new messages, QWK Mail writes them to the message file and creates indexes to those messages in the index files corresponding to the conferences in which the messages are located. Since index files are not required by offline readers, some QWK Mail systems provide an option to turn off index file creation.

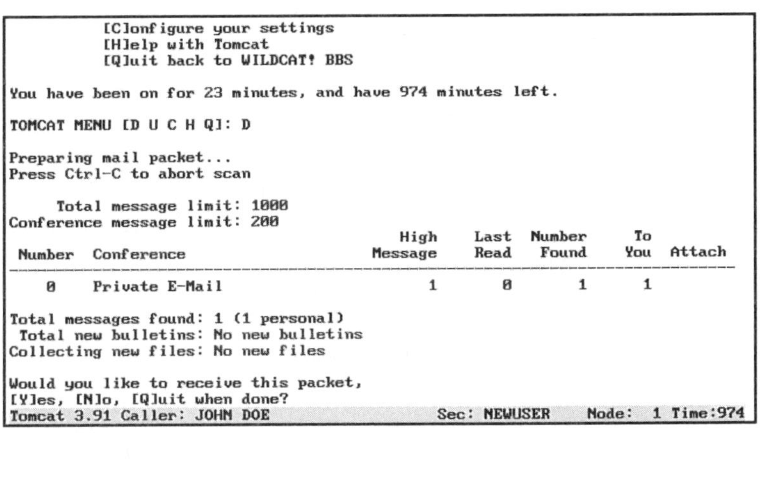

Fig. 14.6
In this QWK Mail session, the user is selecting the download option to receive waiting messages.

Now that the message and index files are created, QWK Mail checks to see if the user has selected services to include in message downloads. If services are selected, QWK Mail makes sure that the user hasn't received each service since the last time that the service was updated. Failing that, QWK Mail includes the appropriate files in the message packet. If the user has received the file service since the last time the service was updated, it's not added to the message packet for download. QWK Mail compares the date and time of a file service with the date and time of the user's last access to tell whether or not a service should be included.

Note

New file lists are special cases. If a user chooses to receive a list of all new files added to the system, QWK Mail builds a message packet which includes a list of files and their descriptions added to the BBS since the user's last login.

Services may also include welcome, good-bye, news, and bulletin files as well as those files specifically set up as services by the sysop. Welcome and good-bye files are typically added to the message packet at the user's discretion (options are provided in the QWK online configuration). News and bulletin files are treated as normal services and are only included if you've updated them since the last time they were added to the user's packet.

If QWK Mail finds file attachments during the scan for new messages and enclosed files are supported, the files are added to the message packet. When we say that components are "added" to a message packet, we actually mean that they're written into a temporary directory on the hard disk. QWK Mail stores the files that make up QWK packets in temporary directories so that they can be easily archived and compressed or, in the case of QWK reply packets, unarchived and decompressed.

After all files that make up the message packet are in the temporary directory, QWK Mail runs the compression utility. The compression utility makes an archive that includes all of the files in the temporary directory and compresses it. Once the message file is created, it's sent to the user as a binary file download. In the case of the Digital Mozart BBS, the file that is downloaded by the user is called "DMOZART.QWK". "DMOZART.QWK" is the name that we gave the QWK message packet in the Basic Components section of this chapter. The user is now ready to read and respond to messages in the QWK message packet.

Getting the Contents of the Message Packet

Now that the QWK message packet is on the user's machine, the user runs an offline reader to read and respond to the messages in the packet. Most readers automatically display a list of message packets for the user to choose from when executed, like the reader shown in figure 14.7. Others provide a menu called "File" from which the user chooses "Open". When the user chooses a file, the offline reader goes to work.

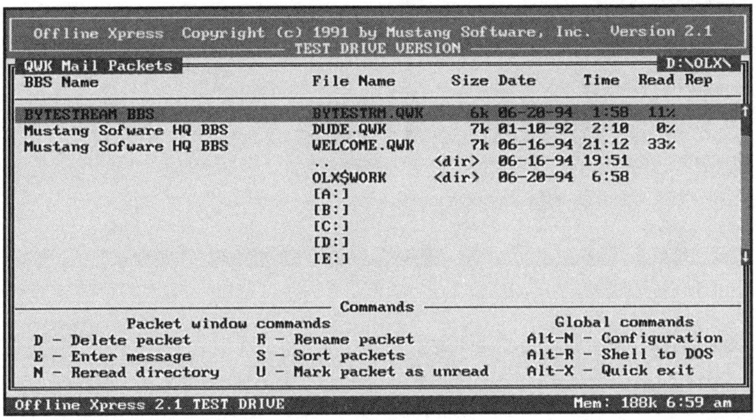

Fig. 14.7
Shown here is the opening screen for Offline Xpress Test Drive, a popular offline reader made by Mustang Software, Inc.

The first task performed by the offline reader is the task of expanding and decompressing the packet. Similar to the QWK Mail system, offline readers use temporary directories to store the contents of message and reply packets. Usually, two separate temporary directories are used for each type of packet so that the contents of the two packets are kept separate; however, this isn't necessary and may not always be the case. The contents of the QWK message packet are expanded into a temporary directory.

After the QWK message packet is expanded and decompressed, the offline reader prompts the user with a menu of options, such as those shown in figure 14.8. On this menu, the user can choose to read bulletins, news files, or messages. Some offline readers also provide an option for viewing a list of enclosed files. If there are no bulletins, news files, or enclosed files included in the message packet, those options are disabled.

If bulletins is chosen, the offline reader displays a list of the bulletin files from the message packet. Upon selecting a file for viewing, the user is rewarded with text or ANSI screens showing the contents of the bulletin. News files are handled like bulletins, except there's only one news file included in a packet; instead of providing a list of files, the offline reader skips that and displays the news file that's included. Bulletins and news files are typically displayed in a viewer that provides cursor key and/or mouse support for navigation.

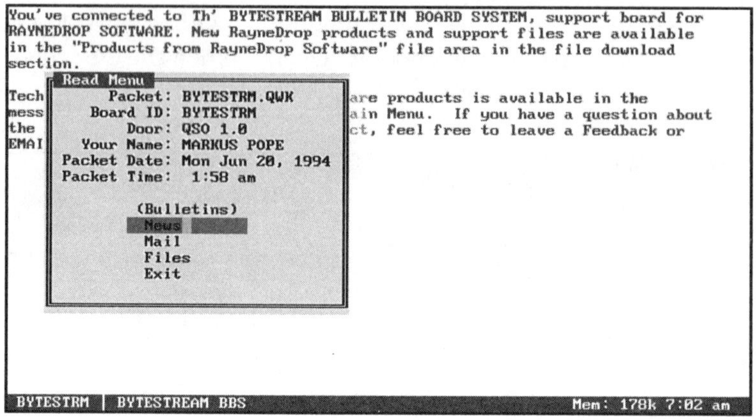

Fig. 14.8
Another snapshot taken from Offline Xpress Test Drive, this time showing what the typical offline reader's main menu looks like.

Retrieving Enclosed Files

Next on the options list is messages (or mail), but let's jump over to enclosed files and cover messages later on, in detail. Files that are enclosed in message packets are listed when the user selects the enclosed files option (sometimes referred to only as "Files"); that is, if the offline reader provides an enclosed files option at all. Additionally, the offline reader may provide a way to view enclosed files just in case they're saved in text format. If the offline reader doesn't provide a way to get a list of or view enclosed files, then it's off to DOS or to the Windows File Manager you go!

Note

Lack of support for enclosed files in offline readers isn't a major issue unless you're using your BBS to provide technical or customer support. In these cases, it's common to see files attached to messages.

Reading and Responding to Messages

At last we come to the core part of the message packet—the messages. When the messages option is chosen, a list of conferences is displayed similar to that shown in figure 14.9, one of which is usually called *personal*. We haven't yet covered the personal conference. Personal is a special conference that's added by the offline reader when the message packet is opened. It contains messages that are addressed to the user. So you're probably wondering how the offline reader knows which messages are addressed to the user, correct?

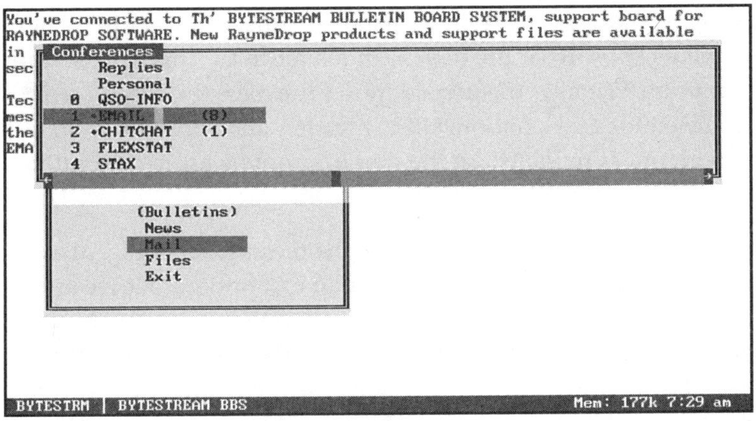

Fig. 14.9
This is the conferences menu displayed by the Offline Xpress Test Drive program. Notice that one of the first conferences is called Personal.

A special index file called "PERSONAL.NDX" is often created by the QWK Mail system and included in the QWK message packet. "PERSONAL.NDX" is used by the offline reader to tell which messages in the packet are addressed to the user who downloaded it. Since the Personal conference contains messages that are addressed specifically to the user, it is usually the first conference read. The Personal conference is followed up by the actual conferences (message bases) provided by the BBS. Let's say, for the purpose of this discussion, that the user chooses to read his or her personal messages and selects Personal.

After the user selects Personal, the offline reader displays the first message in the conference. The first message in the conference is also the first message in the message packet that is addressed to the user. While messages are displayed, users may choose from options such as Next, Previous, and Reply. Next moves to the message following the current message. Previous backs up to the message preceding the current message. And, as you probably figured out by now, the reply option lets the user compose a message in reference to the current one.

Tip

Offline readers provide many more messaging options than those we talk about here. Experiment with your offline reader to get a feel for the features it provides.

Imagine that the user is reading a message from another audiophile and chooses to respond. First, the user selects the reply option and the offline reader opens up a message reply editor. Examining the reply editor, we find that the text of the original message is automatically *quoted* in the body of the new reply. Most offline readers include original messages in replies so that recipients know what the reply is in reference to. This helpful feature is called "quoting." Finally, the user addresses the message, types a reply and chooses the editor's save option. Offline readers allow users to change editors, even though one is provided, so the user may not be using their offline reader's default editor.

When replies are saved, they're added to the message reply file. After the user is finished writing replies, he/she chooses an exit option to leave the offline reader. The offline reader closes the QWK message packet and creates the QWK reply packet. To create the QWK reply packet, the offline reader runs an archive and compression utility. The reply file is compressed, if the utility is configured so, and included in an archive file. As stated earlier in this chapter, this file is given a name that consists of the BBS's identifier and an extension of ".REP". For our sample BBS, the Digital Mozart, this file is called "DMOZART.REP".

Uploading QWK Reply Packets

Finally, the reply packet is ready to go. The user signs onto the BBS again and enters the QWK Mail system. After starting QWK Mail, the user selects the upload option and sends the reply packet to the BBS. When the packet is successfully received by the BBS, the QWK Mail system processes the messages contained within.

The first task performed by the QWK Mail system is that of expanding and decompressing the reply packet. QWK Mail runs an external archive and compression utility, hopefully the same one used by the user, and extracts the message file containing replies from the reply packet. After extracting the message file, it reads each reply and adds it to the message base corresponding to the conference in which the reply was posted. Finally, QWK Mail links replies to their parent messages. A reply's parent message is the one for which it was in reference to.

There you have it—the life of a QWK Mail session from beginning to end. Now you have a good foundation of knowledge that will help you to answer questions about the QWK Mail system.

Installing QWK Mail on a Wildcat! BBS

In this section, we walk through step-by-step installation and configuration of QWK Mail on Mustang's full-featured commercial version of Wildcat!; however, installing and configuring QWK Mail varies only slightly depending upon the BBS software you're using. You will find this section helpful even if you're not installing QWK Mail on a Wildcat! BBS.

> **Note**
>
> QWK Mail is not included with the Wildcat! Lite software accompanying this reference. If you decide to use Mustang's Wildcat! software, we suggest that you upgrade to the full-featured commercial version so that you can take advantage of QWK mail and other features that aren't included in Wildcat! Lite.

QWK Mail is implemented as a *door* on Wildcat! systems. Doors are external, sometimes third-party, utilities or games executed by the BBS software. We cover only the subject of doors as it pertains to the installation of QWK Mail, in this chapter. Doors are covered in much greater detail in Chapter 15. The QWK Mail door included with the commercial version of Wildcat! is called *Tomcat*. You can install other QWK Mail doors on a Wildcat! BBS, such as Silver Express, but this text teaches you how to install Tomcat because it's the most commonly used.

Follow these steps to install Tomcat:

1. Put the installation disk in drive A and run INSTALL.EXE by typing **A:INSTALL<ENTER>**.

2. After pressing the Enter key when prompted for a source disk drive, use the arrow keys on your keyboard to highlight *Install Options*. Press Enter.

3. From the Install Options menu, highlight each installation option using the arrow keys and press the spacebar to change each setting to "No", as shown in figure 14.10.

> **Note**
>
> It's not necessary and can cause problems to install options that are already installed on your Wildcat! system. If you installed Tomcat when you first installed Wildcat!, press Esc twice and press Enter to exit the Wildcat! installation program and skip the installation steps below.

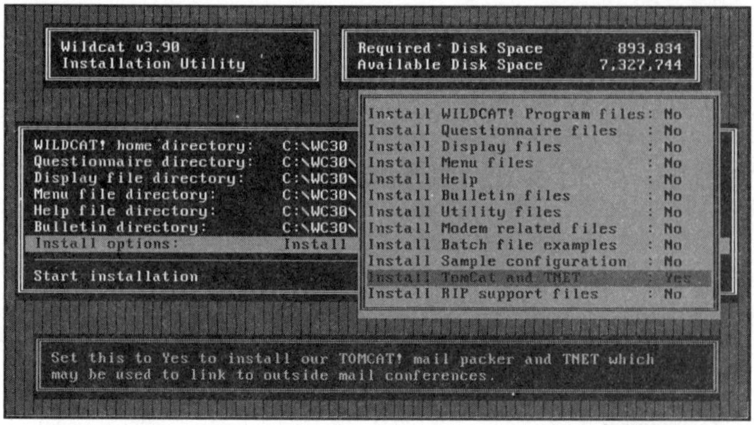

Fig. 14.10
Select options to install from the Install Options menu of the INSTALL program.

4. Highlight the *Install Tomcat and TNet* menu item and press the spacebar to change its setting to "Yes". Press Esc to exit the Install Options menu.

5. Highlight *Start installation* and press Enter to start copying the Tomcat files to your Wildcat! directory.

6. Once Tomcat is copied to your system and INSTALL displays the "INSTALLATION COMPLETE" message box, press Enter to exit the Wildcat! installation program.

Tomcat is installed on your Wildcat! BBS system. We're not quite ready, however, to turn you loose in QWK Mail. Now that Tomcat installation is out of the way, you must give Tomcat information about your BBS—remember our discussions about BBS identifiers, message base name restrictions, archive and compression utilities, etc., from the "Basic Components" section of this chapter? If not, go back and review that section before continuing. Use the TCMAINT utility included in your Wildcat! directory to change Tomcat options.

Do the following to configure the Tomcat QWK Mail system:

1. Change to your Wildcat! directory and run the Tomcat configuration utility. Type **TCMAINT<ENTER>**.

2. At the TCMAINT main menu, select the *Configuration* option. Highlight Configuration using the arrow keys of your keyboard and press Enter.

3. Enter a name (or ID, as it's referred to by Tomcat) for your BBS that is equal to or less than eight characters in length, as indicated in figure 14.11. This name is used as the BBS identifier for your bulletin board. For the Digital Mozart BBS, for example, you enter "DMOZART" as the BBS identifier. If the name you enter is eight characters, TCMAINT automatically moves you on to the next field; however, if the name you enter is less than eight characters, press Enter to continue to the next field.

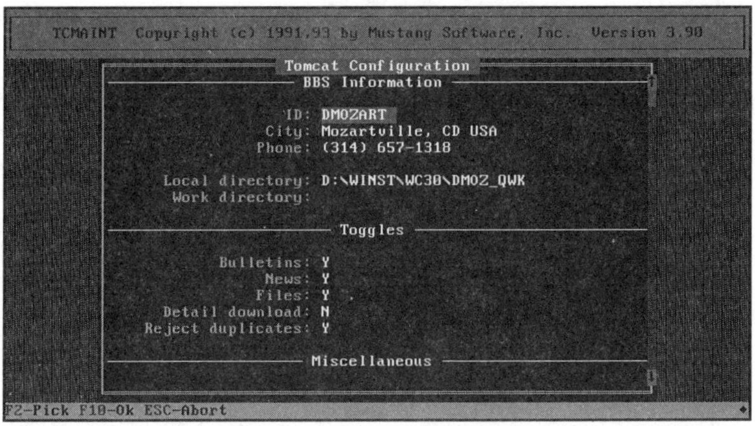

Fig. 14.11
This is the menu displayed by Tomcat when you select the Configuration option from the main menu.

4. Type the city and state where your BBS is located and press Enter. Some sysops enter names that represent their themes. For instance, we may enter "Mozartville, CD USA" or something similar for the Digital Mozart BBS.

5. In the Phone field, enter the telephone number of your BBS just as you want it to appear in the CONTROL.DAT files of message packets—"(314) 555-1357" for example. Press Enter to continue to the next input field.

6. Type the path where you want Tomcat to store message and reply packets for local logins (sysop logins) and press Enter. For example, if you want Tomcat to store message and reply packets in a directory called "DMOZ_QWK" in the Wildcat! directory, type **C:\WC30\DMOZ_QWK<ENTER>**.

> **Note**
>
> If you don't enter a path for local message and reply packets, Tomcat stores them in a directory called "WCWORK\NODEx"—where x is the node number of the session processing a packet.

7. Next, type the path where you want Tomcat to store message and reply packets for remote users, and press Enter. If your BBS is a multiline Wildcat! system, leave this path blank and skip to the next configuration option.

8. Looking back at figure 14.11, the *Toggles* section lets you specify what extra services Tomcat includes in message packets. You can include bulletins, your news file, and/or a list of new files. Press **Y** to include the option or **N** to exclude the option for all three: *Bulletins, News,* and *Files.* For example, press **Y** with the option for News highlighted to include your news file in message packets.

9. *Detail Download* determines how much information is written into the BBS activity file regarding QWK Mail downloads. If you press **N** to exclude this option, Tomcat writes a small entry into the activity log that indicates a download event occurred. If you press **Y** to include this option, Tomcat writes a detailed entry into the activity log showing the number of messages included in a QWK Mail packet from each BBS message base. Press **Y** or **N** to continue the Tomcat configuration.

   As you can see from figures 14.11 and 14.12, there are a wealth of features in the Tomcat utility. It's not necessary for us to cover them all, so we describe only those that are pertinent to basic installation of Tomcat. If you wish to learn more about extra features in the Tomcat configuration, refer to the documentation for Tomcat in the Wildcat! user manual.

10. Press the down arrow on your keyboard four times to skip past the *Reject Duplicates*, *Propeller*, *Prescan Area* and *Save packets*—these options aren't important for the basic operation of the Tomcat QWK Mail system.

11. Notice the *Max Packet* and *Max Conf* options in figure 14.12. Tomcat, like most all QWK Mail programs, lets you limit the number of messages included in a message packet. Tomcat, however, goes one step further than that and allows you to set message limits depending upon

the user's connect rate. For example, you can limit the number of messages included in a user's packet when they call at 2400 baud. Typically, you decrease the maximum number of messages for lower speeds so that users don't spend a lot of time online, downloading large packets.

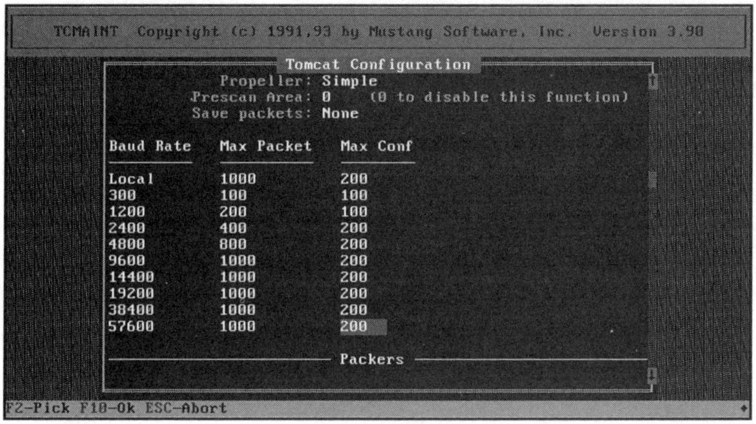

Fig. 14.12
As shown here, Tomcat lets you specify the maximum number of messages and conferences to include in QWK message packets.

For each baud rate shown in figure 14.12, including the local logins, set the maximum number of messages and the maximum number of conferences included in QWK message packets. Press Enter or the arrow keys to move between fields. When you're finished, use the down arrow key to move on to the *Packers* configuration.

12. Tomcat provides users with access to four different archive and compression utilities. In Packers, you can specify the four utilities provided by the QWK Mail system and their associated file name extensions. You can also set the command line syntax used by Tomcat to call each utility—both the command used for creating a message packet and the command used to extract the message file from a reply packet.

Since the defaults include PKZIP, by far the most popular archive and compression utility, press Enter or the down arrow to skip past to *Short conference names*, as shown in figure 14.13.

13. Press Enter to view and edit Short conference names. The Short conference names menu is shown in figure 14.13. Tomcat creates abbreviated conference names for you, but you can edit and change them if you wish. To change the abbreviated name for a conference, use the arrow keys to highlight the appropriate message base and press Enter. Input a name for the conference that is equal to or less than 12 characters and that doesn't contain spaces. After entering a new name, press Enter again. Press Esc when you're finished editing the Short conference names.

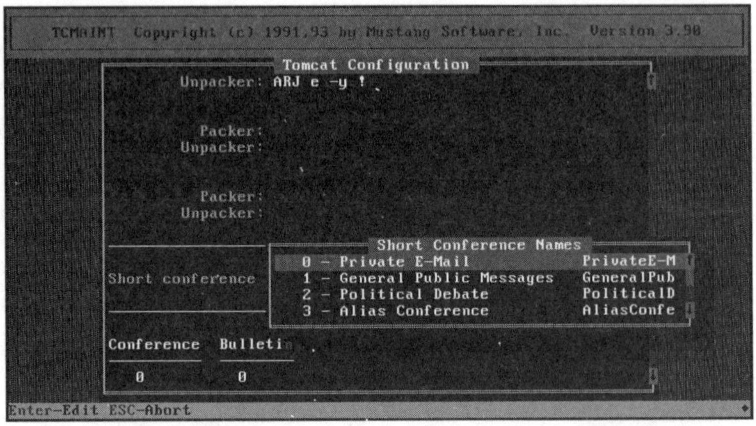

Fig. 14.13
When you select Short conference names, a list of standard and abbreviated message base names appears. Highlight the message base you want to edit and press Enter.

14. Finally, Tomcat lets you exclude bulletin files from QWK message packets. If you don't specify which bulletin files to exclude, Tomcat includes them all. Since we're just getting started with QWK Mail, press F10 to exit back to the TCMAINT menu.

15. Other options are available in TCMAINT but they deal specifically with network mail. Network mail, or FidoNet, is covered in Chapter 19. Press X to exit the Tomcat configuration utility.

Now that Tomcat is installed and configured, you must tell Wildcat! to execute the mail door batch file when users select *Tomcat Offline Msg Door* from the mail menu of your BBS. The mail door batch file runs the Tomcat utility and exits back to the BBS when the mail door terminates—it's called MAIL.BAT and it's located in the Wildcat! home directory. If you're running a multiline Wildcat! BBS, you may choose to call this file MAIL.RUN and locate it in the node directories of each node. When users select the mail door option from the message menu, Wildcat! checks to see if there is a MAIL.RUN batch file in the node directory of the current node and, if there is, renames and executes it in place of MAIL.BAT.

Follow these steps to configure Wildcat! to use the Tomcat offline mail door:

1. Change to the directory in which you installed Wildcat! and run the MAKEWILD configuration utility by typing **MAKEWILD<ENTER>**.

2. Use the arrow keys of your keyboard to highlight the *Menu Definition* option and press Enter.

3. Press Pgdn until *Message Menu Definition* appears at the top of the screen.

4. Once you're at the editing screen for the Message menu, shown in figure 14.14, use the arrow keys to highlight the key that activates the *Call MAIL.BAT* activity.

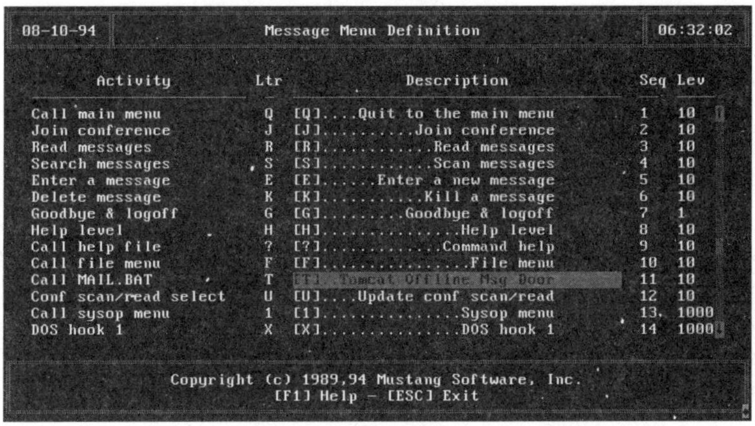

Fig. 14.14
This is the Message Menu Definition screen that appears when you select Menu Definition and press the Pgdn key in the MAKEWILD configuration utility.

5. Make sure the key that activates the Call MAIL.BAT activity is the one you desire. Also, make sure that the text for the menu item is worded appropriately. When you have the desired key selected and the menu item reads the way you want it to appear to users, press Esc to exit the Message Definition menu.

6. Use the arrow keys to highlight the *Door Definition* option and press Enter.

7. After the Door Definition menu is displayed, use your arrow keys to highlight *Mail* and press Enter. Notice that there are two menu selections displayed, *Multiuser support* and *Currently in use.*

8. If your Wildcat! BBS is a multiline system, press **Y** to select "Yes"; otherwise, press **N** to select "No".

9. Press **Y** to enable the mail door option, then press Esc three times to exit the MAKEWILD configuration utility.

10. Finally, press **Y** to confirm exit and **N** to exit without checking for all of the necessary directories (since you previously installed Wildcat!, all necessary directories already exist).

Tomcat is now configured and ready for use! You may want to sign on locally and perform a QWK Mail download to ensure that everything's working. Remember that local QWK Mail downloads are stored in the Local directory that you specified during Tomcat configuration—in the previous example, the local directory is "C:\WC30\DMOZ_QWK".

Installing QWK Mail on Other BBS Systems

Installation and configuration of QWK Mail varies slightly depending upon implementation. Some software packages include installation and configuration utilities, like TCMAINT in the previous section, while others list step-by-step manual installation instructions in the documentation and provide a text configuration file that you must change with a text editor. Similar to Doors, there are three ways that QWK Mail systems are implemented: as executable programs (Doors), as modules, and as integrated libraries or extensions.

In the previous section, we cover one of these three implementations—installing QWK Mail as a Door or executable, although the instructions are specific to Wildcat! systems. Door implementations are typically called with command line parameters and exist as completely separate, or stand-alone, programs. The BBS usually executes a batch file that in turn runs QWK Mail. Sometimes, as is the case with Tomcat, you can even run the utility from a DOS command line. Since external QWK Mail utilities are typically called with batch files, you can perform other tasks when the utility is started and when it's exited.

TBBS, by eSoft, Inc., implements QWK Mail as an add-on module. It's a separate utility, called QSO, that's run using a command line switch with the BBS executable. Even though QSO is a separate utility, it requires TBBS in order to run and it's fully integrated into the BBS software. While QSO is very easy to understand and use, it lacks an installation and configuration program. The QSO manual gives step-by-step instructions on how to install it manually (by copying files using DOS). To configure QSO, you must edit an ASCII text file containing setup options—it has a command interface similar to that of Windows .INI files.

The third method of implementation fully integrates QWK Mail into the BBS System. Galacticom, for example, implements Doors and add-ons like QWK Mail as dynamically linked libraries or DLLs. DLLs are linked into the executable at run-time and appear as seamless additions to the BBS's feature list. Instead of calling a batch file that runs the QWK Mail system, Galacticom simply makes a call to what it believes is just another one of its internal functions.

Because QWK Mail is implemented as a Door on Wildcat! systems, the QWK utility chosen must handle all COMPORT I/O including support for the 16550 UART (which has a 16-byte transmit and receive buffer). While QSO lacks an installation and configuration program, it's a cinch to install and the format of the configuration file is very readable and easy to modify. And even though QWK Mail integrates seamlessly into systems like Galacticom, those systems can get too expensive for the hobbyist sysop. So you see, none of these methods of implementation are better than the others. Your choice depends solely upon your preference.

Disadvantages and Limitations

There aren't too many disadvantages to using offline mail in lieu of answering messages online. One of the biggest disadvantages or limitations of the QWK Mail system is the lack of Network Mail support—support for specific Fidonet node addresses (net mail is discussed in Chapter 19). The only support for network mail in the QWK specification, that this author can find, is a flag in message headers indicating that a message has a network tagline or network mail status. Even though network mail utilities can use the flag and network tagline to import QWK Mail messages into BBS message bases, offline readers don't provide the ability to use these provisions.

Another major disadvantage and limitation of the QWK Mail system is the disheartening lack of message *threading* in offline readers. Threads are groups of messages, or message chains, that are linked together by the BBS. For example, you compose a message and save it in a BBS message base. After that, someone responds to your message. The BBS links the response to your original message and this grouping of messages is called a thread. Message threads are essential when conversing about subjects spanning beyond the scope of a single message and its response. Offline readers don't provide the message "threading" provided by the BBS. Since a user typically sees messages and their responses only once a day, it's easy to forget subjects that messages are referencing to—that is, of course, without the ability to easily reference entire message threads.

So you're probably wondering how the lack of message threading affects you as a sysop. Without threading, message subjects are short lived and unrelated messages start appearing in threads. If you provide technical and customer support on your BBS, it's hard to answer users' questions within the scope of one message. Explaining a topic to a user is a dialogue usually consisting of many confirmation and follow-up messages. Reading responses posted by users that don't have access to entire threads is often like listening to barroom banter and trying to follow the conversations of everyone in the room.

Luckily, as we discussed previously, offline readers support message quoting. Recall that quoting is the ability to include part of a message in a response. To make the threads on your BBS more readable, suggest to your users that they use the quoting feature of their offline readers. If your users include pertinent portions of previous messages in their responses, the lack of message threading in offline mail readers isn't all that frustrating.

Common Questions and Problems

Along with disadvantages and limitations, let's also talk about common problems that come up while using QWK Mail. This short section accompanies the tips and support issues covered throughout this chapter. It gives you supplemental information that you can use when answering questions about the QWK Mail system.

Incompatibility between compression utilities is the most common problem experienced by users of QWK Mail. If the compression utility used by the offline reader isn't the same or compatible with that used by the QWK Mail system, a user can't read and respond to messages; the offline reader can't extract messages from packets and the QWK Mail system rejects packets that are uploaded. In a case such as QSO by eSoft, Inc., the QWK Mail system uses the standard ZIP compression of PKZIP 1.0 and the offline reader uses PKZIP 2.0, users can download messages but the QWK Mail system rejects their reply packets.

Such incompatibilities are easily solved by providing the archive and compression utility used by your QWK Mail system on the BBS for download or by instructing users to configure their offline readers to call compression utilities with special backward-compatibility options. Of course, compatibility options are usually only available when using a newer version of the same software. Using the most recent and commonly used version of compression software will help to keep questions of this type to a minimum.

A commonly asked question among QWK Mail users is, "Why does the file name extension of the QWK message packet sometimes change to something like '.QW0' or '.QW2' instead of remaining '.QWK'?". We answer this question in the "Basic Components" section of this chapter. In review, some QWK Mail systems rename subsequent message packets when more than one is downloaded within the span of a day. This is done so that each new downloaded QWK packet doesn't overwrite packets downloaded previously.

Some users download and respond to QWK message packets from many bulletin boards at once (within the time frame of one day at least). The BBS identifier, a name given to a BBS when the sysop sets up QWK Mail, is included in each reply packet. QWK Mail systems reject reply packets when their BBS identifiers do not match those to which the BBS's packets are uploaded. If users upload reply packets for other BBSs to your QWK Mail system, their packets are rejected and their messages aren't added to your message bases. Typically, users are aware of what they've done after they have read error messages displayed by QWK Mail but, nonetheless, there may be some users that ask questions.

Summary

In this chapter you learned what QWK Mail is, how it works, how to implement it, and why. You've learned that there are several components to the system, including QWK Mail, compression utilities, and offline mail readers. We've shown you some of the more popular offline mail readers and QWK Mail in action. In addition, we've provided you with some tips and tricks that you can use while answering questions for your users. You now have a base of knowledge that you can use to install a QWK Mail system on your BBS and provide support for your users!

Chapter 15

Adding Doors

by Mark L. Chambers

By itself, a good bulletin board program should be able to provide your callers with a set of basic services that everyone uses online: for example, these minimum features should include public and private messages, file transfers, questionnaires, user utilities, and bulletins. In fact, 10 years ago most bulletin boards offered only these features! Some sysops are satisfied with these services, and operate popular bulletin boards for callers whose main interests are participating in message bases and transferring files.

The majority of modern sysops, however, have chosen to expand their services to include much more than the traditional set of BBS functions. Today's BBS offers the caller online recreation in the form of multiplayer games, electronic periodicals, and database search/retrieval programs. Some systems have extended their bulletin boards to augment their business with online shopping and ordering—and even the ability to send faxes.

With options like these, it's no surprise that the bulletin board community is enjoying an influx of new users on a par with major online services like CompuServe, GEnie, and America Online. Why not enjoy local bulletin boards in your area instead of spending money on an online service, especially when local systems are either free or much less expensive? A range of expanded services is essential to attract these new users.

How can you add these online services to your BBS? With external door programs! In this chapter, we'll discuss the various types of doors available for any bulletin board system, as well as describe step-by-step how you can add doors onto your Wildcat! BBS.

Types of Doors

No matter what the function of an external door, it falls into one of two categories (depending on which type of BBS program you're using):

- **External DOS doors.** Network BBS programs that run under DOS (or under a DOS multitasker like DESQview) use specially written external door programs that also run under DOS. These door programs can be written in BASIC, PASCAL, C, or any other language that can control the serial port. When a caller selects a door, the BBS program temporarily releases control and shells to DOS, then runs a batch file that loads and runs the door program. Once the caller is finished using the door, it drops back to DOS and runs another batch file that reloads the BBS program. Of course, the connection is maintained the entire time, so the caller may never know that a door program is monitoring the modem instead of the BBS program; however, if the door encounters an error, there's a chance it may lock your system until you can return and reboot your BBS PC. Popular commercial bulletin board packages that use external DOS doors include Wildcat!, PCBoard, Synchronet, and Searchlight. Popular freeware and shareware programs that use this method include RBBS, Spitfire, and Remote Access. Figure 15.1 shows a screen from a popular external DOS door.

> **Tip**
>
> You can also run standard DOS programs as external DOS doors if you use a redirection utility like Marshall Dudley's shareware program DOORWAY, which intercepts the caller's keystrokes and routes display data from the BBS console screen to the COM port. However, not every program will work as a door, and DOS applications may require more memory or resources than your PC can provide while running a BBS program. If you'd like to run a DOS program as a door, try it first and make sure you test it completely before offering it to your callers! DOORWAY is available on the Wildcat! support BBS.

- **Modular doors.** How can a BBS that never drops to DOS offer external programs? Integrated bulletin board programs like TBBS and Major BBS get around this problem by supporting modules written especially for the particular program—for example, TBBS sysops who buy the TDBS add-on module can run doors written in DBASE language, while doors written for the Major BBS in C language are effectively "linked" into the program, becoming another function of the system. Therefore, doors written for an integrated BBS program cannot run under a BBS that uses external DOS doors, and integrated BBS programs can't run external DOS doors. Just like external DOS doors, your users will probably be unaware that they're running an external door; however, since an integrated BBS program never needs to shell to DOS or pass control to a modular door, these doors tend to load and run faster, and they're much more reliable than external DOS doors. Figure 15.2 shows a screen from a popular modular music database door.

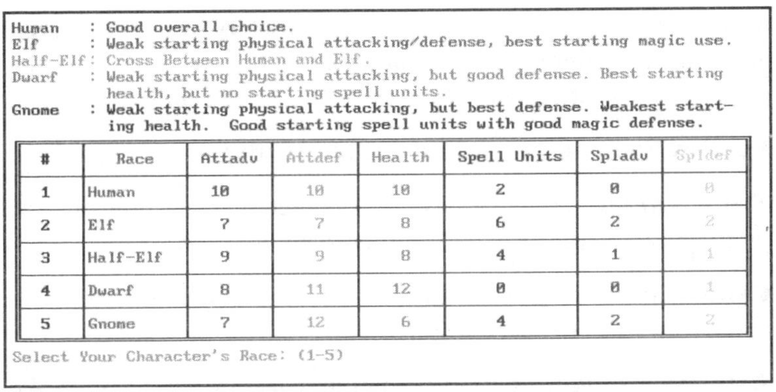

Fig. 15.1
A screen from a typical external DOS door.

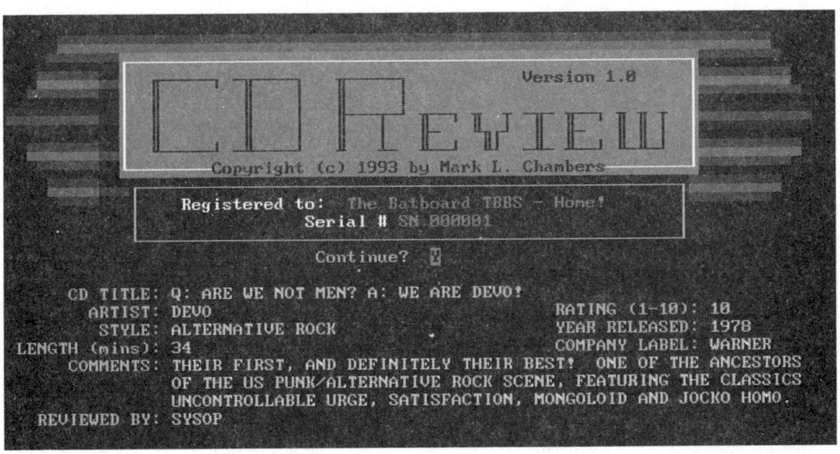

Fig. 15.2
A screen from a typical modular database door.

Now that you understand how doors work, let's examine some of the common types of external DOS doors you can add to your Wildcat! system.

Game Doors

By far, the most popular application for external doors is online gaming, and game doors range from simple single-player puzzles all the way up to multiplayer "Dungeons and Dragons" games. With a single call to your BBS, your users can play blackjack, trade and attack other players in a universe of a thousand planets, and attempt to conquer the world in a full-color ANSI war game—all in an hour!

Most game doors fit into one of the following game genres:

- **Space games.** Players command interplanetary fleets of trading ships and warships, conquer planets, and build a fortune. TRADE WARS, probably the best-known BBS door of all time, fits into this category.
- **Puzzles.** These are generally single-player "brain teaser" games.
- **Trivia games.** A popular pastime, updated for electronic play. Some programs allow the users to add their own questions.
- **Casino and card games.** Las Vegas online! Some casino doors even allow your users to "bet" online time.
- **Role-playing games.** These games may feature ANSI graphics or the classic "Zork" text adventure interface that accepts words or sentences. They usually center around exploration or combat.
- **Simulations.** These doors include sports games, war games, and political simulations.

Some game doors now support RIP graphics as well, and these games really give the player a glimpse of what BBS online gaming will be like a few years from now. As an example, figure 15.3 shows a screen from the TBBS RIP game door Escape from Languor, where a player can move, take items, and battle monsters with a simple click of the mouse! If you're familiar with the graphical games available on GEnie and America Online, you'll feel right at home playing a door offering RIP graphics. RIP games are rare, but they're steadily growing in popularity.

Another type of game door is actually played offline; your bulletin board accepts turn files as uploads from players, processes them as part of your nightly external maintenance event, and makes the new game data available for downloading the next day. The wildly popular space conquest game VGA PLANETS uses this method, which is extremely flexible; in fact, players can play long distance at very little expense, since the only time involved online is spent uploading and downloading turns and game data. VGA PLANETS is even popular on the Internet and CompuServe, since turns can be transferred through e-mail.

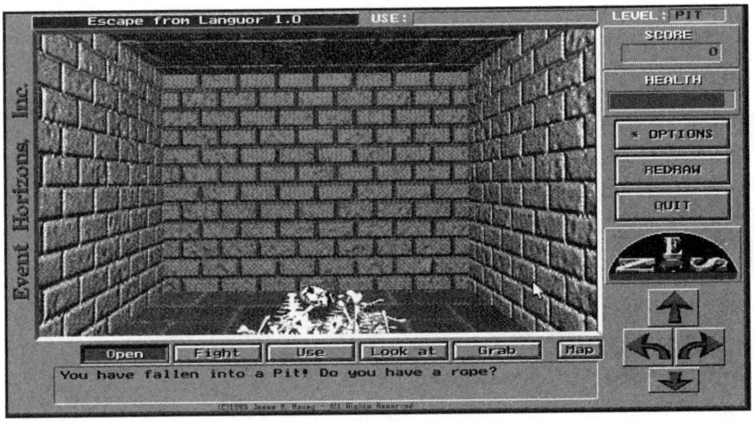

Fig. 15.3
The RIP game door Escape from Languor.

> **Tip**
>
> Most BBS-ready CD-ROMs offer a bewildering variety of external DOS game doors. If you'd like to pick and choose from a large selection of online games for your system (of all types, and all ranges of complexity), pick up one of these shareware BBS discs; you can select your favorites at your leisure, and you won't have to worry about downloading them from another BBS or an online service.

If you're an experienced caller, you may have already played a game door that you wish to offer on your system—if you're not familiar with game doors, however, it's still a relatively easy matter to decide which doors to offer. Check other boards in your local area and ask the sysops which games are most popular and most reliable; chances are, if a hot game attracts players for your competition, it's a good choice for you, too. You might also ask the opinion of other sysops on CompuServe. Finally, it never hurts to ask your callers directly with a questionnaire asking which doors they prefer.

Databases

Database doors have been around since the first BBS list door was written—figure 15.4 shows a typical BBS list database. However, databases covering other topics have been slower to appear than game doors; a database containing the names and mailing addresses of members of Congress, for example, is less exciting in some ways than taking control of a planet or slaying a dragon!

Today, the importance of the online database is rapidly growing around the world. The ability to search for and retrieve needed information from a huge online database is a very worthwhile feature for callers interested in research or specific topics, and many profit and business systems are built around a particular database resource.

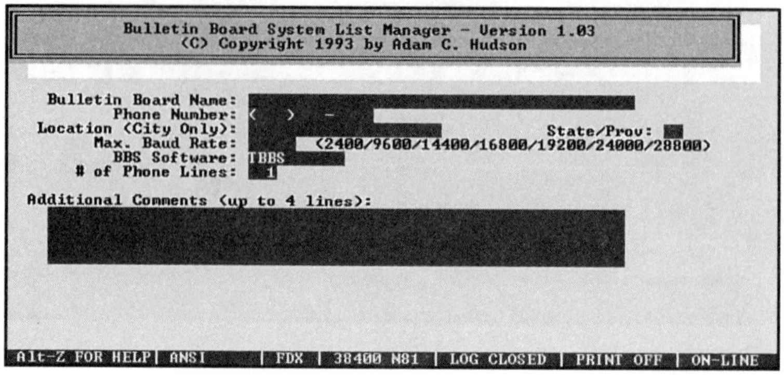

Fig. 15.4
A typical BBS list database door.

For instance, a BBS run by a real estate company might offer a database containing information on available properties; employees on business trips could access the database remotely with laptop computers equipped with modems, while customers could call up and browse the selection of properties directly. Other applications might include genealogy, technical product data, music and video catalogs, and classified advertisements.

Another type of online database door allows you to search for certain words or phrases within a number of full text files (instead of individual records in a database); once you've located the text string, you can view or download the file that contains it. These information retrieval doors make it easy for you to make any type of ASCII text into a database of sorts.

A few database doors even provide graphics for records in your database! In our real estate example, imagine how helpful a full-color image of each house would be for the customer—or, if you were running a "matchmaking" door for your single users, each caller's picture could be displayed with his or her personal data. These graphical databases usually require a special terminal program, which results in much faster transfer times, or the door may send a standard GIF image that can be automatically displayed as the user receives it by popular communications programs like PROCOMM PLUS for Windows. Graphical database doors include Durand Communications Network's DC Genesys, which is compatible with DBASE, and IMAGEN's REAL TIMES, which supports a wide range of display formats.

News/Magazine Readers

As mentioned earlier in the book, electronic periodicals have matured along with the online community; you can now choose from a huge array of electronic newsletters on every subject, creative writing journals, FAQ text files (short for Frequently Asked Questions about a certain topic), magazines, and even the electronic edition of the *USA Today* daily newspaper. Your callers can view these periodicals online with a news or magazine reader door.

Aren't reader doors merely dressed-up bulletin menus? Not at all—unlike a periodical, a bulletin is a simple text file that you'll read only once, without being able to page forward or backward or search for a specific phrase. Reader doors typically include support for an internal table of contents, so that the caller can jump directly to a particular story or article. Many reader doors support archiving, where back issues of the periodical can be downloaded for review offline; these doors also automatically handle new issues when you add them. Figure 15.5 shows a reader door displaying the online edition of *Boardwatch Magazine.*

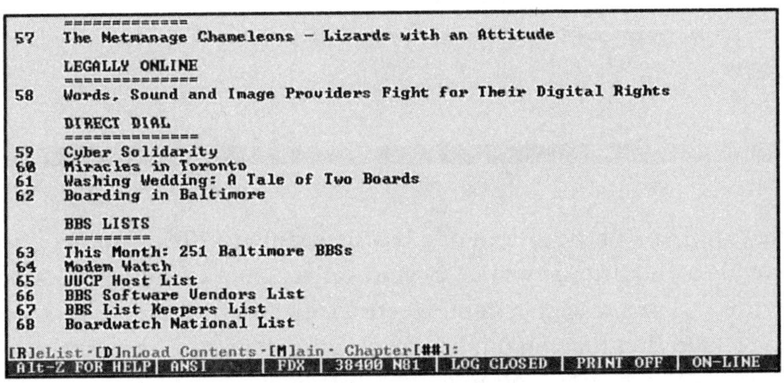

Fig. 15.5
A reader door displaying the online edition of *Boardwatch*.

Adding one of the better electronic periodicals can be expensive (both *USA Today* and *Boardwatch* charge hundreds of dollars annually for their online editions), and you're responsible for retrieving the periodical with a communications program like PROCOMM PLUS or QMODEM. For example, in the case of *USA Today* you'd write a script for one of these terminal programs so that it would call and download the text automatically each night. However, if you can afford the cost, these services can be a real drawing force for your subscribers. You'll be able to advertise that your BBS features the latest news or magazines online on a monthly or daily basis—and, as we mentioned earlier, providing something new on a regular basis increases the value of your system to your callers.

FAX Doors

The idea of sending a fax from your BBS may not occur to your users immediately, but if you offer them a fax service on your system they'll quickly find it indispensable! Fax doors allow a caller to compose a message online or upload a text file, which becomes the body text of an outgoing fax document—some can even attach a PCX format graphics file as a separate page, or you can add it as the fax cover sheet. Once the caller saves the document, the BBS waits until one of your phone lines is idle (or the next event where the BBS drops to DOS) and attempts to send the fax.

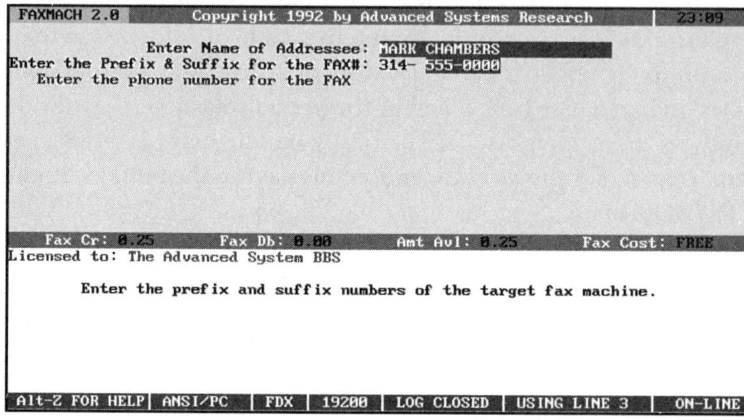

Fig. 15.6
A typical fax BBS door.

If you're running a profit system or a business/support BBS, your fax door may provide an additional service to your callers: a set of prepared fax documents arranged in a *request* system, where a caller can select one or more faxes to receive after logging off. Potential subscribers could request to be faxed a copy of your subscription form, a listing of your services, or a set of instructions for your menu system, while a business could offer technical support documents or product descriptions.

Of course, you'll need a fax modem, but these are now as plentiful and as inexpensive as a modem that only sends data. In fact, some modem manufacturers now make only fax modems! If you're shopping for a fax door, make sure it supports a method of charging the caller; fax services are usually offered only to subscribers, or charged on an individual basis. The door should also have a means of restricting long-distance calls to prevent a user from bankrupting your system.

Currently, several BBS programs (including Synchronet and Spitfire) include support for incoming faxes as well, which rely on the "adaptive answer" function now offered by many modems. These modems can differentiate and report whether a call requires data or fax, and the BBS program handles each case automatically.

Online Ordering Doors

Online ordering doors are a powerful tool for any profit or business/support system, since your customers can call at any time, 24 hours a day, to purchase products or services, browse through your online inventory, or check on the status of an order. In some cases, these doors are matched with a separate text or graphical database door like those discussed earlier in this chapter; other ordering doors feature their own internal databases to handle your inventory descriptions.

Online ordering doors are some of the most sophisticated doors available; these doors allow credit card purchases, calculate sales tax, subtract purchased goods from your inventory database, and print invoices on the sysop's printer. Some online order doors even fax a confirmation of the customer's purchase automatically! Even features like these aren't enough for some online entrepreneurs, however. Many successful online merchandising systems don't use PC bulletin board software at all—instead, they run on custom host systems written especially for online sales.

Tip

If you'll be offering merchandise online, make certain you're charging local and state taxes, where applicable, and obtain a business license if it's required. Take the time to set up your electronic storefront carefully, since you'll be liable if you're not legally covered. Additionally, make sure you're ready to handle merchandise returns and process complaints (either online or through a voice support number).

Galacticomm has built a solid reputation for their Major BBS as the premiere online ordering system in the PC-based BBS market. Their Shopping Mall modular door provides catalog sales, credit card purchases, and multiple online stores, each of which can offer its own inventory arranged into separate departments.

Utility Doors

Utility door programs perform a wide range of functions:

- *CD-ROM* doors are designed to augment the standard file transfer functions offered by your BBS, but they're no longer as common as they used to be; most bulletin board programs now support CD-ROM access and file display directly. The problem with CD-ROMs is that they're excruciatingly slow when accessing and reading files, which can severely degrade performance. A CD-ROM door solves this problem by copying the file(s) you've selected to a temporary directory on your hard drive, where your BBS can access it much faster—this way, your CD-ROM drive is also free for other callers to use on a multiline system.

> **Tip**
>
> One method you can use to help improve the speed of your system's CD-ROM is the use of a CD-ROM software cache, such as the version of SmartDrive shipped with MS-DOS 6.2; although not as effective in a BBS environment as a hard drive software cache, your users will still notice a speed increase. If your BBS will operate on a LAN with a CD-ROM file server, this problem disappears because the file server efficiently handles CD-ROM access.

- *Time Bank* doors allow your callers to "bank" online time and bytes from their current session until a later date, when they can "withdraw" from their account in order to stay online longer or download a larger file (see figure 15.7). These programs directly manipulate your userlog, so the BBS program actually has no idea that the caller's remaining time or byte values have changed. Some bank doors allow your users to purchase "lottery" tickets for a chance to win an online bonus, while others have built-in games like a slot machine or blackjack table where your callers can gamble their time; these are very popular with callers.

- *Callback* doors provide an additional level of security for your system by verifying that the caller is actually using the number entered during registration; these doors are commonly used to upgrade a user from a new user security level to a registered security level. After making sure the number provided by the caller is correct, the callback door takes control of your phone line, sends the modem a dial command, and actually calls the user back. The user must then enter his or her password; if the password is correct, the door upgrades the caller's security level and disconnects. As with a fax door, make sure you turn off long-distance verification if you don't want your system automatically making long-distance calls.

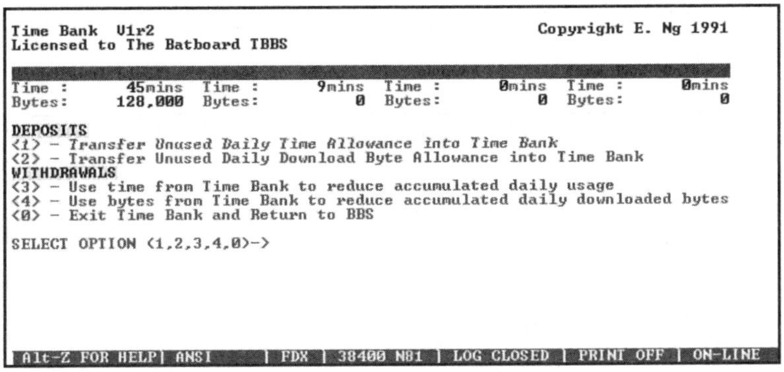

Fig. 15.7
A typical Time Bank door, where a user can store time and bytes.

Adding Doors to Wildcat!

Adding doors to your Wildcat! BBS is a simple operation. Let's cover the process step-by-step:

1. Run MAKEWILD and display Part 1 of the General Information screen, where you can make global changes to your BBS configuration. Change the value for question 8, "Number of external doors," by adding 1 to the current value (figure 15.8). For example, let's assume that this is the first door you've added, so enter **1** as the value. Press Escape to return to the main menu.

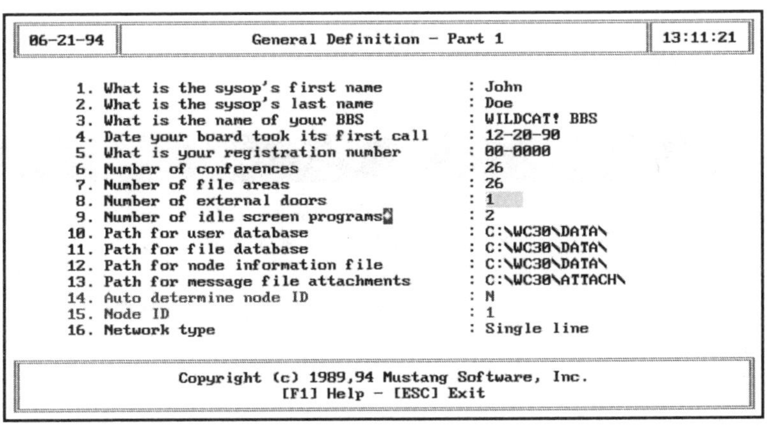

Fig. 15.8
Adding a door on the MAKEWILD General Information screen.

2. Next, display the Door Definition screen; you'll note that an additional number has been added to the default 10 functions (which are controlled like doors). In our example, you've added your first door, so your screen should look like figure 15.9. Exit MAKEWILD, making sure that you save your changes.

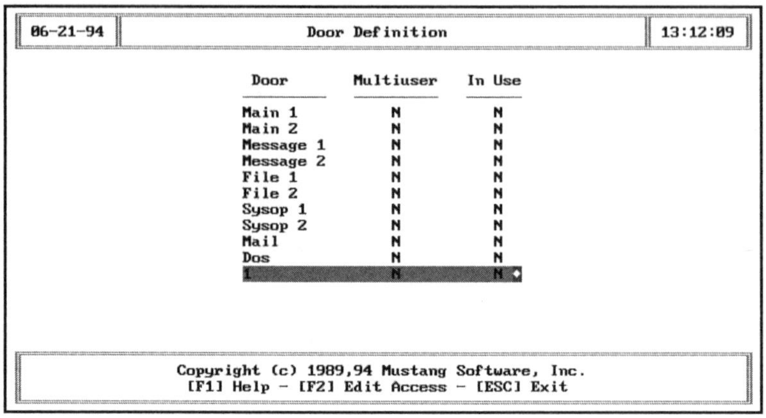

Fig. 15.9
The MAKEWILD Door Definition screen, showing your first external door.

3. Add the name of the door you're installing to the files DOORS.BBS and DOORS.SCR; these are the display files shown to your callers before Wildcat! prompts them for the door to run. Each door is keyed to a number, so an entry might look like this:

   1. Sampo Attack! Defend the Earth against the dreaded Sampo!

   These files must appear in the path you've designated in MAKEWILD for conference display files.

> **Tip**
>
> For additional guidelines on creating your ASCII and ANSI door menus, check the discussion of THEDRAW and WCDRAW earlier in this book. Your DOORS.BBS and DOORS.SCR files should provide adequate descriptions of each door, so make sure you allow space for future expansion when designing them.

4. When the user enters the number for a door to run, Wildcat! searches the Wildcat! home directory for a door batch file you've prepared called DOOR#.BAT, where the # corresponds to the number selected by the

user. The BBS program then shells to DOS and runs the DOOR#.BAT file. We'll discuss tips on how to build these door batch files in the next section.

5. Before shelling to DOS, Wildcat! creates a standard door information file in the DOOR.SYS format, which is recognized by most third-party door programs. DOOR.SYS is created in your Wildcat! home directory. The door program uses this information to determine the user's ID, how much online time the user has remaining, the user's security level, and more. Generation of the DOOR.SYS file before the door runs and its deletion after the door is done are completely automatic.

> **Tip**
>
> Although you can set Wildcat! to terminate completely when running doors in MAKEWILD, it's highly recommended that you use the default method of shelling to DOS instead; shelling to DOS requires no changes to your CAT.BAT file and control returns automatically to Wildcat! after the door is finished. This is also preferred from a security standpoint because Wildcat! never exits completely.

6. You should now configure the door and the door batch file for operation according to the instructions provided by the door's author. Usually this involves editing a configuration file so that it reflects the correct COM port and modem speed you're using, as well as whatever game parameters you need to modify.

7. Once the door has completed, Wildcat! checks a file called USERINFO.DAT for any modifications that have been made by the door program to the user's data—for example, a Time Bank door might have added additional time or bytes to the user's current session.

8. Run Wildcat! and test your door. Note that some door programs do not support local mode operation, so you may have to ask a caller or your co-sysop to help you test your door installation.

If you're running a multiline version of Wildcat! instead of the single-line version provided with this book, some of the steps outlined in this section will change. Because more than one user can be online at once, your BBS will use separate directories for each node. For complete details on multiline door operation, check your Wildcat! Sysop Guide.

Using Doors

As we've discussed elsewhere within this book, your BBS program already has extensive security features built-in—however, each time you run an external door, your BBS is releasing some amount of control, and it's possible that a poorly written door could wreak havoc on your system! To avoid this, make sure any door you run can detect when carrier has been lost (meaning the connection has been broken), so that control can automatically be returned back to your BBS.

How many doors should you run? That's a common question for many new sysops, but there's no one right answer. Of course, if you're running a BBS that specializes in online entertainment, it's in your interest to offer a large selection; sysops of such boards often provide 50 or more doors in a multiline environment, heavily promote them and offer contests to maintain player interest.

On the other hand, if you're running a single-line system or you're working toward a balanced BBS where your game doors are only a part of the picture, having too many works against you—your users will be unable to participate in half of the games you're offering, and they'll end up stagnant, taking up space on your hard drive. Most business/support boards don't offer any doors at all.

The solution for most sysops is somewhere in the middle. Select 10 or so doors that you enjoy personally, and try to spread them out from simple to complex. It helps if you pick doors from different genres, as well; don't add 10 card games and ignore strategy and simulation doors. If your callers seem ready for more, add doors on a trial basis from that point on. Using this method, you'll eventually reach a point of "door equilibrium."

If you do find that a huge door is receiving little or no traffic, you can certainly remove it. However, if the door takes up little or no space, consider keeping it online. As experienced sysops will tell you, doors can go from cold to hot overnight, drawing interest and participation in a very short time. As long as the door isn't using up a great amount of your system resources, keep it for future users to enjoy.

If a number of your users specifically ask for a game, see if you can provide it. This helps your image as well as your possible subscription income. Because most doors are shareware, registering more than a few can get expensive; it's a good idea to ask callers that request a certain door to sponsor it by directly contributing a part of the registration fee. In return, you can add their names to your DOORS.BBS file as the sponsors of the door.

> **Tip**
>
> Don't hesitate to mention your most popular game door in any advertising you do for your BBS! True fans of a door game won't hesitate to call long distance to participate in a good match. If you run a profit board, consider offering a free subscription to your system as a prize for a contest spanning several weeks—these longer marathon contests can help maintain a high rate of participation and interest in a particular game door.

Summary

In this chapter, you were introduced to the two types of doors—external DOS and modular doors—and we detailed the various services you can add to your BBS through door technology. You also learned how to add a door to your Wildcat! BBS, and how your bulletin board and the door program interact.

In the next chapter, "Adding CD-ROM Support," we'll discuss how you can offer your users thousands of download files inexpensively by upgrading your BBS with a CD-ROM drive.

Chapter 16

Adding CD-ROM Support

by Mark L. Chambers

Of the many hardware and software advances made within the last five years in the BBS community, the two that have made the most impact on the average hobby system are the arrival of inexpensive high-speed modems and the appearance of CD-ROM download libraries.

The availability of inexpensive CD-ROM drives and discs mastered especially for bulletin boards has finally made it possible for a sysop to offer a huge file library without painstakingly building that collection of files on a hard drive. Before the CD-ROM, sysops were resigned to downloading files, or receiving them through the mail on floppy disk or tape (which was only marginally better). It took several years and a phenomenal amount of work to build a download library of 600 megabytes, and those files had to be regularly backed up to prevent their loss if that tremendously expensive hard drive happened to fail.

Today, however, CD-ROM drives are becoming standard equipment on most new PCs, and you can add that same 600 megabyte file library to your BBS in under an hour for around $50! Plus, your CD-ROM library will never require a backup, and the CD-ROM files are already virus-checked and fully described in the included BBS directory files. As the files become outdated, you can archive your current CD-ROM library on a shelf and continue to update your library with new CD-ROMs as they're released.

In this chapter, we'll discuss how you can install one or more CD-ROM drives in your BBS computer. You'll also learn more about advanced CD-ROM solutions like a multiple CD-ROM "jukebox" and a networked server devoted especially to CD-ROMs. We'll cover the finer points of selecting, installing, and licensing your CD-ROMs. Finally, we'll finish up this chapter by discussing subscription access to your CD-ROM files—and even how to create your own CD-ROMs!

Selecting and Installing a CD-ROM Drive

If your PC is not already equipped with a CD-ROM, what features should you look for when buying one for your BBS? Compared to an audio CD-ROM player, computer CD-ROM drives are much simpler to operate, and you'll actually spend far less time worrying about features and controls when selecting a CD-ROM drive for your computer. On the other hand, if you're not experienced with installing and configuring PC hardware, your CD-ROM drive can be difficult to add to your system. Figure 16.1 shows a standard computer CD-ROM drive.

Fig. 16.1 Standard computer CD-ROM drives. An internal model is on the left and external on the right.

First, you'll need to know which interface your drive will use:

- **SCSI.** If your PC uses a SCSI hard drive, it's likely that your controller card will allow you to daisy-chain one or more CD-ROM drives as additional devices, so you'll probably need a simple cable instead of an additional interface card. Check your PC documentation, or contact the store where you bought it. SCSI devices have a well-earned reputation as being hard to configure, and sometimes two SCSI devices will not work perfectly together, so before you buy your drive, enlist professional help if you need it!

- **Sound card.** If you currently have a sound card installed on your PC, note that many multimedia sound cards feature CD-ROM interfaces built-in; for example, the Sound Blaster 16 Multi-CD audio card can also provide a connection for many CD-ROM drives. Check your sound card's documentation. While you're looking, see if the card will support multiple drives; if not, you'll probably want to stick with an AT-bus interface, which is considerably cheaper.

- **AT-bus.** Most CD-ROMs use this interface, which you install just like any other PC expansion card—however, that doesn't mean that one card will operate every brand of CD-ROM drive, so you'll have to buy the proprietary interface card as well. A good CD-ROM drive and interface bundle should cost you around $200. Some CD-ROM drives don't even require the interface card—instead, they can be added to your system as the second IDE device if you're using an IDE hard drive. As you might imagine, this saves several steps and many headaches during installation.

Next, decide whether you'll need a double-speed or single-speed drive. Most older or used CD-ROM drives are single-speed, but they will still work fine on a single-line bulletin board. Double-speed drives (which are the current standard) are a better pick for multiline operation. Whichever speed you select, make sure the drive has an average access time of 350-380 milliseconds or less. Older drives sometimes range around 600 milliseconds, which is unacceptable; users will definitely be able to tell the difference. Recently, triple- and quad-speed drives have appeared on the market as well. Although these drives are much more expensive, large multiline bulletin boards with eight or more lines will benefit from the speed improvement—if you're running a smaller system and you'd like to save money, a double-speed drive should be a good pick for your system.

Another consideration is the amount of buffer memory your CD-ROM drive will provide; the more buffer memory, the more data your drive will be able to read at once from the CD-ROM disc. If you're comparing two drives, check their specifications for the buffer each one provides. You can also dedicate additional memory to your CD-ROM by using a software cache like the SMARTDRV program supplied with MS-DOS 6.2; we'll discuss this software shortly.

Like modems, you can choose from internal and external CD-ROM drives—the only difference is that external drives have their own case and power supply. As long as you have at least one free drive bay that has access to the outside of your PC's case, you'll probably want to pick an internal drive. Keep in mind, however, that some older PCs may not have a power supply that provides adequate connections or voltage for a CD-ROM drive, so external drives have their advantages.

There are also two types of loading mechanisms for computer CD-ROMs. *Caddy* drives use a thin plastic cartridge that protects the CD-ROM from dust, and they're slightly more reliable than tray drives, but they're also marginally more expensive. Tray drives hold the disc on a flat tray that extends out from the drive. Either of these mechanisms is fine for a BBS system.

Tip

Because your drive will be in constant use, you may wish to consider an extended warranty for it if one is available at the time of purchase. Also, some drives have an automatic lens cleaning system that's activated whenever you change discs—this is a good feature for drives that see a lot of use.

Of course, the installation process will vary among drive manufacturers, but the following steps illustrate the general procedure of adding a single CD-ROM drive to your system:

1. Determine the IRQ and DMA channels currently being used by your PC—similar to a serial port, you must avoid conflicts between your CD-ROM and your existing devices by selecting a unique IRQ. In almost all cases, the CD-ROM drive installation software will automatically provide the correct values as defaults, so you can simply select the defaults. If you're using MS-DOS 6.2 and your drive doesn't have such an installation program, use the MSD utility to display the IRQ values.

2. Open your PC's case and select an open card slot for the interface card, if you need one.

3. Remove the cover from both the card slot and the drive bay (for an internal installation).

4. If you're using a SCSI drive, check the jumpers to make sure that it's set for a single drive—this is usually the factory default, but it's much easier to verify this before you install the drive! You may have to add a tiny

jumper called a *terminating resistor* to your drive, which indicates to the controller card that this is the last drive on the cable. If you're using an IDE drive, set the jumpers for the proper DMA, IRQ, and base address, as required. Most drives are shipped with default jumper settings for a common installation, so you may not have to make any adjustments to the jumper settings at all.

5. Install the drive and card (if required) into your PC. If you're installing an interface card, make sure it's placed in a matching expansion slot. An 8-bit card will work in a 16-bit slot, but a 16-bit card will not work correctly if you place it in an 8-bit slot.

6. Connect the data cable and an internal power supply cable to the drive. If your PC no longer has a free power supply cable, you can use a cable "splitter" (sometimes called a "Y adapter," which will create two connections from one cable—your local computer store will likely have these adapters.

7. Boot your PC and install the software drivers as directed in your drive manual.

Tip

If your software drivers allow you to reserve additional buffer memory (and you have additional memory to spare), you can significantly improve the throughput of your CD-ROM drive by specifying a larger buffer on your driver's command line. Check your CD-ROM drive manual for more information.

8. Reboot your PC to load the new software drivers. Note that these drivers may require so much conventional memory that they prevent your BBS software from loading—if this is the case, load your CD-ROM drivers into high memory to free up your conventional memory. For more information on loading drivers high, see your MS-DOS manual. If you're running MS-DOS 6.2 or later, use the MEMMAKER utility to configure your memory automatically.

9. Before you replace the cover on your PC, try a test: load a computer game CD-ROM or BBS CD-ROM, switch drives to your CD-ROM drive and try the DIR command. You should be able to read the directory of the CD-ROM just like a hard drive.

The CD-ROM Network Server

The CD-ROM network server is a different animal altogether. A server is a combination of a fast PC and one or more CD-ROM drives. Its sole purpose is to provide the files from your CD-ROM drives to all the BBS nodes on a network; as we mentioned earlier in the book, the server approach provides the fastest access to your CD-ROM library, and it doesn't negatively impact the speed of your BBS nodes. In some cases, the server may also act as a hard drive file server as well. Figure 16.2 shows the design of a CD-ROM file server.

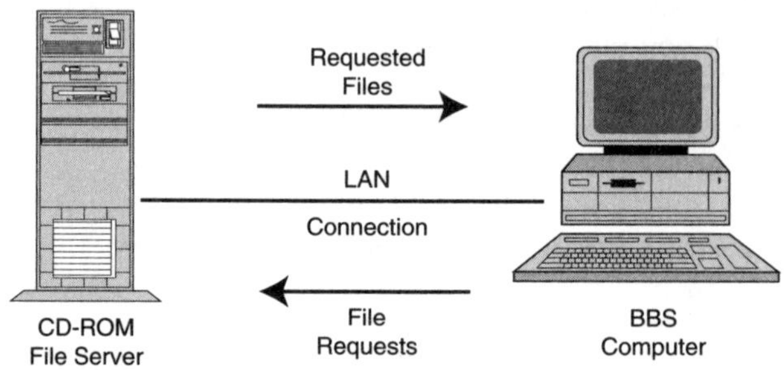

Fig. 16.2
A CD-ROM file server.

The drawback for this approach is obvious: you'll need a LAN and a dedicated computer! The network can be a simple peer-to-peer system (like a LANTASTIC network), or it can be a full-fledged NOVELL network. Since many large multiline profit bulletin boards use networks already to provide the best response, this may not be a problem; for example, a large Wildcat! or PCBoard system may actually have multiple servers online at once.

However, the CD-ROM network server is a huge case of overkill for a BBS with eight lines or less. If you use one of the CD-ROM utility doors we mentioned in the previous chapter, you'll largely avoid the performance disadvantages of a CD-ROM—without the expense of a network installation. For a single-line hobby BBS, a door solution is not necessary either, although it probably offers extra features that you won't find in your BBS program's built-in file system.

Additional Drives vs. the Jukebox

Although most CD-ROM interface cards support two to four drives on the same cable, adding an additional drive can be a problem. Unless your PC case has room for several CD-ROM drives, you'll need external models. The same applies to the power leads provided by your PC's power supply. Each time you add an additional CD-ROM, you'll have to reconfigure at least part of your drive hardware and some of your software settings.

There is an alternative to adding multiple separate CD-ROM drives to your BBS, but—like many "ideal solutions" in the BBS world—it's more expensive. If you're certain that you'll be adding more than two CD-ROM drives to your PC, you should consider adding a CD-ROM "jukebox" instead. These drives hold six or more CD-ROMs, and they usually use a SCSI interface.

Older model jukebox drives operate much like a music jukebox; there's only one laser lens in the case, but the CD-ROMs are rotated into place as your users request files from each disc. This process will slow down the read process slightly, but your users are not likely to notice—once the disc is in place, the drive is as fast as a single-disc drive. Since only a single CD-ROM can be read at once, however, multiline boards must access these jukebox drives through a special download door.

Newer model jukebox drives actually provide a laser for each ROM disc, so the access problems experienced with older drives don't apply; your BBS can read from each disc without rotating them into position. Currently, double-speed jukebox drives that handle six discs are available for less than $1,000, so the price comparison between a jukebox drive and six separate CD-ROM drives actually favors the jukebox!

Jukebox CD-ROM drives are state-of-the art, offering bulletin board users tens of thousands of files and almost 4 gigabytes of storage! With two or three of these massive drives online, it becomes even clearer why the largest PC-based bulletin boards can draw users away from traditional services like CompuServe and GEnie.

Using Your CD-ROM Drive

In this section, we'll discuss the sysop side of maintaining your CD-ROM library. You'll learn how to select a CD-ROM for your system, how to transfer the file directories to your system, and whether your CD-ROM requires licensing. We'll also discuss how you can limit access to your CD-ROM, and how you can archive your entire hard drive file library onto your own custom CD-ROM!

Selecting CD-ROMs

BBS CD-ROMs come in all varieties, from general interest to adult material. Some offer a particular type of file, like games, images, or Windows shareware, while others try to provide your BBS with a complete file library on a single disc. What should a sysop look for in a BBS CD-ROM?

First, decide what type of material you'd like to offer your callers. If you're looking to add a wealth of shareware files to your system, a general interest CD-ROM like the excellent Night Owl shareware series offers thousands of files in dozens of categories, and it makes an excellent single-disc library (figure 16.3). On the other hand, if your BBS has a popular subject for a theme—for example, C programming or raytracing—you may be able to locate a CD-ROM that specializes in the same subject.

Fig. 16.3
The Night Owl 11 CD-ROM directory, showing the wide range of subjects available on a general-interest shareware CD-ROM.

```
[ Night Owl Shareware Version 11 ]
 1 ASP/ASAD Shareware          21 Game Scenery/Utils     41 Personal Appl.
 2 BBS - Doors                 22 GeoWorks               42 Printer
 3 BBS - PCBoard               23 GRPH - Animation       43 PROG - ASM, "C"
 4 BBS - Other                 24 GRPH - GIF             44 PROG - BASIC,QB,VB
 5 BBS - Lists & Info          25 GRPH - JPG/TGA/TIF     45 PROG - Pascal
 6 Business / Finance          26 GRPH - Pgm/Util/Misc   46 PROG - General
 7 Communications              27 HAM / SWL / Scanner    47 Religious
 8 Database / Spreadsheet      28 Hard Disk / CD-ROM     48 Screen/Video
 9 Demo Programs               29 Health / Medicine      49 Sound - MOD/MID/VOC
10 DTP / Clipart / C.A.D.      30 Home Computing         50 Sound - Pgm & Utl
11 DOS/System Related          31 Info / Text / FAQ      51 Text Processing
12 E-Mail                      32 Input Devices          52 Virus
13 Education                   33 Magazine / Books       53 Windows Appl.
14 File Compression            34 Math / Sci. / Eng.     54 Windows Games
15 File Processing             35 Menus & Shells         55 Windows Pgms/Utils
16 Floppy Disk                 36 Misc. & Leftovers      56 Windows BMP/ICO/WAV
17 Fonts                       37 Modem / Comm. Port     57 Windows/NT
18 Food / Nutrition            38 Network / LAN          58 Word Processing
19 Games & Recreation          39 Offline Mail           59 DoorGames Carltonware
20 Game Cheats/Hints/etc       40 OS/2
```

If your BBS has more than one CD-ROM drive, you might consider a combination of both; one drive could offer a general selection of shareware, while the other could rotate through CD-ROMs that specialize in a single type of file on a monthly basis. If you have only a single CD-ROM drive, it's recommended that you rotate your CD-ROMs every two weeks or so; your users will appreciate the variety.

Tip

If possible, create a schedule of what will be offered on your CD-ROM for the next three months, and post it as a bulletin. Also, if your BBS program supports the display of a screen file before or after logon—for example, the PRELOG.BBS file used by your Wildcat! system—display the title of the current CD-ROM as a part of that file.

Other popular manufacturers of BBS CD-ROM discs include:

- **Profit Press.** Profit manufactures the well-known MEGAROM series, which includes both shareware collections and specific discs covering Windows, games, digital audio, images, and adult material.

- **Digital Publishing Company.** Digital manufactures a complete shareware collection especially suited for Wildcat! BBS sysops called Wildcat! Gold, including a directory of several hundred Wildcat! utilities.

- **PC-SIG.** As a distributor of shareware, PC-SIG maintains one of the largest libraries of PC files, and those files are constantly upgraded and improved. The PC-SIG CD-ROM series is the best available for use on your BBS, but—since you must license the disc before distributing any of the files—a PC-SIG CD-ROM is considerably more expensive than other BBS-ready ROMs.

Once you've determined what type of CD-ROM you're looking for, pick up a copy of *Boardwatch Magazine* or *CD-ROM World* and scan the advertisements for BBS CD-ROMs. While you're looking, keep these guidelines in mind:

- **Number of files and total bytes.** It's a common misconception that all CD-ROMs contain exactly the same amount of information; however, just like a hard drive, a CD-ROM holds up to a maximum amount, but it can contain far less. For a BBS CD-ROM, that maximum amount is about 680 megabytes of data. When you're shopping, take the time to find out how many total megabytes are actually contained on the CD-ROM; if the disc offers less than 600 megabytes, it should be considerably cheaper than a "full" CD-ROM, or you're getting a bad deal. Similarly, make sure that the CD-ROM has enough files to hold your callers' interest; some CD-ROMs on the market have less than a thousand files, making them poor choices for a BBS.

- **File dates.** Here's another indicator of how good a particular BBS CD-ROM is—but be careful, as file dates can be misleading. For example, a CD-ROM full of shareware programs should offer the latest file dates possible because shareware files quickly become stale when new versions are released. If possible, the files should be a year old or less. However, if you're shopping for a CD-ROM that specializes in animations or GIF images, file dates mean little or nothing—there's no such thing as a new version of a GIF, and the image maintains its value as a download.

- **Virus checking.** Never buy a BBS CD-ROM that hasn't been thoroughly checked for viruses by the manufacturer—if you do buy such a CD-ROM and you offer it on your BBS, you're asking for trouble. If a CD-ROM you've already purchased is found to contain even a single virus, remove the CD-ROM immediately and contact the manufacturer of the CD-ROM. Remember, it only takes a single file containing a virus downloaded from your BBS to forever brand your system as "off limits" for downloading! As we mentioned in Chapter 8, such a possibility is remote—but why take the chance?

- **Archived files.** Check to make sure that all of the programs and text on the CD-ROM is archived with a popular utility like PKZIP, ARJ, or LHA. To avoid confusing and irritating your users, the archive format should match the archive format you use for your hard drive files if possible. Remember, some files are already compressed—for example, GIF and JPG images—so archiving them will do no good.

- **BBS advertisements.** Many sysops commonly insert ASCII graphics "advertisements" into all the archived download files on their boards. There's nothing wrong with this practice (in fact, it's a good way to promote your BBS), but these advertisements don't belong on a shareware CD-ROM. After all, you're paying for the files, so why should another BBS be advertised when the caller unarchives them?

- **BBS-ready directories.** Here's another hard and fast rule: no matter how attractive you may find the files on a shareware CD-ROM, don't buy it for your BBS if it doesn't come with some type of file descriptions (figure 16.4). Creating those directories from scratch would be a super-human effort. Do the directories feature detailed descriptions? Are the size and resolution of GIF files listed in their descriptions? If the answer is no to either of these questions, it's recommended that you not buy the CD-ROM.

Fig. 16.4 Typical file descriptions provided with a BBS-ready CD-ROM.

```
BOXER600.ZIP  [0]  BOXER Text Editor v6.0 - Top Rated!   <ASP>
                         | v6.0 adds 75 New Features & Options: Point &
                         | Click mouse support in menus, locate differ-
                         | ences automatically in similar files, greatly
                         | enhanced keyboard RECONFIG utility, Replace
                         | Again, improved File Menu & much, much more.
                         | Still: Color Syntax Highlighting, Undo/Redo,
                         | multi-files & windows, mouse support, column
                         | marking, WP, macros, S&R, compilation, more!
BP_31.ZIP     [0]  B/PLAN DEVELOPER v3.1 <ASP> - Write A Plan
                         | Like A Pro & Save $$$$...the goal is to get
                         | your project funded.  B/Plan Developer helps
                         | you create a "market driven" and "investor
                         | centered" business plan that attracts money.
CASLBL20.ZIP  [0]  CASSETTE LABEL v2.0 <ASAD> a simple program
                         | to print nice audio cassette labels which
                         | fit inside the plastic holders. It requires
                         | a printer which can print full IBM
                         | characters (Laserjet, Proprinter, etc) NOTE
                         | SW set 6 month timer when first loaded, DO
                         | NOT distribute a copy you have run only the
                         | original. Req. $12.00
CATAPP.ZIP    [0]  Shareware Author Catalog Entry Program v2.10.
                         | This program gives shareware authors a way to
```

- **Duplicate files.** It's a simple step for a manufacturer of a CD-ROM to check for duplicate files, so any CD-ROM you buy should be free of them. Also, if you're buying a CD-ROM from a series of discs from the same manufacturer, check to make sure that the new disc contains only new files, with no duplicates of files you already have on the previous CD-ROMs in the series.

- **A CD-ROM reader program.** Although you'll be using your new CD-ROM on your BBS for some time, eventually you'll replace it with a newer disc, and you can claim it for your personal use. Most BBS CD-ROMs include a custom CD-ROM *reader* for individual search and retrieve access—a convenient feature when you've loaded your CD-ROM library for your own use offline. Some reader programs can even display GIF files and run the contents of an archive file without copying it to your hard drive. Any CD-ROM you buy should have some sort of reader interface software; figure 16.5 shows the interface from the popular MEGAROM CD-ROM series from Profit Press.

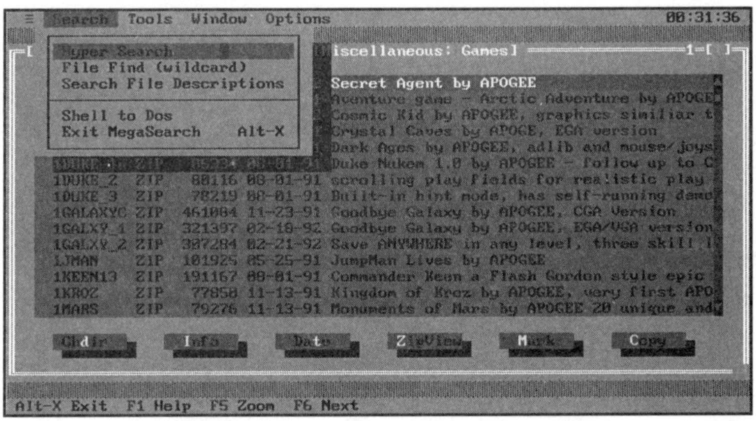

Fig. 16.5
A CD-ROM reader interface, which you can use offline to search and retrieve files from your BBS-ready CD-ROM.

Using CD-ROM Directories with Wildcat!

Your Wildcat! BBS provides basic support for CD-ROMs that will help speed filename and text searches. Because DOS access for CD-ROM file directories is extremely slow, Mustang includes a utility called WCFILE.EXE (figure 16.6) with Wildcat! Lite that will create matching zero-byte files on your hard drive for every file on your CD-ROM.

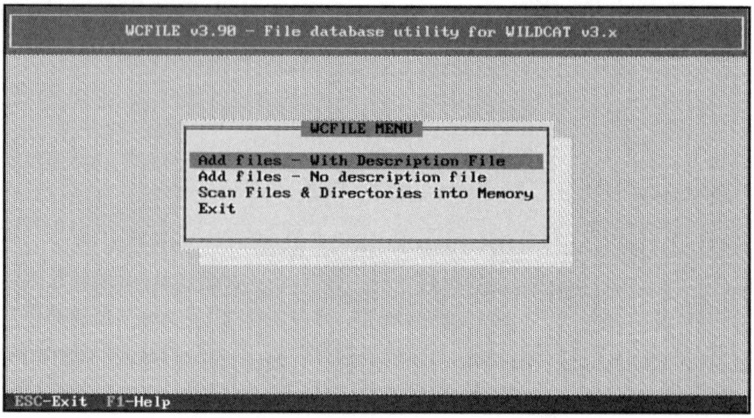

Fig. 16.6
The WCFILE utility Main Menu.

Whenever a caller performs a text or filename search, Wildcat! searches the hard drive pseudo directory instead, taking advantage of your hard drive's speed and efficiency. Once the actual download begins, however, Wildcat! will send the file specified in the "CD Path" field in each file's database record.

You'll still have to manually assign file areas on your hard drive with MAKEWILD, but WCFILE will automatically insert the actual path to the real file on your CD-ROM into the "CD Path" field. WCFILE also handles the importing and conversion of the BBS directory descriptions, flagging each file as "On CD-ROM" in your file database as it's processed.

WCFILE is also a handy utility for adding files to your file database in bulk from your hard drive or offline storage. The program gives you the option of adding files with corresponding descriptions taken from CD-ROM directory files, or you can add just the filenames with WCFILE and enter the description manually for each file. Make sure that you use WCFILE only when your BBS is not running, and that you run it only from your Wildcat! home directory.

Licensing

Only a few CD-ROM discs require you to pay a license fee. Usually these discs are produced by a well-known periodical, user group, or a software distributor—for example, the shareware distribution company PC-SIG manufactures a very popular CD-ROM containing all of the programs in its current library, and requires any sysop using the CD-ROM to pay a licensing fee. The only way to be certain a disc requires no licensing is to contact the manufacturer, but in most cases the salesperson should be able to tell you.

Because commercial CD-ROMs can be read and copied from the DOS prompt just like a shareware CD-ROM, they could theoretically be offered for download on a BBS. As you might imagine, the animations, sounds, and images found on commercial CD-ROM games and multimedia discs should never be distributed! In most cases, such animations and images are several megabytes long as well, so they wouldn't be easily downloaded anyway. To be safe, if any CD-ROM isn't marked as "BBS Ready" or explicitly allows you to use it on a bulletin board in its license, consider it licensed for the sole use of the original purchaser and don't offer it for your callers.

Limiting Access

If you run a profit BBS or a subscriber hobby system, you'll find one of the prime benefits of CD-ROM drives is their tremendous pull on the subscribing user. The opportunity of accessing 680 megabytes or more of new files can make the difference between a caller who's satisfied with free access downloading and a caller who subscribes.

As we mentioned in Chapter 10, an ideal method of enticing users is to provide them a limited amount of access to your system, and the same applies to your CD-ROM libraries. Use this technique to your advantage; for example, if your new CD-ROM has 75 directories, allow your standard level users to download from only 10 of those directories, and make certain they know of this limitation! Your standard level subscribers still benefit from the CD-ROM, so you haven't created any ill feeling on the part of your free-access users, but you've presented your potential subscribers with a powerful benefit for their monetary support.

Wildcat! makes it easy to add this restriction. To limit a directory of CD-ROM files that you've already created to subscribing users:

1. Run MAKEWILD and select the File Area Definition screen.
2. Highlight the file section you'd like to restrict and press F2 to display the Edit Access screen (see fig. 16.7).
3. Select only the subscribing access level and the Sysop access level in the Download Security field.
4. Press Escape to exit MAKEWILD and save your changes.

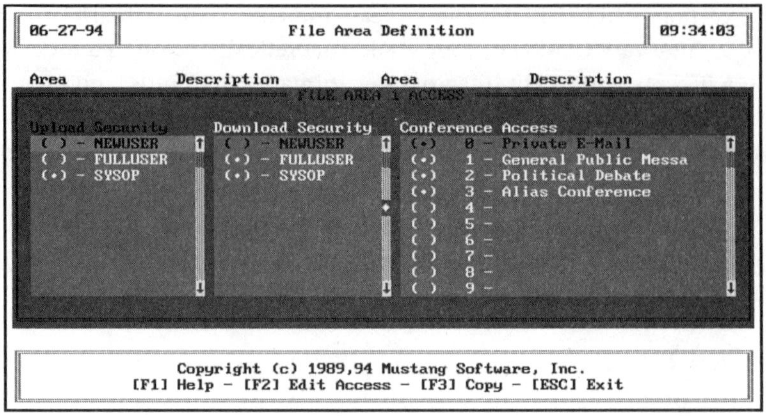

Fig. 16.7
Editing the security access levels for a CD-ROM directory.

Creating Your Own CD-ROMs

So far in this chapter, we've discussed CD-ROMs that you buy from a manufacturer; however, you can also make use of a CD-ROM as an archival tool for your current library of download files that occupy space on your hard drive. In effect, this would free up to 680 megabytes of valuable hard drive space, and place all those files onto a single CD-ROM, with no backup requirements or possibility of viral infection. You could then use that CD-ROM online, and your callers would never know the difference.

Let's carry this idea a step further. Suppose you've been a sysop for some time, and you've collected your hard-drive library of unique and hard-to-find GIF images in the old-fashioned manner: by downloading them from other boards, accepting them as uploads, and swapping them with other sysops. Plus, you've already built extensive descriptions of each file. Perhaps you'd like to offer a CD-ROM of your own!

Although CD-ROM recording units are still expensive—most range from $7,000 to $10,000—many CD-ROM service bureau companies now offer low-cost CD-ROM duplication of data you supply, so it's now possible to create your own CD-ROM discs for your use or distribution. For example, prices have dropped to less than $2,000 for a batch of 100 discs, which provides a handsome profit if you sell each disc for $50. This is exactly how most of today's better-known BBS CD-ROM manufacturers got started. Of course, the price for a single archival disc will be higher, but it will still save you a tremendous amount of hard drive space and backup worries.

How do you deliver 680 megabytes of data to a CD-ROM service bureau? Most companies accept your files on Syquest and Bernoulli removable cartridges, QIC-format and DAT tapes, and even the hard drives themselves (although the possibility for damage is high unless you deliver your hard drive in person). Most bureaus can create an ISO-9660 format CD-ROM, which is the standard for IBM-compatible PC drives.

This industry is almost certain to grow as the popularity and availability of CD-ROMs continues to rise in the PC community.

Summary

In this chapter, you were introduced to the computer CD-ROM and the tremendous value it can add to your BBS. We covered how to select and install a CD-ROM drive, as well as the advanced features of a network CD-ROM server and a jukebox drive that can offer your customers multiple discs.

We also provided guidelines to help you in selecting a CD-ROM for use on your system, as well as how to restrict access to part of the CD-ROM to build subscriber interest. We covered the utility program WCFILE, which Mustang Software provides to add hard drive and CD-ROM files to your Wildcat! file database. Finally, you learned more about creating your own CD-ROM with your own files, either to sell or to use for archival purposes.

Coming up in the next chapter, we'll review other services you can add to your BBS that will enhance its value to your callers.

Chapter 17

RIP Graphics, External Protocols, and Viewers

by Mark L. Chambers

In this chapter, you'll learn the details on how to install three improvements to your Wildcat! bulletin board that are sure to be popular with your users: RIP graphic menus and screens, external protocols, and an external archive viewer program. Although these improvements aren't necessities, they are features that greatly add to the convenience, power, and usability of your system. For instance, RIP graphics can add a "point and click" interface to virtually any character-based BBS, while external protocols and archive viewers make it possible for your callers to inspect an archive before downloading it with the latest in file transfer protocols.

> **Tip**
>
> Depending on your BBS software, you may find that your program offers a built-in archive viewer. Although this is a very convenient feature, check what archive format it uses before you put your system online—your download files must use the same archive format, or the viewer will be unable to display the contents of those files.

Adding RIP Graphics

As we mentioned in Chapter 6, your Wildcat! BBS provides built-in support for displaying RIP graphics to your callers. In this section, you'll learn all the details about how RIP works, and we'll create a RIP screen with the RIPaint program from TeleGrafix. Finally, we'll add that example screen to your Wildcat! system.

How Does RIP Work?

RIP (or more properly, RIPscrip) is a terminal emulation language specifically designed for creating graphical displays with buttons and controls similar to graphical environments like Windows and OS/2. Using RIP, your callers can use a mouse to click a menu command rather than activate that same command by pressing a character. RIP also provides a tremendous step ahead in BBS graphics, providing high-resolution color images in a very short time (version 2.0 screens will be able to display .JPG format photo-quality pictures as well—see fig. 17.1). Unlike ANSI, RIP also allows you to include multiple character fonts in a wide variety of sizes on the same screen, allowing you to vary the graphic impact of text strings to create headlines, titles and captions for your menus and display files—in effect, the sysop can finally design and layout screen "pages," much like a graphic artist. Surprisingly, this new breakthrough in online graphics is based on the simplest of ideas—the transmission of ASCII text, identical to the characters we introduced earlier in our discussion of serial communications. As mentioned in Chapter 6, RIP files are composed of commands containing only 7-bit ASCII characters, which allows the use of RIP graphics on online services and Internet providers that are limited to 7 data bits and even parity. Each line in a RIP display file begins with an exclamation point, and multiple commands may appear in a single line of a RIPscrip file separated with a *pipe* character (|).

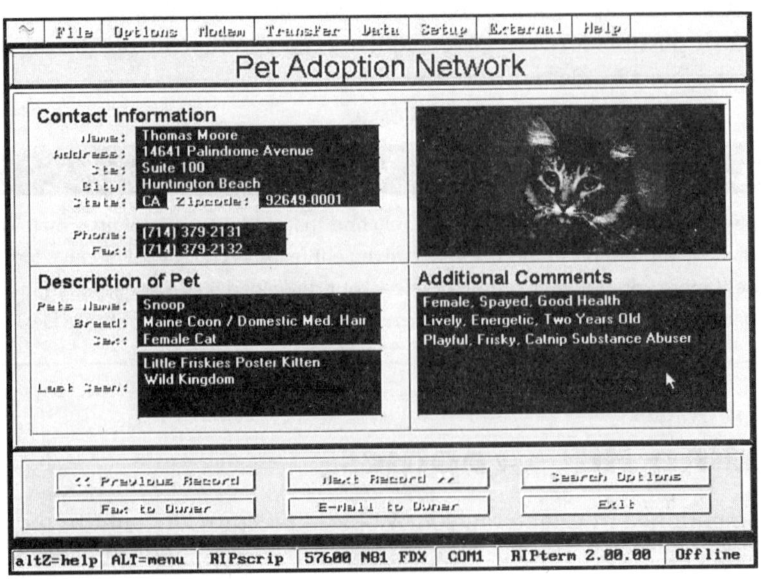

Fig. 17.1
A sample RIP2 screen using a high resolution graphic.

Of course, RIP is completely different than the standard ANSI (or ANSI-BBS) terminal emulation that currently dominates the BBS world, so callers using ANSI would see a string of ASCII characters instead of an image. To use RIP successfully, a caller has two choices: either switch to the freeware RIPterm terminal program (see fig. 17.2), or obtain another shareware or commercial terminal program that offers RIP support. RIPterm offers a very good set of standard features (especially for the price!), and also offers ANSI emulation, so it makes a good general-purpose terminal program for everyday use. At the time of this writing, only Mustang Software's QMODEM PRO and deltaComm's TELIX FOR WINDOWS support RIP as a terminal emulation, but other developers have expressed the intent to add RIP to their terminal programs (including Datastorm Technologies, who will add RIP support to the latest version of their popular PROCOMM PLUS for Windows).

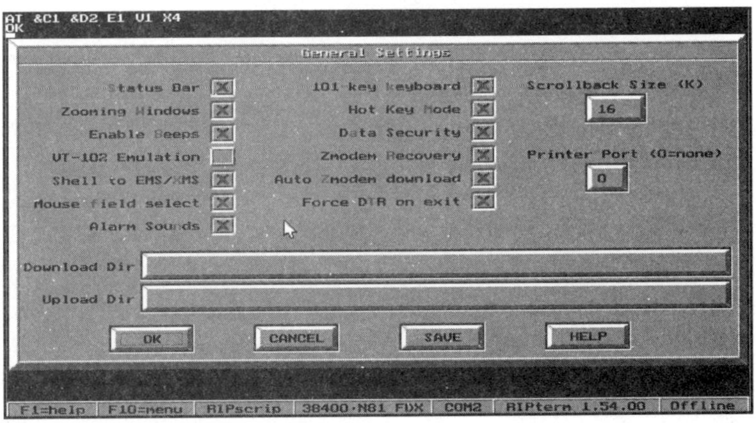

Fig. 17.2
The graphical RIPterm terminal program supplied free of charge by TeleGrafix.

Figure 17.3 shows a typical RIP menu file in its entirety, and figure 17.4 shows the display seen by the caller receiving the RIP menu. As you can see, RIPscrip is a highly-efficient language that can accomplish quite a bit on-screen with a very small file! The smaller the file size, the faster your BBS can send the caller menus, RIP display files, and screen updates. Part of this efficiency is due to the use of a complex method of compressing numbers from a decimal into hexatridecimal format, which requires fewer characters (and therefore, less time) to transmit. Multiple commands can appear in a single line of RIPscrip code, which also adds to the efficiency of the transfer.

As mentioned earlier in the book, RIPscrip has no error-detection or correction built-in—this is also true of ASCII and ANSI emulations—but the popularity of high-speed, error-correcting modems has proven this to be a wise decision on the part of RIP's designers. Callers not using error-correcting modems will be susceptible to incomplete or garbled RIP screens if line noise interferes during a session, but this is a problem with any terminal emulation.

Fig. 17.3
A RIPscrip language menu file (as it exists on your BBS).

```
!|1K|*|w000Y271610|c01|W00|=00000001|R008DHR9P|R0076HR8D|R0067HR76|R005EHR67
!|R004OHR5E|R0042HR4O|R003LHR42|R0037HR3L|R002VHR37|R002KHR2V|R002BHR2K
!|R0023HR2B|R001XHR23|R001SHR1X|R001PHR1S|R001MHR1P|R001KHR1I|L8Z1I749P
!|L8Z1I349P|L8Y1I009B|L8X1I0075|L8U1I005T|L8R1I004T|L8R1I0044|L8M1I003N
!|L3U1I001J|L8Z1I8Z1I|L8Z1IBA9P|L901IFB9P|L931IHR94|L931IHR73|L951IHR5U
!|ZC12UBG2EBK1ZAV1Y1E|Z6H1W6Y1X6V178G191E|ZAW1YAC1YAI178H181E
!|Z8N1K8N2C8B2B772B1E|Z8L1K7S1G7I1U7A2C1E|Z8T1K8R278Z2E9Z291E
!|Z8S1J9K1J9X1WA02A1E|Z7E1P7A226Z296H291E|Z7C1Q6Y1T6K226I281E
!|Z9Y1QA323AC29AQ271E|Z9X1QA91RAM20A0261E|Z5G2F5L235T1Q5R0Y1E
!|Z5Q0X60175W1Y6L1V1E|ZBM2EBF1XBM1HBK111E|ZAN1WB61WBD1FBL0Z1E
!|L804C8040|L804S8054|L9D4L8Z4L|L8D4K7W4K|L8U4E9445|L8U4Q954Y
!|L85468G4E|L8G4P854X|L8X418R4D
!|L9B4C8X4H|L9B4T8X40|L8X528R4S|L8D518J4S|L7Z4S8D4N|L8D4G7Z4D|L8D418J4C
!|Z5G6B4F6B3T663I5W1E|Z5G6B505Z46613I5W1E|ZBK6HBW6NCS6ADE621E
!|ZBL6GBE67CR65DC631E|ZB86ZBV5FC730802N1E|Z802N52ZY5C5B606U1E
!|Z696X6A5A746R806N1E|Z8M60A56LB45JAY6Y1E|Z33603770377241701E
!|Z4G705Z715Y715Z6U1E|ZD066D074DN73C4741E|ZCE73B974B874B8701E
!|F8L2X08|S0B01|F8P4308|F934A08|F994N08|F8W4X08|F8I5108|F844T08
!|F844H08|F8A4808|F8R4L08|S0800|F831X08|F961X08|FA81X08|F6Y2008|F8I3V08
!|F8I4408|F874C08|F8Z4508|F804M08|F8A4W08|F8V2P08|F3E6L08|FDD6008|S0107
!|F8P4K08|#|#|#
```

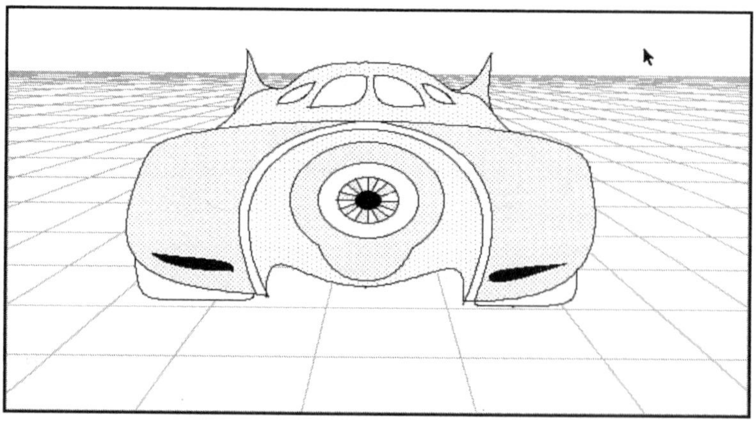

Fig. 17.4
The image seen by the caller who receives the menu.

What makes RIPscrip so exciting to sysops everywhere? After all, the NAPLPS emulation standard has been around for many years, and it provides a high-resolution display for the caller. Even traditional ANSI allows simple animation, and it's universally supported by terminal programs for PCs, Macs, the Amiga, and the Atari ST. What's the secret to the success of RIP?

The answer is that RIPscrip offers not just a high-resolution display, but a complete graphical user interface. Unlike NAPLPS, RIP supports the caller's mouse, allowing your users to simply point and click on a file to transfer, a menu selection, or a game control. Unlike ANSI, RIP supports fully-scalable fonts, bitmap icons, and fill patterns. Combine these with the capability to add RIPscrip menus to existing bulletin board programs—without requiring the sysop to buy and run a proprietary BBS system—and you can see why RIP has caused a revolution of sorts in the BBS community.

Building RIP Files

The additional graphic display possibilities provided by RIPscrip introduce a new element to the creation of RIP menus and display files—unlike ASCII or ANSI files, which we've created with a text editor and THEDRAW (respectively), RIP screens require a more advanced layout tool capable of designing high-resolution objects, icons, and screens in a familiar graphical environment. Since the finished files are in ASCII text format, they could conceivably be created with a text processor, but the work involved would be far beyond human patience! However, a sysop or developer can learn to visually "decode" a RIP file to the point where it's easy to make small modifications to text strings.

A RIP screen designer shares many of the same tools you'd find in a traditional "paint" program, like a freehand drawing pen, functions for adding lines and shapes and the ability to select different patterns and colors. A complete RIP paint program will also provide a set of design tools for adding and customizing icons, buttons, and "hotspots" (areas of the screen without borders that react to a click of the mouse)—although they're not completely necessary for graphic screens, they're required if you're going to create "point-and-click" menus that accept user input through the mouse.

Now that we've introduced RIPscrip and the tools you'll use to design RIP screens, let's create a RIP display file for your BBS. For this demonstration, we'll use the powerful TeleGrafix RIPaint program, which the company sells to sysops and developers who need a sophisticated paint package with support for buttons and hotspots. TeleGrafix also sells the inexpensive RIPdraw, which is suited for artists and users who'd like to create their own RIPscrip images without adding mouse controls.

Tip

As RIP has grown in popularity, several shareware RIP drawing programs have appeared. Although they're slowly improving as shareware authors grow more experienced with the technology, these programs range from serviceable programs to bug-ridden disasters—therefore, you'll have to try each of them to find one you can actually use. However, even the best of the shareware drawing programs can't match RIPdraw or RIPaint. If you're serious about creating RIP images for your BBS, contact TeleGrafix and buy one of these two programs,
or settle on the best shareware program you're able to find. At this time, TeleGraphix does not distribute a shareware version of either of its RIP drawing programs.

RIPaint allows you to build your display visually, without requiring any language editing or modification. Much like other paint programs, you simply save your work once you're finished, and the resulting RIP image—called a *scene file* and usually carries an extension of .RIP—is created on disk, ready to be used on your BBS.

RIPaint also allows you to add icons to your files; these icons can be surrounded by hotspots, making them into icon buttons your callers can select with a mouse. If an icon file you include in your RIP screen is not present on the caller's PC, RIPterm will sense the problem and indicate that the icon is missing, so make sure that your users have all of the icons required by your menu and display screens. Most sysops make an archive of icons available for downloading, so that callers who plan to use RIP can download the file and unarchive the icons directly into their RIPterm \ICONS subdirectory.

From within RIPaint, follow these steps to create a RIP welcome screen for The Digital Mozart BBS:

1. Press Alt-F to display the Font selection box (see fig. 17.5). Click on Bold Font to select it.

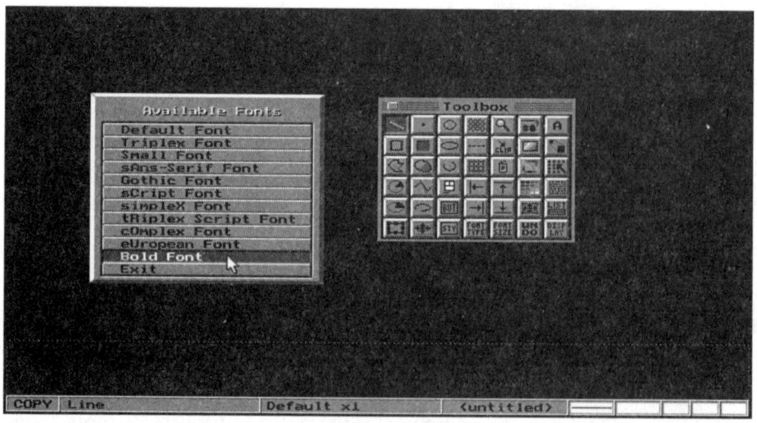

Fig. 17.5 The RIPaint Font Selection box, showing the variety of fonts available on a RIP screen.

2. Next, pick a larger font size by pressing Ctrl-F. Click on the 4x size to select it.

3. Click the Text button on the Toolbox pad to indicate you'd like to add text to the scene. Move the text cursor that appears to the upper-left corner (see fig. 17.6).

4. Click the left mouse button and type **Welcome to...** in the upper-left corner. Press Enter to accept the line and Escape to return to command mode.

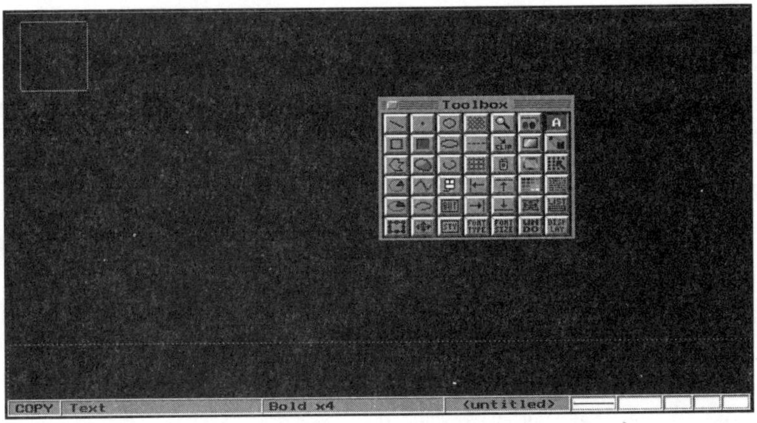

Fig. 17.6
Moving the RIPaint text cursor to the upper-left corner of our scene.

5. Now we'll add an oval shape as background for the BBS name; click the Ellipse button in the Toolbox and draw an oval in the middle of the scene.

6. Click the Fill Pattern button in the Toolbox and select the "chain link fence" pattern from the lower-left corner of the Patterns box (see fig. 17.7).

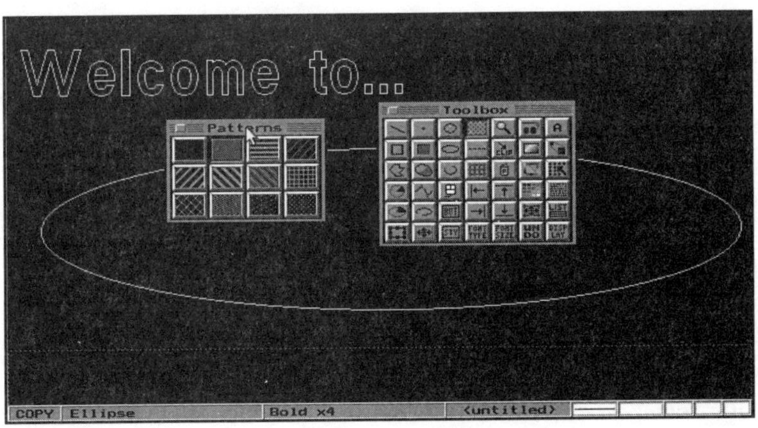

Fig. 17.7
Selecting a fill pattern.

7. Click the Toolbox Fill Color button and select red.

8. Click the Flood Fill button and then click inside the oval shape to fill it with the red pattern.

9. Press Alt-F again and select the Gothic font.

10. Press Ctrl-F again and click the 6x size to select it.

11. Click the Text button and move the text cursor to the far left of the screen.

12. Click the left mouse button and type **The Digital Mozart BBS!**. Press Enter to accept the line and Escape to return to command mode.

That's it! To view your RIP welcome screen, press the spacebar to hide the status line and Tab to hide the Toolbox. Your finished screen should look something like figure 17.8.

Fig. 17.8
A simple RIP welcome screen for The Digital Mozart BBS.

Of course, this is a very simple example, but even this basic welcome screen offers more visual impact and interest than the ANSI screen we created with THEDRAW earlier in the book. The Gothic RIPscrip font works perfectly for our theme—if you have artistic talent, you can use the extensive drawing tools available in RIPaint to improve this basic screen with another few minutes of work.

Adding RIP to Wildcat!

Your Wildcat! BBS program offers excellent support for RIPscrip, including automatic detection of a caller using RIPterm or a RIP-compatible terminal program like QMODEM PRO. If RIP is detected, your RIP menus are enabled; if ANSI support is detected, Wildcat! turns on ANSI color menus. By default, auto-detect is enabled for each new user, but a caller can turn this off from the Main menu by pressing Y for Your Settings.

To prepare your system for RIP graphics:

- Create your RIPscrip menu and display screens. These screens should end with the extension .RIP, and they can be used just like your .BBS and .SCR files. To avoid confusion, make sure that you move your .RIP files to the proper locations; they should be placed in the same directories as their corresponding .BBS/.SCR files. If Wildcat! doesn't find a specific .RIP file, it displays the correct .BBS or .SCR file instead.

- Run MAKEWILD, display Part 3 of the General Information screen and set question 13 (Enable RIP graphics support) to Y.

Wildcat! is immediately ready to display RIPscrip graphics, but you should thoroughly test your system before offering it to your callers. The local sysop console display does not show RIP images—instead, you'll see only the ASCII text being sent to the caller, so you'll have to test your RIP menus remotely.

Adding External Protocols

Your Wildcat! BBS offers seven *internal* file transfer protocols and one *external* protocol, ZMODEM MobyTurbo, which is not built-in to Wildcat!. Your users are asked to choose one of these protocols during the registration process. Whenever a user asks you which protocol to select, recommend ZMODEM; it's fast, easy to use, reliable, efficient, and it's certainly the best pick of the internal protocols. For these reasons, ZMODEM has become the most popular and widely-used protocol for BBS use.

However, ZMODEM is actually not the fastest PC file transfer protocol, nor does it offer the most features. For example, ZMODEM MobyTurbo—which is already configured as an external protocol—offers faster transfer rates. MobyTurbo is a variant of ZMODEM distributed by Omen Technology, the developer of ZMODEM. PUMA (or MPT) protocol is also slightly faster, and BIMODEM allows bi-directional file transfers (where your callers can both download and upload at the same time). Other "alternative" protocols popular with BBS callers include HSLink and SuperZMODEM (or SZMODEM). Wildcat! allows you to add up to 10 external protocols. In this section, we'll discuss the operation of external file protocols by showing you how to add PUMA to your protocol selection. Note that external protocols apply only to network type BBS programs like Wildcat! and PCBoard—integrated BBS programs like TBBS and the Major BBS cannot drop directly to DOS, so they can't run the external protocol program.

As we just mentioned, all file transfer protocols are not "created equal," so it's important to read the documentation for each external protocol you decide to offer before you begin the process of adding it to your system. In particular, check these specific characteristics (each of which we'll describe in detail as we add the PUMA protocol):

- Does the protocol support the transfer of multiple files in a single transfer? If so, you'll have to supply the external protocol program with each filename the caller enters into your BBS program. In the case of Wildcat! Lite, the BBS stores a list of filenames in a separate file, which is then specified on the external protocol program's command line. Other BBS programs store these filenames in predefined variables, which are then passed as separate arguments on the protocol program's command line.

- Does the protocol program require your BBS to specify a baud rate on the command line? If so, this value is usually equal to the "locked" baud rate maintained between your modem and your PC.

- Does the protocol report whether the transfer was successful or not—and, if so, how does it report an unsuccessful transfer? If success or failure is indicated, your BBS program can probably "read" this value—for example, Wildcat! Lite can check an error log named "DSZ.LOG" in the EP directory (which is the standard logfile generated by Omen Technology protocols), or it can check for the existence of a file called TRANSFER.BAD.

Like any other major modification to your Wildcat! system, the process begins with MAKEWILD. Follow these steps:

1. Run MAKEWILD and select External Protocol Definition. The screen shown in figure 17.9 appears.

Fig. 17.9
The MAKEWILD External Protocol Definition screen.

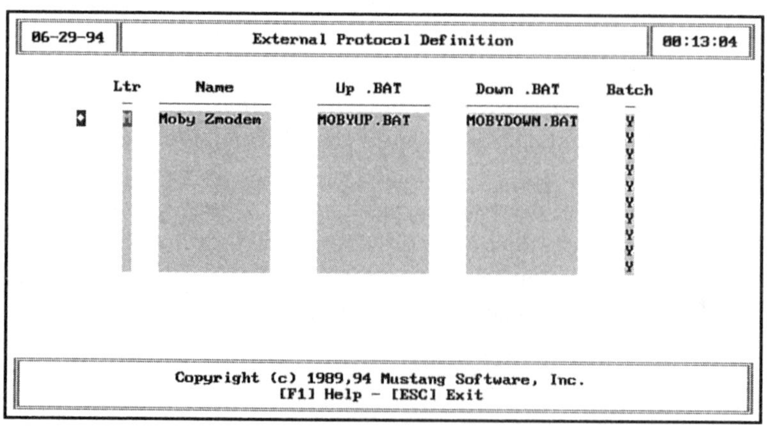

2. Use your down arrow key to move one line down and press **P**, which will identify PUMA, and press Enter.

3. Enter a name of up to 12 characters. For our demonstration, type **PUMA/MPT** and press Enter.

4. The next field names the DOS batch file that Wildcat! will run to receive an upload sent with this protocol. Let's follow the same naming convention—type **PUMAUP.BAT** and press Enter.

5. The DOWN .BAT field names the DOS batch file that Wildcat! will run to send a download with this protocol. Again, follow the MobyTurbo example by typing **PUMADOWN.BAT** and pressing Enter.

6. The last field, Batch, indicates to Wildcat! whether this protocol supports the transfer of multiple files in the same session—like ZMODEM or KERMIT—or sends only a single file at a time, like XMODEM. If you're not sure whether the protocol you're installing has this capability, check the protocol program's documentation. Since PUMA does support batch transfers, press **Y**. Your finished protocol definition for PUMA should look like figure 17.10.

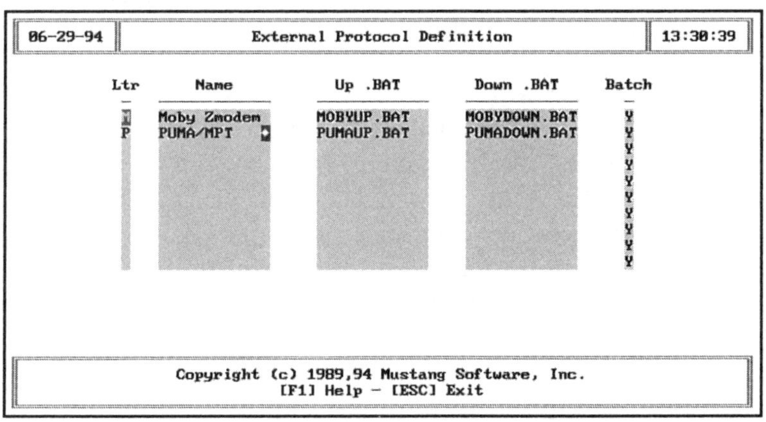

Fig. 17.10
The finished external protocol definition for PUMA.

This concludes the modifications we need to make to your Wildcat! configuration; now you should create the batch files that we named in MAKEWILD. These files vary according to the external protocol program you're installing, so check the documentation for the exact command line options.

Tip

If you're not familiar with writing batch files, you can also ask other sysops using the same protocols on their boards to supply you with example upload and download batch files.

Whenever a user downloads with an external batch transfer protocol, Wildcat! first creates a temporary work directory named \EP for the transfer. If the transfer includes multiple files, Wildcat! also creates file called FILES.LST that contains a list of the filenames to send. In the case of a single file transfer, the file itself is copied to this work directory. The program then shells to DOS and runs the batch file you specified in MAKEWILD, passing the batch file five variables that are usually required by the protocol program. In order, these variables are:

- The current baud rate between your PC and modem (with high speed modems, this value is typically "locked").
- The COM port being used.
- The online time remaining for this caller.
- The current baud rate between your modem and the caller's modem. Note that this value may be different from the first variable.
- The last variable contains the name of the file to send (for single files) or FILES.LST for multiple file batch transfers.

These same five variables are used in your upload batch files as well, but the last variable is empty on batch uploads (since Wildcat! doesn't know the names of the files it's receiving). For more information on how to pass variable values to a DOS batch file, check your DOS manual. Wildcat! automatically deletes the temporary directory after the transfer has completed. Since Wildcat! only shells to DOS for external protocols (just like external events), make sure your batch file doesn't run CAT.BAT or WILDCAT. The EXIT command word is also not required.

Adding an External Archive Viewer

From time to time, your callers may wish to see the files contained in an archive before they download it. For example, a user may check the date on the .EXE file to see if it matches an existing file, or perhaps to see whether the archive contains additional material. Your Wildcat! BBS supports the addition of an external archive viewer program (available with the V command from the Files menu), which can display the contents of an archive online. Some of these programs allow the caller to read ASCII text files "inside" the archive from the viewer, while others even allow your users to download individual files from "inside" the archive without downloading the entire compressed file. Just as with external protocols, external file viewers are suitable only for network BBS programs, since integrated BBS programs can't drop to DOS.

Mustang Software provides you with a basic external archive viewer called VZ.EXE in your Wildcat! Lite home directory, but many sysops have substituted sophisticated programs with additional features. One popular external viewer program among Wildcat! sysops is AVIEWCOM.EXE from Cygnus Data Systems, an excellent shareware viewer designed for Wildcat! that allows the caller to read text files and download individual files from within an archive. Figure 17.11 shows a typical AVIEWCOM screen.

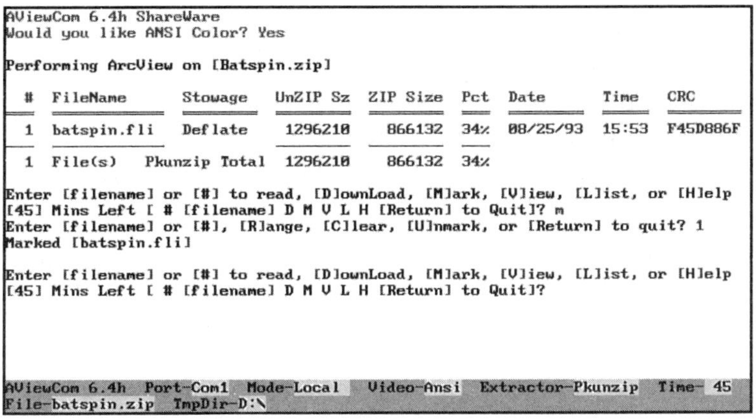

Fig. 17.11
Viewing the contents of an archive file with AVIEWCOM.

Whenever a user chooses V from the Files menu, Wildcat! shells to DOS and runs a DOS batch file called VIEWCOMP.BAT, which must be located in the Wildcat! home directory. Wildcat! also passes the complete DOS path to the file selected for viewing (including the drive, directory, and filename) as variable %1. To substitute your own external viewer program, use your text editor to modify the VIEWCOMP.BAT file and change its contents to the commands detailed in your viewer's documentation. As an example, if you're using AVIEWCOM, the batch file should contain a command line similar to:

```
c:\WC30\AVIEW\AVIEWCOM %1 COM1
```

This command assumes a single-line system running on COM1—as mentioned earlier, check the documentation accompanying your particular viewer program to determine the command you'll need. As with external protocols, Wildcat! only shells to DOS, so make sure your batch file doesn't run CAT.BAT or WILDCAT. The EXIT command word is also not required.

Whenever you run an external archive program, keep security in mind. For example, if you offer adult download files online and all of your users can browse the file listings, it's possible for a minor to use the external viewer to display adult text files inside of an archive (or even download them directly, if the viewer program doesn't directly support security levels for your particular BBS program)! If you're going to allow your callers to view the contents of sensitive files, make sure only those who can download those same files are allowed access to the viewer.

Summary

In this chapter, we discussed the RIP-emulation standard in more detail, and also introduced the RIPaint drawing package from TeleGrafix. You also learned how you can add three popular features to your BBS: RIP display screens, external protocols, and an external-archive viewer.

In Chapter 18, "Understanding External Connections," you'll be introduced to the exciting possibilities of external connections that can link your system with other bulletin boards across the world, as well as the international Internet network.

Part IV

Connecting to the World

Chapter 18

Understanding External Connections

by Mark L. Chambers

In the next four chapters of this book, we're going to focus on *external connections*. That's a broad term, but it fits the topic very well; unlike external doors, where the action remains local to your BBS, external connections link your BBS system with the rest of the world through public messages, electronic mail, files, and chat. For example, with the right external connections, callers on your system can:

- Read and reply to Internet e-mail from correspondents anywhere around the world.
- Download files received automatically through the FidoNet FILEBONE transfer system.
- Chat in real-time conversations with users on another BBS across town—or across the country.
- Access your BBS from hundreds of miles away with a local call.
- Dial another BBS or online service while still connected to your system.
- Play popular modem games like DOOM with other callers connected to your system.

One type of external connection is a particularly hot topic of interest in the media these days. You've probably heard the phrase "Information Superhighway" in the news recently; it refers to the global Internet network and the free passage of information, ideas, and opinions constantly flowing to and from Internet sites around the world, 24 hours a day. No matter what your occupation, background, or interests, you're likely to find a wealth of valuable information by connecting to the Internet.

Until recently, bulletin boards were unable to participate in this worldwide cyberspace community because no PC-based BBS had the complex, powerful software required to exchange messages with the UNIX systems that make up the vast majority of Internet computers. Instead, sysops developed their own worldwide network, called FidoNet, which has also grown tremendously. The two networks were linked through *gateways*, so a limited number of messages could travel back and forth, but bulletin board sysops sometimes felt they only had half a picture when it came to message networks.

All that has changed in the last few years as bulletin boards benefit from the increase in PC processor speed and modem baud rates. Your Wildcat! BBS can now exchange electronic mail and messages over both FidoNet and the Internet, bringing the global community right to your BBS console! In fact, at least one BBS manufacturer—eSoft, maker of TBBS—is developing a direct "plug-and-play" connection between its bulletin board system and the Internet. We'll cover the Internet in detail in Chapter 20.

In these four chapters, you'll explore the exciting future of bulletin board technology: the external connections that allow you and your callers to reach out and communicate with the rest of the world.

Why Expand with a Message Network?

Like other advanced BBS services, external connections are not for every system—although messages were the first service offered on bulletin boards, they're no longer the only game in town! A large percentage of sysops have little interest in connecting their boards to other systems or a LAN, preferring instead to concentrate on improving other areas of their BBS. In fact, as massive as FidoNet is, it still only connects a modest portion of bulletin boards in the United States.

In this introductory chapter, we'll explore the general advantages and disadvantages of adding a message network connection from the sysop side of the console. Once you've read the pros and cons of joining the international community, you'll have a better handle on whether or not your system should eventually add an external connection.

Advantages

When considering the advantages of external connections, keep in mind that most of them may affect your users more than they affect you as the sysop of your BBS. If you're running a subscription hobby system or a profit BBS, it's strongly recommended that you add both FidoNet and Internet connections, because it's a safe bet that your users will enjoy networked public message bases and electronic mail (therefore increasing the value of your system, and attracting subscribers).

Advantages to external connections include:

- **Guaranteed daily message traffic.** A bulletin board with a "slow" message base generates very little activity from your users, and a lack of messages doesn't invite anyone to enter a public discussion. External connections to FidoNet and the Internet can guarantee that your readers will see new message traffic as often as your BBS calls your host system to exchange message packets.

- **Fast international electronic mail.** The Internet is a clear advantage for your users who would like to send and receive electronic mail or subscribe to Internet *mailing lists* (you'll learn more about Internet mailing lists in Chapter 20). On the average, an Internet e-mail message should reach its destination within 10 to 15 minutes after your BBS uploads it to your *UUCP provider* (more about your UUCP provider later in this chapter).

- **Site-to-site file exchange.** Both FidoNet and the Internet allow a user to exchange files with other network sites; however, the current BBS file transfer technology on the Internet is limited to files enclosed in electronic mail. FidoNet allows you to *FREQ* (short for File REQuest) any file allowed by the sysop of another FidoNet BBS. FidoNet also provides the means to automatically receive shareware files through the FidoNet File Distribution Network.

- **Wide variety of message topics.** No matter what your tastes, hobbies, or the theme of your system, you and your users will find something of interest in the tremendous variety of echoes and newsgroups! If you haven't installed a QWK mail system, make sure you add one before you make your external connection; your callers will need QWK mail to read and reply to just a day of message traffic!

- **Technical support via echoes and newsgroups.** Both message networks offer dozens of public message areas (called *echoes* on FidoNet and *newsgroups* on the Internet) where you and your users can receive timely technical support on computer topics, as well as a tremendous number of subjects that aren't related to computers.

- **Familiar BBS interface.** One of the primary advantages of an external connection on your BBS for your users is the BBS interface itself! This is especially true of Internet connections because UNIX systems are confusing—to say the least—to those comfortable with a DOS or Windows environment. On your BBS, however, Internet and FidoNet e-mail and messages are composed and read using your board's standard message commands and editor. Leaving an Internet e-mail message is almost as simple as leaving a local e-mail message for another user on your system!

- **Atmosphere.** Although an intangible, the "international message center" atmosphere created by a FidoNet or Internet connection enhances the perceived value of your BBS, which translates into money from your subscribers. Your bulletin board is no longer an isolated island in cyberspace! In fact, the idea of a message center has been used as a central theme by many bulletin boards.

Disadvantages

Unfortunately, all of the disadvantages of external connections affect only you, the sysop—your users will be largely oblivious to all of the money and time you'll have to invest to install an external connection, join the network itself, and maintain the link after your system is running smoothly on the network.

- **Cost.** Of course, this is a major stopping point for many sysops! Not only will you be required to purchase additional software (and, for some connections, hardware as well), but there's a good chance that your FidoNet host or Internet UUCP provider may be a long-distance call, which adds up to at least one daily long-distance call lasting several minutes. Internet UUCP providers usually charge a monthly subscription for access, while FidoNet connections are free. To be effective, your Internet connection will require several connections each day, and a chat link requires a constant connection with your host BBS for as long as the chat period lasts. Most expensive of all are the X.25 packet and satellite connections; the latter usually requires a separate *nanny* PC connected to your BBS computer that handles message tasks.

- **Line use.** If you're running a single-line or two-line system, your system will be affected to some degree by an external connection because it must tie up one of your lines to place an outgoing call to exchange mail with your host. With a FidoNet connection, a single call per day may be sufficient, and it can be placed late at night; however, as we just mentioned, your BBS will make several calls a day with an Internet connection, and a chat link will busy out one of your lines for the length of the chat period.

- **Difficult installation.** Every external connection requires some form of software installation, and installation time can range from several hours to a day. These programs must work together and in conjunction with your BBS in order for your mail exchanges to be successful, and that can be the biggest headache of all; always allow plenty of time for fine tuning when scheduling the installation of an external connection. Some connections will also require hardware installations—for example, a satellite or X.25 connection—so enlist help if you feel you'll need it.
- **Hard-drive space.** Depending on the number of newsgroups or echoes you'll offer, expect to lose anywhere from 5 to 100 megabytes (or more) of hard-drive space for processing and the extra space taken up by all of those new messages.
- **Maintenance time.** Another important consideration for the sysop is the amount of maintenance time required to keep an external connection running smoothly. Although most connections run automatically once they've been fine tuned, you'll still have to add and delete newsgroups and echoes, check error logs and diagnose problems periodically, monitor electronic mail, and participate in the message conferences you receive for yourself! Of course, the amount of maintenance time increases with the number and size of the echoes and newsgroups you elect to receive.
- **Adult content.** When you open your system to the rest of the world through a FidoNet or Internet connection, you also provide an entry point for messages containing adult language and sexual content. Because FidoNet originated as a BBS-oriented message network, each echo has an appointed moderator who maintains control by issuing warnings (and, in the event of continued abuse, cuts the offending caller's FidoNet connection). This makes FidoNet a much safer message network for sysops who don't allow adult material on their systems. Internet messages and chat links, however, are largely unmoderated, and as such those who participate are allowed to say whatever they wish.
- **Loss of interest in local messages.** As mentioned in the previous section, the addition of public message traffic from an external connection is a great idea for systems with slow local message areas.

However, if your BBS has an active and popular local message base, there's a danger that those local message areas will be lost in the international shuffle after you add an external connection. With all of the networked messages your system receives, your users are likely to spend less time in your local message base.

What Will I Need?

Although FidoNet, the Internet, and nationwide chat links appear to be quite different, they actually share several common elements. In the next three chapters, we'll focus on the specific requirements, installation, and operation of these popular connections, so we won't go into individual features at this point. However, we can discuss those elements shared by all three:

- **An identifying address.** Your system's unique network address is the equivalent of a regular caller's logon name; it identifies you to all other sites on the network, allowing other systems to send messages to your system. If you've installed a chat link, your system ID usually appears next to your callers' names when they type messages. Figure 18.1 shows the components of a typical Internet address.

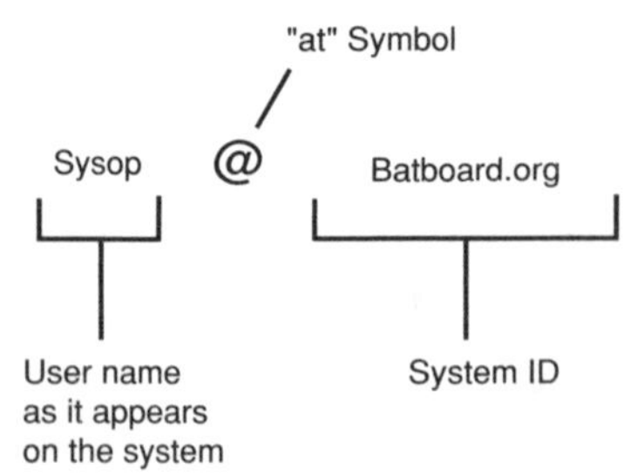

Fig. 18.1 The components of a typical Internet e-mail address.

- **Mailer/front end software.** Unless your system has built-in support for a message network, you'll need a separate program that runs independently of your BBS program; this mailer utility processes incoming message packets and adds them to your message base. It also scans your existing messages and creates a packet containing outgoing messages and e-mail written by your users for others on the network. Typically, this utility also performs the actual dialing process to connect with your network host.

- **A host or hub connection.** Once you've completed the installation of your front-end software and obtained your address, your BBS is a recognized network site—but without a connection to another site, you'll never receive a single message! Depending on the network you've joined, your BBS must dial your FidoNet host or Internet UUCP provider to exchange messages and mail. Typically, your FidoNet host is a much larger BBS called a *hub* that exchanges messages with other FidoNet systems, while your Internet UUCP provider is a UNIX host computer that has a direct wired connection to the Internet using the TCP/IP data exchange standard. These host systems operate 24 hours a day, so you can connect to them whenever you wish to exchange mail. Make sure you check with your provider to find out "peak" and "off" hours because UUCP connections during off hours are usually significantly cheaper than peak hours (similar to the cost for a long-distance call). A chat host is usually a multiline BBS like yours that can dedicate a phone line to connecting with you; messages are exchanged between systems as they're typed.

Figure 18.2 shows an illustration of how your BBS works in conjunction with your mailer, your network ID, and your host connection to transfer mail.

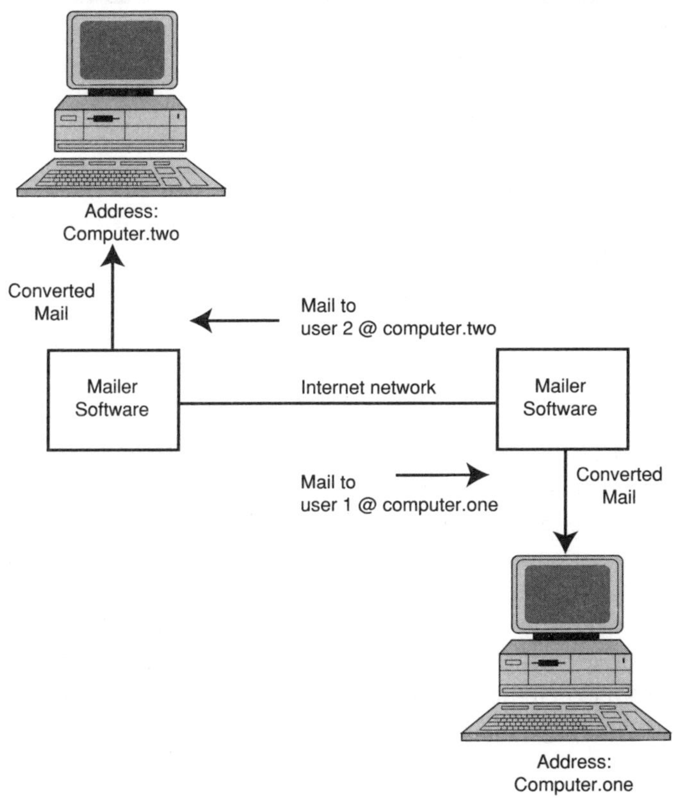

Fig. 18.2
An illustration demonstrating how your BBS uses an external connection.

Help!

If you're technically adept, there's certainly no reason why you can't perform the installation of an external connection by yourself. Although a FidoNet or Internet connection is more difficult to install than your initial BBS installation, each software program will come with its own documentation, and the next two chapters will outline the process.

However, if you're unsure of your technical abilities (or you simply would rather work with a safety net), don't hesitate to call for help anywhere in the process! Possible sources of help include:

- **Direct software technical support.** If you're receiving a specific error message from your BBS or the network mailer, or you're experiencing problems getting the mailer to use your modem, call for voice support for the offending program. Direct software technical support usually addresses only the company's product.

> **Tip**
>
> To save time during a technical support call, try to gather as much information about the problem as possible, and be ready to provide information about your PC and your BBS. Don't forget to have your software and hardware serial numbers handy!

- **BBS manufacturer's support system.** Call your BBS manufacturer's support bulletin board and post a public message to ALL. Describe the problem completely, and request an answer on the BBS. Because many of your peers will have had the same trouble, it's likely you'll receive at least several informed guesses as to what might be causing your problem.

- **Local sysops.** This is really more of a first line of defense—in fact, it's recommended that you request the help of a sysop who's already installed an external connection long before you order your mailer software. Experienced help is your best guarantee that your installation will work right the first time. Although a sysop who uses the same BBS program as you should be your first choice, FidoNet and Internet installations share enough common ground among different BBS programs to allow an experienced sysop to help, no matter what program he or she runs. If you live in an area with several other boards, you're likely to find at least one FidoNet or Internet guru who's helped new sysops connect for several years. Local sysops are also the best choice to help you obtain a network address.

> **Tip**
>
> If you ask another person to survive a FidoNet/Internet satellite installation with you, make sure you treat that person to an expensive dinner to celebrate after everything is running smoothly!

- **Consultants.** Finally, if you're running a larger profit or business/ support system and you would like to make sure your installation and fine tuning will go perfectly (and in the shortest amount of downtime possible), call the manufacturer of your BBS program and request they recommend a BBS consultant. This is a costly proposition that often involves transportation and hotel expenses, but expert help is never cheap.

> **Tip**
>
> Most consultants work on an hourly basis; make sure you have everything prepared so the person can perform the installation process in as short a time as possible. This includes obtaining your network address ahead of time!

Summary

In this chapter, you were introduced to the underlying concepts behind external connections. We outlined the advantages and disadvantages every sysop should know before deciding to add an external connection, and the common elements shared by all external connections. Finally, we covered where you can obtain the help you may need to install and fine tune your external connections.

In Chapter 19, we'll begin our specific discussion of the first major message network available to bulletin boards around the world: Tom Jenning's International FidoNet message and file network, which includes over 20,000 bulletin boards worldwide!

Chapter 19

Connecting to FidoNet

by Dave Gibbons and George Peace

FidoNet is many things to many people around the world. Its name has roots in a BBS package called, appropriately enough, Fido. FidoNet is a distributed BBS network reaching dozens of countries on six continents. It is a network with no central traffic manager and only a handful of rules.

FidoNet nodes connect as needed using modems on regular phone lines installed in homes and businesses. Communication is accomplished through transfer of files containing a wide assortment of messages and data.

In this chapter, you will learn some of the history and evolution of FidoNet as well as what FidoNet is today. The chapter then covers how to connect your BBS to the FidoNet, with some specific directions for Wildcat! users.

Discovering FidoNet

FidoNet is the invention of Tom Jennings, the San Francisco-based author of the Fido BBS software. Tom developed FidoNet because no one had done it before and because it sounded like fun. Tom and other sysops, like his friend John Madill in Baltimore, used modems to call other BBSs and post messages. The process required an abundant supply of time and money and few of 1984's hobbyist sysops had either.

Tom thought software should be able to accept messages posted by local callers, store them, and make a modem call to forward them to their final destinations. John agreed. The pair embarked on a development and testing project that ended in June 1984 with the birth of FidoNet.

Tom's invention, though not immediately recognized as such, has become one of the largest store-and-forward message and file transport networks in the world. The FidoNet store-and-forward technology—no longer exclusive to the FidoNet network—is used in dozens of hobbyist, commercial, and government enterprises.

Laying the Foundation

FidoNet began with just two nodes. Node 1 was in San Francisco and node 2 was in Baltimore. This network, though fragile and far from the sophistication of today's store-and-forward operations, was the beginning of a revolution in communications.

The network quickly grew from its humble beginnings. FidoNet expanded to 50 systems within three months. This growth brought problems. Traffic control and call management were noticeably missing. Tom and the others noticed that delivery of messages to several nodes in the same city required as many calls as there were nodes to call. They also realized that keeping track of the growing list of member BBS nodes was already next to impossible.

FidoNet exploded to over 150 nodes during the winter of '84/'85 and doubled to 300 nodes by summer. No longer a small community of friends, FidoNet had already reached and in some ways exceeded the complexity of older and better-known commercial and government networks.

Maintaining the List of Nodes

Nodelist (the list of nodes in FidoNet) management was moved to St. Louis in September 1984. Tom Jennings wrote software to handle complex routing while the group in St. Louis developed a new expandable nodelist format. FidoNet still uses this "St. Louis" nodelist format to define local nodes and mail routing points.

Ben Baker, an original FidoNet system operator in St. Louis, developed a software package that processed nodelist updates from various collection points in the network. The software, now a shareware package known as *MakeNL* (Make NodeList), is still maintained by Baker and continues to be used throughout FidoNet. The software processes the weekly updates and produces a new nodelist and a weekly *nodediff* (nodelist difference) file. MakeNL is executed at a central collection BBS every Friday and automatically creates and archives the nodediff for distribution throughout FidoNet.

Sysops receive and apply the changes represented by the weekly nodediff. The result of nodediff processing is maintenance of a current nodelist on each FidoNet BBS.

The FidoNet nodelist represents the oldest, largest, and most up-to-date list of BBSs in the world.

Addressing the Mail

FidoNet consists of over 30,000 individually addressable nodes. The size and apparent complexity of the network suggests that an equally complex structure should also exist to communicate among nodes. Node address definition is actually logical and easily implemented, consisting of four numeric parts used both for locating a node and for intermediate routing:

```
zone:net/node.point
```

The *zone* component is the major division within FidoNet and is equivalent to the continent. FidoNet is divided into the following six zones:

1. North America
2. Europe
3. Australia and New Zealand
4. Central and South America
5. Africa
6. Asia

The *net* component identifies the local area within the zone. A network can be a country, a city, or even a special FidoNet component depending on local FidoNet customs and concentration of BBSs in the area. FidoNet has over 700 nets spread over the six zones.

The *node* component identifies the BBS within the local area within the zone. Nodes are the voice of FidoNet. They are the origination and destination of most mail. The node (Tom Jennings was node 1) was originally the only address component. The name and meaning assigned to the component has remained the same through the evolution through node, then network/node, and then zone:network/node.

The *point* component typically identifies a caller or another BBS. Point number zero is equivalent to no point. Addresses 1:270/101.0 and 1:270/101 are equivalent. 1:270/101.0 and 1:270/101.8 are different FidoNet addresses on the same BBS. 1:270/101.8 is commonly referred to as point eight or 270/101 point eight.

Sending Mail Around the World

NetMail is the name given to Network Mail originating at one FidoNet node and sent to another node. The NetMail message is placed into a packet (envelope) containing information used to send or route the mail to its ultimate destination. The message content is most often a personal note but can be a public message addressed to multiple destination nodes or even an attachment in the form of a file.

Packets are processed on each FidoNet node by software referred to as a packer or unpacker after the processes it performs, or simply as a mail processor. Packets can exist in uncompressed or compressed form with an archiver such as PKZIP or ARJ. The mode and format are arranged and configured according to the sysop's preferences and connection requirements. Packets are transferred between FidoNet nodes using FidoNet mailer software such as FrontDoor, TIMS, D'Bridge, or BinkleyTerm to connect to the destination node.

The destination of a message is not always another FidoNet node. FidoNet system operator Burt Juda maintains a *gateway* system (fidonet.org) that translates mail among FidoNet and non-FidoNet addresses and formats. The gateway and a flexible inter-network addressing format allow FidoNet sysops and users to exchange mail with people on virtually any network by using the gateway system as the connecting link.

Sharing Message Bases

A significant event of the early period of exploration and expansion occurred in 1986. Jeff Rush, a Texas system operator, developed software that distributed messages in message conferences to several BBSs. Jeff's software allowed sysops to identify message conferences to be shared or echoed among many FidoNet BBSs. Callers entered messages on one BBS and the software reflected it to other BBSs where it was loaded and available to callers as if entered on those BBSs. This shared message conference phenomenon became known as EchoMail.

EchoMail operation expanded and soon absorbed a series of EchoMail collection and distribution BBSs. The BBSs collected all available EchoMail from multiple sources and packaged it for distribution.

EchoMail distribution in North America is serviced by a four-level collection and distribution system that begins at the BBS level. Three large central EchoMail distribution hubs are configured in a redundant triangle and exchange mail almost continuously. Thirty or more regional distributors provide links between the central hubs and several hundred local distributors who in turn provide services to FidoNet BBSs and callers. Message transport from originating BBS through local to regional to central hub and out to another BBS anywhere in North America is rarely more than one day with many BBSs experiencing three to six hour delivery.

The FidoNet North American EchoMail backbone carries over 20,000 messages totaling over 25 megabytes every day. Over 600 different EchoMail conference topics are available to virtually every FidoNet BBS in North America.

The cost of transporting this volume by modem is significant even with recent technology such as V.34. Some EchoMail distributors use the Internet, satellites, and even tape as alternative transports.

Coordinating the Network

Tom Jennings addressed a 1991 gathering of FidoNet system operators and described the act of coordinating FidoNet as a task similar to herding cats: Both elude our efforts artfully.

Managing the Network

By design, FidoNet is a decentralized network but even such a structure requires a limited amount of management. A multilevel system of coordinators has been established to collect and process nodelist/nodediff changes and to receive and forward NetMail for geographic subdivisions such as local Nets. Coordinators exist at zone, region, net, and hub levels, and are listed in the nodelist at the beginning of the segment they maintain.

Maintaining Standards of Conduct

FidoNet has always maintained the following two basic rules of conduct:

- Do not be excessively annoyed.
- Do not excessively annoy others.

Growth of the network brought with it an increased amount of social influence and a resulting need to clarify the basic rules. The coordinators eventually built a generalized FidoNet policy document to offer more explicit guidelines about obtaining and keeping a FidoNet address. The document tries to offer a balance between rules and tolerance to the extent possible in a network of over 30,000 nodes.

Documenting Technical Standards

The FidoNet Technical Standards Committee, or FTSC, is an internationally-chartered subgroup that maintains documentation covering technical practices within the network. New software is measured against requirements and standards set forth in FTSC documents. FTSC documents are written by sysops and programmers to make sure existing standard practices within the network are maintained in the formal specifications. The FTSC reviews and votes on whether to accept proposals as offered. Dozens of proposals and updates have been presented for review, but only half a dozen have ever been accepted as formal technical standards.

Getting the Word Out

FidoNews is the FidoNet newsletter—a chronicle of FidoNet history. The newsletter has been published since the early days of FidoNet and is an integral part of the network.

FidoNet documents describe *FidoNews* as a binding force and the place where official announcements are made. Article submissions can be sent from any FidoNet node to node 1:1/23. Articles are processed and adapted to *FidoNews* format. The resulting newsletter is published weekly and distributed in electronic form to all zones.

Meeting FidoNet System Operators

The first recorded meeting of North American FidoNet system operators was in June 1985. A small group from San Francisco and St. Louis met in a St. Louis home. The group gathered without an agenda and parted without knowing the significance of this first historic meeting. The meeting cemented a plan to subdivide FidoNet into independently functioning networks and significantly streamline nodelist processing.

Later meetings became somewhat more formal and became a yearly event known as a FidoNet Convention or FidoCon. FidoCons were the first events where sysops from around the world could gather to share experiences. The events have continued and expanded until there are now zone level FidoCons.

Connecting Your BBS to FidoNet

By now, you should have a good picture of how your BBS can take advantage of FidoNet. This section shows you how to make all the right connections, both technically and within the FidoNet community. The examples in this section use Wildcat! Lite, but the general logic applies to just about any BBS software you want to use.

Before you start setting up your BBS to communicate with FidoNet, make sure you have gathered all the tools you'll need. To access FidoNet, you need these elements (in addition to a working BBS, of course):

- **A mailer.** This is a program that attaches to a remote site and sends and receives mail. Popular examples are FrontDoor, InterMail, BinkleyTerm, D'Bridge, and LynxMail.

- **A mail tosser.** This program transfers the mail packets into and out of your mail database. Two popular mail tossers for Wildcat! are WildMail! and GoMail.

- **A FOSSIL driver.** A system driver (most can be loaded as a TSR or as a driver in the CONFIG.SYS) that enhances DOS's communications functions. Most mailers require an active FOSSIL driver to work. X00 and BNU are two common examples.

> **Note**
>
> FOSSIL stands for *Fido/Opus/SEAdog Standard Interface Layer.*

- **A Fido nodelist.** The nodelist is a master list of the names, phone numbers, and Fido addresses of all member bulletin board systems. It is a very large text file (usually available as a ZIP file) that is updated frequently.

- **A nodelist compiler.** In order for the nodelist to work with your bulletin board software, it must be changed from its native ASCII format into a simple database format. WildNode! is a nodelist compiler for Wildcat! BBS software. Your mailer will probably require a compiled nodelist (in a different format from the BBS's compiled version) as well, but most mailers include their own compilers.

- **A full collection of archive utilities.** Because different sysops use different archivers to compress their mail packets, you'll have to be prepared for whatever comes your way. A good cross section includes PKZIP/PKUNZIP (for .ZIP files), PKPAK/PKUNPAK (for .ARC files), LHARC (for .LZH files), ZOO (for .ZOO files), and ARJ (for .ARJ files).

Note

Most of the third-party programs discussed here are available as shareware or freeware on Mustang Software's BBS (805/873-2400). Though this chapter lists what are probably the most popular utilities, several other quality programs are available on the Mustang BBS and other services.

The first part of the process is the mailer program, which can receive or initiate calls to other mailers and exchange electronic mail. These mailers are usually set up either as BBS front ends or as processes that are activated by the BBS at certain times. If the mailer is set up as a front end, it answers the phone all the time, usually with a prompt such as `Press Esc to enter the BBS`. When a user sees that prompt and presses Esc, the mailer starts up the BBS and the user can log on. If another BBS's mailer program sees that prompt, however, it sends a special sequence that identifies it as a mailer and the two programs begin a mail transfer. This setup allows mailers to call any time, day or night, to exchange mail. You don't have to worry about getting unwanted mail or having unwanted parties receiving your mail because you can set up your mailer to communicate with only the BBSs you've specified.

The other type of setup lets the BBS answer the phone all the time and only launch the mailer at scheduled times. Many sysops, for example, set aside a time in the middle of the night when they block out any non-mail calls. This lets even high-traffic BBSs guarantee mail callers a chance to get through without fighting busy signals.

Either way you set up your mailer, FidoNet requires you to observe the Zone Mail Hour (ZMH), which is an hour in the middle of the night when only other mailers can connect with your BBS. The policies are detailed in the file POLICY4.ZIP, available on Mustang's BBS and several other places (Internet users can get it from ftp.fidonet.org).

FidoNet mail is sent from place to place in specially formatted packet files. Because each type of BBS software uses a different format for its message base, the packets must be translated from this generic format into the BBS's format by the mail tosser program. The tosser first reads any outgoing messages and creates a packet to be uploaded to a remote mailer. If you normally call two other BBSs, such as a local FidoNet coordinator for NetMail and a different BBS for EchoMail conferences, your tosser will create one outgoing packet for each of them—one with only outgoing NetMail and the other with any outgoing EchoMail. When your mailer connects with a remote mailer, it will send a packet (if you have any mail to send) and receive a packet of any mail the remote site has for you. It is possible to have a mail session in which neither site sends a packet. If you receive a mail packet, the tosser will translate it into the format your BBS uses for messages and insert them into your message base.

Joining FidoNet is easy—you just have to set up your mailer and successfully send mail to a network coordinator. As you learned earlier in the chapter, FidoNet is a very free, open system with few restrictions. There is only one initiation rite—successfully installing your mailer. You may be able to get some help from other sysops in your area, but most will advise you to struggle through the process on your own for its learning benefits. The lessons you learn setting up a mailer will serve you well during your time as a sysop. In this chapter, we try to smooth the path a little by guiding you through the general steps involved in setting up a mailer.

Finding a FidoNet Feed

The first thing to do when you decide to make your BBS a FidoNet node is find out what other nodes exist in your community. FidoNet volunteers publish a list of all existing nodes in a file usually called NODELIST.ZIP (available on Mustang's BBS and most other FidoNet sites). The file lists the names, phone numbers, and sysops of all the FidoNet sites in the world.

Tip

If you download the nodelist from a BBS, you should also try to get a nodelist reader program. In its native format, the nodelist is very difficult to read, but nodelist reader programs allow you to read and search it comfortably.

Find some other BBSs in your area and try to contact the sysops. They will be able to help you find the local coordinator. Even if you have a network hub in your city, you should try to get your feed from someone lower down the chain, like a local coordinator—hubs are set up to deal with local coordinators, not individual BBSs.

The BBSs in your area will be part of the same numbered *network*, and each will have a *node number* within that network. When you look at FidoNet mail, you'll see addresses such as 1:111/9999. The first part of that address (before the colon) is the zone number, followed by the network number, a forward slash, and a node number. Each continent has its own zone (North America is zone 1), divided into several networks. The network coordinator's node address is always 0, so if you found that all the BBSs in your area were in network 289 (central Missouri), the network coordinator's address would be 1:289/0.

Once you find a local coordinator, send a message through the local coordinator to your network coordinator. This message will have a dummy return address (node requests usually use /9999 after the zone and network numbers). Within two weeks, you should have your own node number.

In the next section, you'll see how a typical mailer is set up, and the steps you go through to send that first node number request.

Working with a Mailer

This section gives you the general steps to configure a mailer program, and shows how those steps are accomplished in FrontDoor, a popular mailer. Each mailer is different, so consult your mailer's documentation for specific instructions on accomplishing each general step.

1. Install the mailer software. In most cases, this involves expanding the archive file for the mailer into a temporary directory, then running its install program. As with any software installation, always check the README file for any special instructions.

   In the current version of FrontDoor, there is no Install program. You have to create the directories yourself. Extract the archive (FD211.ARJ) into an FD directory on your drive, and create NODELIST, MAIL, PACKETS, and FILES subdirectories in the FD directory.

2. Set up the mailer with your FidoNet address and BBS information. You have to tell the Mailer what return address you want to use. Because you won't have a real address at the start, use a dummy address with your zone, network, and /9999. If you are in zone 1, network 289, for example, your temporary address would be 1:289/9999. Your mailer will probably have a section for text about your BBS, so set it up with your name, your board's name, and any other information you want to include with outgoing messages.

Run FDSETUP to configure most of FrontDoor's options. Your site's information is set up in the Global menu's Address option. When you select the Address option, you'll see selections for Address, Site Info, Domains, and AKA matching, but you only have to fill in the first two. Select Address and enter your dummy address (don't worry about the AKA fields, just the Main field—see fig. 19.1). Enter text-based information about your BBS in the Site Info input box (see fig. 19.2).

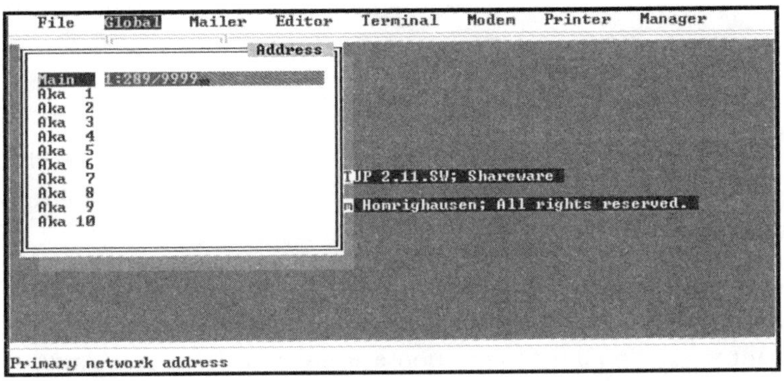

Fig. 19.1
Setting your FidoNet address in FrontDoor's FDSETUP.

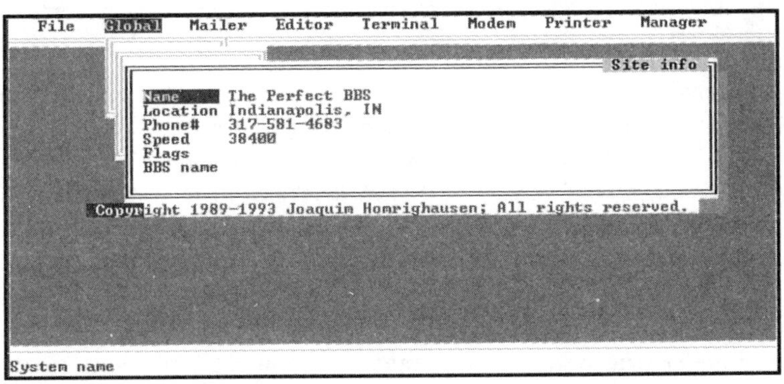

Fig. 19.2
Entering your BBS information in FrontDoor.

3. Set up the directory paths for the mailer. Your mailer software will probably require separate directories for the different types of files it works with: incoming and outgoing mail packets, incoming and outgoing files, system files, and the compiled nodelist. It will also need to know where to find your BBS's message base. Check your mailer's documentation to find out what directories you have to create and how to let the software know which directories to use.

In FrontDoor, use the Filenames option from the Global menu to enter the paths (see fig. 19.3).

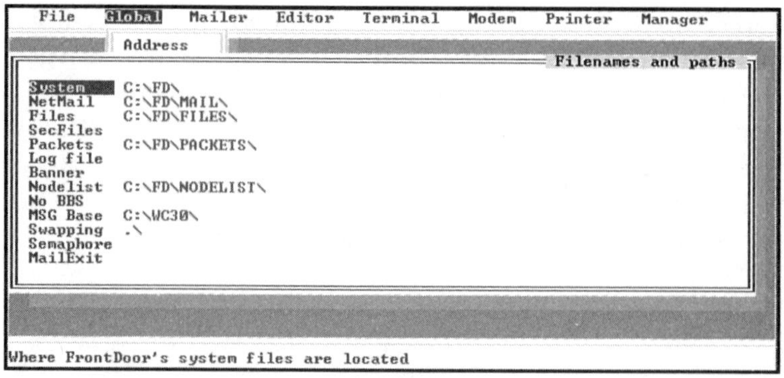

Fig. 19.3 Setting up directories in FrontDoor.

4. Tell the mailer about your modem. The mailer needs to know which port and speeds to use, how to initialize your modem, and some information about how your modem responds to commands.

   In FrontDoor, select the Modem menu to set up any information about your modem. Choose Default Settings, then any of the options you want to set. You'll probably choose at least Hardware and Command Strings to make sure the values match your modem.

> **Caution**
>
> The mailer will use the FOSSIL driver's settings rather than the modem's actual *hardware* settings. The FOSSIL driver, for example, may assign your modem port 1 even if it's on COM port 4. When you're setting up the mailer to use your modem, remember to use the FOSSIL settings instead of the hardware settings.

5. Tell the mailer where you pick up mail. Enter the FidoNet address of your *uplink* (the system or systems where you get mail). You usually won't have to tell the mailer the phone number of the uplink, because it will automatically look the number up in the nodelist.

   FrontDoor uses a text file called ROUTE.FD to determine your uplink's address. Use a text editor to create this file in your FD directory. Enter the following lines:

```
Schedule @ *
  route-to 1:xxx/xxx
```

   Replace the 1:xxx/xxx in the last line with the FidoNet address of your uplink.

6. Define events for the mailer. Most of the time, your mailer will just answer the phone and pass incoming modem calls on to your BBS. At certain scheduled times, however, it has to perform other actions—called *events*. An event might run a batch file that has your mail tosser prepare any outgoing mail, activate a tape backup, or anything else that might happen on a set schedule. One event that is required by FidoNet is the Zone Mail Hour, during which the mailer accepts calls only from other mailers. In the simplest possible setup, your mailer will execute these four events (in this order):

   - The Zone Mail Hour (ZMH).
   - A post-ZMH batch file that has the mail tosser put any new mail into your message database and prepare packets of any outgoing mail.
   - A call to your local FidoNet coordinator's BBS to send and receive any new mail.
   - A batch file that puts any received mail into your message database.

   Select the Manager menu in FrontDoor, then select Events. Press Ins to add new events (see fig. 19.4). Any external event uses X in the Tag field (in this example, the second and fourth events are external) and a DOS errorlevel. See the "Putting It All Together" section later in this chapter for more information on setting and using these errorlevels. The Behavior option lets you change several options about each event (see fig. 19.5). For the first internal event in our example, you'd set the Allow nodes to pickup waiting mail option to Yes, the Attempt to pickup waiting mail option to Yes, and the Inbound Only option to Yes. The second internal event makes a call to the local coordinator, so you set Allow nodes to pickup waiting mail to Yes, Attempt to pickup waiting mail to Yes, and Inbound only to No.

7. Install and compile the nodelist for the mailer. The mailer probably includes a nodelist compiler or a "Compile Nodelist" option in its setup program.

   FrontDoor includes a nodelist compiler called FDNC. Run it from the FD directory after you've set the path for the nodelist in the Global options (see fig. 19.3).

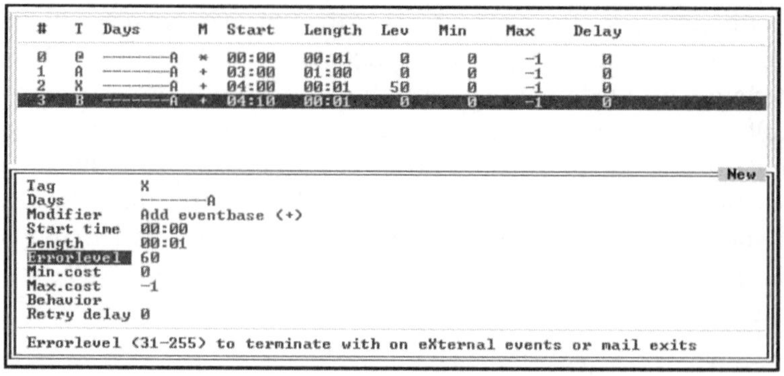

Fig. 19.4
Adding or editing an event in FrontDoor.

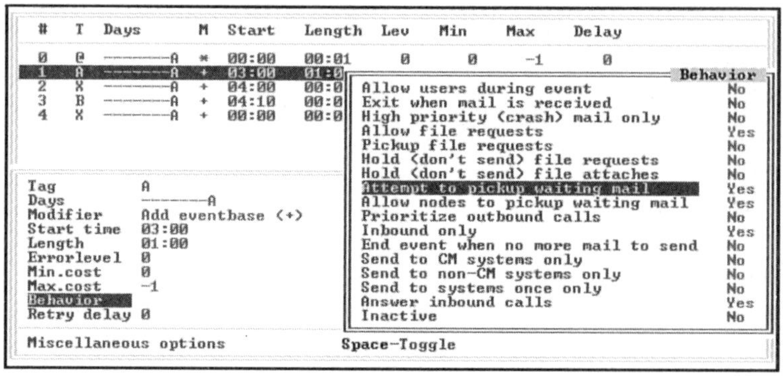

Fig. 19.5
Using the Behavior option to customize events in FrontDoor's Event Manager.

When you complete these steps, you are ready to set up your mail tosser and your BBS.

Tossing Your Mail

This section gives you the general steps to set up your mail tosser. As with mailers, each mail tosser is different, so consult your tosser's documentation for specific instructions to complete each general step.

1. Install the mail tosser software. Expand the archive file for the mail tosser into a temporary directory, then run its installation program. As with any software installation, always check the README file for any special instructions.

   For WildMail, run the WMINSTAL program.

> **Note**
>
> The installation procedure for your mail tosser may incorporate step 2 and/or step 3. WildMail! is one example.

2. Set up the mail tosser with your FidoNet address and BBS information. As with the mailer, you should use a dummy address that ends in /9999 until you are assigned an official address.

   WildMail! sets this address in the installation program. Choose the Install/Upgrade WILDMAIL! option, then select the Your primary address option (see fig. 19.6).

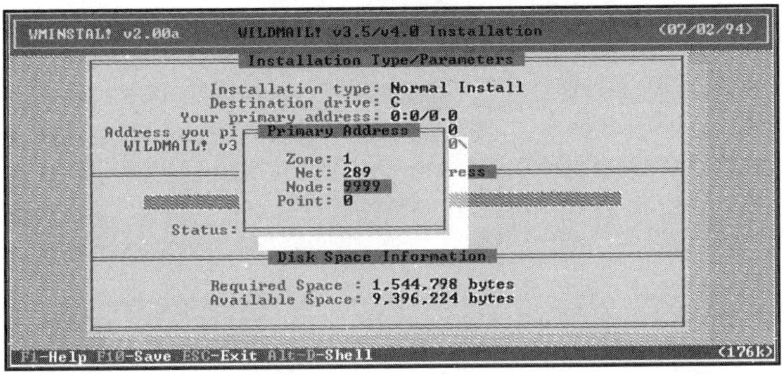

Fig. 19.6 Setting your address in WildMail!'s installation program.

3. Tell the mail tosser where you pick up mail. Enter the FidoNet address of your uplink. The mail tosser doesn't need to know the phone number, as it relies on the mailer to know how to call the uplink.

   Select the Address you pick up mail from option in WildMail!'s installation program (see fig. 19.7) and enter the address of your uplink.

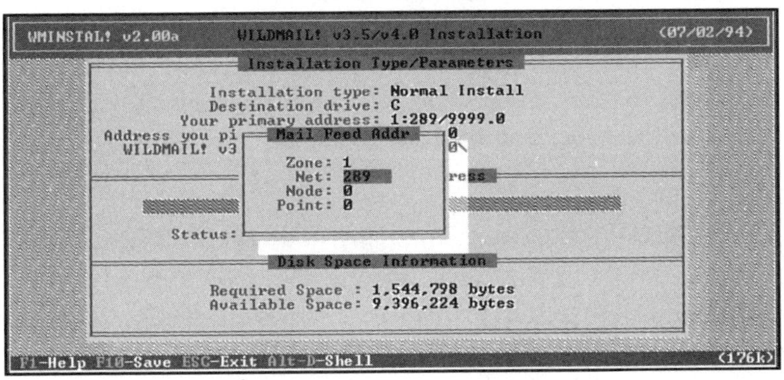

Fig. 19.7 Setting your uplink's address in WildMail!'s installation program.

4. Tell the mail tosser about your BBS. It will need to know the directories where your BBS stores its mail database and configuration files.

WildMail!'s configuration program is WMCONFIG. Choose the System Information option from its main menu (see fig. 19.8). Enter the directory names for inbound packets ("Inbound path1"), outbound packets ("Outbound path"), NetMail packets ("NetMail path"), and rejected messages ("Bad msgs path").

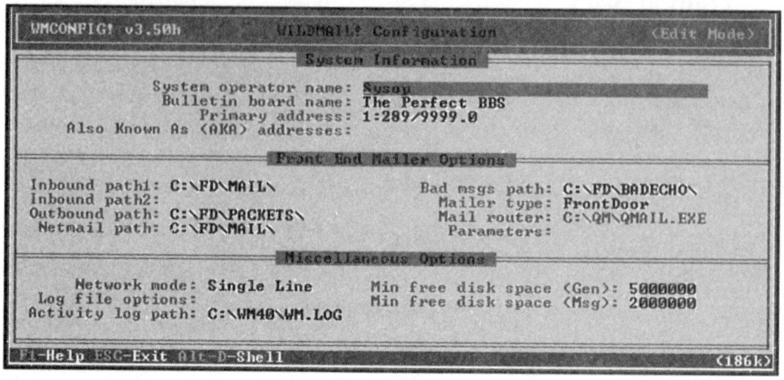

Fig. 19.8
WMCONFIG's System Information menu.

5. Tell the mail tosser about your mailer. The mail tosser needs to know where to put the packets of outgoing mail and where to find the packets of incoming mail. Set up the paths as defined in your mailer configuration program.

   In WMCONFIG, select the Mailer type option and select your mailer from the list (see fig. 19.8).

6. Set up conferences. Your BBS will have one or more numbered conferences set up for NetMail (see the next section). The mail tosser needs to know the numbers the BBS uses for these conferences. If you're receiving EchoMail, you can set your tosser to put messages from a specific echo into a specific local conference.

   Choose the BBS Specific Options selection in WMCONFIG's main menu, and set the NetMail conference number field to the number Wildcat! uses for its NetMail conference (see the "Setting up Wildcat! Lite for FidoNet" section following for more information about conference numbers).

Before you can test your tosser, you need messages to send or receive, so wait until after you've set up your BBS software and created a test message.

Setting up Wildcat! Lite for FidoNet

Assuming you've already installed Wildcat! Lite and it works with your modem, there are only three main things you have to do to get it to work with FidoNet: set up a NetMail conference, give yourself (and your users, if you choose) NetMail credits, and compile the nodelist. The next two sections show you how these steps work with Wildcat! Lite.

Creating NetMail Conferences

This section assumes you're creating a single NetMail conference, but you can take the same steps for as many conferences as you want.

1. Run MAKEWILD.
2. Select Conference Definition.
3. Highlight an available conference and press Enter.
4. In the Conference Definition screen (see fig. 19.9), enter a name (for example, "Net Mail" or "Fido") in the Conference field.

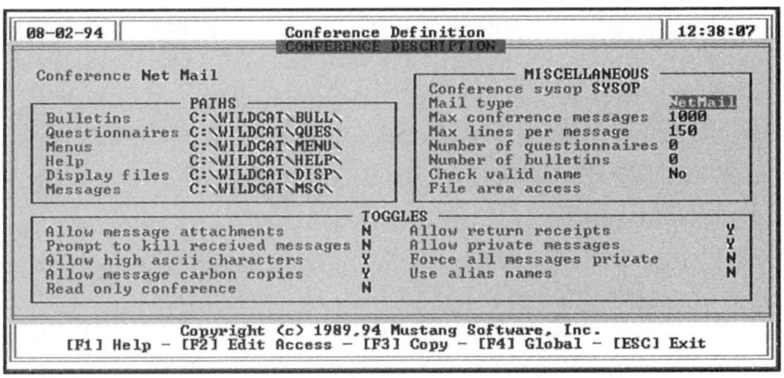

Fig. 19.9
MAKEWILD's Conference Definition screen.

5. Enter **SYSOP** in the Conference Sysop field.
6. Highlight the Mail Type field and press the spacebar to change it from Normal to NetMail.
7. Press Esc.
8. Set the access for the conference. Press F2, then highlight the user level(s) you want to be able to use in the conference (see fig. 19.10) and press the spacebar. A dot will appear beside each access level you choose. Make sure you grant access to at least the SYSOP user level.

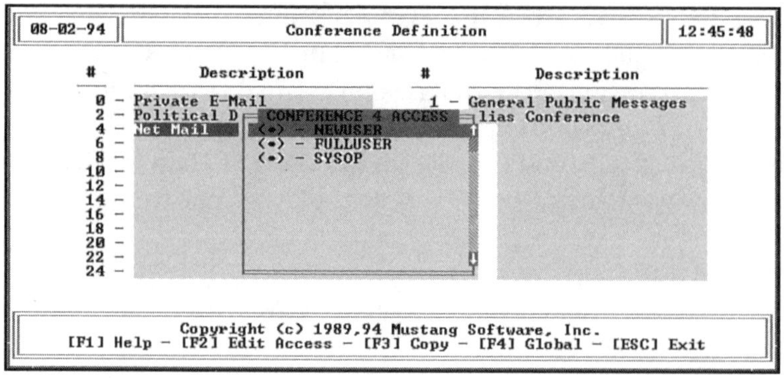

Fig. 19.10 Setting access levels in MAKEWILD.

9. Press Esc until MAKEWILD prompts you with `EXIT MAKEWILD: Are you sure?`. Highlight Yes and press Enter twice to exit the program.

Granting NetMail Credits

Your mailer and BBS software give you the ability to charge users for NetMail access. You could, for example, set up a charge of 15 cents for each message and $1.50 for each international message. If you plan to make the long distance and international calls to send out your NetMail (which could easily get very expensive), you may want to think about charging. If you're using the usual route, sending your mail to a nearby uplink to be distributed through the Fido channel, you probably won't want to hassle with charging your users.

Whether you charge or not, Wildcat! Lite and your mailer will perform some accounting for NetMail users, based on their *NetMail Credits*. In the user definition within Wildcat! Lite (along with the user's name, address, birthdate, and other information) is a field for NetMail Credits. If this is set to the default of 0, the user can't send any messages in a NetMail conference. If you're not charging your users for NetMail access, you can set the accounts up for a dummy number like $9,999.99—even if the mailer automatically debits the user 10 cents for each message, it would take a very long time to exhaust an account that large.

To set up a user's NetMail Credits:

1. Log onto your BBS with Sysop privileges.
2. Go into the Sysop menu and press **U** for users.
3. Find the user record you want to change. If you're testing the system, find your own user record.

4. Type **30** (the number of the N-mail bal. field) and press Enter.

5. Type the number of NetMail Credits you want to give the user and press Enter. If you're not charging your users, enter a large number like 999999 (which Wildcat! Lite will format to $9,999.99).

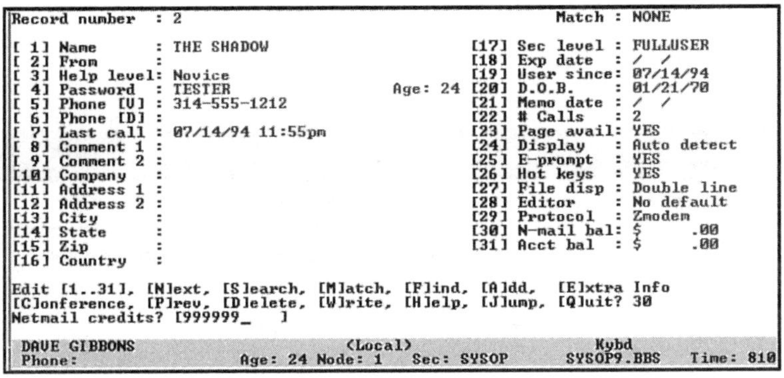

Fig. 19.11
Granting NetMail Credits to a user.

6. Press **Q** and Enter to stop editing users.

7. Logout.

Compiling the Nodelist for Wildcat! Lite

This step requires the WildNode! Nodelist compiler, available on Mustang Software's BBS and several other locations.

1. Expand the WildNode! distribution file (WNODE.ZIP or something similar) into the DATA directory in your Wildcat! Lite home directory.

2. Place an extracted copy of the nodelist in that directory.

3. Edit the WILDNODE.CFG text file. This file sets up the amount each user is debited when the user sends national and international mail. It also defines the phone numbers that should be considered local. Each entry in the nodelist includes an area code and phone number, but if you're dialing into a local number you don't want to dial the area code or the 1 for long distance. When you enter the area code and exchanges that should be considered local, the nodelist compiler strips off the 1 and the area code before any BBS number in those exchanges and strips off just the area code of any other BBS within your area code.

All the options in WILDNODE.CFG are set with different variables (see table 19.1). For example, WILDNODE.CFG uses the COST variable (with two values) to set the charge for national and international mail. To charge 10 cents for national mail (outside your local calling area) and one dollar for international mail, enter this line in WILDNODE.CFG:

```
COST 10 100
```

Table 19.1 Important WILDNODE.CFG Variables

Variable	Syntax and Meaning
NODE	The word "NODE" followed by a space and your node's complete FidoNet address.
COUNTRY	The word "COUNTRY" followed by your country code ("1" in the US).
COST	The word "COST" followed by two variables (long distance and international) showing charge in cents for each type of call. Subsequent lines up to a line that just says "END" are part of the cost table, which sets costs for specific area codes and exchanges. Use these lines to exempt local calling exchanges.
cost table lines	Two variables only—no preceding keyword. The first variable is an access code, area code, and (optionally) an exchange. The second value is the number of cents to charge for each call to that number. For example, if you are in the 314 area code and the 442 exchange, you might use a cost table line like this: "1-314-442 0" to set all calls to your local exchange to no charge. These lines must appear between the "COST" line and the "END" line.

A simple WILDNODE.CFG might look like this:

```
NODE 1:289/9999
COUNTRY 1
COST 10 100
     1-314-  20
     1-314-442 0
     1-314-474 0
END
```

This example uses a dummy node number from Zone 1, Net 289, sets the country to US (1), and sets up a cost table. The cost table sets a 20 cent charge for calls within the 314 area code, but charges nothing for any calls to the 442 and 474 exchanges within the 314 area code.

4. Run WILDNODE. It compiles the nodelist automatically (which can take a few minutes).

Putting It All Together

Now that you've set up your mailer, your mail tosser, and your BBS, you're ready to send mail—almost. Unless you want to manage the whole process manually (which is possible), you have to write up batch files to take over the management. This section lays out the logic for some of these batch files. It assumes a good working knowledge of DOS batch files, including using the DOS errorlevel and branching with GOTO statements. If you don't know how to write your own, then example batch files for various mailers and mail tossers are available on many BBSs, including the Mustang Software BBS.

A batch file to send mail (if your mailer is NOT running the whole time) follows these steps:

1. Load your FOSSIL driver. If you load your FOSSIL driver in your CONFIG.SYS or AUTOEXEC.BAT file, skip this step. For example, if you load the X00 FOSSIL driver from your CONFIG.SYS, you'll have a line like this:

   ```
   C:\FOSSIL\X00.SYS {switches}
   ```

   From your AUTOEXEC.BAT or another batch file, the line would look like this:

   ```
   C:\FOSSIL\X00.EXE {switches}
   ```

   The {switches} notation above refers to the optional command line switches FOSSIL drivers use for information about your serial ports and other configuration options. A typical set of switches might include the port's address and IRQ, the device number you want the driver to use for that port (all set in X00 with a switch beginning with the FOSSIL number), and the baud rate and parity (X00's "B" switch). For example, you could use this line to set your COM4 (this example uses a base address of 2F8 and an IRQ of 5) to FOSSIL device 1 and lock the port at 57600 bps:

   ```
   X00 1=2E8,IRQ5 B,1,57600
   ```

   Refer to your FOSSIL driver's documentation for more information about command line switches.

2. Run the mail tosser to process any outgoing mail.

3. Activate the mailer. If the mailer has a command line option to automatically send mail, use it. The connection process and mail exchange will all be handled by the mailer in this step.

4. Run the mail tosser again to process any received mail.

This type of batch file could be run from within Wildcat! Lite as an event.

If your mailer is running the whole time, answering the phone for the BBS, its batch file works based on DOS errorlevels. When the mailer runs an event (including when it receives a non-mail data call and activates the BBS), it actually closes down and sets a DOS errorlevel depending on what event it's running. It does this so your batch file can tell what's going on and branch to the appropriate section. For example, you might configure it so a "Send Mail" event sets a DOS errorlevel of 40. Your batch file would have a statement like this:

```
IF ERRORLEVEL 40 GOTO SENDMAIL
```

It would also have a subroutine called SENDMAIL, which starts with a line like this:

```
:SENDMAIL
```

A simple batch file to run your mailer and branch to two sections (one to run the BBS and one to process mail) would follow these steps:

1. Load your FOSSIL driver. If you loaded your FOSSIL driver in your CONFIG.SYS or AUTOEXEC.BAT file, skip this step.

2. Set a subroutine called MAIN that runs the mailer, branches on the two errorlevels and then jumps back to its own beginning. For example, if you set your mailer (called MAILER in this example) so it used 40 as the errorlevel for a mail event and 50 as the errorlevel for a BBS call, the MAIN section might look like this:

   ```
   :MAIN
   MAILER.EXE
   IF ERRORLEVEL 40 GOTO MAILPROC
   IF ERRORLEVEL 50 GOTO BBSCALL
   IF ERRORLEVEL 10 GOTO END
   GOTO MAIN
   ```

3. Set up a subroutine called MAILPROC that runs the mail tosser, activates the mailer to send mail automatically, runs the tosser again to process any received mail, then jumps back up to the MAIN procedure. This example shows the syntax for the WildMail! tosser and uses

/SENDNOW as the parameter that makes the mailer run a mail event and exit immediately.

```
:MAILPROC
WM SCAN TOSS NETMAIL
MAILER /SENDNOW
WM TOSS NETMAIL
GOTO MAIN
```

4. Set up a subroutine called BBSCALL that runs the BBS software (CAT.BAT in this case) then branches back to the MAIN procedure.

```
:BBSCALL
C:
CD\WCLite
CAT.BAT
GOTO MAIN
```

Note

This setup assumes you use a high-speed modem with a locked port speed. If you use a lower-speed modem that adjusts its port speed based on the connection speed, you can set your mailer to use different errorlevels for each connect message (CONNECT 300, CONNECT 1200, and so on). Use those errorlevels to branch to separate subroutines that pass the proper connection speed on to the BBS software.

5. Set up an empty subroutine at the end of the batch file, so when you exit the mailer with its "Exit" command, the batch file knows to close down. The MAIN subroutine, preceding, assumes the mailer uses errorlevel 10 when it exits (as FrontDoor does). The last line of the batch file should look like this:

```
:END
```

Summary

FidoNet is a worldwide, all-volunteer association of bulletin board systems dedicated to exchanging electronic mail, news, and files. This chapter discussed the history of FidoNet and its current state, including much of the vocabulary you need to understand documentation and electronic mail conversations on FidoNet. The second half of the chapter walked through connecting your Wildcat! BBS to FidoNet, all the way from contacting a coordinator to setting the right options in your mailer and tosser software.

Chapter 20

Connecting to the Internet

by Dave Gibbons & George Peace

No other network is as large or as remarkable as the Internet. There is no yardstick to measure its size. No effective benchmark has yet been devised to establish its effectiveness. Yet it lives and grows as we watch. The Internet is the world's largest distributed network.

Call it ARPAnet or CSnet or NSFnet after its formal roots or call it The Network. Say it is the model for tomorrow's Information Superhighway or Information Furnace. Call it what you will but it will still be Internet: the total of all the parts from which it grew. The Internet has grown from its original four interconnected networks to the many thousands of independent networks that form it today.

If you are interested in connecting your BBS to the Internet, an understanding of what the Internet is and how it is used is essential. This is covered in the first part of this chapter. After that, you will be ready to connect to the Internet following the guidance and directions in the later sections of the chapter.

Discovering the Internet

Who is credited for development and deployment of the Internet? Surely a project of this size and complexity must have a plan and a leader. We look around and see only obscure faces among the shadows of the network. We credit those many unnamed faces with the growth and success of the Internet. They came from government, academia, and business and built the network—occasionally by accident and often with reverent humor—because it needed to be done.

Accessing the Internet Backbone

Internet connectivity has long been regarded as a privilege reserved exclusively for universities and government agencies. The primary network transport, known generally as the backbone, is funded primarily by the National Science Foundation (NSF). Day-to-day operation of NSFnet, the oldest and best known of the Internet backbone transports, is provided by Advanced Network and Services, Inc. (ANS), a corporation created by NSF for this purpose.

Talking Internet via BBS

Internet access was once reserved for UNIX host systems whose revered keepers frowned upon any other access as inferior, unacceptable, and even dangerous. Ironically, that attitude accompanied comments that users and others were creating too large a load for too few UNIX hosts. The UNIX keepers worried that increasing end user access to their hosts would overload the host machines and present a support challenge they were not prepared to accept or handle. They wanted to see Internet expand into new territories but insisted on maintaining access as it had always been—exclusive and even difficult.

The UNIX/Internet keepers are suddenly discovering that their attitude must change because tens of thousands of DOS- and MAC-based personal computer BBSs are unstoppable.

The BBS is ideally suited for providing Internet access to the masses. A BBS is established explicitly to connect an end user or caller to a service. BBS services have historically focused on offering access to local message and file libraries. The BBS sysop should view Internet access as another service to offer.

The actual task of connecting a BBS to the Internet is not appreciably different than hooking up a CD-ROM drive or installing a modem. The difficulty is in understanding the new and wonderful Internet words and acronyms and translating it all to BBS. A growing number of BBS software vendors and consultants are stepping up to this challenge of connection and translation, positioning the BBS as the on-ramp to the Information Superhighway.

Several levels of connectivity are available to a BBS. They vary from the indirect method offered by UNIX-to-UNIX Copy (UUCP) over modems to more complex and capable SLIP or PPP packet connections over high-speed serial connections.

UNIX-to-UNIX Copy (UUCP)

UUCP offers site-to-site batch exchange of files. The majority of BBS connections use UUCP. The setup consists of software to schedule and supervise connections and to pack and unpack message files. UUCP is not a full-time Internet connection. It is strictly a scheduled or on-demand connection mechanism. A dial-up link is established, files are transferred, and the link is broken. All message and file handling and processing is done between connections.

UUCP-equipped BBSs use programs equivalent to the UNIX uucico program to conduct the actual connection and file transfer. There are several variations of uucico compatibility. Responsibility for compatibility rests with the sysop although many connection points, commonly known as Internet Providers, are familiar with a variety of uucico implementations and will help with setup.

Many UUCP-equipped BBSs call their Internet provider only once a day. Internet connectivity, caller perception, and value can be greatly enhanced if the BBS polls the provider frequently. Many BBSs are able to maintain the image of a full-time mail connection by polling their UUCP provider every few minutes.

Some BBSs are themselves UUCP and Internet providers. This turns BBS connectivity into a hierarchical or multi-hop environment. This typically allows more economical connections, even co-op arrangements, and off loads many second tier BBS connections from already crowded host systems. The process of becoming a UUCP provider can be either a wrenching experience or as easy as flipping a switch in already installed software. One such setup is the widely deployed Personal Internet Mail Processor (PIMP) UUCP connectivity package for eSoft's (303/699-6565) TBBS. *Boardwatch Magazine*'s Jack Rickard (303/973-6038) designed PIMP to install in minutes and offer Internet connection options on all lines for other BBSs as easily as to local callers. Any BBS running the latest PIMP can transition to being a UUCP provider after changing one parameter in one control file.

Transmission Control Protocol/Internet Protocol (TCP/IP)

TCP/IP, introduced in 1974, is the protocol used throughout the Internet backbone structure. TCP/IP is the protocol used to pass information among connected Internet nodes. TCP/IP connectivity is common to virtually all packet-based transfer protocols on the Internet.

Recent years have brought TCP/IP to Local Area Network (LAN) environments. Indeed, many enterprise networks are already registered with the Internet. They use pre-assigned unique addressing to avoid conflicts outside the enterprise. In this way, connection between the Internet and a LAN is nearly as easy as adding another server to the LAN.

Serial Line Interface Protocol (SLIP)

SLIP or TCP/SLIP is a wide-area network protocol designed to support a TCP/IP environment over serial dial-up and private lines. SLIP offers a fully-functional live Internet connection over a modem. The connection can be full-time and fully addressable from any Internet address or it can be on demand as local needs dictate. SLIP, though common for Internet connections, is not a formally-adopted Internet protocol. Its appeal stems from the fact that it is a feature of many UNIX implementations.

Point-to-Point Protocol (PPP)

PPP is also TCP/IP over serial and private lines. It is an advanced implementation offering greater throughput and error recovery than SLIP. PPP is an adopted Internet communication protocol and preferred over SLIP wherever available.

Exchanging Messages via the Internet

The Internet is not all things to all people but there are a few million folks out there who seem to take the challenge seriously. The number of information libraries and data repositories is growing at a dizzying pace and promises not to subside in the predictable future.

Internet Addressing Techniques

Whether sent via Post, express courier, or the Internet, mail must be addressed. The common format of Internet addressing is the two part user@domain format. An @ character separates the user and domain components.

The user (or left) portion of the Internet address is the name of the end user or recipient of the mail. Periods are used as separators between words instead of spaces. As a result, user Philip Brooks is addressed as philip.brooks and user Joe E Brown is addressed as joe.e.brown. Periods in user names present problems. There is no way to declare certain periods spaces and others real periods in an Internet address so user names with periods are not compatible with Internet addressing.

The domain (or right) portion of the address is a logical or symbolic address identifying a specific computer. This component has two or more sub-parts separated by periods. The order of significance is from right to left such that we can follow the domain address mycomputer.mycompany.com from high-level domain com (a commercial entity) to mycompany (the company) to mycomputer (the actual computer).

High-level domains have been established to represent types of organizations such as com, edu, gov, mil, net, and org. Other high-level domains define geographic areas around the world. Examples are us (USA), ca (Canada), and jp (Japan).

Other domain components (left of the high-level domain) are selected by the organization responsible for the individual computer.

Domain names are known as the Domain Name System. Domain name applications are approved by a central registry and tracked by a series of high-level Internet address translation systems referred to as Domain Name Servers.

Electronic Mail (E-mail)

One certainty of the BBS and Internet connection is the availability of e-mail. Internet e-mail provides a great deal of information and reward beyond traditional private person-to-person exchanges. Many of the same services available to full-time Internet connections are available indirectly via e-mail. Services include mailing lists, FTP-by-mail, and even Gopher-by-mail. Access to e-mail services and extraction of data received is occasionally a challenge but the rewards of discovery are no less than from a full connection.

Sysops will do well to consider and exploit the indirect access options available. FTP, Gopher, and other services can be available without installing a full-time connection.

Mailing Lists and List Servers

Mailing lists are variants of e-mail. A mailing list is a one-to-many reflection of e-mail messages. Messages are addressed by individual participants in a topical discussion group to a central reflector site. List server software at that site reflects or forwards the e-mail to multiple recipients.

Many hundreds of mailing lists are available via dozens of list servers throughout the Internet. Mailing lists are not an exclusive phenomenon. Any computer can run list-server software and host one or many mailing lists.

Usenet Newsgroups

Usenet is a particularly interesting part of the Internet culture. Usenet itself is a series of machines that exchange public mail messages called articles organized into topics called newsgroups. Thousands of newsgroups covering virtually all imaginable human interests flow continuously to and from Usenet sites. Newsgroup topics vary from deep academic studies to humor and poetry.

Newsgroup names are formed similarly to domain names with a small number of high-level groups leading down (left) to subgroup hierarchies. These seven high-level groups are generally available via all Usenet sites:

comp	computer hardware and software
misc	groups that don't belong elsewhere
news	general news
rec	recreation and the arts
sci	sciences
soc	social issues
talk	discussion and debate

Other high-level groups are optional and include:

alt	informal groups
biz	business
clar	subscription commercial news stories

Newsgroups can be established to be moderated, to allow open posting, or even one-way posting of articles. Moderated newsgroups are set up so that all news articles must be reviewed and allowed by the listed moderator. These newsgroups tend to maintain topics of discussion better than unmoderated newsgroups because off-topic articles can be filtered.

Accessing Data Through the Internet

Two of the most frequently requested, and certainly the most often associated with full-time Internet, connections are FTP and Telnet. Many callers are unfamiliar with the Internet but are quite certain they *need* FTP and Telnet access. This might be true of course, but it's likely that they need many other things as well. Both are quite useful services to offer or have access to and both afford no end of opportunities for discovery.

File Transfer Protocol (FTP)

This twenty-something-year-old method for transferring files is the most used feature of the Internet. Pretty much every file or document ever released for public access or download eventually makes its way to one of many hundreds of FTP servers.

BBS sysops and callers will most often be interested in public or *anonymous* FTP servers—those that allow anyone to log in and transfer files. The FTPer logs in to an anonymous FTP server as user name anonymous with the user's e-mail address as the password. Access is granted and the FTPer is presented with the system FTP prompt where commands such as DIR, CHDIR, GET, and BYE are used to navigate the directory tree and transfer files.

BBS caller file retrieval via FTP is a two stage process. An FTP *get* transfers the file from the server system to the hard disk on the BBS host computer. Once all files are transferred and the FTP session ends, the caller must download the file to the caller's own computer. Perhaps illogical at first glance, this process is the best way to handle such access. We must consider the usual difference in speed between the BBS's full-time Internet connection and the remote caller's modem connect speed. The connection and transfer between the BBS and the FTP server is handled as efficiently as the high-speed link allows and then the download transfer is handled as efficiently as that link allows. The two stages of file retrieval parallels the two different connections required to complete the process.

Remote Login (Telnet)

Telnet places second on the list of most requested Internet services. This is a process whereby an Internet user on one host machine accesses another host. This allows what many view as free access to remote BBSs and information services. This is because the Telnet session connecting the caller to the Internet host service is conducted over the high-speed Internet connection instead of over a long-distance dial-up link.

Telnet and the process of linking a caller to a remote service is also known as a data switch operation. This turns the BBS into a passive participant connecting the caller to the requested remote service. Callers connected to such a service via Telnet can read messages, download files, join chats, and do whatever else is available on the remote service. The data is simply passed through the connection.

Connecting Your BBS to the Internet

By now, you should know what pieces of the Internet will fit well with your BBS. Though it is possible to offer some of the more advanced functions like FTP and Telnet through your BBS, most BBSs offer e-mail and newsgroups because they are much easier (and less expensive) to implement. This section shows you how to exchange Internet e-mail and newsgroups with another site. The examples in this section use Wildcat! Lite, but the general logic applies to just about any BBS software you want to use.

Most of the "live" connections to the Internet (connections that are active continuously) are on UNIX systems (like mainframes) running through high-speed connections. Because you probably don't want to dedicate the resources to have such a system in your home, you'll probably have to rely on someone else's Internet connection. Unless you offer services that require a live connection (FTP, Telnet, World Wide Web, etc.), your BBS can get by with connecting to an Internet host periodically—anywhere from every 15 minutes or so to every few days—to send and receive e-mail and newsgroup postings. This section assumes you do not have a live connection to the Internet.

Note

Though you can't use FTP without a live connection to the Internet, some sites offer an FTP-by-mail function. With FTP-by-mail, you send an e-mail message with instructions to a special address at the site, then an automated mailer decodes the instructions and sends you (via e-mail) the files or file lists you've requested. Check with your Internet provider to see if this service is offered, or if they can direct you to another FTP-by-mail site.

Because the Internet is primarily UNIX-based, your host will almost definitely use UNIX. To transfer the newsgroup messages and mail between your system and theirs, you'll need a UUCP (UNIX-to-UNIX copy) program that works with your BBS. Two that work with Wildcat! are wcUUCP (by Mustang Software) and WildUUCP (by Online Computer Resources). If you read the FidoNet chapter, you saw that mail involves two functions—tossing and mailing. *Tossing* is getting the mail into and out of your message base, and *mailing* is connecting with another system to exchange mail. As with a FidoNet connection, the mailer and tosser are two completely independent programs, and the two UUCP programs mentioned previously include both mailer and tosser.

Finding a UUCP Feed

Before you can get online with the Internet, you'll need a UUCP feed site. The two most common options here are universities and commercial services. Contact any local universities first to see if they offer UUCP accounts to BBSs. You may also want to check with other sysops in your area to see how they're getting their connections. With the recent popularity of the Internet, many commercial e-mail and newsgroup providers have sprung up. Check *Boardwatch Magazine* and places like the Mustang Software BBS for advertisements. A brief list of commercial sites is also included with wcUUCP.

Your UUCP feed site will work with you to set up a domain name for your BBS (like MYBBS.COM or BOYSCOUTBBS.ORG). Any mail going to that domain name will be automatically routed to your UUCP feed site. You can set up any number of users within your domain—your UUCP feed site doesn't have anything to do with setting up your individual users.

If you plan to carry several newsgroups, you should know that not all sites carry every newsgroup. Most select several popular newsgroups—maybe a few dozen or even a few hundred of the thousands available. If you want a newsgroup that isn't carried by a potential service provider, you can ask them if they'll carry it or choose a different provider. Most of the major commercial providers carry a full selection of newsgroups, so this is really an issue for universities and smaller commercial providers.

Working with a UUCP Program

This section gives you the general steps to configure a UUCP program, with specific examples drawn from Mustang Software's wcUUCP. Each one is different, so consult your program's documentation for specific instructions on accomplishing each general step.

1. **Install the software.** This involves either installing from the distribution diskettes or expanding the program's archive file into a

temporary directory and then running its install program. As with any software installation, always check the README file for any special instructions.

wcUUCP installs from its installation disks. Just run UUCPISNT from Disk 1.

2. **Set up the UUCP software with your site information.** Important information about your site includes your name and the site's domain name.

   To enter this information in wcUUCP, run NETMAINT from your Wildcat! directory. Enter your name in the UUCP Administrator field, the site's full domain name (exactly as assigned by your provider) in the UUCP Domain Name field, and site name in the UUCP Site Name field (see fig. 20.1).

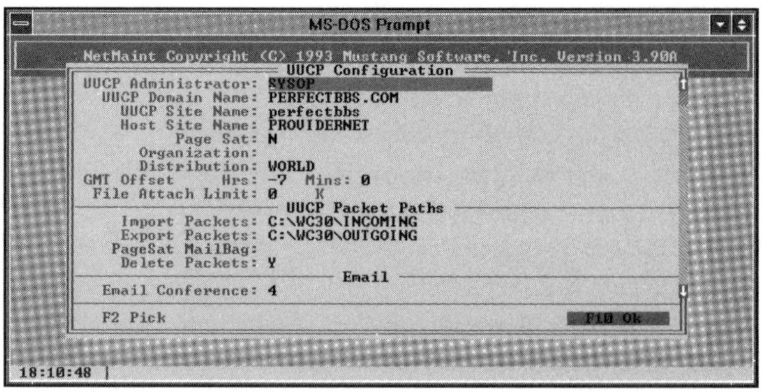

Fig. 20.1
Setting options in NETMAINT.

3. **Set up the UUCP software with your host's information.** The setup program needs to know the site name of your host, as well as the phone number and logon procedure.

   For wcUUCP, enter the host's name in NETMAINT's Host Site Name field (see fig. 20.1). The phone number and logon procedure are set up in a user-modified text file called SYSTEMS, which is automatically placed in the WCUUCP directory in your Wildcat! directory. When you edit the SYSTEMS file, you'll see that it contains its own documentation (over 50 lines of comments) with examples of several ways to set up UUCP logon procedures. Your modifications will be on two lines—one for dialing and one for the actual logon.

The first line contains the name of the site, the word "any" (a placeholder), the name of a modem definition file (a file with the extension .MDM in your Wildcat! directory), a speed, a dialing string, and the optional notation "" <CR> "", which tells the UUCP software to send returns to the host site until it sees a prompt. A typical line looks like this:

```
PROVIDERNET Any HAYES 9600 ATDT1-314-581-4683 "" <CR> ""
```

The logon procedure starts with the name of the site as well, but is followed by one or more single-word prompts and responses. The prompts come from the host site, and the responses are the answers you'd normally type at each prompt. For example, you might see a prompt "Enter your user name:" and respond with "SYSOP7". Since the prompt has to be reduced to a single word, you might pick "Enter" or "name:" for the logon procedure line in SYSTEMS. The entire line might look like this:

```
PROVIDERNET name: SYSOP7 ssword: mypass terminal uucp
```

This example shows three prompts and three responses. The second prompt will match either "Enter your password:" or "Password:".

4. **Set up the UUCP software with your modem information.** It needs to know which port and speeds to use, how to initialize your modem, and some information about how your modem responds to commands.

   wcUUCP uses .MDM files (which are user-modifiable text files) for its modem information. Refer to Step 3 for information about using the SYSTEMS file to choose a .MDM file.

5. **Set your GMT offset.** The Internet codes each message with its creation time relative to Greenwich Mean Time (GMT). Your UUCP software needs to know where you are in relation to GMT. Pacific time, for example, is seven hours before GMT (usually written -07:00), Eastern time is -04:00, etc.

   In wcUUCP, set your offset in the GMT Offset fields (figure 20.1).

6. **Define conferences in your BBS software.** Using your BBS's setup program (MAKEWILD for Wildcat!—see fig. 20.2), define your e-mail conference and any newsgroup conferences you want to use. The e-mail conference should use the "force all messages private" option, but in most cases, the newsgroup conferences should be public. Keep in mind

that you don't have to use the same name for your conferences that the Internet uses for its newsgroups—you could pick up the alt.fishing newsgroup and carry it on your BBS as "Happy Hooking," for example.

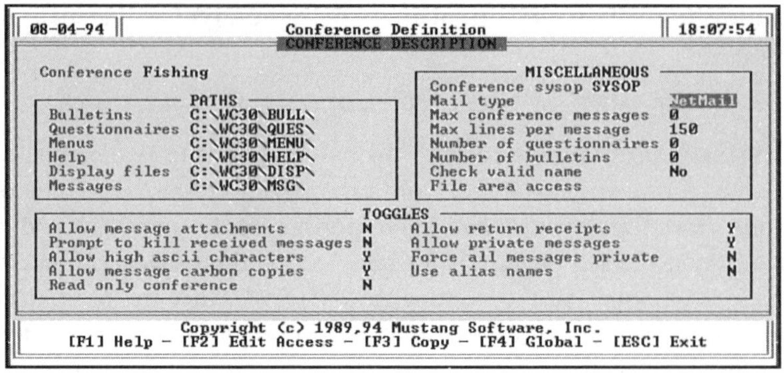

Fig. 20.2
Defining conferences in MAKEWILD.

7. **Define conferences in your UUCP software.** The tosser included with your UUCP software needs to know where to send incoming and outgoing newsgroup and e-mail messages. Set it up with the conference number of the e-mail conference. Then match up the newsgroups with their appropriate BBS conferences.

   In wcUUCP's NETMAINT, for example, you can choose newsgroups from a pick list and match them up with any numbered conference in Wildcat! (see fig. 20.3).

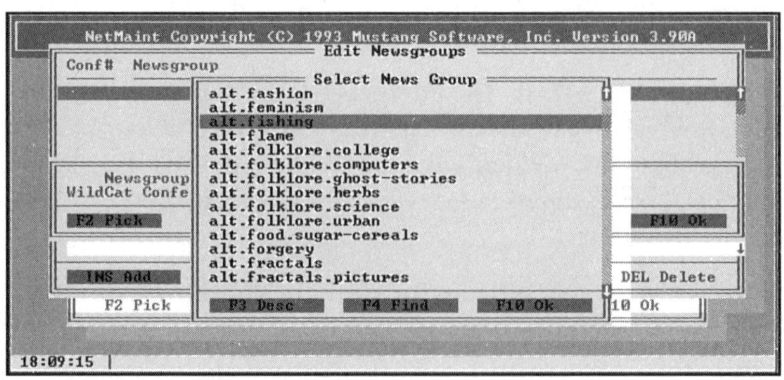

Fig. 20.3
Selecting newsgroups in NETMAINT.

8. **Set up events in your BBS software.** The BBS needs to know how often it should try to exchange mail with your provider. In very busy settings, this could be every 15 minutes or so, while if your traffic is very low, you may want to check in every few hours or even once a day.

The mailer will run on a batch file (see the next step), so set up events in your BBS software that trigger that batch file.

In Wildcat!, for example, you'd log on to the BBS with sysop access and choose Event Management from the Sysop menu. Choose A to add an event, then enter **6** to make it a batch file event (see fig. 20.4). You'll see a list of days. Choose **E** to make the event take place every day, or select the days you want to call the provider, then press **S** to save the setting. The next option lets you make the event **F**lexible (which means it takes place during non-busy hours), **S**oft (which runs the event on time or as soon afterward as it can), or **H**ard (which kicks any user off the BBS, if necessary, to execute the event on time). Pick the way you want the event to take place by pressing the appropriate letter. If you choose Soft or Hard, you'll then be asked when to execute the event. Enter the time you want the event to run, in 24-hour format. Select **S** for "**S**hell" if you want the batch file to run in a DOS shell within the BBS, or **T** for "**T**erminate" if you want the BBS to exit at the specified time. Finally, enter the name of the batch file (see the next step for information about writing the batch file).

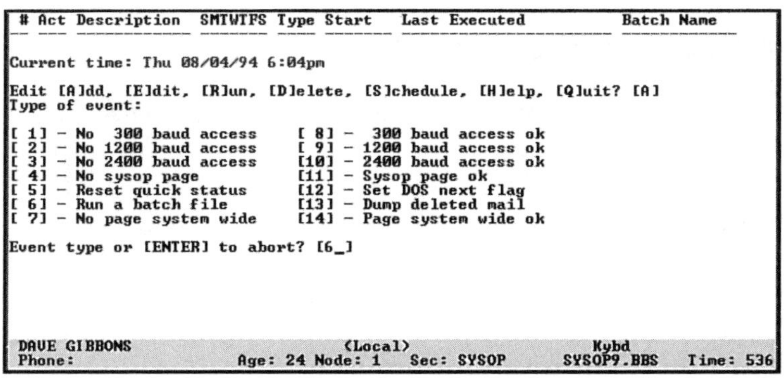

Fig. 20.4
Defining an event in Wildcat!.

9. **Create a mailer batch file.** Your UUCP software probably won't have scheduling capabilities, so it is run in a batch file by the BBS software. The batch file does the following three things:

   - Scans the message base for outgoing mail (wcUUCP uses the command line "WCUUCP /E" to export mail).
   - Has the mailer program contact the Internet provider (wcUUCP's mailer program is UUCICO).

- Tosses any new mail into the message base (wcUUCP uses the command line "WCUUCP /I" to import mail).

A simple mailer batch file for wcUUCP might look like this:

```
WCUUCP /E
UUCICO -SPROVIDER
WCUUCP /I
```

As you saw in Step 3, UUCICO uses a user-modifiable text file called SYSTEMS to define logon procedures for any of the systems you might call. Each line in the file starts with the name of a system, such as

```
PROVIDERNET Any hayes 19200 ATDT5551212 "" <CR> ""
```

which sets up the dialing parameters for a service called PROVIDERNET. You could define any number of services, each with a different name. The "-SPROVIDER" parameter on the second line of the preceding batch file tells UUCICO which of the listed services to use.

When you have completed all these steps, your BBS should activate the mailer batch file as an event per your schedule.

Live Connections

The previous section showed you how to link your BBS to e-mail and newsgroups, but what if you're a little more ambitious? You can give your users all the tools they'd find on the big online services—Telnet, FTP, World Wide Web, Gopher, and others—and it only takes a lot of money and some technical genius. If you don't have the technical genius, you may be able to use someone else's—we used IQuest, an Indianapolis-based provider with a direct link to the Internet backbone, for much of this information about the current state of live Internet connections on BBSs.

First you'll need to find a provider that offers high-speed access—and we don't mean V.Fast modems over regular telephone lines, this access is through more expensive leased lines. Don't start by calling the phone company to get your leased line, as your provider may be able to help you get special rates that wouldn't normally be available to you. Check *Boardwatch* and other BBS magazines for providers with high-speed access.

The next hurdle is the equipment. Your high-speed modems probably won't connect to leased lines (though some have both leased line and standard telephone functions), so you'll need to get at least one CSU-DSU—a purely digital modem, more or less, which sells for $500 to $1,000. You'll also need a bridge router ($1,500 or more), which is a stand-alone unit that transfers data back and forth between the CSU-DSU and an Ethernet connection. That means you'll need an Ethernet-based network to link the bridge router to the PCs that run your BBS.

The Internet is built on UNIX, so all those popular programs—Gopher, Telnet, FTP, etc.—are written for UNIX. Thankfully, most of them are free, and you even get the source code in case you want to make any changes. Of course, you'll need to base your BBS on a UNIX system to take advantage of those tools.

Tip

If you don't want to shell out the money to buy a copy of UNIX, you can get a completely functional free version called LINUX. Many systems on the Internet offer it for downloading, as do some BBSs. You can also order it on CD-ROM from some shareware CD-ROM companies.

And you'll need UNIX-based BBS software to take advantage of all those tools. Unfortunately, as of this writing there aren't any widely-available UNIX BBS packages that let you use the "live connection" functions. As with anything else, though, if the market opens up more, somebody's bound to come up with a professional package. Until then, many sysops have found themselves writing their own BBS software to provide live connections. Check with your Internet provider to see if a package is available when you read this, or if you can use some of the programs the provider had to write to get it to work.

Summary

This chapter told you about the past and present of the Internet, from its roots in the military and education to its current status as the fastest-growing community in history, and how you could be part of its future. It discussed some of the terminology and standards you'll need to know to get connected, and walked through an installation of a simple e-mail and usenet connection for your BBS. The last section told you some of the things you need to take the next step—setting up a live connection between your BBS and the Information Superhighway.

Chapter 21

Advanced External Connections

by Mark L. Chambers

In this chapter, we'll discuss the more advanced and specialized external connections currently available for bulletin boards. These services are typically more expensive than the FidoNet and Internet message network connections we've covered in previous chapters, but their potential value to your callers is also higher than just about any addition you can make to your BBS. The installation process for three of these connections—a satellite system, LAN connection, and an X.25 packet connection—involves hardware upgrades or additions as well.

It's important to keep in mind that the power and features offered by bulletin board hardware and software are constantly improving, so limitations noted in this chapter may disappear in a year or two. If you'd like to know exactly what the requirements and features are for a particular piece of hardware or software that is mentioned in this chapter, contact the manufacturer directly.

Satellite Systems

For under $1,000, would you equip your BBS with the following:

- FidoNet echoes and FidoNet file distribution areas—all of them?
- Internet newsgroups—all of them?
- Smaller networks like RIME, ILink, and RBBS-NET?
- National Weather Service weather information and maps?
- Daily national TV program listings?
- Online periodicals like *USA Today*?

If you would—and most sysops would eagerly volunteer—then consider a satellite system for your bulletin board. A satellite is the ultimate external connection for those sysops who'd like to offer *all* of the messages that FidoNet and the Internet can offer, as well as a rapidly-expanding list of secondary data (for example, TV listings and weather information).

Figure 21.1 shows a basic schematic of how your bulletin board is connected to the satellite antenna, as well as the intermediate hardware and software required to convert data so that your bulletin board program can toss the new messages into the correct areas.

Fig. 21.1
A typical BBS satellite system.

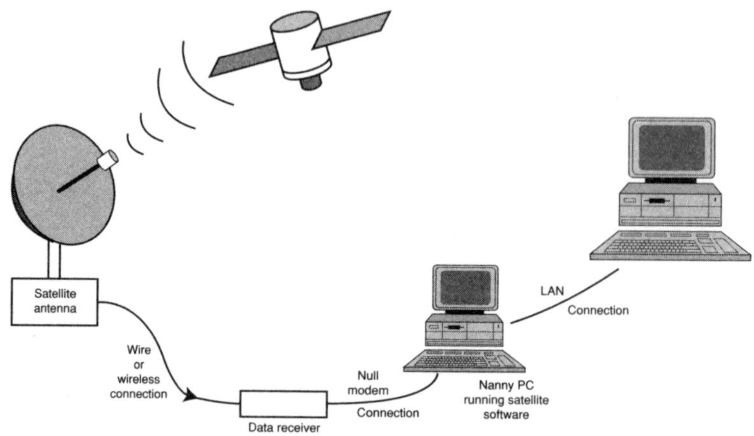

Components of a Satellite System

For many sysops, the idea of adding a satellite system to a BBS sounds far too technical and complex, while installing an outside satellite antenna would prove too difficult. In fact, the installation of the antenna itself is probably the easiest part of adding this service to your system; plus, there are surprisingly few components required to go online.

To familiarize you with the operation of a satellite system, let's examine each component in detail:

- **The satellite antenna.** Antennas for these systems operate on the C and KU frequencies. C band antennas are 6 to 10 feet in diameter, while KU antennas are 2 to 3 feet in diameter. Depending on the size, you can mount the antenna on a pole, the roof, or even a wall of your home. The antenna is connected to the receiver by a null modem cable or a wireless antenna.

- **The satellite receiver.** This is a receiver similar to those used for video satellite reception, but it handles data instead—typical download baud rates average about 19,200 baud, while some newer receivers can handle "burst" delivery at up to 57,600 baud.
- **A dedicated PC.** Unless you're able to run the satellite software under a multitasker like DESQview—which is not recommended unless your BBS PC is far faster than it needs to be—plan on purchasing a dedicated PC (usually called a *nanny* machine) to run the satellite software. The nanny PC is connected to your BBS computer with a Novell LAN or simple peer-to-peer network like LANtastic.
- **The system software.** The nanny PC will continuously run this software, which is provided by the satellite company as part of your subscription. As data is received, the satellite software is responsible for processing and saving it as mail packets and archived files.

The entire satellite system is automatic after you've configured the satellite software, synchronized the antenna direction with the satellite (which takes 15 minutes or so), connected the null modem between the antenna and the receiver (if required), and set up the message and file areas on your system. This last step could very well take the most time and effort, so make sure you allow plenty of time and add a certain number of message areas and file sections each day for a week or two.

Advantages

In addition to the sheer number of messages you receive with a satellite system, this form of external connection offers you the following advantages as well.

- **Reduced long-distance charges.** Of course, this is a primary attraction for a sysop. If you must call long distance to connect with your current UUCP provider or FidoNet host, a satellite system will save you almost all of those charges. Your BBS receives everything except e-mail through the satellite, but your board cannot upload replies; therefore, the only time you'll need to dial your UUCP provider or FidoNet host is to send outgoing mail and pick up any e-mail.
- **Continuous feed.** Your satellite system continuously updates your BBS with information as fast as the satellite company receives it, eliminating the wait between calls to your UUCP provider or FidoNet host for new messages.

- **Current weather information.** You're likely to be surprised how popular current weather maps and radar images are with your callers; you'll find many users will connect several times during the day to monitor weather changes. Of course, if you're running a profit BBS or a subscription hobby board, these services will attract additional subscribers to your system. TV listings are less of an attraction for most callers.

Disadvantages

There's no such thing as a free lunch! Satellite systems also have their disadvantages, such as:

- **Initial expense.** A satellite connection requires a large initial investment, including the antenna itself, the receiver, the local peer-to-peer network, and the nanny PC that will handle your message processing. Over time, this initial cash outlay will pay for itself in the long-distance charges you save, but you may decide that the cost and effort required to get the system running doesn't outweigh the benefits.

- **Additional hardware.** Prepare your BBS corner for expansion when you add a satellite system! You'll need as large a BBS hard drive as possible to store the megabytes of messages you'll receive, and the nanny PC will take up additional room.

- **Subscription rates.** Depending on the number of networks and secondary services you receive, you'll pay a monthly subscription to the satellite company. Current minimum subscription rates vary from around $30 to $50 per month.

- **Reliance on the satellite company.** Once you've purchased the antenna and equipment, you're essentially relying on the satellite company to provide your download feed, locking you into the pricing and service provided by that company. This may change in the future, however, as *service-only* providers could appear to offer download feeds to those who already have antennas.

At the time of this writing, only two companies offer BBS satellite services. Both of them feature similar equipment and data feeds, so contact both and check on current pricing before making your decision.

- Planet Connect Inc. Voice: 615/623-8751

- PageSat Inc. Voice: 800/227-6288

LAN E-mail and Logon Connections

Although LAN connections are usually internal to a company, they do count as external connections. In most cases, a business/support BBS attached to a LAN will offer simultaneous service to callers dialing in and users logging in over the network; the connection method is largely irrelevant because both users interact with the BBS in exactly the same way. This allows a remote user dialing in to exchange e-mail with a user logged in through the LAN. Figure 21.2 illustrates a BBS with a LAN connection.

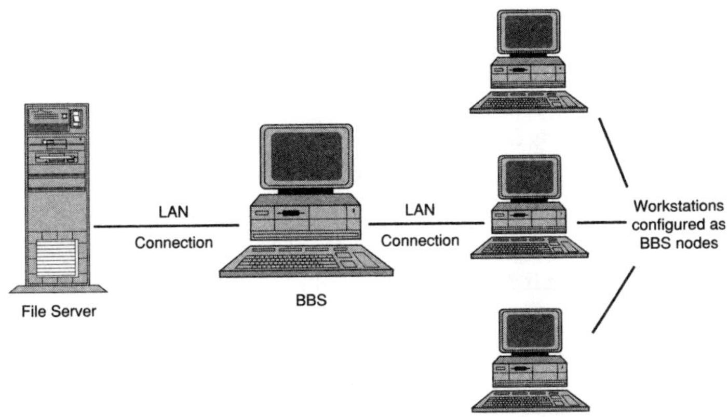

Fig. 21.2
A BBS system with LAN connection.

If you're running a multiline network BBS, of course, there's a good chance you're already offering a LAN *logon terminal* for general use. The logon terminal is simply an inexpensive PC or AT computer with a copy of the BBS program on its local hard drive (or, alternately, the terminal can run a copy of the BBS program from a network drive). Other employees with PCs on the LAN can logon to the BBS in the same manner. Your Wildcat! system supports the Novell IPX data transfer protocol for LAN communications.

Mustang Software sells a utility called WCMHS that imports and exports messages in Novell's MHS (short for Message Handling Service) format, which allows your Wildcat! system to send and receive e-mail and public messages with other e-mail and messaging systems that support MHS.

Integrated systems are suitable as company-wide LAN e-mail systems as well. The Major BBS has specialized in local LAN support for several years, and takes full advantage of Novell's IPX protocol.

A local LAN logon with a network communications software program—for example, the network version of PROCOMM PLUS—is also a good way for a sysop to upload files to be added to the board's file library and perform maintenance tasks without taking the BBS down. Throughput is usually good through a Novell LAN, with baud rates around 19,200 being normal.

X.25 Networks

Another external connection that generates a tremendous amount of caller interest is an X.25 packet link (sometimes called a *time sharing* network). This feature allows long-distance users to dial a local number and connect with your bulletin board, much like the "big guys"—online services such as CompuServe, GEnie, and America Online. X.25 providers include Sprint, Tymnet, and Autonet.

In practice, an X.25 link is quite simple. A caller dials a local access number (which is usually restricted to 2400 or 9600 baud) and specifies a host name that identifies your system—for example, if you wanted to connect to CompuServe, you'd enter the name CIS. From that point on, the caller begins the logon process, just as if the connection had been made over a modem.

In fact, the link between your system and your caller's modem actually shares a high-speed connection with other user sessions. Data blocks (or packets) from multiple calls are sent one after another in an alternating fashion, each identified by a specific host address, which allows more than one person to use the same high-speed link (figure 21.3). This is one of the reasons why large online services seem to pause for seconds at a time before responding to the commands you type; you'll also notice slower transfer rates and slower scrolling during peak hours, when your link to the online service is actually being shared by many other users.

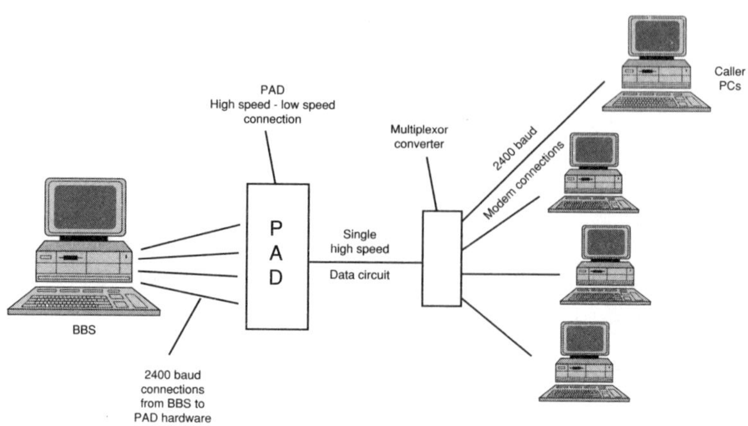

Fig. 21.3
The operation of an X.25 time sharing network.

Although an X.25 connection seems like a dream come true to your users, it's so prohibitively expensive that only the most profitable of bulletin boards can afford to offer such access, no matter how users are charged for it. The hardware required for a packet connection is quite sophisticated and expensive, while the monthly rates you'll pay often range from $500 to $1,500! Unless you're searching for a connection method for your business/support system, X.25 is almost certainly too expensive to consider.

Chat Links

Another external connection that has arrived recently on the BBS scene is the *chat link*. The idea behind linking multiple chat systems on multiple bulletin boards is a simple one, and it has proven very popular with users: it's much more fun to interact online with 250 users around the country than it is to chat with five users logged in locally on the same BBS! As we described earlier in this book, the traditional multiline BBS oriented toward online chatting can be very popular in larger towns—but what about sysops living in rural areas?

Chat boards are particularly successful when the sysop charges for connect time, often only when the caller is chatting. The rest of the BBS is essentially free, providing extra incentive for users to connect even when they're not immediately interested in chatting; however, the BBS program usually displays a message when other users logon, so it's a safe bet that the caller will probably decide to chat for at least a few minutes before logging off!

Chat links are external connections patterned after the huge CompuServe CB Simulator, a familiar feature for most users of that online service. Each caller's location or home bulletin board is typically displayed before the message, making it easy for others to tell "who's where" as well as "who's who." The Major BBS and TBBS allow configurable action words and macros to be sent to others in chat, and these also work across chat links—for example, one user might use the action word "HUG" to send a virtual embrace to another, and the sentence `User 1 just hugged User 2` would be sent to every BBS connected in the chat network. These action words help generate interest and add personality to individual callers. Some systems also provide interactive "teleconference" games that can be played without leaving the chat area. The new WCCHAT module from Mustang Software brings this same functionality to version 4 of the Wildcat! BBS program.

As mentioned earlier, tying your system into a chat network involves dedicating at least one line of your system for an automated connection several nights a week with one or more bulletin board running the same BBS software (figure 21.4). Although the specific software varies between bulletin board programs, the general procedure for adding a chat link to a BBS remains the same:

1. Determine what hours you wish to offer a chat link. If you have a utility that can determine what hours of the day your BBS receives the most calls, use it to determine a period of one to four continuous hours when the link should be active; or, if you don't have such a program, monitor your BBS over the course of two or three days during the evenings and make your best guess. Traditionally, the hours of 7 p.m. to midnight are prime chat hours.

2. Join a chat link network and "sign up" your BBS for those hours. You should be able to locate a link network for your BBS on the manufacturer's support BBS; leave a public message requesting more information if necessary. If the manufacturer has a support newsletter or magazine, check it for chat link advertisements.

3. Since a chat link typically requires only a single line for the connection to your network host, select one of the last lines in your hunt group and configure your link software to take control of that line at the appointed hour. If chatting is particularly popular, you may consider offering it every day—otherwise, it's recommended that you offer your chat link at least two nights during the week, and always provide it on Saturday.

4. Most link programs use a simple script that you write yourself (or a standard script supplied by the BBS manufacturer) to dial the other system and logon as a chat network member. If you need to customize this script or schedule an event to trigger it, do so now.

5. At the next scheduled chat period, check to make sure your BBS dialed out correctly, and join in the chat. If anything seems difficult to follow, consider writing a simple help file that you can distribute to your users to educate them on how the chat link works.

6. Once the link has started and stopped automatically with no problems, advertise your new service and watch your users enjoy themselves!

The larger chat networks use SprintNet or other X.25 packet networks for the lowest possible hourly connection costs—typically as low as $1.50 to $2.00

an hour for members. Members of smaller chat networks dial other members directly, hoping that the interest and user activity generated by a chat link will pay for the long distance call in subscriptions.

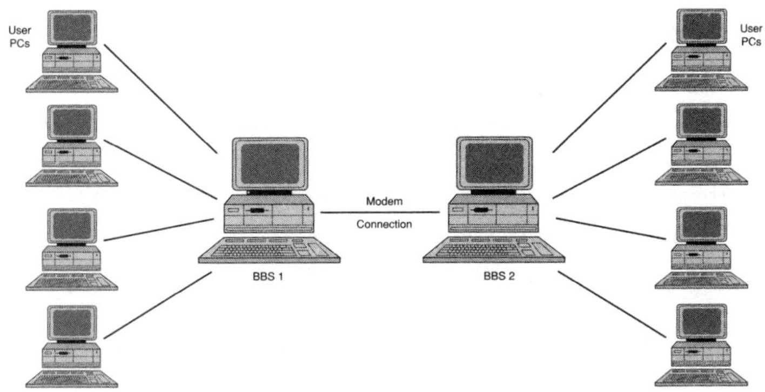

Fig. 21.4
A BBS chat link connection.

This technology is also a growing favorite among sysops because it provides a method of tapping the popularity of the largest boards specializing in multiline chat without the expense of offering 16 or 32 lines. Chat networks also solve a problem that has plagued the sysops of multiline chat systems for years: how do you maintain user interest in chatting when few or no other users are online at the same time? As a member of a chat network, you're virtually guaranteed that your users will have a respectable number of other callers available to chat.

If you're running Galacticomm's Major BBS, a popular network is the ChatLink/NetACCESS nationwide service, which advertises rates of as low as $1.50 per hour. This service even offers electronic mail (complete with attached files) and over 200 separate discussion forums. In a similar vein, eSoft's TBBS program can be upgraded with the UltraChat link module, and several TBBS sysops have organized their own direct-dial chat networks.

Outdial Connections

Next, we'll cover a new external connection that promises to greatly expand the range of user applications for multiline bulletin boards—the *outdial connection*. This term refers to modules being offered on integrated BBS programs like the Major BBS and TBBS that allow your users to take control of one of the bulletin board's telephone lines and call other systems. So far, the process sounds very similar to a chat link connection—however, the big difference is that the caller is not hooked automatically into a chat function. Instead, the BBS acts much like a terminal program, and simply routes data (including ANSI color graphics) between the remote system and the user.

In effect, your caller has used your BBS to connect to another system, and your BBS "disappears" from the scene until the connection with the other remote system is broken. Typically, the caller terminates the connection by either selecting the Goodbye function on the remote BBS, or presses a sequence of characters to alert the outdial program that the modem should disconnect from the remote BBS. Figure 21.5 shows a typical editing screen from a TBBS outdial program; you can see the strong resemblance it bears to a terminal program "phone book."

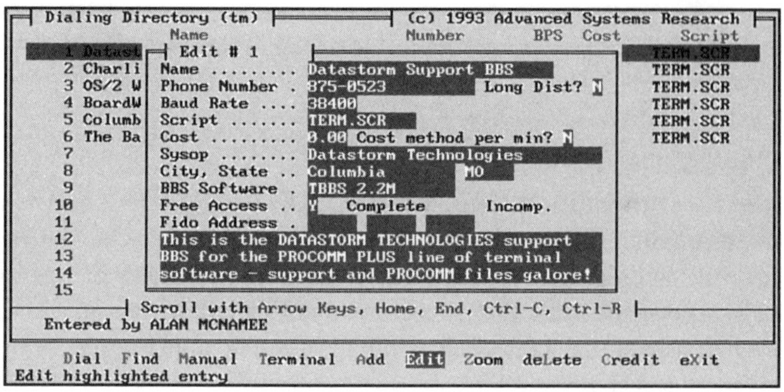

Fig. 21.5
A "Dialing Directory" provided by an outdial program.

Although most outdial programs are operated by your users, the connection can also be automatic; for example, if our hypothetical Digital Mozart BBS system did not have the hard drive space for an extensive selection of online games, you could link an outdial program to the menu command "Play Games." Whenever the command is selected, the outdial program automatically calls another local BBS that specializes in online doors, the caller logs in and begins using the doors on the other BBS. Other than the delay needed to initialize the modem and dial the other system, your user need not even be aware that the connection is being made.

In this same vein, integrated systems like TBBS and the Major BBS can use outdial connections to provide true external DOS doors. As you learned earlier in the book, these integrated programs can't drop completely to DOS, so they normally can't use the standard DOS external door programs available to network BBS programs. However, if you use an outdial module, a null-modem cable can provide a serial connection to a second PC dedicated to running doors. In practice, the serial connection is almost instantaneous, so your users may not even realize they're using doors that actually reside on a second PC.

Profit bulletin boards can charge for outdial access, and these programs also make sense for business and support systems. Subscribers and employees can make a local call to the BBS and use the outdial program to connect to a long-distance host system, thereby avoiding the charges for a direct long-distance call.

Passthrough Connections

Our last connection type is brand new and rather specialized, but it delivers something that takes advantage of a very popular innovation in the game software industry: user-to-user passthrough connections for "head-to-head" modem games.

If you've never enjoyed a modem game like the wildly successful DOOM, the connection involves one player calling another from within the game itself (usually with the most basic of modem controls). The player being called instructs the modem to automatically pick up, and the game synchronizes the transfer of data between the two players so that they can play interactively. As modems become more and more plentiful and game software becomes more and more complex, most game players would rather connect and compete with another human being than the game's built-in computer player.

Recently, modules and programs have become available for multiline integrated systems like TBBS and the Major BBS that allow callers to link up directly over separate lines on the BBS to play these games. When such a *passthrough* connection is made, the BBS acts much the same as it does during an outdial session—it simply allows data to flow between the two separate lines without changing or adding characters to the data stream. Some passthrough programs offer extensive features like paging (where your callers can send each other requests to join in a game) and a "waiting for a player" display (so potential players can see who's online and what game title they'd like to play).

Although passthrough connections are highly specialized, they do demonstrate how BBS developers are constantly exploring new connection technologies—if an application or its data can be transmitted over a serial connection, chances are that someone is working on bringing it within the grasp of BBS sysops!

Summary

In this final chapter, we've explored the less common methods of extending your BBS services through external connections. You learned what components make up a satellite-BBS connection, as well as several advantages and disadvantages of adding a satellite to your system. We examined the possibilities for using your BBS as a company-wide LAN e-mail system. We also covered the advanced (and expensive) X.25 network and how it provides long-distance callers with transparent local access to your BBS. We introduced the idea of chat networks that allow your users to chat in real-time with users of other systems. Finally, we explored the outdial external connections currently being offered on modular BBS programs and passthrough connections that provide the ability to pass data from modem-based games between users.

Although these advanced external connections will require much more time and expense than a simple FidoNet or Internet connection, their rarity may make them worth adding to your system—in a world of competing bulletin boards, most of which offer almost exactly the same services, it's important to stand out as a high-tech leader to attract more users!

Part V

Appendixes

Appendix A

Popular Bulletin Board Packages

by Mark L. Chambers

In this appendix, you will learn about the top commercial, shareware, and freeware bulletin board packages available today. These programs are generally considered to be the best available, and—since new BBS packages are appearing every year and there's no way to include a description of each—they make a good cross-section of the myriad of BBS software from which you can choose. You'll note that most of these programs also provide features and advantages unique to that particular program.

Commercial Systems

As you learned earlier in this book, commercial bulletin board software is generally:

- **More reliable.** Like most other commercial applications, the commercial BBS software you purchase has been tested in-house and by beta testers outside the company. A BBS program is online 24 hours a day—so imperfections usually show up quickly—and the sysop community is a close-knit group, so if a particular commercial bulletin board package is prone to errors, it won't last long in the marketplace.
- **More powerful.** Commercial BBS software can handle more lines and offers more features than shareware and freeware packages. Instead of the one or two programmers who typically develop a shareware program, a BBS software manufacturer can devote considerably more money, resources, and skilled-employee hours into the development of a commercial package.

- **Better supported.** A commercial bulletin board package is likely to provide better documentation and technical support, and there's also a very good chance it will be better supported by third-party programs like doors and utilities. Many commercial bulletin boards take a "one package" route, and provide everything they have with the BBS program itself; other programs offer the BBS as a base package, and offer additional functionality in modules that you can buy separately.

- **More expensive.** Naturally, you'll be paying extra for the preceding advantages! As you learned earlier in the book, most commercial BBS programs are offered in varying line counts: the more lines the software will support, the higher the cost. Some manufacturers provide a discount when trading up to a higher line count, while others credit you with the full price of the original software when upgrading.

Wildcat!

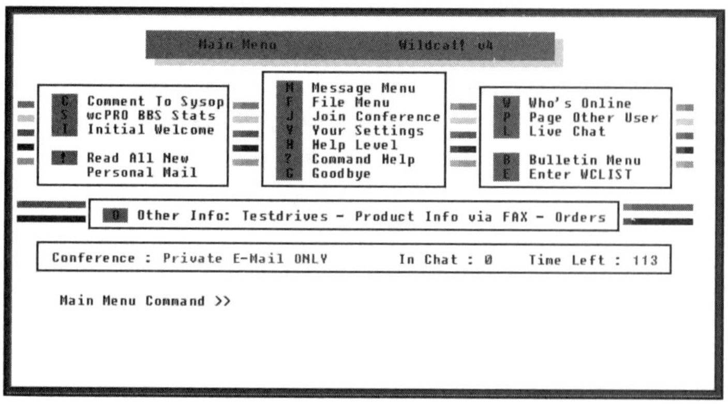

Fig. A.1
A representative Wildcat! menu.

Manufacturer: Mustang Software, Inc.
Voice telephone number: 805/873-2500
Current version number: 4.0
BBS type: networked
Maximum line count: 250

One of the oldest networked-PC BBS programs available today, Wildcat! began as a system that appealed to sysops of business/support systems. The earliest versions of the program stressed electronic mail features, making it a standout for those who wanted to supplant their office electronic mail system with a BBS system for remote users. Wildcat! used a standard menu design that you can still see reflected in Wildcat! Lite, with hardcoded menus and commands. In effect, Wildcat! bulletin boards in the past looked very much alike in their command structure and layout.

With the recent release of version 4.0, Wildcat! has provided BBS sysops with a new level of tremendous versatility and power. Menus and BBS command keys are now totally configurable and the sysop has a set of standard Wildcat! functions that can be performed anywhere within the menu structure (instead of only from certain menus). The new WCCODE module—which is modeled after the BASIC programming language—allows you to completely customize your BBS with exactly the features and functions you need. WCCODE programs can operate as doors, events, or even appear as "seamless" commands inside your Wildcat! system. In other words, Mustang Software now provides what may be the ultimate in "design-it-yourself" BBS programs (along the lines of TBBS and version 15.x of PCBoard).

The Wildcat! file library system has traditionally been a very strong advantage. Wildcat! was a leader in delivering support for file tagging and extended descriptions, and version 4.0 provides support for CD-ROMs (vastly improved over earlier versions) and automatic addition of external file descriptions. Along with the ability to provide GIF "thumbnails" (which allow a caller to determine whether or not to download a particular GIF image), WildCat's file library system remains the best of any commercial BBS program. Other advanced features new with version 4.0 include spell checking for messages and scrollback for the sysop console.

As in Wildcat! Lite, external DOS doors are available, and you'll find a large number of third-party utilities available. The improved WCPRO, which is also available from Mustang Software, provides a fully-integrated screen development system, which allows you to mock up a complete BBS design in a short time, edit and refine it, and finally test it just as your callers will see it! Other modules include WCGATE (a combined Internet, QWK mail, and MHS mail connection package) and an enhanced CHAT module. Mustang will offer all of these individual modules bundled together in a single box—and, if you're serious about your BBS and its capabilities, the BBS SUITE is a singular advantage by itself!

Summary: Wildcat! is probably the most advanced BBS program available today, and Mustang Software has a proven record of continuing feature upgrades, technical support, and customer service. The program is an excellent all-around system especially suited for networked multiline bulletin boards centering on file transfers and doors.

The Bread Board System (TBBS)

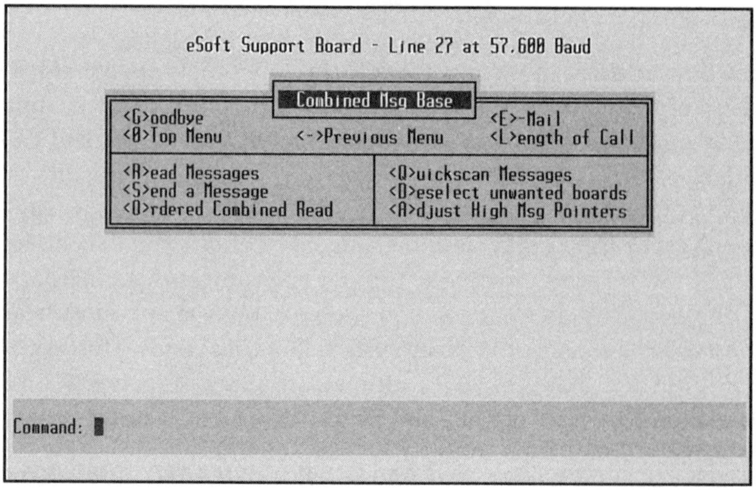

Fig. A.2
A representative TBBS menu.

Manufacturer:	eSoft, Inc.
Voice telephone number:	303/699-6565
Current version number:	2.3
BBS type:	modular
Maximum line count:	96

TBBS has been considered the predominant player in the integrated BBS market for several years. When TBBS was initially released for the TRS-80 line of computers, it was one of the first systems to make widespread use of hotkeys, and it was also one of the first PC-based bulletin boards to offer an integrated multitasker.

The program is best known for its near-total configurability (hence the name The Bread Board System, which refers to the circuit board used by hobbyists to build a new device). A TBBS menu system is "built" from a selection of commands, each of which performs a certain function. On the positive side, this allows your menu structure to take almost any form and offer any commands you wish because nothing is hardcoded beforehand; the disadvantage is that some experience and study will be required before you totally master the SDL (or System Definition Language) you'll use to create your menus. SDL offers techniques that you'll find in popular programming languages, including macros and files. Until you're up to speed, however, you can use one of the three sample menu systems built automatically by the installation program. The installation program also automatically configures most popular modems for use with the BBS.

TBBS was also the first BBS to use a flexible system of security "flags" to control access to specific commands, along with a standard base access level; external doors can change these flags during a call, or they can be reset during an external event. If you've decided to charge your users, TBBS features separate billing classes that you can use to charge subscribers for online time, as well as an expiration date for each user.

Compared to networked bulletin board programs, TBBS is rather expensive, but callers appreciate its ease of use. High on the user-friendly list is the TBBS message base, which has been copied by many shareware BBS packages. At the time of this writing, file handling is mediocre, with no built-in support for file "tagging" or advanced CD-ROM features like copying a ROM file temporarily to the hard drive (except through an external door).

External door modules for TBBS are written in TDBS (or The Data Base System), a complete dBASE language that is functionally very similar to dBASE III Plus. If your primary interest as a sysop is in providing large amounts of database information online for quick search and retrieval, this is an excellent BBS package. Although game doors are available for TBBS, there are less of them than you'll find for the Major BBS. You'll also find there are fewer third-party programs available for TBBS.

Most of the expansion possibilities for the basic TBBS package are offered by eSoft directly, including a .QWK mail processor called QSO, the SYSOM DOS command prompt emulator, a chat link connection called ULTRACHAT, the INTERCHANGE dial-out terminal, and a FidoNet connection package called TIMS. eSoft also sells a RIP menu configuration kit. A third-party module called PIMP is available to handle Internet e-mail and newsgroups, and at the time of this writing, eSoft is beta testing an impressive new Internet connection that will allow callers FTP and Telnet access.

Summary: Although pricey, TBBS is a BBS program well regarded for its reliability and total configurability, and it can provide an impressive line count without a network. It's especially suited for multiline bulletin boards centering on messaging and database applications.

PCBoard

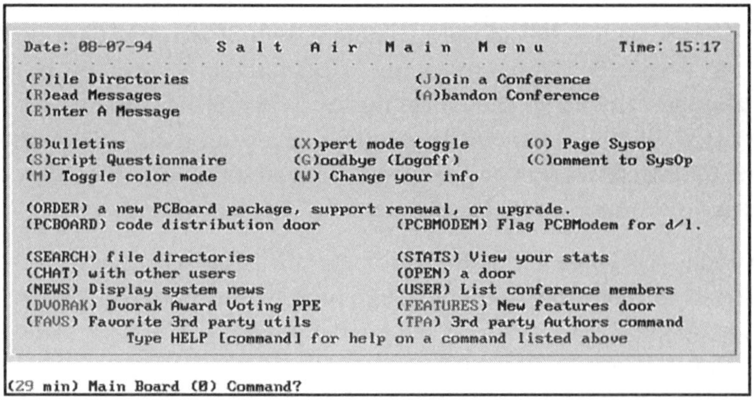

Fig. A.3
A typical PCBoard main menu.

Manufacturer:	Clark Development, Inc.
Voice telephone number:	801/261-1686
Current version number:	15.1
BBS type:	networked
Maximum line count:	Over 1000

Like Wildcat!, PCBoard is another well-known and well-respected "old-timer" in the networked BBS world that has outgrown a hardcoded menu system. It offers the PCBoard Programming Language Compiler (or PPLC) that operates similarly to WCCODE programs. PCBoard sysops can add seamless, integrated doors and commands inside their systems with PPLC, and a significant third-party PPLC developer group has quickly appeared to offer PPLC programs for PCBoard sysops who'd rather not learn the language.

PCBoard's traditional advantages are a powerful file library system, exceptional configurability, excellent door support, and a fully-featured message system. In addition, the latest revisions of PCBoard include Digiboard support, OS/2 compatibility, and RIP support within PPLC code. At the highest line counts, PCBoard is more expensive than even most other commercial programs, but it requires no additional modules or add-ons, relying instead on PPLC and external doors to provide extra functionality.

PCBoard has also long been a leader in sheer message and file capacity, making it a natural for profit boards with many CD-ROM drives or FidoNet and Internet connections. A PCBoard multiline BBS is a good selection for a sysop planning on adding a satellite or a large number of FidoNet echoes.

PCBoard is a favorite among experienced sysops because of its advanced configuration options, but it can confront the user with a higher-than-normal learning curve. In its default configuration, the program is nowhere near as user-friendly as TBBS or Wildcat!—therefore, if ease-of-use is important to you, plan on spending a week or two modifying menus and adding PPLC programs to simplify the look and feel of your PCBoard BBS.

Summary: PCBoard is an advanced, high-performance BBS package that appeals to experienced sysops running networked multiline bulletin boards. Although the default menu system is not the easiest to use, PCBoard delivers everything needed for a powerful BBS with a large number of lines, especially for file transfers and doors.

The Major BBS

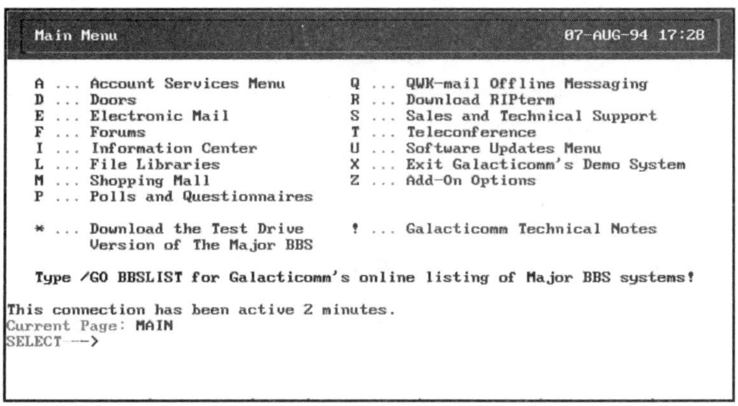

Fig. A.4
A representative Major menu.

Manufacturer:	Galacticomm, Inc.
Voice telephone number:	305/583-5990
Current version number:	6.2
BBS type:	modular
Maximum line count:	256

Like TBBS, Galacticomm's Major BBS has been very popular with sysops looking for an integrated solution to a multiline system. It runs on a single PC, it's extremely stable, and it's less costly than a local area network installation. However, the Major BBS has different strengths than TBBS, and it has been steadily improving on those advantages to set it apart from its "older cousin."

The Major BBS uses a somewhat static menu system, with some features hardcoded, but the default menus score reasonably well on the ease-of-use scale. The newest version supports RIPscrip to a higher degree than most bulletin boards—RIP menus can be automatically generated, and RIP terminal software is autodetected, just like your Wildcat! Lite system. RIPaint is even available as an option module, so you can customize your RIP screens without requiring a separate program. The Major BBS has traditionally been known for its exceptional entertainment/chat module and door games, its support for "credit" billing and subscriptions, and its sophisticated array of sysop controls and accounting reports available from the console. The Major package also boasts a robust, highly-configurable security system and a completely-revamped file library (with CD-ROM and full-screen tagging support, of course).

Major BBS external door programs are written in C, and the source code for various modules and the BBS itself is available for a price—therefore, third party game, utility, and database door programs are much more plentiful for the Major BBS. In fact, if you have the money and the need, the Major system can be outfitted with an amazing number of features through modules provided directly by Galacticomm. These modules include the entertainment and chat package (which includes chat link support), a new search and retrieve database with GIF graphic support and Boolean keyword search, a complete online shopping system, a dial-out module that allows users to use your lines to connect to other systems, and a fully-featured Internet mail connection. Galacticomm also sells its own multiport serial cards and hardware.

Although the installation program offers considerable power in determining the structure of your default system, the Major BBS is suited more for experienced and advanced sysops. A beginning sysop can eventually take full advantage of the Major BBS, but the power and flexibility of the BBS program will take time for a novice sysop to harness. The accounting options available within the Major BBS will prove invaluable to sysops operating profit bulletin boards.

Summary: Galacticomm's Major BBS is well suited to sysops of profit bulletin boards, as it has a sophisticated billing system—plus, it offers all the services a profit BBS sysop needs to attract and keep users. The strongest advantages of this package include its online chat module, a wide variety of third-party door selections, its online shopping module, and the new graphical search and retrieve module.

Synchronet

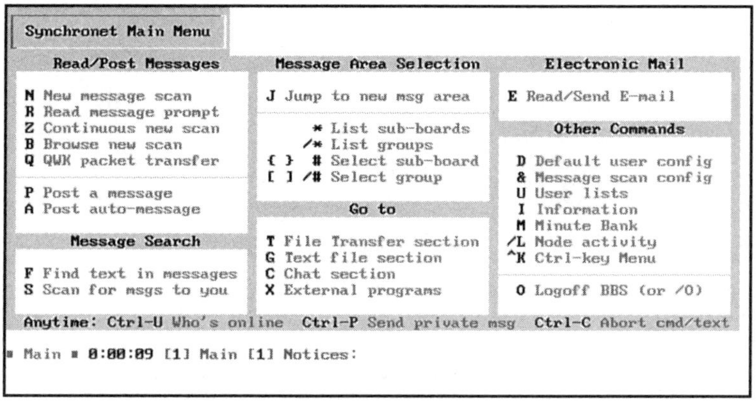

Fig. A.5
A representative Synchronet main menu.

Manufacturer:	Digital Dynamics
Voice telephone number:	714/529-6328
Current version number:	2.0
BBS type:	networked
Maximum line count:	250

Digital Dynamics made quite a splash a few years ago with the introduction of Synchronet, and it has built a dedicated following. Like PCBoard, Synchronet includes everything it has to offer in a single package with no option modules to expand the functionality of your system, and version 2.0 includes a programmable command and menu language called Baja that mirrors PPLC. Like Wildcat! and PCBoard sysops, Synchronet owners can write programs in Baja to customize the menu structure, add functionality, or create integrated doors—however, it's much less expensive, with a full 250 node license for under $500.

Synchronet stresses its extensive connectivity, with built-in support for QWK mail and QWK networking, RIME/PostLink, FidoNet, incoming fax, and Novell LAN connections. The program also has a distinct advantage in the area of serial ports because it can use a fossil driver to provide up to 10 lines—just in case, though, it provides support for Digiboard multiport serial cards as well. Advanced features include caller ID support, RIP graphics, and an upcoming OS/2 version.

The Synchronet system is well suited to sysops of any experience level—it's well designed, easy to configure, and the default system makes a good starting point for a beginning sysop. The command structure is intuitive and fast, so most users will also find Synchronet easy to handle. While the program provides only mediocre multiline chat support, Synchronet is well known as an excellent external DOS door platform (providing direct support for 11 different door data files).

Summary: If you're interested in external connections, give Synchronet a try—this BBS provides an inexpensive platform for any sysop concentrating on providing a wide range of messages from nearly any source available today. You can also look to Synchronet for continued additions of "cutting edge" technology like caller ID and fax transmissions.

Searchlight

Fig. A.6
A typical Searchlight menu.

Manufacturer:	Searchlight Software, Inc.
Voice telephone number:	800/988-5483
Current version number:	4.0
BBS type:	networked
Maximum line count:	unlimited

Searchlight Software wants you to think of a single BBS program when you consider RIP, and if you're interested in providing your users the latest in a BBS graphical user interface, their Searchlight BBS is the most integrated RIP platform available on the PC. Searchlight cannot only generate automatic RIP menus—it's currently the only BBS capable of displaying RIP graphics on the sysop console screen at the same time they're sent to the caller! Of course, ANSI and ASCII are also supported for those users who just don't seem to need all the graphical niceties provided by RIP.

This comprehensive RIP support is especially welcome in the Searchlight file library, which features Windows-like scroll bars, point and click tagging, and a full group of command buttons to replace a traditional menu. Another

Searchlight advantage in the graphics area affects sysops who offer DOS text applications online as doors. Unlike other bulletin boards, Searchlight doesn't require a "doorway" redirection program. It has built-in direct video support, so it's easier for you to offer your users special applications that wouldn't be available otherwise.

Searchlight appeals to beginning sysops, with an excellent default menu system; if you'd like to customize your menus, however, the program allows you to configure them with any number of commands in any order. DESQview is the multitasking software of choice, and Searchlight offers an unlimited number of lines on a network for less than $400, so expansion should pose no problem! Searchlight includes only FidoNet capability built-in, so you'll require third-party programs to provide Internet and QWK connectivity. The Searchlight message base is quite good, and the file library offers tagging and comprehensive keyword search functions.

Summary: If the idea of a graphical BBS makes your heart beat faster, look no further than Searchlight. Even without RIP, Searchlight is a fully-featured, well-established BBS package—although it lacks some of the advanced features offered by more expensive programs, it makes a good choice for a beginning sysop.

Shareware and Freeware Systems

Shareware and freeware BBS programs are generally not used by larger multiline bulletin boards, but they offer the following advantages of their own.

- **Less costly.** Unlike their commercial counterparts, most shareware BBS programs are usually not "crippled" or limited, so you can try them in a full configuration immediately. Once you decide to register a shareware system, it usually runs hundreds (and even thousands) of dollars less than a commercial BBS with the same number of lines. As mentioned earlier in the book, freeware BBS programs like DLX are distributed without cost, but typically with little or no technical support except for help from other sysops running the same program.

- **Latest technology.** Surprisingly, shareware and freeware programs usually offer the latest technology—for instance, fax support and CD-ROM handling—quite a bit earlier than commercial BBS programs. Since a shareware program is usually developed by one or two programmers, new technology can be implemented much faster.

- **Source code.** Freeware bulletin boards like DLX and RBBS often provide the BBS sysop with original source code, allowing you to modify the BBS as you like.

DLX

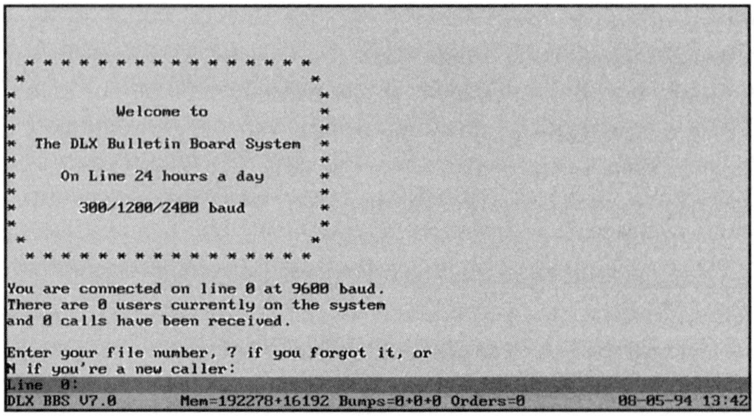

Fig. A.7
The DLX sysop console.

Manufacturer:	Freeware. Available from CompuServe.
Current version number:	7
BBS type:	integrated
Maximum line count:	32

DLX is a popular bulletin board package that specializes in multiline chat services, and as such, it's a great representative of the species. Unlike the other BBS programs we've discussed, DLX requires far less in the way of RAM, hard drive space, and system horsepower. At the same time, its file library is quite limited, and its public message base is nearly non-existent. Yet, DLX was a success as a commercial BBS system—its author recently released it into the public domain as freeware—and it has a large following. Why?

The answer is the recent surge in popularity of online chat, leading to hobby and profit systems built around a social theme. Callers connecting to a DLX chat BBS don't expect to transfer files or exchange static messages on a traditional message area—instead, they're calling to communicate in real time or exchange electronic mail, and the functionality that allows them to do so in DLX is extremely powerful and well designed!

DLX users have access to two different types of online chat: *private* chatting between individuals (where no one else on the system can read what's being typed) and *public* chatting, which works much like the CompuServe CB simulator or a large chat link network (all users can participate). Much like a sysop chatting with a user, DLX sends each character as its typed in a private chat.

On the other hand, public chat text is sent line-by-line to everyone as soon as a caller presses Enter. Public chat can be further subdivided into *channels*, each of which can be joined or abandoned, and users can be *paged* on other lines to join in the fun. DLX also carries the same design to system electronic mail, which can be either private between individuals or public to all; public mail can be divided into categories, so DLX does provide a rudimentary message base of sorts, but with nowhere near the number of commands and features offered by most other bulletin boards.

Another distinct advantage to the DLX system is its ease-of-use for both sysop and caller. DLX is a breeze to setup in its default form, with no separate configuration program; however, you can alter the behavior of the system through a parameter file if necessary. Many DLX sysops operate systems with no changes to the default configuration. The sysop can modify a basic set of system display files, but the area where most DLX sysops spend the most time customizing their systems is the system prompts file, which can be changed with any text editor. These custom prompts can go a long way in adding to the atmosphere and fun of a DLX social BBS.

Another important DLX feature is its support for five multiple choice-style questionnaires and one essay-style questionnaire. As we discussed earlier in the book, matchmaking doors are popular among social bulletin boards, and the DLX questionnaires fulfill that function; users can "browse" the answers provided by others, constantly opening up possibilities for new online relationships. These questionnaires can also perform other tasks, such as an online voting booth, new user registrations, and even taking subscription information.

Summary: Although DLX is severely limited when it comes to file and message support, and it doesn't support doors, it performs the task for which it was designed perfectly: it creates an online meeting place where up to 32 users can meet, chat, and interact! The source code for DLX is now publicly available for free, so if you're a programmer, it can be modified (and even redistributed) without royalties—expect to see a number of DLX-clone BBS packages in the future, each of which will likely have different additional features added to the original code.

Spitfire

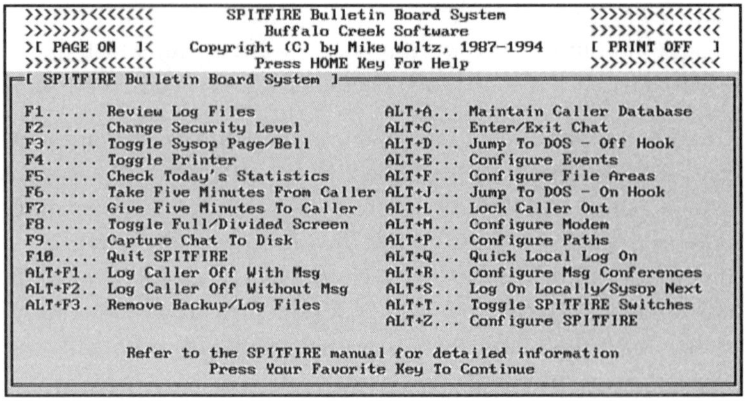

Fig. A.8
The default Spitfire main menu.

Manufacturer:	Buffalo Creek Software
Voice telephone number:	515/225-9552
Current version number:	3.5
BBS type:	networked
Maximum line count:	255

Spitfire is a well-respected shareware BBS that concentrates on ease-of-use (especially from the sysop's standpoint), and it's representative in features and appearance of most of the shareware bulletin boards available today. Installing a Spitfire BBS is as simple as unarchiving the program files, editing the BBS batch file, and typing SF—the BBS automatically creates its own subdirectory structure, prompts you for your personal information, and creates your userlog entry. In fact, unlike other BBS programs, Spitfire doesn't have a traditional external configuration program; any changes you need to make to the program's operation are handled from the Waiting for Calls screen or the program's command line.

This extremely simple setup and operation makes Spitfire a particular favorite among beginning sysops, as well as those who don't want to devote a large amount of time making changes or don't feel they need to customize a BBS. Spitfire can be run on a LANTASTIC or Novell network, so it provides a high maximum line count. The program also runs under Windows 3.1 or under DESQview, so it makes a good choice for sysops who cannot dedicate a PC entirely to a BBS.

The downside to this ease of use is that Spitfire lacks some of the advanced features offered by more complex BBS programs, and a sysop has less opportunity to fine tune the operation of a Spitfire BBS. For example, the Spitfire system supports only external events, and with far less flexibility than programs like Wildcat! The program supports only a few preconfigured modem types. Basic security features are provided, and they should be sufficient for you and your callers, but Spitfire lacks advanced security settings for co-sysops or sigops. CD-ROM support is limited, with no option to copy files temporarily to the hard drive for downloading. Compared to most BBS software, the program's default ANSI menus are utilitarian, and it also provides only a limited number of display files and insertion parameters.

Even with its simple design, Spitfire incorporates most of the features we've covered in this book, including RIP support. With a class 2 faxmodem capable of adaptive answer, Version 3.5 even allows your BBS to accept incoming fax transmissions!

Summary: Spitfire makes an excellent beginning hobby system, and it's easy to setup your entire BBS within half an hour! If you'd like to offer your callers online external doors, local message bases, and a file library service with a minimum of cost and trouble, Spitfire is a proven and well-supported choice!

PowerBBS

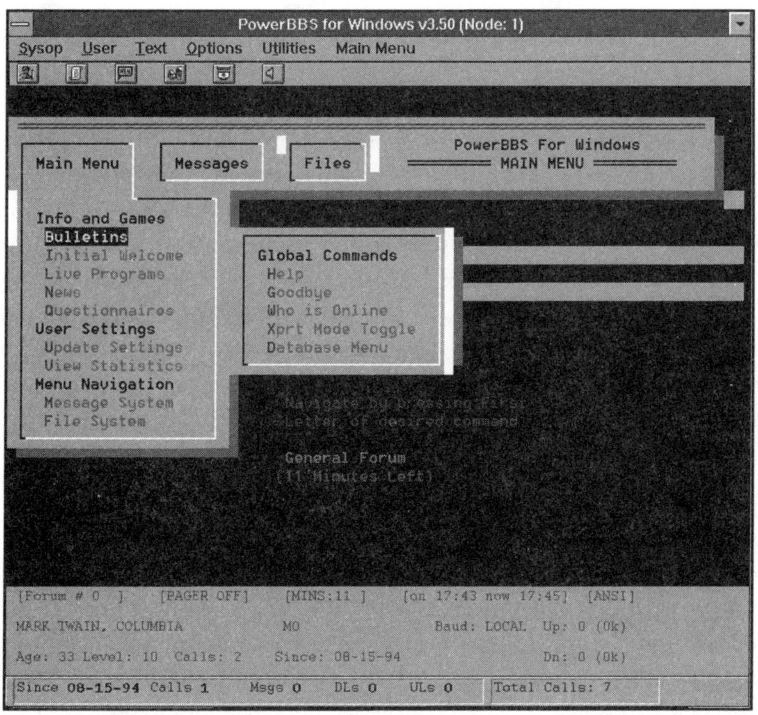

Fig. A.9
The default PowerBBS main menu.

Manufacturer:	Russell E. Frey
Voice telephone number:	516/938-0506
Current version number:	3.5
BBS type:	networked
Maximum line count:	unlimited

At the time of this writing, PowerBBS is the only fully-featured, widely-used BBS program specifically written to run under Windows 3.0 and 3.1. As such, it offers you the chance to run a bulletin board under today's most popular multitasking environment; while your BBS operates in the background, you can run other Windows applications and still use your PC.

Although the ability to multitask a BBS under Windows is the primary advantage to PowerBBS, it also has an impressive feature list, including fax capability, FidoNet and Internet connectivity (including telnet), caller ID, graphical sysop's utilities, internal QWK mail, CD-ROM support, a built-in scripting language, and RIP graphics. PowerBBS provides support for external DOS doors, as well as an integrated dBase-compatible online database called PowerBase. The default menu system presents callers with an ANSI "drop down" menu bar—which looks much like the Windows interface itself—and the menus can be navigated with the arrow keys or hotkey commands.

However, PowerBBS is not the perfect solution—in part, this is also due to it being a Windows application. If you're running more than one line, a 486-based PC is suggested, and you'll need a minimum of 4 megs of RAM—the more lines you offer your callers, the more memory PowerBBS will need. Depending on the speed of your PC, the number of users online and the application you open locally, your callers may experience delays and time lags. Also, the 3.x Windows environment has proven a less stable BBS foundation overall than the custom internal multitaskers provided by DOS programs like TBBS and the Major BBS. As you learned earlier in the book, your bulletin board will be more reliable if you can devote an entire PC to it, rather than trying to "share" the PC with your BBS program. If you're considering running a profit BBS or a business/support system, then the idea of running a Windows-based BBS is less attractive.

Summary: Although PowerBBS is probably not a good selection for a multiline system larger than two or three lines, it makes a good choice for a sysop who can afford only a single PC and must continue to use the computer while the BBS is running. PowerBBS also has a wide range of built-in features that help to consolidate external connections and advanced services like fax and online database access. The popularity of Windows and the abundance of Windows applications virtually assures a following for this BBS program.

Appendix B

ANSI Tables

The following table lists the ANSI character codes used to store characters in memory and in files. The ANSI (American National Standards Institute) code table is a superset of the ASCII (American Standard Codes for Information Interchange) codes, which cover the first 128 codes. The ASCII codes were originally developed for teletype communications. The first 32 codes are the control characters, although only four of them are used in Windows applications. The codes from 32 through 127 are the normal typewriter characters, and codes 128 through 255 are the extended characters. Note that the extended codes used in MS-DOS applications differ from those shown here for Windows applications, which use the ANSI standard.

Table B.1 ANSI Codes

Character	ANSI Code
Backspace	8
Tab	9
Line feed	10
Carriage return	13
Space	32
!	33
"	34
#	35
$	36

(continues)

Table B.1 Continued

Character	ANSI Code
%	37
&	38
'	39
(	40
)	41
*	42
+	43
,	44
-	45
.	46
/	47
0	48
1	49
2	50
3	51
4	52
5	53
6	54
7	55
8	56
9	57
:	58
;	59
<	60
=	61
>	62

Character	ANSI Code
?	63
@	64
A	65
B	66
C	67
D	68
E	69
F	70
G	71
H	72
I	73
J	74
K	75
L	76
M	77
N	78
O	79
P	80
Q	81
R	82
S	83
T	84
U	85
V	86
W	87
X	88
Y	89

(continues)

Table B.1 Continued

Character	ANSI Code
Z	90
[	91
\	92
]	93
^	94
_	95
`	96
a	97
b	98
c	99
d	100
e	101
f	102
g	103
h	104
i	105
j	106
k	107
l	108
m	109
n	110
o	111
p	112
q	113
r	114
s	115

Character	ANSI Code
t	116
u	117
v	118
w	119
x	120
y	121
z	122
{	123
|	124
}	125
~	126
	127
Ç	128
ü	129
‚	130
ƒ	131
„	132
…	133
†	134
‡	135
^	136
‰	137
Š	138
‹	139
Œ	140
ì	141
Ä	142

(continues)

Table B.1 Continued

Character	ANSI Code
Å	143
É	144
‘	145
’	146
“	147
”	148
°	149
–	150
—	151
~	152
‰	153
š	154
>	155
œ	156
¥	157
P	158
	159
Space	160
i	161
¢	162
£	163
⊗	164
¥	165
¦	166
§	167
¨	168

Character	ANSI Code
©	169
ª	170
«	171
¬	172
-	173
®	174
¯	175
°	176
±	177
²	178
³	179
´	180
µ	181
¶	182
•	183
¸	184
¹	185
º	186
»	187
1/4	188
1/2	189
3/4	190
¿	191
À	192
Á	193
Â	194
Ã	195

(continues)

Table B.1 Continued

Character	ANSI Code
Ä	196
Å	197
Æ	198
Ç	199
È	200
É	201
Ê	202
Ë	203
Ì	204
Í	205
Î	206
Ï	207
Đ	208
Ñ	209
Ò	210
Ó	211
Ô	212
Õ	213
Ö	214
×	215
Ø	216
Ù	217
Ú	218
Û	219
Ü	220
Ý	221

Character	ANSI Code
þ	222
ß	223
à	224
á	225
â	226
ã	227
ä	228
å	229
æ	230
ç	231
è	232
é	233
ê	234
ë	235
ì	236
í	237
î	238
ï	239
Ò	240
ñ	241
ò	242
ó	243
ô	244
õ	245
ö	246
÷	247
ø	248

(continues)

Table B.1 Continued

Character	ANSI Code
ù	249
ú	250
û	251
ü	252
´y	253
b	254
ÿ	255

Table B.2 ANSI.SYS Cursor Position and Screen Commands

Command Name	Command Sequence	Description
Cursor position	ESC[#; #H	Moves the cursor to a specified position on the screen.
Cursor up	ESC[#A	Moves the cursor up a number of lines without changing columns.
Cursor down	ESC[#B	Moves the cursor down a number of lines without changing columns.
Cursor forward	ESC[#C	Moves the cursor forward without changing lines.
Cursor backward	ESC[#D	Moves the cursor backward without changing lines.
Horizontal/ vertical position	ESC[#; #f	Has function identical to cursor position command.
Save cursor position	ESC[s	Saves, in memory, the current position of the cursor.
Restore cursor position	ESC[u	Restores the cursor to the position it occupied when the previous save cursor position command was issued.
Device status report	ESC[6n	Requests that ANSI.SYS issue a cursor position report.
Cursor position report	ESC[#; #R	Reports the current position of the cursor.

Command Name	Command Sequence	Description
Erase display	ESC[2J	Erases entire display and positions the cursor at the home position.
Erase line	ESC[K	Erases from the cursor to the end of the line.

Table B.3 ANSI.SYS Commands for Controlling Display Screen Attributes

Command Name	Command Sequence	Description
Set graphics rendition	ESC[#;...;#m	Sets the screen display attributes using the following attributes:

Attribute Parameters	Meaning
0	All attributes off. Normal display
1	High intensity display on
4	Underscore on. Underscore will not work with a color display
5	Blink on
7	Reverse video on
8	Concealed on. No display
30	Black foreground
31	Red foreground
32	Green foreground
33	Yellow foreground
34	Blue foreground
35	Magenta foreground
36	Cyan foreground
37	White foreground
40	Black background
41	Red background

(continues)

Table B.3 Continued

Attribute Parameters	Meaning
42	Green background
43	Yellow background
44	Blue background
45	Magenta background
46	Cyan background
47	White background

Index

Symbols

A

B

C

D

E

F

G

H

I

J-K

L

M

N

O

P

Q

R

S

T

U

V

W

X–Y–Z

Customer Access

We want you to be happy with *Wildcat!* BBS. The special *Wildcat!* v3 Lite software included with this book is easy to setup and fully documented. The information in this book should provide answers to most of the questions you may have about *Wildcat!* BBS. We recognize, however, that you may need help with the installation and setup of your *Wildcat!* v3 Lite BBS software.

An excellent choice for support is our *Wildcat!* Support System BBS at (805) 873-2400. Feel free to look around, download any files on the system that may be of use to you, or leave a public message in the appropriate area if you need a question answered. This method of obtaining support is especially good if you want expert guidance regarding the more advanced features from MSI staff and other callers.

Voice Support

Voice technical support for *Wildcat!* v3 Lite is limited to initial setup help. If you are unable to find the answer to a question or just need a quick explanation, please give our Technical Support Department a voice call at (805) 873-2550 between 9:00am and 5:00pm PST. We must, however, limit support calls to those problems not resolved after reading the manual. Full voice technical support is available to our registered *Wildcat!* 4 customers for as long as they own the product.

Availability

Wildcat! 4 BBS and its associated utility packages are available through your local software retail stores and mail order outlets. Most retailers carrying *Wildcat!* BBS have the Single Line package on the shelf with MultiLine versions as well as wcPRO, wcGATE and wcCODE available via special order. Mail order outlets usually carry the complete line of Mustang Software products. Both retail and mail order outlets offer very competitive prices as well. We have included a discount order form for ordering directly from us on the next page. Although any software store should be able to get our software for you, the following is a list of retailers that normally stock *Wildcat!* 4 BBS:

Retailers:

CompuUSA .... (800) 266-7872
Software, Etc. .... (800) 328-4646
Software City .... (800) 222-0918

Mail Order Outlets:

Dustin Discount .... (800) 274-6611
Programmers Provantage .... (800) 336-1166
BBS Technologies .... (209) 498-0200
On-Line Services .... (800) 597-6160
Star Ware .... (800) 523-0702
Computability .... (800) 554-9924

Wildcat! 4 The World's Most Popular BBS Software.™

Mustang Software unveiled the first Wildcat! BBS in 1986. Since its initial release, Wildcat! has emerged as the world's most popular Bulletin Board System (BBS) software with more than 30,000 Sysops worldwide.

Wildcat! is packed with more intelligent features and value than any other BBS product available. Callers can send, receive and view messages and files, access external applications, and chat 24 hours a day.

Intelligent features include:

- A .GIF thumbnailer that lets your callers and preview a sample of multiple .GIF files in one combined bitmapped file;
- A spell-checking editor to allow your callers to audit their text before posting their messages;
- RIPscrip graphics to provide your callers with a graphical user interface (GUI) and allow them to navigate the BBS with their mouse;
- Support for over 32,000 message conferences and file areas to give your BBS plenty of room to grow;
- Sysop-defined language files that allow your callers to select the BBS language interface of their choice;
- wcDRAW BBS display screen editor that lets you customize the look of your BBS interface;

Mustang Software is the Number 1 BBS supplier worldwide. Our liberal upgrade policy allows Sysops to start with our Single Line version and trade it in later for full credit to any of our MultiLine products.

An Exciting Array Of Add-On Packages.

Our powerful collection of add-on utilities will enhance any Wildcat! 4 BBS. These utilities have the same easy-to-use interface as the rest of the Wildcat! 4 family, and are fully supported by Mustang Software.

- ***wcPRO Utilities For The In-Control Sysop***

  wcPRO provides powerful user, message and file database maintenance capabilities. You can create custom reports of online statistics, use command macros for nightly batch processing, and export BBS data into other formats for external applications.

  The wcPRO package also includes our fax-on-demand processor, wcFAX, so your callers can request data online and receive product literature, registration forms, and price list documents via their fax.

- ***wcGATE Internet/MHS Messaging Gateway***

  wcGATE enables your callers to send and receive Internet E-Mail and news right from your BBS, and has built-in support for satellite connections. wcGATE also allows you to transfer BBS messages to your company's favorite MHS-compatible E-Mail system using Novell's Message Handling Service.

- ***wcCODE Custom Online Development Engine***

  wcCODE allows you to develop custom applications to enhance or change Wildcat's operation. BASIC-like syntax and over 200 built-in functions makes it easy to use. wcCODE applications will work on any Wildcat! 4 BBS. Sample applications like our wcLIST BBS Lister and an on-line order system are included.